Lines of Dissent

Lines of Dissent

Writing from the New Statesman 1913–1988

◆

Edited by
STEPHEN HOWE

VERSO

London · New York

This collection first published by Verso 1988

Verso
UK: 6 Meard Street, London W1V 3HR
USA: 29 West 35th Street, New York, NY 10001-2291

Verso is the imprint of New Left Books

British Library Cataloguing in Publication Data

Lines of Dissent: writing from the
    New Statesman 1913-1988.
    1. General essays in English — Anthologies
    I. Howe, Stephen   II. New Statesman
    082
ISBN 09-86091-207-8

Typeset by Leaper & Gard Ltd, Bristol, England
Printed in Great Britain by Bookcraft (Bath) Ltd, Midsomer Norton, Avon

CONTENTS

FOREWORD

I come from a family which took the *Daily Mirror*, mostly for the crossword. My political mentors were Cassandra, and Richard Crossman who then wrote a column in the newspaper. Both were fine, populist writers. I came later to the *New Statesman* and perhaps for that reason have always been slightly awed by a sense of its almost monolithic past. Since it has not always met the standard of writing set by Cassandra, I have not read it regularly enough to dispel that feeling.

It's for these reasons that I find this collection quite liberating. Here in abundance is fine writing with a sense of purpose and principle; and a plurality of view which the magazine should never have abandoned. Historical essays, like Christopher Hitchens's introduction to this volume, and Adrian Smith's profile of the first editor, Clifford Sharpe (in the *New Statesman*, 7 January 1988), together with the mass of gossip about the magazine's past which you soon hear when you join the staff, has further encouraged me. Here is an enterprise on a human scale: magnificently certain and miserably fearful; shifting sharply in political position and sometimes drifting without any at all; edited at times by editors who are drunk or mad, and on occasion both.

I am in no doubt that the *New Statesman* can regain a wide readership; at least, if the modest resources necessary can be found. There are many fine writers who already contribute to the *NS*, and many more who will respond to a magazine with a renewed sense of purpose. The magazine's most splendid times have always been founded on a backbone of political purpose – like, for example, the commitment to decolonisation.

The spirit of the times calls out now for a major crusade to radicalise democracy, assure liberties and assert the values of citizenship, not only in this country but throughout the world. Up to 1940, in a limited way, Britain could take pride in being at the forefront of democratic life. No more. Now it is Western Europe which is more democratic, and the United Kingdom which is less so. Mrs Thatcher's abuses of state power have revealed how undemocratic, because it is unwritten, the fundamental British constitution really is. She has used a uniquely powerful executive and centralised state apparatus to narrow the range of democratic decision-making and restrict competition for political power. The *ancien régime* lies upon civil society like an incubus which crushes the life out of radical politics and sucks the democratic instincts of the people.

The *New Statesman* has frequently led attempts to bring democracy and freedoms to the British people. Through all the inconsistencies of the recent past, the magazine has persistently exposed official secrecies and the abuses of big government, and stood up to official harassment in order to do so. In more than words the magazine has stood for freedom. For the future we mean to give political and intellectual substance to these journalistic instincts.

Stuart Weir

PREFACE

When I was eighteen, my notion of the ideal job was to edit the *New Statesman*. It wasn't an ambition as such, nor even an aspiration. But the *NS* was crucial to the way I was coming to view the world, almost ubiquitously pervaded my ideas about politics and the arts. The dream of directing that flow of ideas, perching on the fountainhead from which flowed so many of the sources of my imagination, thus became almost equivalent to the impossible idea of controlling my own life.

Mine *should*, in a way, have been a *New Statesman* adolescence by descent: my parents, left-leaning professionals from working-class backgrounds, living in Metroland, interested in ideas, were ideal *NS* readers. As it happened, though, they didn't buy the paper. I discovered it for myself, with an excitement so strong that it's tempting to go way over the top and echo Hazlitt on the Lake Poets' awakening of his intellectual life.

Ten years and more later – having read the paper very nearly every intervening Friday, combed its back issues, learned something of its history, seen a little of life in its offices – the *NS* editorial chair is a place whose occupants I admire but would never again dream of envying. Often it seems to have been purgatorial: too many editors – indeed almost all – have left in bitterness or in sorrow. The *NS* offices have, one gathers, not always been happy places to inhabit. Yet the voices coming from them have almost never been depressed (though they might have been tragic), or weary (though they might be strident) or dull (though they might be pompous). The *NS* may long have been an 'institution', but it's avoided becoming a museum piece, a monument to its own or any other past.

Everyone, so it seemed as I talked and read about the paper's history, has their own least favourite *NS* era. I was always being told how dull it was under Clifford Sharp, how insufferable in Martin's last years, how claustrophobic in Crossman's day, how Spartish with Bruce Page at the helm. Just today, as I write, Robert Harris in the *Observer* complains that wit could only feature in the *NS* 'pre-Year Zero'. Goodness knows which Year Zero he has in mind: the bizarre mental slide which associates this most open of journals with Pol Pot is a classic instance of what the *NS* has always fought against. Anyway, he's as wrong as the other inverted nostalgists. For me the *NS* over the years has always been interesting, and usually fun, to discover or rediscover. (And Harris, you're too intelligent, surely, to play the young fogey: also too young, most designated YFs being, in my observation, not even biologically youthful.) *NS* voices have invariably been diverse to the point of cacaphony.

Here I offer a selection of those voices, drawn from three-quarters of a century's *New Statesman* writing. The choice is mine, though others have given generously of their opinions. I lament, but shan't apologise about, all the things I've had to leave out. The piles of xeroxed second choices, third choices, private loves and pet hates, things one would want to reprint if Verso had given one 500,000 words to play with, have become a major traffic hazard for my cats' progress over the study floor. I wanted them all in: what *is* in doesn't satisfy me and so hasn't a paper-heap-ensnared cat's chance of pleasing anyone else. So it goes.

I hesitated about reproducing material which has appeared in previous *NS* books, notably Edward Hyams's fiftieth birthday book, *New Statesmanship*: but since that's long out of print and there are a few pieces in it that I couldn't bear to miss, there is a small overlap. I have not sought to cater especially for historians of British politics, although I'm one myself and the *NS* files are among our richest sources. Still less have I tried to indulge *NS* in-house nostalgia or self-congratulation. I haven't attempted to give a cross-section of the journal's contents: the bias is towards political coverage (thus, alas, desperately little of the incredible richness of *New Statesman* poetry and short stories or of its book, cinema, theatre, dance, music or sport reviews is included here) and slightly towards the fairly recent past.

To anyone dissatisfied with this selection, then, a reminder that, as Orwell commented, a year's bound issues of most magazines will contain more worth reading after a lapse of years than almost any book. Go off to a library and dig around in the files. While you're at it, take notes of possible choices for the centenary anthology.

Thanks to all the helpful *NS* staff past and present, and notably Malcolm Imrie, John Lloyd and Stuart Weir. My especial gratitude, for her help and hospitality, to Jane Thomas. *NS* editors, so far, have always been men (and I'm painfully aware of how few women contributors there are in this book); but Leonard Woolf noted decades ago that it was always the Editor's secretary – equally invariably a woman – who *really* kept the paper going. Seeing Jane in action I suspect it's still true, and she has been invaluable to me. Finally, thanks to M2 who kept distracting me.

Stephen Howe, 29 November 1987

* * * * * * * * * *

As this book went to press, it was announced that the *New Statesman* and *New Society* were to merge. The implications of this are not, as I write, yet clear. The causes are painfully so: a precipitous decline in the finances of the *Statesman* and still more in those of its stablemate. The British Left's radical middle-class constituency, it seems, cannot today sustain more than one non-specialist, non-sectarian weekly journal. The question remains whether it will support even one.

The market economy and its present political apostles – whatever party label they may sport – have no more sentiment for institutional traditions than for social justice. Yet there is no market parity in determining which institutions live and which die under this dispensation. The new harshness exposes the vast disproportion in private means between apparent equals. This week the wife of another magazine's young editor (ostentatiously styling herself thus rather than in her own name) holds a birthday party. Mrs Charles Moore will be 'at home' to 500 guests in London's Guildhall. The difference between the journal whose social network sustains such display and that which must struggle to survive lies in a few thousand readers; and in a well-rewarded political alignment.

At the risk of lapsing into gloomy heritage-mongering – a socialist Young Fogeydom – this seems the place to lament past glories. Tomorrow, in other places, the search for the possibilities of renewal and the more ruthless settling of accounts with the old to which both Stuart Weir and Christopher Hitchens point.

Evidently, an epoch has closed. But it seems uncertain whether this anniversary volume must now be also a valedictory. There have been several previous mergers in the career of the *Statesman*, most notably that with the venerable and distinguished *Nation*. In each case, the *Statesman* has effectively subsumed its smaller partner within its organically evolving identity. In each case, though financial necessity has been involved, there has been a clear intellectual rationale for the amalgamation. There has been a meeting of minds, not a shotgun marriage. There has been a continuity of commitment both to a liberal culture and to a radical socialist politics. Full editorial independence has been retained. Not least in importance, the name of the *New Statesman* has always stayed on the masthead. In at least some of these respects, things have been done differently today, and not for the better. If they should prove to have been wholly for the worse, for the name and character of the *New Statesman* to have been lost, this volume must be the partial, inadequate memorial. If not, it will show something of the depth, the breadth, the diversity of the roots from which the radical writing of the future can grow. Then the suggestion that readers think about choices for a centenary anthology may still stand.

S.H., 24 February 1988

INTRODUCTION

Most people can place events in their 'private' lives by reference to
certain dates or benchmarks in what we may still unironically term 'the
public arena'. This mnemonic ability may be trivial, as when some
relation speaks of a distant kinsman who was wed in the year of the
Golden – 'no, I tell a lie, it was the *Diamond*' Jubilee. With more
solemnity, some apparently serious people think it important to tell you
just where they were standing, or what they were doing, when they
heard the news of the assassination of John F. Kennedy. (I once
received some hate mail, when, recalling the 1962 Cuba missile crisis, I
detailed my exact whereabouts and emotions on the day the boy
President nearly killed *me*. Many readers, I learned, like their historical
allusions to be kept strictly orderly.)

In fact, I don't much depart from the norm. Nineteen fifty-two was the
year of the Coronation because it was the year I was taken to the cinema for
the first time. I can conjure flickering images of Suez and Hungary by
reference to the early days of family television ownership, and I recall a
double hanging taking place because it was scheduled to occur during
breakfast on the last day of a school term; a day of incongruous
emancipation. But I can very distinctly evoke the day when the negative
was reversed, and I could place the 'political' time from a 'private'
experience. I was sitting in a study room at a Methodist boarding school
in Cambridge, reading a volume I had found in the library. The book
was an anthology called *New Statesmanship* and its editor, I remember,
was Edward Hyams. I suddenly began to bang my head on the arm of
my chair, as a particular nuance in the argument before me engaged
with some rather inchoate sympathies and suspicions of my own. With
my finger still between the pages, I got up and stamped about a bit. I
began to practise some of the phrases and arguments, probably with the
intention of trying them on the Debating Society and a few chosen
friends. The article I had hit upon was 'Britain and the Nuclear Bombs',
by J.B. Priestley. It had been published in the *New Statesman* on 2
November 1957, when I had been eight years old, and I was reading it
as if it had just written. I would now guess, placing the memory in
context, that this was the year of grace 1966 – the beginning of the

1

sordid ebb-tide of Wilsonism. Years later, working at Great Turnstile
and hearing the *NS* described by Anthony Howard as 'a missionary
outpost to the middle classes', I joined in the laughter of self-
deprecation but remembered the traffic humming by on Fen Causeway
that evening and thought – yes. That's what it *ought* to be. That's where
I came in.

Dates become easier and more difficult as one lives through more
'turning points'. It must have been 1978 or 1979 when I took a train
from Blackpool with a verbal challenge still in my ears. 'I doubt,'
Edward Thompson had said, 'that your editor will want to use it. Or
not all of it at any rate.' He and I had been addressing a conference
fringe meeting about yet another Official Secrets frame-up (by now, we
were in the sordid ebb-tide of Callaghan–Footism) and he had told me
that he wanted to break silence. The last time he had approached the
NS had been about the British torture of prisoners in Cyprus, and the
young whipper-snapper Paul Johnson had let him down on a promise
to publish. If the paper wanted his new essay – all of it – then fine. If
not, then nothing was lost. I silently disagreed with the second of these
opinions.

I had my differences with Bruce Page but when he emerged from his
office with that heavy manuscript and said, 'I see no reason not to
publish all of this at once', I felt that there was a certain fitness to
things. Priestley's 1957 article strikes me now as a shade John Bullish,
and more than a touch sentimental. Edward Thompson's essay (The
Secret State Within the State) which so intricately filiated such grand
matters as the Cold War, the nuclear system, individual liberty and
personal honour, still strikes me as containing the essence of New
Statesmanship. The heart on fire: the brain on ice. Thompson's own
background and formation contain elements both of the middle class
and the missionary. Yet it would be a dull or foolhardy person who
employed either term as a sneer in this instance. The tradition, which
extends from the foes of the Poor Law to the Friends of India, is *our*
tradition in ways which cannot be escaped.

Ought one even wish to escape it? The *NS* has never done well
when it has apologised for, or felt uneasy with, the strain of English
radical reformism. Editors and writers who flinched at jibes like 'elitist',
'academic' or (all purpose) 'Hampstead' have tended to under-perform.
The best course, as many of the succeeding pages here will
demonstrate, is to find opinionated, arrogant, radical originals and to
let them feel that they will not be inhibited. This will hold good for
literary matters as it does with more overtly 'political' questions, and
will often call upon the gifts of the same kind of people. The twentieth
century has taught the Left (has it not?) that 'the masses' are composed

of 'individuals' and that any vulgar counterposition of the two will bring
forth horrors. (It is invariably the suppression of individuality, for
example, that necessitates the equal and opposite *grotesquerie* of the
'cult of the personality'.) Many of the *New Statesman*'s natural stable, I
would venture to say, are *elite* but not elit*ist*. Writers such as Gore
Vidal, Bertrand Russell, Graham Greene, Kenneth Tynan and others
are and were effective precisely because of the low value they put on
any kind of consensus. 'Commitment', to them, is and was not to be
understood as merely 'alignment'. The *NS* has no choice but to try and
be the resort of such authors – not because they are 'names' but
because before they were 'names' they knew an intelligent and
independent paper from a simply politicised and sympathetic one.

If this doltishly obvious precept is followed with any care, it will
confer one crucial advantage among many. It will allow a paper to be
wrong, and to rise above its mistakes. The important question to ask of
any serious party or any serious magazine is not *what* it thinks but *how*
it thinks. (The same, clearly, goes for any serious person.) Conor Cruise
O'Brien, in a clever but rather flippant spectre-at-the-feast job on the
Statesman's fiftieth birthday entitled 'Chorus or Cassandra?', was able to
make telling points about the paper's consistency – its 'line' if you like –
during the late thirties. One doesn't grudge him his fun. The editors
had then wanted two contradictory things: the defeat of Fascism and
the avoidance of rearmament and world war. Neither aim was exactly
ignoble, but the pursuit of *both* sometimes deserved the appellation so
often visited on the less convincing efforts of English do-gooding;
which is to say that it was silly. Other manifestations of the Fabian
conscience and method during that time were a little worse than silly. I
recently looked up H.G. Wells's conversation with Stalin, which the NS
ran with a straight face on 27 October 1934, and found it as
unimprovably writhe-making as I had remembered it:

WELLS: I am very much obliged to you, Mr Stalin, for agreeing to see me. I
was in the United States recently, I had a long conversation with President
Roosevelt and tried to ascertain what his leading ideas were. Now I have come
to you to ask what you are doing to change the world.
STALIN: Not so very much.
WELLS: I wander round the world as a common man, and, as a common
man, observe what is going on around me.

Quite. It's difficult to decide what or how Wells thinks here (and one
ought to add, for the sake of fairness to the good name of Fabianism,
that George Bernard Shaw did contribute an article ridiculing Wells's
style as a questioner). As a result, the re-reading of those yellowed

pages is still vital and instructive. The contortions of the *bien-pensants*, as they made the painful discovery we all have to make – which is that the wrong people can have the right line – form part of our common intellectual history.

So, in its way, does Kingsley Martin's most celebrated dereliction during that devil's decade, which was his decision to suppress George Orwell's dispatches from Barcelona. This (described euphemistically by Edward Hyams as 'a very difficult decision – to refuse to publish Orwell's articles against the Spanish government at the height of the Spanish Civil War') is a famous story by now and I have only two excuses for bringing it up again. First, it illustrates my general point. By declining to print the facts about Stalinism in Catalonia, as reliably witnessed and reported, the *NS* did more than miss the opportunity to publish a modern classic. It betrayed its commitment to the inconvenient fact, and to the inconvenient writer. Kingsley Martin admitted at the time, and confessed in his memoirs, that he had good reason to believe Orwell was telling the truth. It was a case of our old friend and enemy, the concept of unripe time. It was also an appearance by our other old friend 'objectively', who sometimes goes under the alias of 'giving ammunition to the enemy'. In this unprincipled utilitarianism we have an example of what I meant by failure, not in what the *NS* thought, but how.

My second justification takes the form of a postscript. In 1980 or so, when Bernard Crick's biography of Orwell was published, I was given it for review in the *NS* by David Caute. In my article, I took it upon myself to apologise to Orwell's memory for the Kingsley Martin decision. The only letter taking the opposing view came from Paul Johnson, who wrote from his new den on the extreme Right in a sulphurous defence of Martin, the editorial prerogative, the necessity for authority in such matters, and much windiness besides. In his later *History of the Modern World*, Mr Johnson found it possible to review General Franco himself in a more indulgent historical light. I offer this anecdote as a corrective, both to those who think they know about 'giving ammunition to the enemy' and to those who claim Orwell as a conservative founding father.

The distinction between commitment and alignment shows itself in grand matters and in paltry ones. The *New Statesman* has been judged by its attitude to Empire, to Stalinism, to the Bomb and to the publication of small ads by homosexuals and the marketers of contraceptives. It has also had to expend a lot of editorial breath on questions like the Gaitskell–Bevan split, the 'Clause Four' episode and the unending battle for what some believe to be the 'soul' of the Labour

Party. The paper's founding articles speak of a commitment to socialist ideas but of a determined independence from party and faction. I should say that during the Wilson years this delicate balance began to be badly upset. In his by-Auden-out-of-Byron 'Open Letter to Richard Crossman', composed in 1970 and not published in the *NS*, James Fenton wrote:

> And then, besides your Parliamentary
> Heavies, come the great masters of connivance
> Who, when they have to empty Labour's jerry
> Of all its filth, will stop at no contrivance.

Fenton was like a number of people at the end of the sixties. He had had all he could take of the grisly hypocrisies of party politics:

> I simply can't abide Labour's top brass
> And will not tag behind them where they go
> οὐ γαρ τι μοι Ζευς ἦν ὁ κηρυξας
> Ταδε/οὐδ' ἡ ζυνοικος των κατω
> θεων Δικη,* Dicky, as Sophocles has
> It in *Antigone*. The rest you know

Indeed. But as Fenton also wrote:

> I once heard HOPE explaining how a cause
> That ceases to bring in enough returns
> Must soon, according to well-proven laws,
> Be shouldered off. Slowly the *Statesman* turns
> Its back, and all its influence withdraws
> It's something every young idealist learns –
> *The paper must survive the policy.*
> The example that he gave was CND.

Francis Hope, whose death in a Paris air crash can still convene the most diverse people in *ad hoc* ceremonies of regret, was being playful rather than cynical. But Fenton's point against detachment still needs its answer. He wrote his poem *against* ossified Labourism but in favour of a more audacious and subversive – yet *consistent* – editing. His example, the mixture of defiance and affirmation that is contained in the hieroglyph CND, was the result of a chance conversation in the ghastly Bung Hole wine bar opposite the old *NS* premises at Great Turnstile. But it is a suggestive one, given that the battle of nuclearism,

---

* Because I am not the herald of Zeus,
And nor does justice dwell with the gods below

and the related battle over British possession of the Bomb, have allowed the *NS* to make its two most distinct irruptions into the moral and political life of the country: Priestley and Thompson – names which could denote some Victorian expedition, or could adorn an honours board or a war memorial.

Between the decline of 'Aldermaston' and the rise of 'Greenham', the paper actually paid very little attention to what any fool knows to be the great issue of our time. When Edward Hyams concluded his history of the first half-century of the *NS* in 1963, he struck a note of generalised self-satisfaction with the social and national progress registered thus far. And he spoke of New Statesmanship by reference to what Hippolyte Taine had so admired: 'That sense of responsibility towards "the people" (one might almost write simply "people") and not merely towards the nation, which distinguishes a small but important section of the English upper and middle classes'. This seems to me to differ in application from Howard's aphorism cited earlier. A missionary operation *to* the middle classes is not the same as a missionary operation *from* the middle classes. As a result of this slightly complacent paternalism, and of its analogue in a too-warm relationship with the Labour establishment, the *NS* can be said in a sense to have 'missed the sixties'. It took an honourable position on Vietnam and on many other critical matters, but it appeared to the emerging radical generation more as a survival than as a beacon. It wrote *about* that generation, in tones of civilised curiosity to be sure, but not *for* it.

This 'break' in the paper's evolution, which has led to a long-run decline whose outcome is uncertain, had to do with the eclipse of two related institutions. The first is the British Labour Party and the second is the British Empire. The two have not declined in quite the same way or for quite the same reasons. But their respective sunsets have both left the Fabian tradition in a definite shadow. As Hyams puts it in his history of the *NS*:

> The Webbs were imperialist and so was [Clifford] Sharp. It was not so much that these Fabians objected to Indians or Africans having self-government, as that they seem to have objected to fragmentation of a Commonwealth which might, perhaps, be turned over intact to Socialism as one huge rationally governed unit.

Fabianism and the Empire was the title of one of the most important tracts put out by the parents of the *New Statesman*. Sidney Webb, in his incarnation as Lord Passfield, was the most assiduous and the most reactionary of any Colonial Secretary appointed by a Labour administration. Deeply embedded in the Fabian idea was an impression

of British greatness. It was Kingsley Martin's achievement to have
turned the paper somewhat away from Fabian imperialism, but it is
impossible to read his memoirs without imbibing from every page his
magnificent conceit about the standing of the *NS* and himself in the
emerging Third World. (Visiting India for the *NS* in 1979–80, I myself
caught some of the last exhalations of this.) The role of the paper in
forwarding a relatively humane decolonisation cannot be, but often is,
overstated. The *Encounter* school of Anglo-Americanism still tends to
blame the current state of the Third World on the unsoundness of
doctrines propagated by the *NS* and the LSE. Anyway, the real difficulty
came after this accomplishment. As British life developed increasingly
insular characteristics, why should Bengalis, Iraqis, Cypriots and
Malawians continue to read the paper? Shorn of this relevance,
furthermore, what was its continued appeal to Americans, Germans,
Australians? The subscription lists tell their own story. On the two
outstanding post-imperial issues that were still of urgent interest to
domestic readers – Ireland and Palestine – the *NS* had a wavy and
erratic 'line'. Priestley's 1957 polemic, which as redolent with appeals
to British moral authority and global stature, in retrospect very likely
marks the last great utterance of the Fabian imperial tradition.

And what of Labour – whose policy in office Edward Thompson was
excoriating in *his* great piece? Fenton could only have guessed at it but
his satire on Crossman was published at the opening of a longer period
of decay than even he had anticipated. In a 1963 article in the paper,
and in a later essay in the anthology *Towards Socialism*, Crossman had
written scathingly of the disease of 'ex-ministeritis' which had 'blighted
the self-criticism which should have made the political wilderness
blossom with socialist ideas'. Under the dread editorial initials *RHSC*,
and the yet more dread Diary pseudonym *Crux*, the paper became
committed more and more but to less and less. With Labour in
opposition and Crossman released from Cabinet responsibilities, ex-
ministeritis became a scourge. The *NS* became more politicised and
uniform than it had been under Paul Johnson's fairly lenient and
eclectic sixties' reign. The problem was that, to the accompaniment of a
crass and vulgar pictorial re-launch, it urged Labour to occupy
abandoned Conservative ground.

'Speak for England,' cried the anti-Munich Tories in 1939, when
Arthur Henderson rose to move Labour's challenge against
Chamberlain. 'Speak for Commonwealth preference,' mumbled the Old
Guard, as Crossman wheeled all the *Statesman*'s guns to deploy against
Britain's entry into the Common Market. It was an incomparably
depressing period, as a glance at the back numbers will attest. The *NS*
even published a pamphlet, of which I still retain a mouldering copy,

urging that the country cling to the eroded battlements the Tories had surrendered. A little England meant a paltry *Statesman.*

In retrospect, Labour's last stand against Europe does not even possess the virtue of quixotry. What it did possess was all the elements – of post-imperial dudgeon; of the romancing of outdated industry; of the reverie of sovereignty; of the bitter split between 'enlightened' middle and 'resentful' working classes; of the constipated conception of the nation-state – that have brought us to the present slough. There is only one piece of writing from that leaden 'Great Debate' that would deserve re-reading today and it (Tom Nairn's 'The Left Against Europe?') was printed by the *New Left Review* and snapped up by Penguin; neatly leap-frogging the *New Statesman*'s potential readerships.

Look in the *NS* for the remainder of the seventies, as Anthony Howard strove to staunch the haemorrhage of readership and interest that had been started by Crossman, and you will see water being trodden a good deal of the time. The most distinctive and spirited voice, allowed far more than its due meed of space and emphasis, was the long withdrawing roar of Paul Johnson who, having loudly seconded Crossman's anti-European crusade, now compared an etiolated Labourism to 'Auschwitz and the Gulag'.

Put it any way you like; by the end of the seventies it was not only the United Kingdom that had lost an empire and not yet found a role. In the wider culture, and in the journalism that reflected it, there was the beginning of the uninteresting confrontation between the nihilism of punk and the narcissism of the yuppie. (One calls the competition uninteresting because it utterly lacked the dimension of ideas; not because it did not foreshadow the 'style' of many subsequent confrontations between parties, factions, newspapers and even social classes.) I felt protected, in the early stages of this *dialogue des sourds*, by having *NS* colleagues like Martin Amis, James Fenton, Julian Barnes and Duncan Campbell. In their different ways, they all had something of 'the project of the whole man' about them; a genius that does its best work alone and because it must, but which does so with some intention of sharing the good news. I still brood sometimes about what might have happened if we had succeeded to editorial control over the paper in 1978, as we modestly proposed ourselves to do. ...

Reviewing the celebrated *Two Cultures* exchange between C.P. Snow and F.R. Leavis, Lionel Trilling wrote that it was the only example known to him of an English debate where both antagonists were Roundheads. Passing swiftly over Putney, where presumably the same characteristics obtained, one can grant the usefulness of this point. Most of the great clashes, whether between Gladstone and Disraeli, Paine and Burke, Browning and Wordsworth, Elgin and Byron, Wilberforce and Darwin, Tynan and Hobson, partake in some way of our famous and ahistorical choosing of sides. But some do not, and many are not quite as they seem. Was Paine or Burke the Puritan? Was Orwell or Kingsley Martin the Roundhead?

The question has its implications for New Statesmanship, and for the Left in general. Radicals are invariably accused by their foes of being *either* grey and humourless *or* vapid and idealistic. I have a profound conviction that the success of the *New Statesman* in its first few decades had to do with its ability to confound this 'Morton's fork'; wielded so deftly by the world's most sinuous and resourceful conservatism. It was one thing for our betters to joke about the solemn Mrs Webb and her calibrated schemes for human amelioration. It was another for them to cackle at the satires upon their mode of production as they were presented by John Maynard Keynes. At their best, *NS* articles and essays always had the *x* factor; the Cavalier ingredient of originality and verve that modified the Roundhead prescriptions from the realm of necessity. If you look back over the contributions of Claud Cockburn, A.J.P. Taylor, Bertrand Russell and others, you will find insights that were written *for* the readers of the *Statesman* but from, as it were, 'the other shore', by people who had been there and who knew what they were talking about, and who could decode the encrypted language of the Establishment. (A forgotten example here might be the post-war series on the significance of nuclear weapons by Professor P.M.S. Blackett.) This combination of Dreyfusard gallantry and 'insider' familiarity was very often what was implied when a reactionary critic reluctantly described an *NS* article as being 'well-written'.

This would not have been enough on its own, needless to say, without the element of conviction and the nerve of outrage. Even as it is scavenging ideas for its own survival from a Maynard Keynes, the old gang is not quite deaf to the tones of an H.N. Brailsford or a Fenner Brockway. These tones, apart from any moral resonance they may have, serve to remind those in the saddle of what may happen if they are ever unhorsed. A *régime* that does not want to become *ancien* does well to pay attention. The evidence is that, in the transition from the Hungry Thirties to the Butskellite Fifties, the *NS* played a considerable role in civilising the British ruling class – a class that, as Aneurin Bevan liked to say, is never happier than when wearing the medals of its defeats and pretending that reform was all its own idea.

This line of reflection again returns us to the problem of relevance. An empire (more or less) amicably wound up; a domestic social pact (more or less) concluded; a general access to literacy and culture (more or less) established – what was there left for Fabianism and reformism to *do*? It could either become dull, repetitive and piecemeal, or it could settle to the enjoyment of diminishing returns with a satisfied conscience, or it could join some febrile movement of 'new ideas' – prominent among them the 'idea' that its old battles had been a waste of time. If it lacked the conviction to do any of these properly, it could become a notice-board which broadmindedly publicised the doings and sayings of a heterogeneous rainbow. Meanwhile, the quirks and arcana of the Competition and 'This England' would keep the older customers happy.

George Bernard Shaw prefigured this dilemma during his resignation from the *NS* board in 1916. As he wrote rather unfeelingly to Beatrice Webb, the brainchild could be:

> Like the old Thames Steamboat Company or the *Westminster Review*, it will struggle on long after all creation shrieks for its interment. But if you and Sidney put a violent end to it I shall not be greatly grieved. The longer I live, the more I perceive that Napoleon's rule of six years as the effective lifetime of a general applies to all public bodies and all papers. Three years ago, the *NS* was young; today it is about eighty. ... A paper, unless it is to be frankly a dull paper for dull people, like the *Spectator* (which now suits my elderly taste remarkably well) must live by adventures.

Shaw, once again accidentally upholding the honour of Fabianism, had been reacting furiously to the chauvinist position adopted by the *NS* during the opening stages of the First World War. Not until Crossman was the paper to descend to such depths again. 'In Germany,' intoned Clifford Sharp in an editorial, 'the Socialists cannot refuse to countenance the defence of Teutonic civilisation against the Russian peril.' A Fabian pamphlet of 1916, seeking to impose measures of *étatiste* nationalisation by the surreptitious rear entrance, was blazoned with the patriotic title *How to Pay for the War*.

Faced with this, Shaw adopted all the fine irresponsibility of the Cavalier, daring to tell *NS* readers in November 1914 that: 'Mr Asquith himself, though serenely persuaded that he is a Liberal statesman is, in effect, very much what the Kaiser would have been if he had been a Yorkshireman and a lawyer instead of being only half English.'

At all events, it is both sobering and heartening to know that, when it was only three years old, the *New Statesman* was compared by one of its progenitors to the luckless Thames Steamboat Company and the *Westminster Review*, to say nothing of the *Spectator*. It reminds us of the persistence of the difficulty. The production of a readable, combative, diverting, radical weekly in England is something that requires more than good intentions. If there is a cliché in the editorial and a train-wreck sentence in the Diary it is more than likely that the entries in 'This England', supposed to be undetected ironies, will in fact be old clippings of news stories that were originally published as intentionally funny. It has been rare, in the past few years, not to find an issue that contains all three of these (I think related) offences. And articles of general significance – those that combine a kind of erudition with a kind of curiosity, and that yet have an unmistakable commitment to them – have migrated, with their authors, to the *London Review of Books*, to *Granta*, to *New Left Review* and even to *Marxism Today* ('Theoretical and Discussion Journal of the Communist Party'). It may be no coincidence that at least the first three of these titles employs an absolute minimum of design, thereby quietly emphasising a reliance upon words. (One word, in intelligent journalism, is and always has been worth a thousand pictures.)

Attention to style and literacy is a necessary but not a sufficient condition for the avoidance of intellectual torpor. There must be the willingness to 'live by adventures' too. Of recent years, the long contest between Duncan Campbell and the secret state has given an imperishable example of this kind of commitment. 'Official Secrecy' in Britain is not merely an outrage to democracy and free expression. It is emblematic of much else besides – the shamefaced subordination of Britain to Reagan's strategic planners; the erosion of Parliament by the *nomenklatura*; the cretinisation of the press and broadcasting; the survival of class-based attitudes that tell the lower orders and the other ranks that they are not paid to think, or even supposed to. Campbell's extended challenge to this superstructure of deceit, with its arrogation of unchecked, unvoted powers of life and death over the citizen, has been an education for a generation. I myself took a small part in one of the sub-plots, wherein it was revealed that the authorities were vetting juries without the knowledge or consent of defence counsel. In the specific case of a 1978 trial involving Campbell and his *confrères*, this vetting amounted to packing. The exposure was salutary. To have helped preserve the integrity of the English jury system might have been thought enough for one journalistic career; Campbell had combined it with an expansion of the very area in which politics itself can be deliberated. He also furnished many people with a reason to keep on reading the *NS* when its fortunes were generally reckoned to be poor. He deserves his place in the great tradition that he has both upheld and updated.

It is time to say something about the *New Statesman* and its celebrated 'back half'. As so often, Richard Crossman has bequeathed us an encapsulating statement that is so wrongheaded and philistine as to allow a general critique. 'It is recognised,' he wrote in may 1956, 'that left-wing politics are digestible only if they are coated with a thick sugar of arts, entertainments and book reviews, not to mention "classified ads" which enable the superior reader to assure his Tory friends that he always starts reading at the last page and works backwards.'

Allow for some of the notorious Crossman tongue-in-cheek, forget the obvious question 'recognised by who?', and you still have a perfect statement of how *not* to think about the literary aspect of New Statesmanship. Lionel Trilling once described the meeting point of politics and literature as 'the bloody crossroads'. He was actually speaking of the engagement of many twentieth-century writers with Fascism, Communism and the culture of disillusionment, so that his observation is only a partial counter to Crossman's vulgar, Fleet Street presentation of the relationship. But most thoughtful people have come to understand two things that are rather difficult to make compatible. They know that there is *some* connection between the literary and political aspects of culture. But they also realise that nothing is more annihilating of a culture than its politicisation. The *NS* was rather favourably placed by history and geography to make the most of this ambiguity. It shared some editorial identity with the 'Bloomsbury' school, but did not allow this to become identification. It was able to make a natural bridge to modernism, and was printing poems by Auden and Eliot while other papers were only reviewing them. It never became part of the doomed tendency to 'party writing' that so disfigured the idea of 'committed literature' between the wars. Yet it could usually find a measured way of uttering the 'public' thoughts of poets like Spender, novelists like Arnold Bennett or historians like Ensor and Taylor. When a piece of literary work possessed an unarguably political dimension, the *NS* was often at its best in simply giving it presentation. The perfect example here is Yeats's electrifying poem 'Easter 1916', which appeared in an issue of the paper devoted to the Irish crisis in October 1920.

In the fifties and sixties, the *New Statesman* was one of the platforms available to the regional and plebeian writers who oscillated between the so-called Angry Young Man school, the insights of Richard Hoggart and the 'arts for the people' tendency represented by Arnold Wesker, Joan Littlewood and others. This whole period of levelling and experiment looks in retrospect a great deal less exciting, as well as a good deal less innovative, than it felt at the time. But in the moving of the country, artistically speaking, beyond the age of the Lord Chamberlain and of what Kenneth Tynan called the 'Loamshire' style, the *NS* played an honourable role. And perhaps it is mistaken even to try to periodise writers and critics too strictly, or to make generalisations about cultural tendency. During this same time, people bought the *NS* simply in order to read Eric Hobsbawm on jazz or John Berger on painting. There was no 'trend' there, except in favour of people who wrote with gusto and knew and cared what they were talking about.

References to the magazine in contemporary fiction generally portray it as having an image of worthiness, seriousness and honesty. These references, which one comes across in novels as diverse as Graham Greene's *The Human Factor* and Barbara Pym's *A Glass of Blessings*, are often slightly dowdy in their effect. George Orwell used the paper's name as a kind of synonym for 'safe' right-thinking liberalism. Simon Raven has employed it to denote the world of exacting standards and stern principle. Yet all of these tributes are, even when oblique, fairly flattering. They show the *NS* appearing to the English public mind as un-snobbish and un-parochial; as open and decent. On the terrible English 'brow' test, which can be almost as excruciating as the test of accents, the *NS* would come out, if it was a person, as being well-educated, non-specialist, unafraid of jousting or mixing with highbrows but wary of being too impressed by them. This makes, or made, a reasonable 'fit' with the concept of a civilising mission to the middle class.

In recent years, with the intensification of showbiz values in publishing and in mass media generally, the *NS* has not found a voice in which to speak with much confidence. In particular, it has looked and felt uneasy in trying to keep up with the 'avid consumer' style of iconoclasm, where writing and criticism is little more than the monitoring and publicising of new waves. This sort of coverage *does* conform to Crossman's pretended ideal: people buy colourful anarchic rags in order to find what's on and feel no corresponding obligation to peruse the frantic essays and interviews in the 'front half'. One doubts, however, that they have many Tory friends to whom they must apologise for this lapse.

To borrow in a rather obvious way from Molière, it can be said that people make history without realising it. This can be true in alarming ways as well as in the wholesome, democratic sense that the *New Statesman* was founded to propagate. Not very long ago, *Granta* published an intimate account of the quotidian lives of the young scientists whose career path had been speeded up by their recruitment to the laboratories of SDI. They were depicted convincingly as having no reflective capacity worth speaking of, and as passing their leisure time reading trash and eating ice-cream. When I read it I thought of what C.P. Snow (then a director of the *NS*) had written in the magazine as long ago as October 1956:

Harwell and Windscale have just as much spirit as Los Alamos and Chalk River: the neat petty-bourgeois houses, the tough and clever young, the crowds of children: they are symbols, frontier towns.

The recently released Cabinet papers for 1957 show that Harwell and Windscale both nearly melted down shortly after Snow wrote these ambivalent phrases, and that the near-catastrophe was covered up in the abiding interests of the 'special relationship'. Was this calamity quite related to his second observation?

When you meet the younger rank-and-file of scientists, it often seems that they do not read at all. ... When you ask them what they read – 'As a married man,' one says, 'I prefer the garden.' Another says: 'I always just like to use my books as tools.' (Difficult to resist speculating what kind of tool a book would make. A sort of hammer? A crude digging instrument?)

While this 'project of the whole man', as Lukács termed it, remains so distant, and while the very idea of public and social conscience has come under attack on such a broad front, it will be idle to say that radical and critical journalism has any want of subjects. On the contrary, there are innumerable areas of urgent interest and concern that only lack the proper attention and the apposite mode of expression. It has been very lowering to see, over the past few years, the atomisation of the 'good brave causes'; the erection of ever more intensely reified sectarian and minority definitions. As Edward Thompson put it, in *The Poverty of Theory*:

In the old days, vulgar Political Economy saw men's economic behaviour as being *lawed* (although workers were obtuse and refractory in obeying these laws), but allowed to the autonomous individual an area of freedom, in his intellectual, aesthetic or moral choices. Today, structuralisms engross this area from every side; we are *structured* by social relations, *spoken* by pre-given linguistic structures, *thought* by ideologies, *dreamed* by myths, *gendered* by patriarchal sexual norms, *bonded* by affective obligations, *cultured* by *mentalities*, and acted by history's script.

This fragmentation may be part of the widespread discredit of the 'socialist' or 'collectivist' outlook: a fashionable and ahistorical discredit which forgets that collective and even statist solutions are actually mandated by reality itself, and that the Right and the bureaucracy are quite capable of setting themselves such tasks if the Left rushes to forswear them. The whole process has been accompanied by a distinct rise in the jargon level and by a surly defection, to short-term and banal or to outright selfish politics, of many of the potential audience of the *NS*. Never has there been a more pressing need for a tough, ironic, omnivorous, *synthesising* style, which takes up fresh questions in order both to understand and to change them.

We would have to recreate the field of opportunity. But there might be some agreeable surprises in this undertaking. While nobody has been looking, the Cold War has inverted its own cherished premises and become a literal as well as metaphorical absurdity. While nobody has been looking, Europeans have begun to think more in common and even as we ourselves appear to revere it less and less – to adopt English as a *lingua franca*. While nobody has been looking, the once 'Third' World has been differentiating in startling and often encouraging ways. Once, at the Reichstag Museum, which is built into the very structure of the Berlin Wall, I came across an old poster from the radical days of German Social Democracy. It showed a horseshoe magnet spanning the divide between the halves of the continent. The magnetic pole planted in the East read *Democracy* and the equivalent in the West read *Socialism*. I admired the ambition and the mutuality of this image. A magazine that took that as its cause, *and* that drew on the traditions that led up to it, *and* that employed the resources of the English language as more than a means of communication, could probably still make a name for itself.

Christopher Hitchens
Washington–London, January 1988

PART ONE

◆

1913–1930

Low, 27 February 1926

The New Statesman *was born out of Fabianism, a child of Beatrice and Sidney Webb's plan to 'permeate' influential opinion with collectivist (not then specifically socialist, still less pro-Labour) ideas. Their choice for Editor was Clifford Sharp (1883–1935), whom Beatrice called a 'hard-minded conservative collectivist'. Sharp edited the paper into the late twenties, though with his effectiveness increasingly undermined by chronic alcoholism. The paper's board eased him out at the end of 1928, and Charles Mostyn Lloyd – who had in any case effectively been running the show since 1926 – stood in until Kingsley Martin's appointment in 1930.*

In the years before his health was broken, Sharp's editorial skills were generally admired. He had clear if narrow preferences: logic, 'common sense' and persuasiveness rather than literary grace; a fierce disdain for anything that seemed to him like sentiment; strong personal antipathy toward Lloyd George; a growing closeness to Asquithian Liberalism which estranged him politically from most of the NS's founders, staff and readers. His own writing at best – as for instance in his reactions to the Easter Rising in Dublin and to the General Strike, reproduced here – shows the strengths of these attributes. His heavy editorial hand, which made him ever more enemies, displayed their weaknesses.

Among those Sharp estranged was the most famous and controversial of all the early contributors, GEORGE BERNARD SHAW. Here he is, in typically provocative style, on the issue *which dominated political debate in the paper's early months: Ireland.*

A Note on Irish Nationalism

The world seems just now to have made up its mind that self-consciousness is a very undesirable thing and Nationalism a very fine thing. This is not a very intelligent conclusion; for obviously, Nationalism is nothing but a mode of self-consciousness, and a very aggressive one at that. It is, I think, altogether to Ireland's credit that she is extremely tired of the subject of herself. Even patriotism, which in England is a drunken jollity when it is not a Jewish rhapsody, is in

Ireland like the genius of Jeremiah, a burning fire shut up in the bones, a pain, a protest against shame and defeat, a morbid condition which a healthy man must shake off if he is to keep sane. If you want to bore an Irishman, play him an Irish melody, or introduce him to another Irishman. The modern Irish theatre began with the *Kathleen ni Houlihan* of Mr Yeats and Lady Gregory's *Rising of the Moon*, in which the old patriotism stirred and wrung its victims; but when the theatre thus established called on Young Ireland to write Irish plays and found a national school of drama, the immediate result was a string of plays of Irish life – and very true to life they were – in which the heroines proclaimed that they were sick of Ireland and rated their Nationalist husbands for sacrificing all the realities of life to senseless Fenian maunderings, and the heroes damned Ireland up hill and down dale in the only moments of enthusiasm their grey lives left possible.

Abroad, however, it is a distinction to be an Irishman; and accordingly the Irish in England flaunt their nationality. An Englishman who had married an Irishwoman once came to me and asked me could I give him the name of any Englishman who had ever done anything. He explained that his wife declared that all England's statesmen, all her warriors, all her musical composers, all her notables of every degree were Irishmen, and that the English could not write their names until the Irish taught them. I suggested Gladstone. 'She says he was an Irishman' was the reply. After this, it was clear that the man's case was desperate; so I left him to his fate.

From this you may gather that the reaction against the Nationalist variety of self-consciousness does not, unfortunately, mean a reaction against conceit, against ignorance, against insular contempt for foreigners, against bad manners and the other common human weaknesses which sometimes masquerade as patriotism. Ireland produces virulent varieties of all of them; for it is, on the whole, a mistake to suppose that we are a nation of angels. You can always find something better than a good Englishman and something worse than a bad one; but this is not so in Ireland: a bad Irishman is the vilest thing on earth, and a good one is a saint. Thackeray's Barry Lyndon is a very accurate sketch of the sort of thoroughpaced scoundrel Ireland can produce, not when she is put to it, but quite wantonly, merely for the fun of being mischievous. In point of conceit, Ireland, especially northern Ireland, can stagger humanity. The Ulster Unionist is not a shrewd calculator who, on a careful estimate of the pressure of public opinion on any Government which should try to coerce Belfast into submission to a Dublin Parliament, concludes that he can safely bluff Home Rule out of Ulster: he really believes, as so many of the Boer farmers believed, that he can fight and conquer the British Empire, or any other empire that is not Ulster and Protestant. This is not a respectable infatuation; and if there were nothing else to be considered except the salvation of the Ulsterman's soul, it would be a positive duty for the British Empire to blow him sky high to convince him that even a Unionist God (and he believes in no other, and therefore does not really believe in God at all) has occasionally to look beyond Down and Antrim. A new siege of Derry under a capable commander would be an invaluable corrective to the old one, as it would last about ten minutes, and end in an ignominious surrender of as much of Derry as might be left. But these military moral lessons, fashionable as they are, cost more than the souls of the regenerated (not to mention the bodies of those they kill) are worth; and it would, I think, be more sensible to make Ulster an autonomous political lunatic asylum, with Sir Edward Carson as head keeper, and an expensive fleet and a heavily fortified frontier to hold against the Pope, than to thwart its inclinations in any way. The alternative, if England would stand it, would be to make Ulster a province of England, and have the Education Acts and the Factory Acts applied in the English manner; but I doubt if Ulster would tamely submit to be identified with a country where men touch their hats to a Roman Catholic Duke of Norfolk, and meet him at dinner as if he were their equal. On the whole, the notion of a Kingdom of Orangia (Ibsen invented the name in *The Master Builder*) is the more amusing. When it came to paying for the frontier fortifications and the new Harland & Wolff fleet, the South would smile sunnily.

What will finally settle the Ulster question, probably, is just the old-fashioned romantic Nationalism of which the South is so deadly tired. That hackneyed fisherman who saw the round towers of other days in the waves beneath him shining, pursued his not very lucrative occupation on the banks of Lough Neagh, and was no doubt an Orangeman. Now it happens that the true Ulsterman is a harsh father; and his son's chief joy when he is old enough to dare to differ from his violent and bigoted parent is to profess every opinion that can defy and exasperate the old man. And, indeed, it is clear, as the world is now constituted, that prudent young men should aim at being as unlike Orangemen and as like human beings as possible, even as in the South the young men are discovering that in point of insufferableness there is not a halfpenny to choose between a Nationalist and an Orangeman. Thus, though the Protestant boys will still carry the drum, they will carry it under the green flag, and realise that the harp, the hound, and the round tower are more satisfactory to the imagination than that stupidest of decorative designs the Union Jack, which, it must be admitted, is, considered merely as a decorative design, the most resourceless of patterns. And the change can be effected without treachery to England; for, if my personal recollection does not deceive me, the Gaelic League began in Bedford Park, London, W., after a prolonged incubation in Somerset House.

It is not very long since I stood on the coast of Donegal and asked two boys how many languages they had. They had three. One was English, which they spoke much better than it is ever spoken in England. The second was Irish, which they spoke with their parents. The third was the language invented by the Gaelic League, which I cannot speak (being an Irishman), but which I understand to be in its qualities comparable to a blend of Esperanto with fifth-century Latin. Why should not Ulster adopt this strange tongue? Its very name suggests Scotland, which is what the present vernacular of the north also suggests.

The truth is that all the Nationalist inventions that catch on now are not Irish at all. For instance, the admirable comedies of Synge, who, having escaped from Ireland to France, drew mankind in the manner of Molière, and discreetly assured the public that this was merely the human nature of the Blasket Islands, and that, of course, civilised people never admired boastful criminals nor esteemed them according to the atrocities they pretended to commit. The Playboy's real name was Synge; and the famous libel on Ireland (and who is Ireland that she should not be libelled as other countries are by their great comedians?) was the truth about the world.

George Bernard Shaw, 12 July 1913

The Irish rising of Easter 1916 won little support at the time, but gained mass retrospective approval through the blundering brutality of the British response. CLIFFORD SHARP, typically, attacked that response not as immoral but as irrational.

Nothing, it seems to us, is more to be regretted in connection with the Dublin tragedy than the hasty decision of the authorities to execute three of the ringleaders. We question not the justice of the decision – as human justice is generally reckoned – but its wisdom. *Cui bono?* If the answer is that these men had caused a great deal of innocent blood to flow and richly deserved their fate, we certainly shall not dispute it; but that answer is equivalent to a confession that the executions were inspired by mere righteous indignation, rather than by any consideration for the future of Ireland – which, after all, ought to be the Government's main concern. Moreover, if the sentences were a matter of abstract retributive justice, why, out of the captured signatories of the Rebel Manifesto, were only three ordered to be shot, after an inquiry which cannot conceivably have been sufficiently searching to establish relative degrees of guilt? If the three executed men had been killed in the fighting, few would have regretted them; or if, while the fighting was still going on, the Commander-in-Chief had considered it necessary to make an example of them in order to put a speedy end to the rebellion, we do not doubt that his action would have been generally endorsed. But the rebellion was already completely crushed; and the executions, therefore, though they were carried out by the orders of a Court Martial, must be regarded not as a military but as a civil and political measure – directly authorised presumably by the civil Government in London. The only alternative plea, namely, that it was necessary to deal sternly with the ringleaders in order to deter other Irishmen from following their example in the future, is not one that will be put forward by anyone who has the smallest knowledge of Ireland or Ireland's history.

A week ago these three men were recognised as foolish firebrands who had imperilled the welfare of their country, and as such they were execrated by the great mass of their fellow-citizens. But now they have atoned for all their mistakes by paying the full price, and in the heart of every Irishman their names are already added to that long list of heroes and martyrs who have died at English hands for the sake of Ireland's freedom. That is what the Court Martial has done for them. Was it worth it? But we suspect that the Government never took time to consider whether it was worth it. We suspect it was a case not so much of considered action as of automatic reaction to the charges of indecision which have been brought against them. They wished, we suppose, to show that they could act sternly and decisively when they chose. In such a case, however, conscious strength would have shown itself in merciful rather than in retributive justice – but that would have been strength of a quality which, perhaps, it needs a Lincoln to exhibit.

Clifford Sharp, 6 May 1916

*LENNOX ROBINSON, the week after Sharp's editorial, had his finger
more surely on the pulse of the Irish nationalist temperament.*

A Sinn Feiner

One spring day eight, or perhaps nine, years ago, walking down the
village street, the contents bill of a newspaper caught his eye. The title
was not entirely unfamiliar to him; even in the columns of the Unionist
papers, which were the only journals he saw, from time to time a
sentence of careless scorn had been thrown at something called 'Sinn
Fein', but what exactly those mysterious words stood for (he knew no
Gaelic) he had only the vaguest idea. So he went into the little shop
and asked for a copy of the paper. The woman behind the counter
could not supply it, had never had a copy; the contents bill had been
sent down as wrapping paper by the Dublin newsagent; but, of course,
if he wished, she would order it for him. He did wish it, and from that
time onward read it weekly.

He was young then – little more than a boy. He came of Unionist
parents, and the difference between his opinions and theirs – afterwards
so great – was then only shyly beginning to appear. God knows what
vagrant wind sowed that strange seed in his heart, but the little paper
with the queer name fostered its growth. Perhaps big things had always
– in a sense – oppressed him, and he turned in relief from the big city
to the village, from limitless tracts of country to local places well
known, from the vast, world-flung British Empire to tiny Ireland.
Whatever the reason, he quickly grew to believe (in his young, ignorant
way) that it was possible that Providence had not strangely unfitted
Ireland to govern herself, that she even might some day exist as an
independent nation; but this last was a dream too vague and vaporous
to be spoken of; other things lay nearer at hand, and must come first.

The other things were, often, mundane enough. There was, for
instance, besides the newly-found poetry of Ireland, the newly-found
Irish tweed. A descent to bathos, possibly; yet in a country so fruitful in
religious orders it was not difficult to connect the clothing of the body
with a dedication of life and mind, nor is it an exaggeration to say that,
with the donning of that tweed, a certain conscious act of dedication
had taken place (oh, not priggishly, he hoped, rather shyly and
secretly), and that for the future he lived for something bigger and
better than himself.

He has never once regretted that act of dedication, never tried to
free himself from those vows. Religion – in the ordinary sense – as he
grew older receded farther from him, it touched him less and less, and,

knowing his own weakness, he is glad of that image he raised (false god though many may call it); he knows it has kept him cleaner, straighter, truer.

His work – not unconnected with that image – did not, in his opinion, allow him to join himself with any political organisation. He regretted this; it cut him off from his fellow worshippers, and even, years later, when his work changed and left him more free, a tangle of circumstances still kept him apart. But their image, their dream, was his, too; and as, month by month, he saw his country grow more confused, unguided, unhelped, groping like a sick man in a darkened room, he rejoiced at the strong body of independent criticism that was rising up under the name of Sinn Fein.

The body of Sinn Feiners swept past him in an eager troop. He stood on the fringe of the crowd and lifted his hat to them. They were the youngest, the cleanest, the best of the country. . . . They swept past him, their rifles flashing in the sun. He followed them in his heart.

But only in his heart. And there lies the peculiar ache that he feels now; there is the pain-point – that so many he knew and honoured have fought, lost all for the dream's sake, died – while he has stood aloof. Aloof, not altogether because of circumstances, aloof also because he believes them to have been madly mistaken, because he believes they have done to death the thing they and he loved. But the image of Pearse – most gentle of men – risking everything, fighting, wounded, court-martialled, shot – drives him to search his own heart in terror for some weakness that has preserved him safe without risk or loss.

He would be prouder and happier to-day could he count Pearse and the others as his comrades. Passed away for ever now are those words of scorn: 'gun-shy ganders,' 'fine Sunday afternoon soldiers'; be their cause good or ill, they fought a hopeless fight with tenacity and high courage, and regular soldiers, without hesitation, spoke comparatively of Loos and Gallipoli. And they fought, cleanly and with order, without excesses, without drunkenness. He was not mistaken in his estimation of those bright marching lads. He raised his hat with a cheer as they passed; he raises it now, with sad reverence, standing by their graves.

Lennox Robinson, 13 May 1916

Irish events – this time the bitterly fought Dublin industrial struggle led by James Larkin in 1913 – also extracted from SIDNEY WEBB

something as near to passion as he ever came, in this classic defence of
the right to strike.

Strikes and the Law

The uneasiness of 'the City' and the comfortable classes with regard to
strikes and rumours of strikes is a social phenomenon of some
consequence, with reverberations that are penetrating, we believe, even
to Cabinet Councils. Starvation, indeed, may perhaps be winning back
for Mr William Martin Murphy an industrial Dublin of which the whole
nation has become ashamed. But if the successive food-ships of the Co-
operative Wholesale Society fail to raise the siege, if the hoped-for
Australian remittances fail to arrive, if, in short, 'Larkinism' is by the
apathy of the Irish Parliamentary Party temporarily crushed, things will
not be quite as they were in Irish politics, or, for that matter, in English
politics either. The failure of the Irish Executive to control its police; its
refusal to inquire into their conduct; the neglect of the Castle even to
take steps to compel the enforcement of the humane provisions of the
Poor Law, by which the women and children might have been saved
from the horrors of starvation – all this is debited, and is, in our
judgment, rightly debited, to Mr Asquith's Cabinet, which is, whatever
its opinion on Mr Larkin's manners, responsible for seeing that Dublin
– whether or not the employers persist in the lock-out which Sir George
Askwith has condemned – does not die in the streets. But we can close
our ears to the miseries of Dublin. More alarming to folk in Great
Britain is the decision of the Miners' Federation to seek an alliance of
forces with the railwaymen and the transport workers, with the express
object of securing that when again the coalminers have to strike there
shall be carried no 'tainted coal,' from Belgium or elsewhere. The
National Union of Railwaymen have voted, by a huge majority, to give
the necessary notice to terminate the elaborate scheme of Conciliation
Boards which was forced on them. Up and down the country, where
the first faint signs of a coming fall of in trade are being recognised,
employers are wondering what sort of reception their contemplated
reductions of wages will meet.

No one can pretend to view with equanimity the misery and
suffering, the anger and demoralisation – to say nothing of the
economic waste – that are involved in strikes and lock-outs. But there is
something hypocritical in the attitude of a community which avowedly
leaves the livelihood of its labourers to be settled by 'supply and
demand,' and then cherishes resentment against them if they strike for

higher wages, or are locked out by the employers for refusing to accept their terms. It may be absurd for a professedly civilised country to leave these things to the arbitrament of what is really civil war on the economic plane. But if we insist on 'free competition,' and deliberately tell each employer to buy his labour on the cheapest market, we cannot decently turn around and complain when the parties to the bargain come to a deadlock. It may be highly inconvenient that the railway companies and the railway workers should refuse to enter into a wage-contract. But what alternative is there? We have, as a nation, chosen this method of settling the conditions of life of the wage-earning millions. We have been hypocritical enough to advise them to combine, and to praise them for their capacity for co-operation; whilst secretly feeling sure that there would always be found sufficient blacklegs to keep the railways working, so that the workmen's combinations would not really be successful. If, however, the railwaymen, the coalminers, and the transport workers effect a genuine alliance, with an aggregate trade union membership of considerably more than a million, where will the nation find itself? There would be a cry that the mines must be kept going, and the railways kept working, even if the sailors of the fleet and the soldiers from our regiments have to take over the management. But this would be for the Government to fail to keep the ring, to abandon its position of neutrality, and to interfere on behalf of the employers. If the Government once took over the management of the mines and the railways, would it ever be allowed to give them back?

Slowly the nation is being brought to understand that the 'supply and demand' and 'free competition' theory of wages is not one to which we can afford to commit either the standard of life of our workers or the smooth running of our industries. Step by step we have been driven to intervene, and in the public interest to prescribe by law, one after another, the minimum conditions of the contract which employers or wage-earners shall be permitted to accept. We do not leave the parties quite free to bargain as to the hours of labour. In trade after trade, for class after class of wage-earners, we fix a legal minimum of recreation time (by prescribed maximum hours of work, stated meal-times, holidays, early closing, etc.) on which not even the most grasping employer or the most shortsightedly industrious operative is allowed to trench. In industry after industry we fix by law minimum conditions of sanitation and safety which no careless worker is allowed to dispense with, in return even for higher wages, and no heedless employer is permitted to escape, even if his whole margin of profit is thereby destroyed. And now, learning from the extraordinarily successful Australasian experience, we fix by law, in half a dozen sweated trades and imperfectly in coal mining, the lowest rates of wages which, in the interests of the community as a whole, any employer shall be allowed to pay and any worker permitted to accept. An this 'Policy of the National Minimum,' once denounced by the employers as 'Jack Cade legislation,' because it 'robbed them of their right to cheap labour,' is now the principle that our Cabinet professedly accepts, however much particular Ministers in their respective departments may fail to carry it out. 'Every society is judged,' Mr Asquith has expressly laid down, 'according to the material and moral minumum that it *prescribes* to its members.'

This plan of fixing by law, through the machinery of Trade Boards or other representative joint committees, the minimum conditions which the community will allow, and enforcing this minimum by criminal prosecutions – this last point not yet conceded to the coalminers – does not put any compulsion on either employers or workmen to enter into contracts of service. No employer is required to go into business, or to keep his works running, or to take on any men whatsoever. All that the law requires is that if he does choose to go into business he shall not do so under conditions – such, for instance, as those revealed at Dublin – as are injurious to the commonweal. Similarly no workman is required to engage himself, or to accept any particular wages, or to work with any particular associates. All that the law requires is that if he does work he shall not do so under conditions judged injurious to the nation. Thus a Legal Minumum Wage, like the best possible Factory Acts, does not afford a complete guarantee against strikes or lock-outs. But twenty years' experience proves that, by preventing on the one hand the degradation of the worker, and on the other the occasional tyranny or oppression of particular employers – by bringing to bear on the Murphys and Larkins the collective judgment of their respective classes – a Minimum Wage Law and a complete Factory Act do avail, in practice, to prevent the happening of nineteen industrial stoppages out of twenty.

We must distinguish in this connection between what is commonly referred to as 'Compulsory Arbitration' and a Minimum Wage Law. *The latter does not fix the wage.* Like the Factory Acts, of which it is an extension, it only prescribes a minimum. The decision of an Australian Wages Board, or of an English Trade Board, declaring that the minimum wage shall be a pound a week, does not impose any obligation, legal or moral, on any workman to demand no more, or on any employer to offer no higher figure. As a matter of fact, both in England and Australia employers pay more than the minimum, and there have been strikes, and successful strikes, for higher rates than the minimum that the Board has declared. This bilateral right to pay more and to demand more must be carefully preserved. Very different is the case with arbitration. An arbitrator in a trade dispute fixes, after hearing the parties, the rate of wages and other conditions at which he thinks that the combatants ought to resume work. Compulsory arbitration means that to such an award the force of law is to be given. Thus once the award is made every employer in the trade would presumably be required, under pain of prosecution, to take on workmen at the wage fixed, even if his business was thereby rendered unprofitable. Every workman belonging to the trade would be compelled to accept employment at the wages fixed or be summonsed in default. This, in fact, is quite impracticable, and hence the idea of preventing all strikes and lock-outs by compulsory arbitration is a dream. And seeing that, in practice, it would mean that the workers and their trade unions would find themselves attached for contempt of court if they ventured to make a stand for more than the award – the employers would have other ways of escaping its scope – the Trades Union Congress is right in persistently rejecting any idea of compulsory arbitration. On the other hand, the extension of the Trade Boards Act, and thereby of the Legal Minimum Wage enforced as a minimum by criminal prosecutions, to agricultural labour, to the railway service, to all occupations in which wages under thirty shillings per week are being paid, and in due course to all industries whatever, on the lines that Mr Asquith himself has suggested, is the most pressing of all industrial reforms. Until this is done the workers, counting the dire cost to themselves and their families, are as right to strike against what they feel to be oppression as any nation can be to undertake a war of liberation.

Sidney Webb, 18 October 1913

Ireland apart, the issue most preoccupying debate before the deluge of 1914 was the women's suffrage movement. Suffragette leader CHRISTABEL PANKHURST put the case for militant direct action, and against the right of any male morally to judge women's action, in terms which would be instantly recognisable within feminism today.

Militancy

Militancy is, as it were, the flowering of the woman's movement for equality. Women's long existing, hidden discontent with their conditions of inferiority, and the patient and law-abiding Woman

Suffrage campaign of the last century, were the preparation for militancy.

The non-militant suffrage agitation was of the nineteenth century; the militant agitation is of the twentieth. The anti-militant Suffragism of the present day is, in the opinion of the militant women, an anachronism. Militancy is a political weapon used by women as the only discoverable substitute for the vote. But it is more than that. It is a means of breaking up the false relation of inferior to superior that has existed between men and women, and it is a means of correcting the great faults that have been produced in either sex by the subjection of women.

Subjection had made women unnaturally diffident and unnaturally submissive. Their dominion over women has made men overbearing and vainglorious. Militancy is a sign and an expression of the fact that women have shaken off their diffidence and their servility. Women's militancy is an education to men, because it shows them women not any longer appealing to them – 'coaxing them,' as Mr Lloyd George has put it – but, instead, denying their title to withhold the vote.

Anti-militancy involves an admission that men ought to be obeyed and their laws obeyed by women in spite of the disfranchisement of women. Anti-militancy is therefore perilously near to anti-Suffragism. It is, in fact, indistinguishable from the policy of the patient Griselda. For Suffragists to be law-abiding at any and every cost is an evil, because this flatters the self-importance of men and disinclines them to concede a demand so meekly made of them. Militancy has not only educated men by proving that there is a limit to women's endurance, but it has roused the best in them. Never since the days of John Stuart Mill, who, with other men of a most exceptional quality, made the Woman Suffrage cause his own, have men so greatly served this cause as during the days of militancy. The spectacle of women fighting for liberty and literally facing death for its sake has more power to rouse men's sense of justice than have any words, however wise and eloquent.

There has been much vague denunciation of militancy, but not a single valid argument has been brought against its use. As a political method it holds the field to the exclusion of every other, save that of voting. It is idle to point to other countries in which women have won the vote by peaceful means. These other countries are not Britain. Politics and political activity do not in any other country hold the same high place in the interest of men as they hold in Britain. Ours is an old country. Prejudice and conservatism in the ugliest sense of that term are entrenched here as they are entrenched nowhere else, unless it be in Turkey. The British man's attitude towards women – above all the British politician's attitude towards women – is a matter of contempt and derision in our Colonies, in America, and in all those enlightened countries where women have the vote. Comparisons between Suffrage conditions in Britain and Suffrage conditions elsewhere are in the highest degree misleading. Besides, it is impossible to ignore the fact that it is since the beginning of British militancy, which has called to attention the whole civilised world, that the greater number of Suffrage victories have occurred. Nothing can be more unprofitable than for a British Suffragist to be day-dreaming about the victories won by peaceful methods in countries more enlightened than her own. There is for her no wisdom save in reflection upon the past political history of her own country, in observation of the conditions now existing there, and in the invention of a policy based upon historical knowledge and upon a knowledge of the temperament of her countrymen and the existing political conditions of her own land. For the British Suffragist militancy is the only way. Militancy will succeed where all other policies will fail.

The virtue of militancy proceeds from the fact that government rests upon the consent of the governed. When the unenfranchised become ungovernable, then is enfranchisement given to them. The only reason why militancy has not long ago resulted in the conquest of votes for women is that not enough women have been militant. The number of militants required to create a situation from which the Government will be driven to escape by granting votes for women is a matter which experiment alone can determine. To those who still doubt the necessity of militancy, the final answer is this. Consider the men who now are at the head of the political parties, consider the men not yet advanced to leadership who are likely to succeed them, and then say whether you believe that the Asquiths, the Lloyd Georges, or the F.E. Smiths, of the present or of the future, are likely to be moved to give votes to women by reasoned and patient appeal – by anything save sheer compulsion!

The case for militancy as a political method is unassailable. Attacks upon militancy have, however, been made chiefly on the score of morality. Militancy, we are told, is wrong, and lawlessness and violence are wrong. The breach of a law, as John Hampden and others have taught by word and by example, is right or wrong according to the nature of the law and the authority possessed by the law-giver. Bad laws made without due authority ought not to be obeyed, but ought to be resisted by every honest man and woman. It is such laws that militant Suffragists have broken. By marching to Parliament Square they have broken laws which seek to prevent them as voteless citizens from using the only means available to them of claiming the redress of their grievances. But apart from that, all the laws on the Statute book are, as they affect women, bad for want of lawful authority in those

who have made them. Women's claim to the vote implies a denial of
the validity of any law to which their consent has not, through their
duly elected representatives, been obtained. Violence is wrong, say the
anti-militants. Nothing could be more untrue. Violence has no moral
complexion whatsoever. In itself it is neither right nor wrong. Its
rightness or wrongness depends entirely upon the circumstances under
which it is used. If violence is wrong in itself, then it is wrong to break a
breakfast egg, it is wrong to hammer in a nail, it is wrong to pierce a
tunnel through the rock, it is wrong to break into a burning house to
save the life of a child. Yet, as we know, all these actions are entirely
moral. This is because, though violent, they, like militancy, are justified
by the motive of those who do them and the object with which they are
done. If there are any who still condemn militancy, then they must
condemn nature herself, the Arch-Militant, who to achieve her
purposes works so much violence.

The strange fact is that many fervent anti-militants are themselves in
favour of militancy – when it is the militancy of men. Some of the
foremost amongst them vigorously upheld the South African war, with
all its accompaniments of farm-burning and concentration camps. Their
souls were thrilled to sympathetic approval when men were militant in
Turkey at the time of the revolution, when men were militant during
the Chinese revolution, and when men were militant in the Balkan
States. Approval of all this militancy was publicly expressed by the
leaders of anti-militant Suffragism. Even women they will allow to be
militant provided they are not militant in the cause of votes for women.
Thus in the official organ of the law-abiding movement we read these
words:

> The world is governed by ideas, and force is helpless against them. Not the
> arms of France, but the faith of Joan of Arc turned the tide of fortune against
> the English in the Hundred Years' war. Not the arms of William of Orange,
> but his spirit and the spirit of his people, their patriotism, their religion, wore
> down the innumerable hosts of Spain.

These words represent precisely the view held by the militants,
though they come strangely from the pen of women who condemn
militancy. It is the conviction of the militants that their lesser force will
overcome the greater force directed against them by the Government.
This will happen because of the faith that is in the militants, and
because of the spirit of which militancy is the expression. But that does
not mean that Suffragists can win without the use of force. If Joan of
Arc had relied upon faith without force it is not unlikely that the
English would have been in possession of France at the present day. If
William of Orange had trusted to spirit, patriotism, and religion and

nothing more to win his battles, his military successes would have been inconspicuous indeed! The truth is that violence in such cases is itself the expression of the faith, spirit, patriotism and religion of those who employ it. It is then that we have militancy. Violence that is not inspired by spirit and illuminated by faith is not militancy, it is brutality. It is the Suffragettes who are militant, while the Government seek to overcome them by brutality.

People have said as an argument against militancy that it 'rouses the beast in men' – the beast that, as they say, civilisation has put to sleep. If there are men possessed by a familiar spirit so unpleasant as to deserve this name, it is time that that spirit were driven out of them. Better far that well-fed, self-reliant, happy women should undertake the task of luring forth the beast and slaying it than its victims should be, as now they are, white slaves and other unhappy, exploited women. It would seem that the anti-militants take a less favourable view of the nature of the opposite sex than do the Suffragettes. The Suffragettes pay men the compliment of believing that the brutal is not an essential and unchangeable part of them to be drugged into quiescence, but never to be eradicated.

There are people, again, whose objections to militancy seem to be based on the fact that it involves the destruction of property. They would appear to forget that human liberty may, after all, be worth some broken windows or a blaze or two. Whatever may happen, militancy done for the sake of votes for women is not likely to be so destructive to the material interests of the country as was the South African war, waged for the sake of votes for men.

In answering objections to militancy, the Suffragettes have regard to the objections raised by the women rather than to those raised by men. To men critics a sufficient reply is this: 'If you don't like militancy give us the vote, and that quickly!' It ill becomes men to prate of mere property and the Suffragettes' destruction of it, while the nation is being ravaged by venereal disease and innocent women in thousands are being infected by such a disease.

The opposition to women's militancy is founded upon prejudice, and upon nothing else. For the very same acts of militancy that militant women commit would, if they were committed by voteless men, be applauded. The moral law which the Suffragettes have defied is not the moral law accepted for themselves by men. It is slave morality that the militant women have denied and defied – slave morality according to which active resistance to tyranny is the greatest crime that a subject class or a subject sex can commit.

Christabel Pankhurst, 1 November 1913

For a time – a brief time – both Irish and women's affairs were swept from attention by the collapse into war. In the short interval between the killing of the Archduke at Sarajevo and the outbreak of war J.C. SQUIRE, one of the most prolific and thoughtful columnists on the early NS staff, reflected on the history and morality of political assassination.

Political Assassination

The assassination of princes is a practice as old as the world. It is as old as generosity, as old as envy, as old as revenge, and as old as lunacy. Harmodius and Aristogeiton were not the first of their race, and Aristotle in his *Politics* devoted several pages to an analysis of the several kinds and causes of political murders. Under the Empire the crime was so prevalent that, as Gibbon says, 'Such was the unhappy condition of the Roman emperors, that, whatever might be their conduct, their fate was commonly the same.' But genuine concern for the public interest as a motive seems scarcely to have occurred to Aristotle, and certainly not to most of the Roman assassins. A Brutus may (possibly) have sacrificed his prince (*de facto*) and himself in the interests of Republicanism just as later on a Guyon offered up his enemy's life and his own on behalf of the Catholic cause. Common such motives have never been until the last forty years. In no previous epoch, so far as history tells, have so many of the governors of mankind been killed, not by their rivals, but by their humbler subjects. Think of the list: Alexander of Russia, Humbert of Italy, Carlos of Portugal, Presidents Carnot, McKinley, and Lincoln, the Grand Duke Sergius, a Shah of Persia, King Constantine of Greece, Franz Ferdinand of Austria, with Ignatieff, Min, Bobrikoff, Boutros Pasha, Canalejas, Prince Ito, Plehve, and scores of other ministers and officials. Modern history streams with the blood of murdered authority. And most of it has been shed, however mistakenly, with the object of serving the public interest. 'No man,' as Bacon says, 'doth a wrong for the wrong's sake.' Where there is no private motive you could safely assume a public one, even were such a one not invariably announced by the modern assassin. Most of the murdered rulers we have mentioned were neither worse nor better than other rulers or than other men. By obscure men either of their own race or of another they were killed because they held their offices, because they represented dominance of family, caste, wealth or race. Even the cretin Luccheni, who stabbed the unoffending Empress of Austria, had in his insane brain the glimmering of an idea that he was assisting the progress of mankind. Moonshine on a dunghill, perhaps; but the light was there.

It is a commonplace that assassinations are least common in the Teutonic and more advanced countries. In England we have never known many of them. Voltaire remarked of us that 'it was the characteristic of this nation ever to commit murders with the law on their side.' He may or may not have been correct, but it is significant that the only political murders committed of recent years in the United Kingdom were those of Cavendish and Burke by a band of revolutionary Irishmen and that of Sir Curzon Wylie by a revolutionary Indian. Governing Englishmen are killed overseas by members of subject races who consider themselves oppressed, but they are not killed at home. No doubt that is largely due to our traditional political freedom. We are accustomed to regard our rulers when they err as faithless servants rather than as cruel tyrants. But the logical Teutonic temperament, always inclining us to act by reason, must also have something to do with it, for Germany shares our immunity without sharing our democratic institutions. Even in America the last important murder was committed not by an American, but by a Slav, who had learnt his views of Government elsewhere.

In the assassination areas political murders are most frequent where a subject race or a depressed class have most reason for complaint. They are foam on the wave of protest. But their effectiveness and excusableness vary enormously with circumstances. 'I think,' we heard a lady say in an omnibus on Monday, 'that these Anarchists ought to be shot at sight.' She got out, as we knew she would, at the Army and Navy Stores. But, on the whole, if militant Anarchists were only identifiable at sight (say, by horns, hoofs, and tail), we should certainly agree with her. Anarchists who murder on theory because they object to all constituted authority are really homicidal monomaniacs. A man sits down, by himself or with six friends, in the middle of a community which, whatever its grievances, does not agree with him, and decides that government must be abolished by the removal of the governors. The horror and the absurdity of the theory was put epigrammatically by Shakespeare when he made Brutus cry:

> Stoop, Romans, stoop,
> And let us bathe our hands in Caesar's blood
> Up to the elbows, and besmear our swords.
> Then walk we forth, even to the market-place,
> And, waving our red weapons o'er our heads,
> Let's all cry Peace! Freedom! and Liberty!

And we know from experience that these murders committed by individuals and small groups of conspirators are as unfruitful as they are revolting. What difference did the death of Carnot, of King Humbert, of McKinley make? What difference could they have made? One man steps off the scene, another man steps into his shoes. All goes on as it was before. Political murders by individual cranks never have either reason or result. They may be inevitable as long as grave social disorders exist; conditions which distress ten millions of people may well send ten people mad. But madmen never yet did any good, and the usual type of modern political murderer is a man who has gone mad because of an inordinate sensitiveness to the sufferings of himself or his fellows combined with an inordinate vanity which makes him believe he has discovered that murder is a panacea for them.

But there is another kind of political assassination to which resort is had by a much saner sort of man, and for which a much more presentable defence can be put up: we refer to assassination systematically used as one weapon out of many in what is virtually a war between classes or between races. 'You must know then,' remarked Machiavelli to his Prince, 'that there are two methods of fighting, the one by law, the other by force; the first method is that of men, the second of beasts; but as the first method is often insufficient, one must have recourse to the second. It is therefore necessary to know well how to use both the beast and the man.' The doctrines of that most honest of political philosophers are held to-day by large classes of oppressed men. The murder of the late King of Portugal was a deliberate step in a successful revolution. It might have been avoided; if it was unnecessary, it was indefensible (we assume for the moment the point of view of the 'reforming' party); but it was a reasoned and calculated act which quite sane men may have expected to be effective. The Russian murders are also episodes in a war. The Tsardom, backed by its officials and its army, stands on one side: the mass of the people on the other. A permanent state of war exists; no quarter is given on either side; the revolutionaries believe that if the man is mingled with the beast their enemies may be terrorised into submission. Their aim has been to make it not worth anybody's while to take a job under the despotism. Some of the most dignified and heroic figures in Russian annals have been murderers. Stepniak himself killed a man, and the heroic, intellectual, virtuous and broad-minded girl who receives the lash and goes to Siberia for tyrannicide is a commonplace of Western journalism. Whether assassination in Russia has done anything is a point on which reasonably men may differ; and it is at any rate arguable that it might have done much had the body of murderer-martyrs been larger and better organised. The Russian political assassins may have been mistaken in thinking that assassination could ever be wholesale enough to be a really effective revolutionary weapon: but they at any rate were not all cranks or lunatics, and they could at least put up a serious case. We conceive that circumstances might arise in which a conquered race might hold the same sentiments when confronted by a distasteful and unyielding government.

That the most recent of political assassinations is the outcome of any such general popular movement we see no reason to believe. There were certainly reasons why the Orthodox Serbs should have wished the Archduke to be removed, but there is no evidence that the murder was part of any reasoned plan of campaign. The Archduke's political idiosyncracies and influence being what they were, this may possible prove one of those rare modern cases in which a single murder makes a big difference. But, whether or not Prinzip's hopes were vain, every man who knows human nature must feel some compassion for him. Mentally degenerate, morally one-eyed, though a Prinzip and a Moral may be, who knows what abysses of suffering, what awful exultations and despairs they may not have experienced before and after resolving to sacrifice themselves for their fellows? The gradual conviction of a calling, the nightly horror of the law's grip and the rope, the wild imaginings of shots fired and a wolfish crowd pouncing on one to carry one off to death, the strange glow of triumph in a tremendous deed done: it makes one shiver to think of it all. Even around the most degraded of those who throw their lives thus away clings something of the glory of that Winkelried who clasped a score of the enemy's spear-points to his breast. 'Shot at sight' they should be, perhaps; but if so, then not without reverence and not without humility before the awful agony, the sublime courage and strength of which human spirits are capable.

J.C. Squire, 4 July 1914

The great historian Sir LEWIS NAMIER was in some obvious ways an un-New Statesmanly figure: a high Tory and something of a snob. None the less he was a regular and always stimulating contributor, whether reviewing, expounding the Zionist idea or, as here, dissecting the background to the Russian Revolution.

Russian and the Bolsheviks

De Tocqueville, in explaining the origin of the French Revolution, lays emphasis on the equality of condition, education, and manners which had existed between the nobility and the Third Estate, and the galling inequality of rights. The result was the political revolution of 1789. The present social revolution in Russia is the outcome of a similar contrast. There is hardly a country in Europe where the equality of men is as real as in Russia, and where the economic contrast of classes is equally acute. France has her small rentiers and her conservative peasantry; England her well-to-do artisans, her office clerks and shop-assistants; Russia possesses practically none of these types in any considerable numbers. The peasant-holding in Russia is not a fixed, economically sufficient unit, like a farm in England or France or a *Bauernhof* in Germany, but a strip of land in the open fields. By subdivision among heirs this strip has been reduced below the minimum which, under the present backward system of tillage, could satisfy the needs of its owner. He therefore cries out for more land, for 'a new lot' to be got by breaking up the big landed estates. There is hardly another social type, except perhaps the miner, which has an equally strong consciousness of its separate individuality as the peasant. The peasants were actuated by class-consciousness ages before anyone discussed the matter. Peasant revolts, jacqueries, and *Bauernbündlerein* are the oldest form of class warfare; and conditions have made the Russian peasant into a revolutionary proletarian. In the Russian towns, on the other hand, work which in English offices is done by unskilled experts in the art of writing and counting without understanding anything of what they do, is performed by men of a very different mental calibre. There is the poor intelligentsia, men who in education and outlook are as much the equals of the biggest bourgeoisie as the bourgeois of pre-revolutionary France were of her nobility. But that intelligentsia consists largely of proletarians. The absence of them in England accounts for the mental poverty of our labour movements, their presence in Russia for the acute consciousness of the social conflict. Russia is rent between the bourgeoisie and the proletariat, and the present Revolution is mainly social.

But for the sake of Russia and the future of the world civil warfare between classes has now to be prevented. She has to fight out the present war to the end which her best idealists desire, she has to preserve her integrity and help in redeeming the liberty of those small nations in Eastern Europe which look to her as their safeguard against German dominion. The vast masses of the Russian people know but very little about these problems and ideas; no one has ever taught them, they have been merely driven like cattle into slaughter. Professor Pares, a reliable eye-witness, has told us recently that when Russian units went into action, no matter whether victorious or unsuccessful, losses amounting to half or even three-fourths of the effectives were expected.

The old regime cared as little for the lives and well-being of the soldiers as for their opinions. They have paid with their lives and with untold misery for the peculation and the crimes of their rulers. Can one, then, wonder at what has happened? The Revolution did not start in villages and factories, but in the Army. And when the peasant behind the front cried for land and the workman in the towns for bread, the soldier at the front cried out for liberty and peace. Could be be expected to credit his past rulers implicitly with high idealism and righteousness? Here are these immense illiterate masses asking why they should fight; here are these masses distrustful of the bourgeoisie almost as much as they were of the old regime, lumping the two together as 'rulers'; and educated men come forward who confirm them in their dark beliefs.

These men are the Bolsheviks. Roman law taught us *in servorum conditione nulla differentia est* – a slave cannot be possessed of any legal rights. The Bolsheviks believe that there can be no difference in the morals of masters, because masters have no morals. The Bolsheviks will not enter into the rights or wrongs of a war which has been started by capitalist societies; they say there should be no capitalist societies. No settlement of the war in terms of these societies counts for much with them. The real liberty and the whole liberty can come through social revolution alone. As Friedrich Adler, the murderer of Count Stürgkh – who, like Liebknecht, is one of the most prominent German-speaking Bolsheviks – said on his trial, it is no good for him to discuss these problems with men who think in terms of the bourgeois or of the Moderate Socialist parties, because, as for distance, the two points of view might be held on different planets. Still, with regard to peace, the Bolsheviks put forward a programme which nothing except a Bolshevik revolution in the Central Powers, or a victory of the Entente involving the break-up of Austria–Hungary could realise – complete, unfettered self-determination for all nationalities.

In Russia, say the Bolsheviks, no delay should be admitted in carrying out the social revolution. No compromise should be entered into with bourgeois parties – this would be an infinitely worse crime in their eyes than fraternising with German soldiers at the front is to us. There are Bolsheviks in every white community, but they are unimportant. They have much wider influence in Russia, where, under the old regime, ideas were developed far away from the reality of politics and business, and splits frequently occurred in Socialist parties over questions as subtle and hypothetical as those which separate the different 'free reformed new seceders' in the Churches of Scotland. No doubt, by experience, many an honest Bolshevik would be brought down to our planet; but is there time for such long journeys? Meantime, in the incomprehensible theological disquisitions of the

Bolsheviks, peasants and soldiers hear their own cries for an immediate new distribution of land and for peace. It is a truly magnificent evidence of the deeper sanity of Russia that the power of Bolshevism should not be greater than it has proved hitherto. Perhaps it is the instinct of self-preservation which guides the Prussian people. For, naturally, the Germans have fastened on to the party which preaches armistice and an immediate social revolution as a channel for instilling poison into Russia. Before the Revolution her Socialist parties were honeycombed with Government spies and *agents provocateurs*; they were to be found even among the chief leaders – to name but Azev. It remains to be seen how many of the German agents among the Bolsheviks have merely passed from the service of one reactionary Government into that of another. But to represent the typical Bolshevik as a German agent, or as a soldier who flies from the front and turns into a bully or robber at home, is just as clever and fair as to try to make out that an IDB from the Rand or a fraudulent company-promoter is the type of a British Imperialist.

Whilst the bulk of the Bolsheviks want immediate social revolution and peace, the Cadets (using that word to cover all Russian Liberal bourgeois parties) realise the truth about the present war. Russia must be saved, and a disastrous and humiliating peace must be prevented; thousands among the Cadets would willingly sacrifice their lives and all they possess merely to achieve the salvation of their country. But, then, there is also the other side to their programme. They do not want social revolution, either now or ever; many because they recognise the impossibility of such violent transformations and the danger inherent in attempts at achieving them, others (whose number, as men are, is probably larger) for more selfish reasons. The result of their attitude on social problems is that those who, almost alone in Russia, possess experience in business and administration, and count in their ranks the most prominent statesmen, are distrusted by the masses, and have a comparatively small following in a country rent by class divisions.

Between the Cadets and the Bolsheviks stand the Moderate Socialists. They understand the problems of the war as well as its dangers. They wish to make certain that it will not be continued for a day longer than is necessary, and that the side on which Russia fights does not put among its war-aims anything incompatible with the principles of democracy – either in the direction of the *Morning Post* or in that of the *Labour Leader*. They know that should Russia fail in the struggle and collapse before militarist Germany her own liberty as well as that of the small nationalities of Eastern Europe would be jeopardised. They know that it is equally impossible at present to carry on the government of Russia without the Cadets, but that it is impossible to govern Russia whilst disregarding the desires, be they half-conscious desires, even of the illiterate masses. To the Cadets they offered a guarantee that the war will be carried on for Russia's salvation, to the Bolsheviks that Socialist reforms will be carried out as soon as it is possible to do so. The extremists of the Right hate them because they affirm the need of Socialist reform, the extremists of the Left because they enter into a compromise with the bourgeois parties and help them to power. They have to sustain attacks from both sides without committing themselves to either. They know that, were they to make common cause with the Bolsheviks, they would betray Russia (which does not, however, mean that all the Bolsheviks are conscious traitors), but that, were they to make common cause with the Cadets against the Bolsheviks, they would run the danger of betraying those interests of the people which they have promised to uphold. And they alone stand between Russia and the mad convulsion of an implacable class-war which would ruin Russia or the future of her working-classes, or, most probably, both.

The whole scene is dominated by the singular figure of Kerensky. It may be hard for us to descry its real outlines through the heroic legend on the one hand and the idle scandal on the other which have become attached to it. Yet already the policy and public actions of the man seem to give the basis for a provisional estimate. Feeling and understanding marked out for him the line of all-round compromise which sane policy also would have dictated. He has tried to win the confidence of the people and the co-operation of the upper classes. He did not want to coerce or terrorise either. Critics accuse him of weakness, of being a man of many words. But the power of his words has for half a year bridged the abyss into which rash action might have plunged Russia, and even if now the time has come for much more decisive action, such action might have proved disastrous if undertaken prematurely. Kerensky tried to educate where others would have attempted to impose obedience. He poured out his soul and endangered his life in addressing mutinous crowds where others would have used machine-guns. The fact which confronted him was that to try to overcome the ignorance of the people by machine-guns would have been to kill the soul of the Revolution. Is it so inexplicable that he refused to deal in that way with the child-like, trusting masses which had put confidence in him and whose main sin was ignorance?

A very heavy blow was inflicted on the cause of moderation by the rising of General Korniloff. Yet, as soon as the strength of the Revolution had been proved, Kerensky persisted in the course mapped out for him by the needs of Russia. No repression was applied to the parties of the Right, but, on the contrary, a Cabinet was formed –

including the best from among the Moderate Cadets. Was this the act of a weak man or of a demagogue? But the crowd did not understand Kerensky's motives, and a movement towards the extreme Left set in among the working classes. The Soviets passed into the camp of the Bolsheviks. Had it not been for the ill-fated rising of Korniloff the Bolsheviks would never have been able to enact the Petrograd Commune and fratricidal war might never have come.

A strong Government must now arise. Condemnations and executions can hardly be avoided. In future men will perhaps have to suffer even for opinions, delusions, and ignorance. Russia must be saved at any price, and will be saved. Her greatness is indestructible. But that period of the Revolution which is most characteristically Russian is probably drawing to an end. For six months a nation in which certain wild, cruel instincts are still latent has been in full revolution; passions were at their highest pitch, and yet the country was governed without violence. Kerensky will be able to say of this period what Plutarch reports as the dying words of Pericles – that no fellow-countryman has had, by any act of his, to put on mourning. Kerensky may yet disappear in the maelstrom, but his name will not die. He will be remembered for his passionate self-immolation, for the suffering through which he did his work, and for his deep human feeling. He did not set himself up to be a judge over men, perhaps he was not even a judge of events. But Russia's heart spoke through him.

Sir Lewis Namier, 17 November 1917

In sharp contrast to Namier's detached, analytical view of the Bolshevik revolution were JULIUS WEST's eyewitness dispatches from Petrograd. Here he is in the Smolny Institute as the revolution hangs in the balance.

The Bolshevik Revolution

Smolny Nights

Petrograd, November 10th

When the Provisional Government of Russia had decided to give the Taurida Palace a new coat of paint by way of preparation for the Constituent Assembly to be held therein, it was clear that the tenants could not remain where they were. Other accommodation had to be provided, and the Smolny Institute was selected. Now the tenants of the State Duma building were the Petrograd Soviet of Workers' and Soldiers' Delegates, the All-Russian Executive of the Soviets, and innumerable organisations and departments connected therewith. The Smolny, on the other hand, had been a school for the girls of the Russian aristocracy. It is a huge three-storey building with convent-like corridors and a general air of the Regency period. After some little rowdiness due to the Soviet's action in annexing the Government's furniture the move was made, and the local aristocratic female ghosts shuddered. During the last few days I have felt particularly conscious of their perturbation.

The Smolny Institute – architecturally, at any rate – is all a young ladies' seminary should be. It has two wings, one on each side, a pediment supported by pillars with Corinthian capitals, a forecourt, and a public garden in front. But on, say, the morning of November 8th, 1917, it would have hardly passed for what it once was. The forecourt was filled with motors of every variety, from cycles to armoured cars. A creature belonging to the tank family performed a clattering waddle amongst its smaller relatives, as if inspecting some distant and youthful cousins. A few quick-firers were perched up in front of the entrance. Machine-guns in various stages of usefulness pointed themselves at the universe. Soldiers with fixed bayonets and sailors carrying rifles pervaded the place generally, apparently filled in beautiful unanimity with the one desire of inspecting credentials. Occasionally little processions entered containing, as a nucleus, a member of the Provisional Government, or a Cadet or two, belonging to one of those few units suspected of supporting that effete institution. So much for the outside.

The inside impressed the sense of smell most of all. A blind man would diagnose it as consisting of peasant soldiers, tea, black bread, freshly-printed-upon paper, vegetable soup, apples, tobacco smoke, cigarette-ends, and a very small number of women. These, in fact, are the ingredients or revolutionary atmosphere. But atmospheric conditions, after all, do not determine organisation. Let us take a look round. There are fewer book and pamphlet stalls than usual. The wares are heavily Marxian; there are no pamphlets translated from the English, and very few books. Philip Gibbs's *The Soul of the War*, in Russian, is prominent. The British Constitution and the social legislation of New Zealand are approvingly described by several menshevik writers. A room where once young ladies embroidered table-centres contains the Military Revolutionary Committee, and is the actual headquarters (if any) of the revolution. A young ensign is sitting at a table with a telephone, receiving written or telegraphic reports from messengers lined up in a queue which passes before him. The ensign, generally speaking, reads the wire or message and puts it down. Most of the messages report all well and call for no action. Sometimes, however, he has to use the telephone or give an order. Such is the Intelligence Department of a revolution.

The All-Russian Conference of Soviets (which is really the cause of our being here) meets in the large hall of the Smolny – a hall on which the architect has lavished no imagination, and which holds, with an effort, about two thousand persons. There is a platform, there are a number of pillars neatly arranged in two rows, and the conference in progress; Thursday's session, for example. It was called for 1 p.m., but at that hour the delegates were still sleeping off the effects of the previous day's conference, which had gone on until half-past five in the morning. Besides, there were all manner of fractional and committee meetings to be held before the conference could meet. So we sit about and improve on one another's rumours. The Bolsheviks would form a coalition Government with the Social Revolutionaries.

'What! With Chernov and Avksentiev?'

'Certainly not. Only with the extreme left SRs.'

'But they've just refused to support the Bolsheviks.'

'No; that was the SR Internationalists.'

'You mean the SR Maximalist fraction. I've just had it on good authority that they've been offered two posts in the Cabinet.'

'I don't believe it. ...'

Which is untrue. Everybody believes everything, and nobody gets impatient. At half-past eight a few people walking in the middle gangway get a great reception. The hall is immediately overcrowded. The platform is occupied by people who talk to one another for forty minutes, apparently forgetting all about the conference.

Lenin's appearance gave me a feeling I had already made his acquaintance in some previous incarnation. A short man with a large head, clean-shaven (for purposes of disguise), the expression of a pained humourist, considerable obstinacy, equally considerable ability. But the clothes seemed all wrong. And then I remembered. It was Auberon Quin I had been really thinking of. Apart from the fact that revolutionists do not wear frock-coats, Lenin is a precise reproduction of Mr Chesterton's own pictures of his Napoleon of Notting Hill. And when Lenin explained his projects the approximation of fact and fiction became almost oppressive.

At ten minutes past nine we begin. There is apparently a definite procedure in accordance with which Russian conferences are supposed to be conducted. But its details are known to few and are jealously guarded. Anyhow, this is what happened. First a delegate read a declaration from his group condemning the entire conference. Then a delegate representing a fraction of a fraction of a fraction made a speech denouncing the attitude of another fraction of his particular fraction of a fraction. After which a delegate from the Donetz Basin reported that disturbances were taking place down that way, and that Kaledin and his Cossacks were expected. Another delegate arose and read out a political programme passed by his Soviet. Then Lenin got up and announced the practical measures to be taken to obtain peace. Presumably England knows all about them, so they need not be repeated. England, however, probably does not know that Lenin stated his belief in the special efficacy of his appeal on British labour, on the grounds that the Chartist movement had shown the peculiarly sensitive class-consciousness of the English working-man. It was a movement to be copied in all countries ... This amazing reference should not lead anybody to suppose that Lenin's speech was that of a theorist. It was (to me, at any rate) surprisingly practical. He admitted that even his peace proposals might not be accepted and that Russia would have to go on fighting. Yet, even as he recited the difficulties confronting him, the audience visibly came under his spell. In twenty minutes he had finished.

Short speeches became the rule; and a leader who can hypnotise a Russian Conference into making short speeches is a leader indeed. Poles and Letts, Lithuanians and Ukrainians declared their approval of the proposals. So, too, did various quasi-Bolshevik speakers belonging to other parties. Lenin replied, emphasizing the difficulties of the proposal; it was put to the vote and carried *nem. con.* to tremendous cheering. Universal peace settled after a discussion of an hour and a quarter, a bourgeois newspaper correspondent cynically observed. But it was impossible for anybody present not a cynic to check the rising feeling that Lenin's speech might turn out to be a landmark in human history. Two thousand crowded enthusiasts and a stuffy room have a curious effect upon one's convictions.

At twenty minutes to eleven the chairman, Kamenev, announced that the meeting would now proceed to abolish private property in land, so far as owners who did not themselves cultivate their own property were concerned. Another proposal of earth-shaking importance was handled in another twenty minutes' speech. Again delegates rose and approved. One or two asked for a committee to consider details, but the details were already worked out, and if they didn't like them they had only themselves to blame, said Lenin. After all, they had had about eight months to decide what they really did want, and if they hadn't made up their minds yet a committee wouldn't be likely to help them get much forrader. However, some fractions insisted that they ought to consider the matter separately. Very well, said Lenin, let's adjourn. For how long? Put to the vote, it was settled that the interval was to last half an hour, and it lasted two hours.

When we met again it appeared for some time that we had forgotten all about the land. A soldier from the Macedonian front protested against a Russian army fighting so far from home, in the company of the beastly French, too. A Bolshevik appeal against pogroms was read. An Ukrainian soldier demanded independence for his part of Russia, and said the Ukrainian republic would always regard Russia as an elder sister. Then the land proposal was voted upon and carried unanimously.

It was somewhere about this time that somebody said something that aroused cheers rather louder than usual. A delegate began to sing the Internationale. The whole meeting rose and sang too. Then somebody else said that the dead must not be forgotten. The audience rose again and sang the unforgettable 'Eternal Memory' with which the Russian revolution honours its fallen. The deep voices of the men, unaccompanied, singing words for which the moment made all differences seem as trivial as they really were, left an impression upon the meeting which never really wore off. From about 2 to 6 a.m., when it broke up, the conference, whatever its dissensions, was filled with the faith that makes miracles not merely possible but obvious.

The land proposal had been carried unanimously; but that did not settle it. Various delegates now rose and moved amendments. It had been proposed to exclude deserters from the benefits of the measure. Somebody now moved that this disqualification be deleted. Deserters, he said, were manufactured by Kerensky's Government, and ought not to be punished for what was not really their own fault. An officer replied. He agreed that desertion was a misfortune rather than a crime, but maintained that the best men did not desert, and that the disqualification should remain. Then the meeting began to express its feelings, and the officer became inaudible. Lenin smoothed the troubled waters by saying that the Government would consider the matter. How quickly Parliamentary technique can be mastered!

At half-past two Kamenev said that the new Government had been formed. We all knew it had long ago, but the new Cabinet had already acquired the vice of keeping the public in the dark. Besides, there was the novelty of legislating without knowing who was the Government. And then we were told that the Government was to be called the Council of National Commissars, that Lenin was Premier and Trotsky Commissar of Foreign Affairs. And the cheering was terrific, although some of us may have wondered what sort of a reception the new Ministers would get from their departmental subordinates, and the matter was discussed acrimoniously, and carried unanimously, and the conference was declared at an end.

Such were the proceedings during two nights, during which those present believed that the fate of Russia was in their hands.

Julius West, 8 December 1917

Few book reviews are worth reading after sixty-five years: not all that many of their subjects are either. Dame REBECCA WEST's thoughts on Lawrence, though, are as fresh as Women in Love *itself, even for those (like me) who had to look up Mr John Collier.*

Many of us are cleverer than Mr D.H. Lawrence and nearly all of us save an incarcerated few are much saner, but this does not affect the fact that he is a genius. It does, of course, affect the fact of his being an artist. *Women in Love* is flawed in innumerable places by Mr Lawrence's limitations and excesses. His general ideas are poor and uncorrected, apparently, by any wide reading or much discussion; when he wants to represent Birkin, who is supposed to be the brilliant thinker of the book, as confounding the shallow Hermione with his power over reality, he puts into his mouth a collection of platitudes on the subject of democracy which would have drawn nothing from any woman of that intellectual level, except perhaps the remark that these things had been dealt with more thoroughly by Havelock Ellis in his essay on the spheres of individualism and Socialism. He is madly irritable. 'The porter came up. "A Bâle – deuxième classe? – Voilà!" And he clambered into the high train. They followed. The compartments were already some of them taken. But many were dim and empty. The luggage was stowed, the porter was tipped. "Nous avons encore?" said Birkin, looking at his watch and at the porter. "Encore une demi-heure," with which, in his blue blouse, he disappeared. He was ugly and insolent.' We are not told anything more about this porter. This is the full span of his tenuous existence in Mr Lawrence's imagination. He has been called out of the everywhere into the here simply in order that for these two minutes he may be ugly and insolent. This is typical of Mr Lawrence's indifference to that quality of serenity which is the highest form of decency. He thinks it natural that everybody should take their own Grand Guignol about with them in the form of an irritable nervous system and that it should give continuous performances. This prejudices his work in two ways. It makes him represent the characters whom he wishes to be regarded as normal as existing permanently in the throes of hyperaesthesia. When Gerald

Crich and Gudrun stay in London on their way to the Tyrol, her reactions to London, which she does not appear to like, are so extreme that one anticipates that Gerald will have to spend all his time abroad nursing her through a nervous breakdown, which is in fact not what happened. It also shatters the author's nerves so that his fingers are often too clumsy and tremulous to deal with the subtleties which his mind insists on handing them as subjects. There is, for example, a scene in an inn at Southwell, where Ursula has an extraordinary crisis of delight at some physical aspect of Birkin. At first reading it appears that this is simply a sexual crisis which Mr Lawrence is describing according to his own well-worn formula, and one reflects with fatigue that Mr Lawrence's heroines suffer from molten veins as inveterately as Sarah Gamp suffered from spasms, and that they demand as insistently just a thimbleful of union with reality. But then if one is a conscientious reader one perceives that this is wrong. There is something else. Ursula seems to have caught sight of some physical oddity about him, to have noticed for the first time that he was really Siamese twins. One thinks crossly, 'Unobservant girl.' But if one has a decent sense of awe one realises that the author of *Sons and Lovers* is probably trying to say something worth hearing, and one reads it over again, and in the end perceives that Mr Lawrence is simply trying to convey that mystical sense of the sacredness of physical structure, quite apart from its aesthetic or sexual significance, which is within the experience of nearly all of us. Ursula, contemplating her lover's body, had a sudden realisation that flesh is blessed above all other substances because it is informed by life, that force of which there is such a stupendous abundance on this earth, which has such divine attributes as will and consciousness, which has so dark a past and so mysterious a future. It is a reasonable enough emotion, but Mr Lawrence is so nerve-shattered by these extravagant leaps, which suggest that somebody has lit a little gunpowder under his sensorium, that he is unable to convey the spiritual incident save as a hot geyser of sensation.

But *Women in Love* is a work of genius. It contains characters which are masterpieces of pure creation. Birkin is not. The character whom an author designs as the mouthpiece of truth never is; always he is patronising and knowing, like 'Our London Correspondent' writing his weekly letter in a provincial newspaper. But there is Hermione Roddice, the woman who stood beyond all vulgar judgment, yet could be reduced to misery by the slightest gesture of contempt from any servant because she had no real self and, though she could know, could not be. Mr Lawrence could always conjure imaginary things into the world of the eye, and he makes visible the unhappy physical presence of Hermione, with her long face and her weight of heavy dull hair, her

queer clothes, her strange appearance that made people want to jeer yet
held them silent till she passed. In the scene where she sits at Birkin's
table with Ursula and plays with the cat and coos Italian to it, and
scores a barren victory by making the girl feel raw and vulgar and
excluded by exercise of that static impressiveness which she has
cultivated to conceal her dynamic nullity, he discloses the pathetic
secret of her aching egotism with a marvellous appropriateness. He has
found there the incident and the conversation that perfectly illustrate
the spiritual fact he wishes to convey. There are also Mr and Mrs Crich,
the mineowner and his wife, though their creation is not so indisputably
pure as that of Hermione. One suspects that they were called into being
in consequence of Mr Lawrence's readings in German philosophy, that
they are not only post but propter Nietzsche and Max Stirner. But they
are great figures: the father, who loved to give to the poor out of his
faith that 'they through poverty and labour were nearer to God than
he,' until in time he became 'some subtle funeral bird, feeding on the
miseries of the people,' a creature damp with continual pity; the
mother, like a hawk, loathing the rusty black, cringing figures of his
parasites, despising him for his perpetual indulgence in the laxer,
gentler emotions, and bending over his dead body at the last in bitter
contempt because his face was so beautiful, so unmarked by pride or
the lordlier emotions. The persons who are most intimately concerned
in the development of the main thesis of the book are not so
satisfactory because that thesis deals with love. It is in itself an excellent
thesis. It is a stern answer to the human cry, 'I can endure the hatred
the world bears me, and the hate I bear the world, if only there is one
whom I love and who loves me.' It declares: 'No, that is not how it is.
There shall be no one who loves you and no one whom you love, unless
you first get in on loving terms with the world.' Gerald Crich refuses to
enter into an alliance of friendship with Birkin. He, the materialist, has
no use for an expenditure of affection in a quarter where there is no
chance of physical pleasure, and stakes his all on his union with
Gudrun. This concentration itself wrecks that union. She finds him
empty of everything but desire for her; he has had no schooling of
altruistic love; he does not help her out of her own fatigued desire for
corruption and decay, the peace of dissolution; and she breaks away
from him. Thereby, because he staked everything one her, he is
destroyed. It is not really very abstruse, nor very revolutionary, nor very
morbid. In *Antony and Cleopatra* Shakespeare permitted himself to say
much the same sort of thing about the quality of love that arises
between highly sexual people. But when Mr Lawrence writes of love
he always spoils the matter by his violent style. In an exquisite phrase
Mrs Mary Baker Eddy once remarked that the purpose of the

relationship between the sexes is to 'happify existence.' There are times when Mr Lawrence writes as if he thought its purpose was to give existence a black eye. His lovers are the Yahoos of Eros, and though Beauty may be in their spirits, it is certainly not in their manners. This is not represented as incidental to their characters, but as a necessary condition of love. it is a real flaw in Mr Lawrence's temperament; but it is so marked and so apart from the rest of him that it no more spoils the book than a crack in the canvas spoils a beautiful picture.

There are, of course, many obvious distortions of life in *Women in Love* which it is easiest to consider as sheer meaningless craziness. There are, for instance, the extraordinary descriptions of the women's clothes, especially of Gudrun's stockings. She was more decorative about the legs that anybody has ever been except a flamingo. There are also incidents that flout probability or even possibility. There is that amazing scene when Hermione, who is supposed to be an effete aristocrat of unimpeachable manners, comes up behind Birkin, who is sitting on the sofa reading Thucydides as good as gold, and hits him on the head with a paperweight of lapis lazuli. This is certainly not the done thing. All this is without doubt not life as we know it, but the smallest reflection shows that it is not crazy and it has a meaning. The trouble is with Mr Lawrence that he is so much of a poet that it is difficult for him to express himself in prose, and in particular in the prose required of a novel, and that he finds it impossible to express what he wants save by desperately devised symbols. He has felt that there is a quality about many women which makes them wear gay clothes and go actively yet not purposively about the world, and promote events that are never of the highest importance yet often interfere with others that are, which makes them, in fact, build a dome of many-coloured glass to stain the white light of eternity. He feels that every time that Gudrun appeared she was this quality made manifest to the eye, and he is at a loss how to convey it. In sheer desperation he ascribes her to these astonishing stockings. When one visualises those shapely, coloured ankles moving swiftly on those restless errands of destruction, one perceives that the touch is not meaningless at all, though it is clumsy. And the incident of Hermione and the paperweight also is a desperately devised symbol. He has wanted to express that a woman like her, bitter with a sense of spiritual insufficiency, would in the end turn against the lover whom she had wooed because of his extreme sufficiency, and become envious because she could not steal his sufficiency and try to destroy him. In his impatience he has dragged into his novel this very dark scene which, though it is a distortion of life's physical appearances, nevertheless succeeds in conveying the spiritual truth with which he is concerned at the moment. To object to this on the ground that an author has no right to distort life's appearances for his own ends is to subject literature to an unreasonable restriction. It is not imposed on the art of painting. The greatest artists, such as Velasquez and Michaelangelo, have managed to express their vision of reality without tampering with appearances, but there is also El Greco, whose right to manipulate form for his own purposes no sane person would now dispute. Those who deny Mr Lawrence's right to be an El Greco of literature had better not plume themselves that they are actuated by admiration for Michaelangelo's and Velasquez's fidelity to true form; if they can remain unmoved by Mr Lawrence's genius it is much more likely that they are actuated by a longing for the realism of Mr John Collier.

Rebecca West, 9 July 1921

G.D.H. COLE wrote on almost every conceivable political subject for the NS *from 1918 until his death. Can anyone in the late eighties read his thoughts from 1924 on the 'collapse of Socialistic doctrines' without a shiver of recognition?*

English Socialism in 1924

Nothing is more significant in the world of to-day than the collapse of Socialistic doctrines. Only a decade ago the outlines of the Socialist policy seemed well-defined, and Socialism itself a body of doctrines and a programme as clear as the sun at noon-day. When a man said he was a Socialist, you could tell within narrow limits what he stood for and what he believed. There were differences as to method and rapidity of change. Some Socialists thought of Socialism as a product of revolution, and some – the greater number – as the result of a prolonged course of evolutionary change. But as to the end itself they were substantially agreed. The State, democratised by the extension of the franchise and the growth of popular education, would take upon itself the full burden of conducting the national affairs. Industry and commerce would become departments of State action; we should all become Civil Servants and work for the State in a spirit of mutual service. Such an outcome was in line with the actual tendency of political affairs. It was in line also with the development of industry. The trust was the forerunner of nationalisation.

To-day, all that structure of Socialist ideas lies in ruins. Men still call themselves Socialists, probably in greater numbers than ever before. But now, when a man calls himself a Socialist, he conveys by the name little information about his ideas and beliefs. A few – very few perhaps – still cling to the simple State Socialist faith; far more, including nearly all the younger converts, regard the State and its works with an aloof and critical hostility. Socialism is still no doubt a faith; but it is, like the faith of some modern Churchmen, a faith that has discarded all its doctrines – a disembodied faith in the soul of a dead idea.

All this has come out very clearly in the proceedings of the past fortnight at the Summer School conducted by the Independent Labour Party. The ILP is, or is reputed to be, the pioneering propagandist body of Socialism, as well as the tail that wags the dog of political Labour. It is supposed to supply the ideas which the great Trade Unions then accept and finance. What the ILP thinks to-day the Labour Party will think tomorrow. But the puzzle is to discover what the ILP is thinking to-day. The discussions at the Cloughton Summer School leave us with the impression, not that the ILP has a policy which it is endeavouring to press upon the Government, but that, having recognised the inadequacy of the old Socialist policy, it is seeking feverishly everywhere for a new policy to take its place.

In one sense, this is a healthy sign; for it means that the leaders of the ILP are trying to take stock of their position in the light of present realities. There was a notable tendency to concentrate discussion at Cloughton on actual problems of to-day and to-morrow, and to propound and argue positive remedies meant for early application. There was much said about next steps in agricultural policy, in the control of banking, and in industrial legislation, and little about plans to be realised on the morrow of the Revolution. The talkers were really trying to face things as they saw them in the world of fact. But – and this is the really significant thing – they were facing the facts in a strictly empirical and particularist spirit, as if each problem stood by itself and had to be judged on its merits. There was no indication of a clear unifying principle in the light of which all problems could be seen in their true aspect. In short, in this representative gathering of Socialists, there appeared no common basis of Socialist doctrine.

Much that was said at Cloughton was excellent. Especially on the agricultural question, the ILP with its plan for collective control of imports and marketing is, we believe, working along sound lines. But the disappearance of the old State Socialist faith is manifest here also. Gone are the days when the Socialist, confronted by the rural problem, could declare for nationalisation of the land, and look round triumphantly, as if that settled the whole matter. The ILP proposes, indeed, State control of the industry; but the distance it has gone from the old faith is measured by the form which the proposed control is to take. No longer is the Civil Servant to be the agent of Socialism; State control is to be administered through the farmers and rural workers organised into a representative authority for agricultural affairs. Guild Socialism, if it has not secured acceptance for its own schemes, has at any rate made short work of State Socialism in its traditional forms.

It is evident that the members of the Socialist bodies have an uneasy sense that the old dogmas of Socialism are melting away. This appears plainly in their attitude to the Labour Government. Those who defend the Government most warmly say that it is not Socialist, and is not pursuing a Socialist policy. Now it is the mission of the ILP to make the Government Socialist and to ensure that it shall launch a Socialist programme. But what is this programme to be? In discussing the Government, the Cloughton Summer School spoke with two voices. One voice commended the Government's practicality in facing immediate issues; the other blamed it for wandering from the straight path of Socialism. Speaker after speaker urged that, while it should continue to deal with the problems of the day much as it has been dealing with them, it should also make a plain declaration of its Socialist faith by introducing into Parliament really Socialist measures and challenging defeat on this fundamental issue. So much was easily said; but on what issue was the fundamental challenge to be made? Nationalisation of mines or railways, or even of banks? All these are challenges, in a sense. They would arouse the necessary opposition; but would they evoke the no less necessary enthusiasm on the Socialist side? There were not wanting at Cloughton speakers who held that these things are not Socialism. Perhaps they are not; but, if they are not, what is?

Socialism lives as an idea; it is no longer living as a programme. And, even as an idea, can it live long in its disembodied state? Communism has arisen to challenge it, and to beat it at its own game of bourgeois-scaring. Socialism, now that Communism is in the field, has no longer the attraction of seeming to be on the extreme left. It has still, no doubt, a faint aroma of human brotherhood, and this is its remaining source of strength. It still appeals to men's pacific and friendly impulses and emotions, whereas Communism has stolen its old appeal to their fighting instinct. But a political creed cannot live on moral impulses, however generous. It must include a policy as well as a moral rule of life, or it will cease to be a gospel for the workaday world and become even as the Musical Banks in *Erewhon*.

The ILP leaders, understanding this, are trying hard to find for the old soul of Socialism a new bodily habitation. They may succeed in devising a new policy and a good one suited for the needs of the day.

But we doubt if it will be recognisably a Socialist policy, unified by any principle reasonably to be called 'Socialist'. It will pick and choose, as the Labour Government has picked and chosen, among proposals drawn from many schools of thought. It will bring forward plans not vitally different from those which might be drafted by clever business men, or clever Liberals, or clever Conservatives. There will be indeed this difference, that the new Socialism, more regardful of the claims of the wage-earner, will be less regardful of vested interests in property. But, as the plain declarations against confiscation made at Cloughton show, this divergence is less deep than on the surface it appears. The new Socialism makes to property concessions of expediency which differ little in practice from admissions of right.

The new evolutionary Socialism of the ILP – if we are still to call it Socialism – is already in conflict and will before long be in violent conflict with the revolutionary doctrines of Communism. Communism is as definite as Socialism is now eclectic and accommodating, except in Russia, where, having achieved power, it has also had to face the realities of government. Communism in England or France can be a faith, because it has no need to be really a policy. It lives on its possession of just that simplification of issues which is no longer possible for the ILP. It stands where Socialism stood forty years ago. If it succeeds, it will dissolve, as Socialism has dissolved, in the deep waters of its own success.

But there is this difference. The old Socialism was not merely a faith, but a scheme. It wanted this and that – definite things to be done, the sum of which was Socialism. In urging these things, it has left its mark everywhere. No party, no body of political or economic opinion, but has been deeply influenced by the Socialist ideas whose full application it has rejected. This power to influence diverse streams of thought was the strength of Socialism. Communism, on the other hand, is a 'take it or leave it' sort of doctrine. It is not a programme in the same sense; it does not admit of eclecticism and partial applications. Communism is all or nothing.

And, as in this country with its living tradition of accommodation and adjustment, Communism cannot be all, it is doomed, we believe, to be nothing. The virtue which has passed out of Socialism has not passed into Communism. It has passed to no definite group of men, or body of doctrine. It has diffused itself through men of many different groups. In a sense this is weakness, for only defined groups have the cohesion necessary for effective action. But this is only to say that, while the old groups are in dissolution, the new are yet unformed. The new principle of unification is yet undiscovered. It is hoped for, not only by the ILP, but wherever men of goodwill are gathered together for the discussion of public affairs. When it is found, it will group men anew – to their surprise often and mortification at their strange new companionships. Till it is found men will grope on, trying to find in old faiths firm anchorage for changing opinions. There is upon us a time of transition in ideas, when party labels mean ever less, and men uneasy in old faiths cling to them only in default of new. 'Lord, I believe,' says the Socialist of to-day. But he adds, 'Help thou mine unbelief.'

G.D.H. Cole, 6 September 1924

None of CLIFFORD SHARP's friends have recalled humour as being among his more outstanding characteristics. It is thus entirely probable that his proposal to hang Winston Churchill after the General Strike should be taken at face value. Sharp seemed to many observers to be at heart a Tory, and he affected to despise the idea of abstract justice, but his reaction to the strike shows where his heart really lay.

Should We Hang Mr Churchill Or Not?

By the spirit and manner in which Mr Baldwin ended the great strike he almost atoned for the way in which he precipitated it. For there is no longer any doubt that it was precipitated by the action of the Government, and, what is more, quite deliberately precipitated. It is, of course, a matter of common knowledge now that the strike need not have occurred, that is to say that at the very moment of the breaking off of negotiations the Prime Minister had come to an understanding with the Trade Union leaders, which, though it would not have solved the problem of the mines, would have prevented the other Unions from coming out. The inexplicable abandonment of negotiations – which was condemned by all independent critics, including those who habitually support the Conservative Government – at such a stage has been generally attributed to a sudden panic in the Cabinet created by the action of the *Daily Mail* machinists. Let us quote the account of the negotiations given by the Attorney-General, Sir Douglas Hogg, in the *British Gazette* of May 11th:

> While the Cabinet was discussing the document [*i.e.*, the peace formula which had been drawn up by Lord Birkenhead, the Prime Minister and the Trade Union leaders] news arrived that the Natsopas had declined to allow the *Daily Mail* to appear with a leading article entitled 'For King and

Country', ... It was thus clear that a General Strike had not only been
threatened but had actually begun.

The action of the Natsopas had, of course, nothing to do with the
threatened General Strike. It was an act of mutiny which the Trade
Union leaders would instantly have condemned and repudiated, since
they were still hoping that there would be no strike at all. They were
offered no opportunity, however, either of repudiation or of
explanation. They had heard nothing of the events in the *Daily Mail*
office, and when they returned to the conference room with the agreed
formula they found it dark and locked. The Cabinet had declared war
and gone to bed.

These facts are not disputed. All that remains uncertain is their
explanation. We, like most people, attributed the Government's critical
decision to momentary panic which would have been dissipated if they
had listened to explanations or waited until the morning. The truth,
however, appears to be even more discreditable to them. What actually
happened, it seems, was this. The Prime Minister, Lord Birkenhead,
and Sir Arthur Steel-Maitland were fighting desperately for peace,
whilst a section of the Cabinet, led by Mr Winston Churchill, Mr
Neville Chamberlain and Mr Bridgeman, were itching for a fight. The
peace party succeeded in arranging terms based on the Royal
Commission's Report, upon which the strike would be called off and
the miners left, if they would not agree, to fight alone. With these terms
they returned in triumph to the Cabinet room only to find Messrs
Churchill and Chamberlain in charge and a clear majority in favour of
war at all costs. The Baldwin-Birkenhead terms were accordingly
turned down, and when the Prime Minister proposed nevertheless to go
forward with the negotiations and avert the strike, he was faced with
the immediate resignation of seven of his colleagues – Churchill, Neville
Chamberlain, Bridgeman, Amery, 'Jix,' Cunliffe-Lister, and one other
of whose identity we are not sure. So he gave way. He ought not to
have given way, of course, but excuses may perhaps be found for an
utterly exhausted man who, having fought the Trade Unions for days
and nights, found himself called upon at the last moment to fight his
own colleagues. Mr Churchill was the villain of the piece. He is
reported to have remarked that he thought 'a little blood-letting' would
be all to the good. Whether he actually used this phrase or not there is
no doubt about his tireless efforts to seize the providential opportunity
for a fight.

So much for the way the strike began. When it ended Mr Baldwin
had regained control of his Cabinet and had acquired so enormous a

personal popularity in the country that he could afford to let all his colleagues resign if they wanted to. He took charge of affairs without consulting anybody, and without any Cabinet authorisation – which would certainly not have been forthcoming from the fight-to-a-finish section – he declared peace and insisted upon peace. Thereby he atoned for his previous surrender. 'Victimisation' was being attempted in almost every industry. Men were being asked to return to work as new hands, at much lower wages, under humiliating conditions and so on. The Prime Minister stopped all that within twenty-four hours, by his insistence upon the necessity of forgetting the past and looking only to the future. Some of his colleagues and many of his supporters railed at him for his 'weakness'; but this time he stood firm – and gave us peace. His atonement, we think, should be accepted. He blundered on that Sunday night in agreeing to war, but ever since then he has fought for peace, and fought with an extraordinary measure of success.

We do not know whether there is anybody left who still honestly believes that the strike was a 'revolutionary' attempt to subvert the British Constitution. Its real nature, at any rate, was shown clearly enough by the actual course of events. It was a strike 'in furtherance of a trade dispute,' and nothing more; and in so far as it secured for the miners – if they would but have seized the chance – a better hearing than they would otherwise have had, it may not unreasonably be claimed to have been a successful strike, despite the inevitable, and in our view timely, 'surrender.' Not only was it not a strike against the Constitution, it was not even a strike against the Government. If it had the appearance of a strike against the Government, that was only because the Government had intervened – and of course rightly, though very ineffectively, intervened – in the struggle between the miners and the mineowners. If it had not intervened the strike would have taken place just the same; but then the truth would have been clear to everybody – namely, that it was a strike against the inefficiency and grasping obstinacy of the mineowners – nothing more and nothing less. The Constitution was never threatened either by word or by deed.

The general result of the strike is not unsatisfactory. It has shown that an enormous industrial upheaval can take place, in this country at any rate, without the loss of a single life. But what is far more important, it has shown that the weapon of the General Strike is practically worthless in the hands of those who are not prepared to go to all lengths of revolutionary violence. It is a weapon, of course, which revolutionaries (being a tiny minority) could never wield; yet unless it is they who wield it, it is blunt and ineffective. And so from henceforth we may hope that it will be discarded by the Trade Union movement. It has been tested and broken, and we all know where we are far more clearly than we did a month ago. The Trade Unions of Britain stood by their comrades in the mines, and perhaps by their wonderful solidarity they achieved something for them; but certainly the majority of them will never again wish to resort to so desperate a measure. The currency of the phrase, a 'General Strike,' has been so depreciated that we are not likely to hear it again save from the mouths of that minority which never has, and never can, learn anything from experience. The TUC decreed its own failure when it ordered its men to avoid conflicts with the police or the volunteers.

For a General Strike without violence cannot succeed; it is almost a contradiction in terms. With violence, on the other hand, it amounts to a revolution – which the Trade Union world does not want nor seems ever likely to want. Everybody understands this now, and that is why the strike was perhaps worthwhile. We have bought experience at a pretty high price; but we have got it; and no section of the community, we suppose, is more satisfied with the bargain than the 'constitutional' leaders of the Labour movement. The irrepressible left-wingers are silenced; their dreams are dissolved; they must set about the Sisyphean task of converting the Trade Unions of Great Britain to revolutionary ideas, or admit failure. For having so notably helped to teach us all this, ought we to thank Mr Churchill or ought we to hang him on a lamp-post for the incorrigible 'blood-letter' that he is? We are really not quite sure what is the proper answer to that question; but probably – to be on the safe side – it would be best that he should be hanged.

Clifford Sharp, 22 May 1926

PART TWO

◆

1930–1945

Low, 12 May 1956

Kingsley Martin made *the* New Statesman. *For thirty years he and it were linked together with a closeness which perhaps only C.P. Scott and* The Guardian *can parallel in the history of British journalism. Clifford Sharp's* NS *came from the Fabian tradition's aspiration to passionless rationalism. Martin grew up, as he tells in his two splendid (if often unreliable) volumes of autobiography, in 'the way of dissent'; the English Nonconformist radical-liberal tradition with its constant alertness to injustice. The mixture was sometimes uneasy, even occasionally ludicrous: Edward Hyams speaks well of Martin's 'capacity to be surprised and angry when the man whom he expected to punch him on the nose, punched him on the nose'.*

The results included a great deal of empty moralising – varied, as notoriously with some of the NS*'s writing on Stalin, with an intermittent spurious anti-moralism – a fair dose of inconsistency and a lot of self-righteousness; but also some of the finest, most individual and most influential political journalism of the century. These were also the years when the 'back half' of the* NS *featured at one time or another what Martin, with typical but perhaps excusable hyperbole, boasted was 'almost everyone who could claim to be a thinker or a writer'.*

The radical-liberal strand on the paper was strengthened when, simultaneously with Martin's accession, the distinguished but penurious Liberal weekly the Nation *merged with the* NS. *It brought with it an ethos which chimed well with the liberal side of Martin's personality, and the towering presence of John Maynard Keynes. Keynes's role was a little like that of Shaw in the early years – frequently at odds with the editorial line (notably over the issue dearest to Martin in the 1930s, opposition to Appeasement) but providing an invaluably provocative stimulus to disagreement.*

Keynes, of course, was never a Socialist. Martin saw himself wholeheartedly as one (in his French Liberal Thought *he even speaks approvingly of the idea of socialism as secular religion), but was neither a Labour party loyalist nor even peripherally a Marxist. None the less under his editorship the* NS *grew closer – as a candid friend or semi-loyal intellectual opposition – to labour; and the 1930s growth in attraction to Marxism among intellectuals was strongly reflected in its pages. One of the most brilliant though unorthodox converts, EDMUND WILSON, sought in 1932 to explain the appeal.*

Marxist History

It is curious to consider how Marxist history and criticism have grown
up separately from the rest of modern thought.

Marxism has now been developing and spreading for something like
seventy years; it is now an international culture just reaching its phase
of full maturity. It is apparently the only really vital intellectual
movement in the western world. Yet all the rest of our literature and
learning still put up their barriers against it. The old bourgeois culture
does not know about it; or if it does know about it, ignores it; or, if it
speaks of it, misrepresents it. Nothing seems to me to bear out more
convincingly the Marxist's own contention as to the influence of class
interests on people's opinions than the way in which the bourgeois
writers on history, economics, politics, literature and art refuse to read
the Marxist books even for the purpose of condemning them, will not
discuss the Marxist ideas even to point out their fallacies, and manage
to leave the great Marxists out of their cosmoses in spite of the fact that,
however much one may disapprove of them, they must certainly be
recognised as among the great geniuses and leaders of the time.

I have recently had striking experience of this in the case of three
highly intelligent friends of mine, all professional historians or critics,
who have taken the most violent exception to recent articles of mine on
Marxism. One of them is a brilliant music critic with whom I have for
many years been in the habit of conversing about literature and life on
what seemed to be a basis of generally sympathetic points of view. Now,
however, when I go to see him, scarcely am I inside the door when I am
greeted with complaints and reproaches. What he reproaches me with
particularly is the attempt to degrade art by relating it to the social
situation of the artist when it ought properly to be regarded as a
creation entirely spiritual, having its existence on a super-terrestrial
plane.

Now the truth is that all these years my friend has known perfectly
well that I saw a connection between works of art and the environments
in which they were produced, and that he himself has also seen this
connection. We have frequently had engrossing discussions of the role
played in the work of various artists by factors of period, nation, race,
and social status; and, as a matter of fact, it was precisely the early
essays of this writer which first made me see the relation of music to the
age and environment of the composer. My friend, I think, had been
influenced by Taine – at any rate, he admired Taine and pursued a
method which somewhat recalled Taine's and which set him off rather
sharply from his immediate predecessor, Huneker. He could perfectly
understand and accept Taine's 'race, milieu and moment' for any

moment of the past or for any milieu of the present inside the bourgeois culture sphere. But when it came to an objective consideration of the influence on modern art of the fundamental social differences and conflicts of the present, he abandoned his Tainian approach and ascended into the realms of aesthetic metaphysics where I found it very difficult to follow him.

Another writer, an able historian of nineteenth- and twentieth-century America, has recently taken me to task in print for what he considers a betrayal of art for politics. Yet he has himself in the past been largely preoccupied with politics. He is the author of several valuable political histories, and I had always assumed that he considered – as I certainly do – the writing of history an art. I had been aiming myself, in the articles to which he objected, at writing a little contemporary history. But the point is apparently that though it is legitimate to write the history of Populism, for example, or of bourgeois municipal reform, it is not legitimate to write the story of contemporary labour agitation which raises questions of Marxist theory. He further accused me – one of the commonest defences against Marxism – of having accepted Communism as a 'religion.' And he concluded with what seemed to me the hysterical statement that for his part he preferred the companionship of such 'jailbirds' as Dostoevsky, Cervantes, Defoe, and E.E. Cummings – though so far as I know I have never written a word, and should under no circumstances consent to write a word, calculated to discourage or dissuade him from consorting with these high spirits; and though, if jail be the test of the elite, it is equally true that Lenin and Trotsky and W.Z. Foster have all had their doses of prison.

A third writer, an Irish woman of unusual range of reading, social experience and travel, has also criticised articles of mine severely from the point of view of an ignorance of Marxism and of a misunderstanding of what I was trying to say, which seemed to me at first amazing on the part of one who had grown up in the midst of Irish politics and who had taken part in the Irish rebellion against English cultural domination. Yet the point was here again that it is one thing to understand, to share, the Irish grievances against England, another to understand, to think out one's relation to, the struggle between capitalism and the classes it is dispossessing. When I last saw my Irish friend, she mentioned as if with impatience that the chief question that the young people of Ireland seemed to be interested in today was the electrification of the Shannon. The Irish of her generation are like our Southerners in that they are all the farther from recognising the urgency of the problems of the transition to a socialistic from a capitalistic society because they are only just coming to recognise the problems of the transition to an industrial society from an old-fashioned agrarian one.

All three of these people, of course, have recognised the French Revolution – they have recognised the American revolution. They understand and are ready to appreciate the eighteenth-century enlightenment which led up to them. They are themselves partly the products of that enlightenment, still carrying on more or less its tradition. But they have never really accepted the Russian revolution, and they will not see that the culture of Marxism corresponds in our own time to the culture of the French enlightenment in its. As that lit the way for the rising bourgeoisie about to seize political power, so Marxism prepares for Socialism and the classless society of the future.

Marxism is, then, not a religion, though *Das Kapital* is the Bible of warring sects and though Communism has tended to call forth the qualities, emotions and types of character which have been identified with religions in the past. It is not a fixed body of dogma. It is not a diabolical conspiracy for substituting propaganda for art. The work of art is a work of art for the Marxist as for the non-Marxist – though he may also interest himself in examining it, as the non-Marxist will not do, as a record of the needs which have evoked it, as the botanist and the ornithologist must examine even the most beautiful birds and flowers. What Marxism is, is a scientific point of view which schools itself to be independent of class in order that it may for the first time in the history of thought study society and culture realistically in the light of the relationships of classes. The eighteenth-century philosophers were utopians who had never really studied economics and who thought that the general good will of men would be enough to promote general prosperity. The Marxist has a more realistic grasp: he has had time to study revolutions and the things that happen after them, and he has worked out a veritable engineer's technique for analysing society and manipulating its various forces. But the intellectual work of Marxism, like its political work, is far from finished. It has many discoveries still to make, and it must be flexible and daring to make them. Whatever official formulas may be put forward by the present regime in Russia or anyone else, Marxism is not an official set of formulas, but a new vision of human life and a new method of dealing with it. This is what you learn from reading the great Marxists: Marx and Engels, Lenin and Trotsky – though it is not always what you gather from their disciples.

From the point of view of intellectual controversy, it is one of the unfortunate features of Marxism that the Marxist can always blackmail the non-Marxist. When the heretic or suspected witch failed to give the answer desired, the inquisitor could always say: 'The devil put that into your mouth!' The Marxist can always reply: 'Your income – or your social habits – made you say that!' (The amateur psycho-analyst can do the same thing, for that matter.) And it is true that Marxism may be exploited as a cheap way of always appearing to be right or simply of making oneself disagreeable with a semblance of justification. This situation will not, however, deter me from saying that I can see no sound philosophical reason why middle-class readers and writers of unusually wide culture such as the persons I have mentioned above, should ignore the great creative force of Marxism and denounce for all the stupidest extravagances of Marxists another middle-class writer like myself who tries to call attention to it.

The result is, at any rate, that Marxism remains, as I have said, largely in a separate compartment from the rest of contemporary culture. The two streams run parallel to one another, the latter slackening its current as the former gathers power. There are a certain number of people, to be sure, who try to make the best of both worlds, who try to apply Marxist technique within such limits that it will not lead to any disquieting conclusions. For example, Charles A. Beard, who is said to regard Marx's *Eighteenth Brumaire of Louis Bonaparte* as one of the most brilliant historical analyses he has ever read, could scarcely have written his history if the author of *The Eighteenth Brumaire* had never existed; yet he hardly ever writes an article nowadays about the embarrassments of the present day without expressly repudiating Marxism. But the position of people of this kind is uncomfortable. In general, it is surprising how promptly the writers are lining up in one or other of the two camps, and how readily their antagonisms are developing.

I do not mean in the least that all the good writers are coming into the Marxist camp. The Marxists are far from all being geniuses, and some of our best writers are far from Marxism and, from all appearances, likely to remain so. Marxism is not a touchstone for artistic or intellectual or moral excellence. But if we compared those men of genius outside it with those whom it has inspired, we should recognise it – if we had no other means – as the great political–intellectual movement of the time. That other world is dying at the end of its blind alley; but this other, just coming to maturity, has its immense creative work to do.

Edmund Wilson, 15 October 1932

Wilson exemplified the intellectual and emotional pull of Marxism in the thirties. One of the great voices of the liberal conscience, E.M. FORSTER, sympathetically debated the attraction, but warned that that way lay moral disaster.

The Long Run

Dying for a cause in which he believed, the late Christopher St John Sprigg would not desire to be reviewed with any posthumous tenderness. These essays ('Studies in a Dying Culture', published under the pseudonym of Christopher Caudwell) were written by him shortly before he was killed in Spain, they hit hard, and no one who reads them will feel that a Communist makes a comfortable neighbour. They are never abusive, and are often cogent and brilliant, but they are always fanatical. They riddle the bourgeois' arguments and would like to riddle his body, for Caudwell believed that everyone who has not joined the Third International is wrong and must be doing wrong, and is consequently better out of the way. He had faith; and, as has often been pointed out, these modern political creeds have borrowed the passion and the ruthlessness which have hitherto been confined to religion. Regarded as propaganda, the book is surely a mistake. A wise and persuasive writer like Mr John Strachey may well make converts to his cause, and so may a warm-hearted, matey writer of the type of Mr Jack Common. But Christopher Caudwell is what has been called in Bolshevik diplomatic circles 'an error in exportation.' He ought not to be read outside the fold. He will only cause unbelievers to clutch at their pocket-books and thank their God that Mr Chamberlain and Herr Hitler excluded the Reds from Munich.

Some of us think that our pocket-books will be lost in any case, indeed, that everything is now lost except personal affection, the variety of human conduct, and the importance of truth. If we feel like this, we can read Caudwell with pleasure. We are bound to read him with admiration, for he is a sincere man and an able critic.

In the first part of the book he is concerned with some of his erring seniors – Shaw, the two Lawrences, Wells, Freud. He points out, quite rightly, that they all of them feel uneasy; whether they are scientific, amusing, poetical or practical, they are worried, and whether they confess or conceal their worry, their plight persists. He ascribes their uneasiness to their refusal to recognise the trend of the society into which they have been born – that trend being, of course, towards Communism. Bernard Shaw, though more satisfactory than his fellow thinkers because he has read Marx, clings to the bourgeois illusion, that man is naturally free; he will not accept man's dependence upon society, he remains 'a brilliant medicine man, theorising about life,' and rejecting the discoveries of science when they get in his way. T.E. Lawrence freed the Arabs, it is true, but freed them for what? To participate in the diseased French or British political systems; half-aware of the infection he had communicated, Lawrence escaped in remorse into the ranks of the army, where he found 'a kind of Arabian desert in the heart of the vulgar luxury of bourgeoisdom, a stunted version of his ideal, barren of fulfilment, but at least free from dishonour.' D.H. Lawrence and H.G. Wells are also crippled, one of them because he cannot do without class or the dark past, the other because he cannot do without cash. They are all 'pathetic' figures, pathetic being an expression of contempt; Caudwell gives them a little genuine sympathy and much platform-pity, and dismisses them as failures.

He handles his case so well that he leaves us feeling that there is nothing else to say. But there is something. All intelligent and sensitive people to-day are worried – there's no question about that and Caudwell may account for their worry correctly. But have not these worried people sometimes written readable books? And may not the malaise, the lack of adjustment, be the speck of grit which causes the oyster to secrete the pearl? His answer to this would be that in the Classless State we shall have no specks of grit, and that if maladjustment causes art, art must go; a valid answer from his standpoint, but he has not faced the fact that books do give pleasure; he has not discussed art at all, and he is prohibited from discussing it, although he possesses plenty of aesthetic reactions. He dare discuss nothing except opinions. For him, a book is only good if it stands in a sound social relation to its age, and consequently no book can be good to-day unless it is communist. *Kipps, The Plumed Serpent, The Seven Pillars* need rewriting, and what matter if, when rewritten, they are unreadable? Literature has nothing to do with enjoyment.

Through all these essays, and linking them together, runs the idea of Liberty. Liberty is a leaky word, and it is surprising that Communists should venture on board of it. Fascists prudently keep away; they have promulgated that the individual must be enslaved to the state, and thus they avoid many difficulties, both practical and argumentative. But Communism is less sound than Fascism because it is more human; it does care about ultimate happiness, its final aims are thoroughly decent, and so it gets entangled in some of the difficulties which it diagnoses in democracy. Liberty is the most tiresome of these. So long as Caudwell attacks the bourgeois conception of liberty, he goes on gaily enough. It is in the first place indefinable. In the second place, although some people are comparatively free they cannot if they are decent enjoy their freedom while their less fortunate brethren are suffering. Both these points are incontestable, and Caudwell goes on to argue that the more the 'free' assert their 'freedom' the more will they enslave the unfortunate: 'bourgeoisdom crucifies liberty upon a cross of gold, and if you ask in whose name it does this replies, "In the name of personal freedom"'. Our great mistake, he says, is the mistake of Rousseau: the belief that freedom is an escape *from* society instead of something which must be realised *through* society.

Something? Well, what thing? We now look for the positive, the communist, definition of freedom, and Mr Strachey in his introduction promises us that we are going to get it. 'One can only find salvation for oneself by finding it for all others at the same time,' says Caudwell – sound mysticism, but is it sound dialectic materialism, too? 'Somehow,' says Mr Strachey (observe the semi-mystical 'somehow'), 'we must make men understand that they can find liberty not in the jungle, which is the most miserable coercive place in the world, but in the highest possible degree of social co-operation.' The first step towards this has to be the dictatorship of the proletariat. The dictatorship must presumably work through a bureaucracy, as it does in Russia, but the bureaucracy will not establish itself as a bourgeoisie – oh no! In some unexplained way the dictatorship will one day 'wither,' and Karl Marx will turn into Father Christmas, and present humanity with the Classless State. This idealism and warmheartedness is the inspiring force in Communism, the quality that distinguishes it from Fascism eternally. But what has happened to its logic? Just as we reach the summit of the exposition, and, our bourgeois illusions demolished, are expecting a positive goal, the exposition collapses. This collapse occurs in all religions – first the careful reasoning, the analysis of existing ills, and then the desperate jump to glory. Communism, like Christianity, jumps. And the shock is the bigger because of its previous aridity, its harsh technical arguments, economic and psychological, its contempt for all that is pleasant, wayward and soft. On we move, through the dictatorship of the proletariat to the full consciousness of the causality of society — and then we get a surprise-stocking. We open it: to discover that liberty means doing what is best for everyone else.

Talking with Communists makes me realise the weakness of my own position and the badness of the twentieth century society in which I live. I contribute to the badness without wanting to. My investments increase the general misery, and so may my charities. And I realise, too, that many Communists are finer people than myself – they are braver and less selfish, and some of them have gone into danger although they

were cowards, which seems to me finest of all. Yet, if I contribute to the
badness of contemporary society so do they; Caudwell's book, like my
review of it, is printed upon bourgeois-produced paper by bourgeois
printers, and profits the economic system which he condemns. And
though they may be better individuals than I, they are none the less
individuals; they emphasise the very category against which they
protest. And as for their argument for revolution – the argument that
we must do evil now so that good may come in the long run – it seems
to me to have nothing in it. Not because I am too nice to do evil, but
because I don't believe the Communists know what leads to what. They
say they know because they are becoming conscious of 'the causality of
society.' I say they don't know, and my counsel for 1938–9 conduct is
rather: Do good, and possibly good may come from it. Be soft even if
you stand to get squashed. Beware of the long run. Seek understanding
dispassionately, and not in accordance with a theory. Counsels of
despair, no doubt. But there is nothing disgraceful in despair. In 1938–
9 the more despair a man can take on board without sinking the more
completely is he alive.

E.M. Forster, 10 December 1938

Soon after Hitler's seizure of power, the NS *scored a minor* coup *in
unearthing these intriguing memories of the obscure Munich café
politician of the early twenties by W.W. CROTCH.*

Early Recollections of Adolf Hitler

The first time I heard the name of Adolf Hitler mentioned was shortly
after the end of the war, when a man named Franz Xavier Huber, a war
veteran who had a leg shot away before Verdun in 1917, told me the
stories of a curious fellow who had been in his regiment at the front. He
was a garrulous chap, and, sitting in that same Bürgerbraü Keller in
Munich (where in 1923 Hitler took his first plunge into revolutionary
activities by firing off his army revolver at the ceiling and declaring the
morrow would see him victor or dead although it saw him neither the
one nor the other, but unscathed, a helter-skelter fugitive in the
Bavarian hills), he used to tell tales tragic and humorous of his
campaign experiences.

The thing that had struck him about 'Private Hitler' was his
grandiloquence. He was neither popular nor the reverse with his

fellows; they just smiled at him and his vague rambling speeches on everything in the world and out of it. He acquired very swiftly the reputation of being what in the British Army is called 'an old soldier.' That is, he showed distinct talent in avoiding disagreeable tasks, but he knew on which side his bread was buttered. He interested himself particularly in the important question of seeing the officer's washing was done or doing it himself. This secured for him the good graces of the colonel, who removed him from the more constant dangers of the trenches and appointed him runner between regimental headquarters and the front line.

These duties brought him frequently in contact with the men and he would sit for hours in a dug-out and hold forth on Socialism, of which it was evident he had only very hazy notions. Old Social Democrats used to laugh at him, but no one debated seriously with him. He could not brook contradiction and used to fly into terrible rages if anyone ventured a word of dissent. Though he got the Iron Cross of the second class, no one in the regiment ever looked upon Hitler as any sort of hero; indeed they rather admired him for the skill with which he avoided hot corners. The regimental records contain not a line concerning an award of the Iron Cross of the first class to Hitler, though in latter years he has taken to wearing it prominently on his self-constructed uniform.

In those days in Munich I lived in the Thiersh Strasse, where nowadays the Hitlerite organ *Völkischer Beobachter* has its offices in a sumptuous building, and I frequently noticed in the street a man who vaguely reminded me of a militant edition of Charles Chaplin, owing to his characteristic moustache and his bouncing way of walking. He never wore a hat, but always carried a riding whip in his hand with which he used incessantly to chop off imaginary heads as he walked. He was so funny that I inquired from neighbours who he might be: most of them, owing to his Slav type, took him to be one of these Russian émigrés who abounded in Germany at that time, and they freely talked of his being probably a trifle mentally deranged. But my grocer told me it was a Herr Adolf Hitler from Braunau in Austria, and that he was leader of a tiny political group which called itself the 'German National Socialist Workers Party.' He lived quietly enough as a boarder in the apartment of a small artisan, wrote articles for an obscure paper called the *Völkischer Beobachter*, and orated in hole-and-corner meetings before audiences of a dozen or two. His closest friend was a Russian émigré from the Baltic Provinces, a certain Herr Rosenberg, who was joint owner of the paper. Out of curiosity I bought the paper once or twice, and found it a scatter-brained collection of wild anti-Jewish stories and articles interlarded with panegyrics on the Germanic race. My obliging grocer closed his information on Hitler by remarking that he frequently purchased things in his shop and was, despite his eccentric appearance, quite a pleasant fellow, though inclined to talk sixteen to the dozen about anything and everything.

Sometime later I became a frequent customer of a little wine saloon in the Schelling Strasse, called the 'Osteria Bavaria.' It was an historic place in its way, for it had been the haunt of the philosopher Schelling. The public in this inn was mostly composed of Bohemians, artists and art students, members of the staff of *Simplicissimus*, the famous satirical weekly; musicians and poetasters sat around of an evening and listened to Gulbransson or Thöny giving forth their views on art, politics and the price of a pound of meat. Discussions ensued that lasted far into the night, over tankards of beer and bottles of excellent Chianti. Hitler was an almost daily visitor; he had, I learned, been a house painter in his early days in Vienna, but he was rather sore on the subject, and posed as an artist. He was very fond of airing his views on art and architecture, which, however, were not taken seriously by any of the artists who frequented the place.

Hitler was often accompanied by one or two friends who, I was told, were members of his little political group. The most sensible of the band was a chemist named Gregor Strasser, a very sound fellow with whom I often spoke. Hitler's closest friend at that time, however, seemed to be an ex-army captain named Roehm, who later became chief of the Storm Troops, while his friend, Baldur von Schirach, was entrusted with leadership of the 'Hitler Youth,' the boy scout organisation of the National Socialist movement.

One thing that struck me about Hitler was his extreme abstemiousness. He ate every night a dish of vegetables, and mineral water was his only drink. He never smoked. This reminds me of an amusing incident when Hitler became Chancellor. The German vegetarians have a central organ of their league, and this paper came out with flaming headlines:

FIRST GREAT VICTORY OF GERMAN VEGETARIANS.
HITLER BECOMES CHANCELLOR

Sometimes instead of regaling us with chaotic speeches, Hitler would sit for hours on end in front of his mineral water, staring into space, not uttering a word, and apparently quite oblivious of his surroundings. If on these occasions someone suddenly addressed him, he would start as if out of sleep, and stroke his forehead with his hand several times before coming back to reality.

Apart from politics and art, Hitler's chief topics of conversation were

Italy and clairvoyance. He had never visited Italy, but had apparently read a great deal about it, and he would sometimes talk for half an hour on end about the glories of ancient Rome and the greatness of the Caesars. There was something about his talk that made one think of the prophets of the Old Testament: he spoke as if he believed himself to be inspired. The only thing that dispelled the illusion was his frequent use of words that are not found in the dictionary of a cultivated German.

One day I remember a man came in who, for the price of a plate of soup, read hands and told fortunes. Hitler retired with the soothsayer into a corner and spent a whole hour with him in earnest conference. When he got back among us, he turned with anger upon a student who made a slighting remark about clairvoyance, and launched out upon an eloquent defence of occultism of every kind, and especially of astrology. He made a confidant, too, of a Jewish charlatan named Steinschneider who had taken to himself the name of Hanussen, and consulted him frequently. Hanussen, who subsequently founded and ran a weekly newspaper on astrology, devoted to indirect propaganda for Hitler, became for a few weeks after Hitler's accession to power almost as important a factor in Germany as Rasputin had been in Russia. But his end was a tragic one. He was found murdered in a field in the environs of Berlin. Accounts vary regarding his death. Some say he knew too much; others that he had warned Hitler that the stars were unfavourable to him and that in the beginning of the winter of 1933 he would collapse. Others again ascribe his death to the jealousy of professional colleagues. However that may be, the incident does not appear to have shaken Hitler's faith in astrology, and one of Hanussen's chief rivals, a man named Mücke, has been appointed by Hitler 'Federal Commissary for Occultism.' This, I believe, is the first time in modern ages that a state has officially recognised sooth-saying and turned it into a government department.

But there is one extraordinary feature about Hitler's faith in the occult which gives rise to intriguing speculation. As everyone knows, he has adopted the Swastika as the emblem not only of his party but of the State. But curiously enough this Swastika is reversed, and anyone acquainted with Eastern beliefs and superstitions knows that this is to be regarded with positive horror. An inverted Swastika is indicative not of endless life but of the flood and flame of life leading to a violent destruction.

Did Hitler know this when he foisted it upon the German nation? Is the reversed Swastika just another sign of the man's half-baked conceptions of things, even his beloved mysticism? Or is this a last vestige of the irony of his political faith?

Hitler was not without devoted adherents in the 'Osteria Bavaria.'

Some students after a while became seized with a sort of hero-worship regarding him, and hung on to every word he said with wrapt attention. But there is no doubt his chief admirers where the two waitresses, buxom Bavarian wenches, who listened open-mouthed to him and danced attendance on him in a way that formed the subject of many jokes among the habitués of the place. Hitler's relations with women indeed are a strange and obscure chapter. I saw a great deal of him at that time, and I can certify that he was in these matters as abstemious as in regard to food and drink. The only woman he seemed to care for at all was the lady to whose villa in the hills he fled after his inglorious collapse in November, 1923. He used to correspond with her a great deal and spend frequent week-ends at her place. Latterly he is said to have fallen in love with Winifred Wagner, but I can hardly imagine the Hitler of 1921 in love. Another thing that struck me was the man's utter incapacity to deal with important details. When he spoke of Italy, or the German race, or occultism, or the Jews, his talk was a succession of vague generalities, couched in attractive if flowery language, but showing in every case either complete ignorance or at least complete contempt for detail.

Though he insisted in season and out of season on the greatness of 'pure Germanism,' I never met a German who was so entirely un-German. His speech, his thought, his outlook upon men and things were far more Slav than Teutonic. He loved everything foreign while he denounced it. His race theories came from the Frenchman, Gobineau, and the English renegade, Houston Chamberlain. His famous phrase 'the Third Reich' was the invention of the Dutchman, Moeller van den Bruck. The party salute was an Elizabethan stage convention – a subterfuge adopted by actors to imitate Roman. His regimental standards were a pale imitation of Roman eagles. His uniforms are anything but Germanic. They are a sort of cocktail of French, Austrian and English uniforms with most of the bad points to all three. But I will say this, as the result of those long evenings spent with him: he was, and probably still is, passionately, almost ferociously, sincere in all he says and does, even when it appears hypocritical and insincere.

W.W. Crotch, 29 July 1933

D.H. LAWRENCE contributed poetry and short stories to the NS but nothing as vividly terrifying as this prophetic letter, written in 1928 but not published until 1934. Lawrence's own politics were decidedly eccentric, of course. Here, though, he achieves an extraordinary insight into what a later historian of Germany was to call the politics of cultural despair.

D.H. Lawrence's Letter from Germany

We are going back to Paris to-morrow, so this is the last moment to write a letter from Germany. Only from the fringe of Germany, too.

It is a miserable journey from Paris to Nancy, through that Marne country, where the country still seems to have had the soul blasted out of it, though the dreary fields are ploughed and level, and the pale wire trees stand up. But it is all void and null. And in the villages, the smashed houses in the street rows, like rotten teeth between good teeth.

You come to Strasbourg, and the people still talk Alsatian German, as ever, in spite of French shop-signs. The place feels dead. And full of cotton goods, white goods, from Mülhausen, from the factories that once were German. Such cheap white cotton goods, in a glut.

The cathedral front rearing up high and flat and fanciful, a sort of darkness in the dark, with round rose windows and long, long prisons of stone. Queer that men should have ever wanted to put stone upon faithful stone to such a height without having it fall down. The gothic! I was always glad when my card-castle fell. But these goths and alemans seemed to have a craze for peaky heights.

The Rhine is still the Rhine, the great divider. You feel it as you cross. The flat, frozen, watery places. Then the cold and curving river. Then the other side, seeming so cold, so empty, so frozen, so forsaken. The train stands and steams fiercely. Then it draws through the flat Rhine plain, past frozen pools of flood-water, and frozen fields, in the emptiness of this bit of occupied territory.

Immediately you are over the Rhine, the spirit of the place has changed. There is no more attempt at the bluff of geniality. The marshy places are frozen. The fields are vacant. There seems nobody in the world.

It is as if the life had retreated eastwards. As if the Germanic life were slowly ebbing away from contact with western Europe, ebbing to the deserts of the east. And there stand the heavy, ponderous round hills of the Black Forest, black with an inky blackness of Germanic trees, and patched with a whiteness of snow. They are like a series of huge, involved black mounds, obstructing the vision eastwards. You look at them from the Rhine plain, and know that you stand on an actual border, up against something.

The moment you are in Germany, you know. It feels empty, and, somehow, menacing. So must the Roman soldiers have watched those black, massive round hills: with a certain fear, and with the knowledge that they were at their own limit. A fear of the invisible natives. A fear of the invisible like lurking among the woods. A fear of their own opposite.

So it is with the French: this almost mystic fear. But one should not insult even one's fears.

Germany, this bit of Germany, is very different from what it was two and a half years ago, when I was here. Then it was still open to Europe. Then it still looked to western Europe for a reunion, for a sort of reconciliation. Now that is over. The inevitable, mysterious barrier has fallen again, and the great leaning of the Germanic spirit is once more eastwards, towards Russia, towards Tartary. The strange vortex of Tartary has become the positive centre again, the positivity of western Europe is broken. The positivity of our civilisation has broken. The influences that come, come invisibly out of Tartary. So that all Germany reads *Men, Beasts and Gods* with a kind of fascination. Returning again to the fascination of the destructive East, that produced Attila.

So it is at night. Baden-Baden is a little quiet place, all its guests gone. No more Turgenevs or Dostoevskys or Grand Dukes or King Edwards coming to drink the waters. All the outward effect of a world-famous watering-place. But empty now, a mere Black Forest village with the wagon-loads of timber going through, to the French.

The Rentenmark, the new gold Mark of Germany, is abominably dear. Prices are high in England, but English money buys less in Baden than it buys in London, by a long chalk. And there is no work – consequently no money. Nobody buys anything, except absolute necessities. The shopkeepers are in despair. And there is less and less work.

Everybody gives up the telephone – can't afford it. The tramcars don't run, except about three times a day to the station. Up to the Annaberg, the suburb, the lines are rusty, no trams ever go. The people can't afford the ten Pfennigs for the fare. Ten Pfennigs is an important sum now: one penny. It is really a hundred Milliards of Marks.

Money becomes insane, and people with it.

At night the place is almost dark, economising light. Economy, economy, economy – that, too, becomes an insanity. Luckily the government keeps bread fairly cheap.

But at night you feel strange things stirring in the darkness, strange feelings stirring out of this still-unconquered Black Forest. You stiffen your backbone and you listen to the night. There is a sense of danger. It is not the people. They don't seem dangerous. Out of the very air comes a sense of danger, a queer, *bristling* feeling of uncanny danger.

Something has happened. Something has happened which has not yet eventuated. The old spell of the old world has broken, and the old, bristling, savage spirit has set in. The war did not break the old peace-and-production hope of the world, though it gave it a severe wrench. Yet the old peace-and-production hope still governs, at least the consciousness. Even in Germany it has not quite gone.

But it feels as if virtually, it were gone. The last two years have done it. The hope in peace-and-production is broken. The old flow, the old adherence is ruptured. And a still older flow has set in. Back, back to the savage polarity of Tartary, and away from the polarity of civilised Christian Europe. This, it seem to me, has already happened. And it is a happening of far more profound import than any actual *event*. It is the father of the next phase of events.

And the feeling never relaxes. As you travel up the Rhine valley, still the same latent sense of danger, of silence, of suspension. Not that the people are actually planning or plotting or preparing. I don't believe it for a minute. But something has happened to the human soul, beyond all help. The human soul recoiling now from unison, and making itself strong elsewhere. The ancient spirit of prehistoric Germany coming back, at the end of history.

The same in Heidelberg. Heidelberg full, full, full of people. Students the same, youth with rucksacks the same, boys and maidens in gangs come down from the hills. The same, and not the same. These queer gangs of *Young Socialists*, youths and girls, with their non-materialistic professions, their half-mystic assertions, they strike one as strange. Something primitive, like loose, roving gangs of broken, scattered tribes, so they affect one. And the swarms of people somehow produce an impression of silence, of secrecy, of stealth. It is as if everything and everybody recoiled away from the old unison, as barbarians lurking in a wood recoil out of sight. The old habits remain. But the bulk of the people have no money. And the whole stream of feeling is reversed.

So you stand in the woods above the town and see the Neckar flowing green and swift and slippery out of the gulf of Germany, to the Rhine. And the sun sets slow and scarlet into the haze of the Rhine valley. And the old, pinkish stone of the ruined castle across looks sultry, the marshalry is in shadow below, the peaked roofs of old, tight Heidelberg compressed in its river gateway glimmer and glimmer out. There is a blue haze.

And it all looks as if the years were wheeling swiftly backwards, no more onwards. Like a spring that is broken and whirls swiftly back, so time seems to be whirling with mysterious swiftness to a sort of death. Whirling to the ghost of the old Middle Ages of Germany, then to the

Roman days, then to the days of the silent forest and the dangerous, lurking barbarians.

Something about the Germanic races is unalterable. White-skinned, elemental, and dangerous. Our civilisation has come from the fusion of the dark-eyed with the blue. The meeting and mixing and mingling of the two races has been the joy of our ages. And the Celt has been there, alien, but necessary as some chemical reagent to the fusion. So the civilisation of Europe rose up. So these cathedrals and these thoughts.

But now the Celt is the disintegrating agent. And the Latin and southern races are falling out of association with the northern races, the northern Germanic impulse is recoiling towards Tartary, the destructive vortex of Tartary.

It is a fate; nobody now can alter it. It is a fate. The very blood changes. Within the last three years, the very constituency of the blood has changed, in European veins. But particularly in Germanic veins.

At the same time, we have brought it about ourselves – by a Ruhr occupation, by an English nullity, and by a German false will. We have done it ourselves. But apparently it was not to be helped.

Quos vult perdere Deus, dementat prius.

D.H. Lawrence, 13 October 1934

The Italian invasion of Abyssinia in 1935 was a crucial formative moment in the evolution of African nationalist politics. KINGSLEY MARTIN saw one of the first flashes of that awakening and responded with sensitivity, though not unfortunately without condescension ('surprising eloquence').

A London Diary

The meeting was not a big affair – a couple of hundred coloured people, and perhaps fifty white. But I have never seen an Albert Hall meeting which impressed me as so significant an omen as this little gathering in Farringdon Street, called to enlist support for the Emperor of Abyssinia. Mussolini has appealed to the war spirit and declared a White crusade against Black barbarism. Naturally, the response is Black defiance of White barbarism. The speakers came from the West Indies, the Gold Coast, Kenya, Somaliland and Abyssinia itself. When they expressed a hope that the League of Nations or the British Government would see justice done, the audience was silent or ironical. When they declared that coloured people everywhere would fight and die free men rather than submit to the subjugation of the last independent native kingdom, the meeting yelled with enthusiasm. For Blacks to pour contempt on White civilisation is easy: Europe is not a good advertisement for civilisation, and civilised peoples have seldom behaved in a civilised way to the uncivilised. You had only to say the word 'civilisation' to set this meeting jeering. Soon it was persuading itself that Abyssinia was the centre of true civilisation, and Europe of barbarism. Unconscious of irony, these coloured speakers, who have often surprising eloquence and use the language of Shakespeare and Milton better than most English speakers, were quoting Biblical passages about Ethiopia stretching forth her hand and reading Wordsworth's sonnet to the black hero of Haiti. All the literature of freedom – the product of white civilisation – is available for the discomfiture of white tyrants the world over. Africa was described as 'the home of the free.' We were reminded that 'the British Empire is a coloured Empire.' (A good and proper point this.) Most significant of all, the world war they prophesied was not between black and white, but between coloured and white; Japan, the most powerful coloured race, was called upon to champion the cause of international justice!

Kingsley Martin, 3 August 1935

In the decade of recession, revolution and the looming threat of war, a small coup in Greece – not many dead – might have passed unnoted in Britain, had CYRIL CONNOLLY not happened to be there.

Spring Revolution

The boredom of travel! There is an acute condition which develops in enforced lulls before the wholesome drudgery of getting from place to place makes a brute of one again. If you knew how bored we were in Athens! Stagnation and self-disgust engender a low fever that wastes the curiosity and resolution that might have cured them. The weather was too bad to go anywhere and the nearest sun was in Egypt. Sleeping late to shorten the day, one went to the window and found the Acropolis and the Parthenon blocking the horizon. A thing of beauty, that is a joy once or twice, and a standing reproach afterwards. Downstairs it would be nearly lunch-time. In the bar, which was an embottled corridor smelling of gin and Gold Flake, the Greek businessmen jollied each other up in cinema American and Trocadero English. The sombre dining-room was like the Dickensian coffee-room of a Midland hotel. The French dishes all tasted the same, like food on a liner; the Greek joints seemed made of sweetened gelatine. Coffee was served in the lounge amid the engineering papers, and snatches of conversations.

'I hope you are never troubled by the green-eyed monster.'

'Pliss, Mr Ansull?'

'Why, you know what the green-eyed monster is! Jealousy!'

'O yais, Mr Ansull. Pliss?'

A walk in the afternoon. Tram-lines, blocks of yellow houses, demolition, everywhere the metamorphosis of a tenth-rate Turkish market town into a tenth-rate Californian suburb. A pause in the book-shop where one must choose between expensive art books of the Acropolis and diseases of the stomach, or sixpenny editions of Edgar Wallace and Wilhelm Meister. There were also the newspapers, and glancing at them phrases would enter with a little stab and begin to fester. 'Ruskin, one felt, would have disapproved,' 'wherein promise and achievement touch hands very agreeably,' and 'Bébé is painting a portrait of Baba.' Before the Dragoman's ingenious vulgarities I would gape like a mesmerised chicken.

In the hotel thé dansant would have begun. A hundred bearded ladies have brought their black little daughters. The ballroom reeks with stale flowers and cheap scent. All the tables are taken. The fathers in spats and clean collars try to eradicate from their faces the expression which forty years of Levantine practices have implanted. The mothers employ the vocabulary of the underworld of elegance. 'Très réussi ... convenable ... on aura dit ... ça se remarque.' The daughters fidget. The young men attempt polish. All move in the psychologist's wonderland which is revealed to us when we watch charmless people trying to be charming. The band strikes up 'Come on, uglies, do your stuff!'

At dinner a piano and a violin play evening music, with *Peer Gynt*, *Rosamund*, *Chansons sans Paroles*, *Toselli*, wistful and gallant compositions that empty over one all the slops of capitalist sentiment. Afterwards, there are the cinemas with wooden seats and German films unknown to the Academy, and a few places for supper. In Greek cabarets one is not allowed to sit with a woman unless one has champagne. The sexes are therefore divided on opposite sides of the floor. If a young man dances with a 'hostess' he scurries back at the finish like a male spider trying to escape from the nuptial embrace before he is eaten. The girls are sulky, the whisky bad. Back in the room there are mosquitoes in February and the *Continental Daily Mail*,

four days old, with an article saying that our greatest living stylist is Mr
Somerset Maugham. This day, repeated ten times, was typical of
Athens. As boredom gathered momentum one felt all the ingredients of
personality gurgling away like the last inch of bathwater. One became a
carcase of nonentity and indecision, a reflection to be avoided in
mirrors. Why go abroad? Why travel? Why exchange the regard of a
clique for the stare of a concierge?

On the day of the elections the sun was shining. It was one of those
Sundays in early spring when there is an air of displacement. A
sensation of keels lifting from the mud, of new skin, and of new
acquaintances. We motored to Kephissia for lunch. The butter was
good. Refugees paraded about in their hideous best, and gramophones
played in Tatoi. At Hagios Mercurios we looked down over the plain to
the blue lake of the Aegean, Chalcis, Eretria, and the snows and forests
of Euboea. In the wet weather we could not conceive a reason for being
here, in a moment it became impossible to imagine being anywhere
else.

Everyone had voted when we got back to Athens. The bars and
cinemas were closed, and in the restaurant wine was served from tea-
pots and drunk in cups as in an old-fashioned speakeasy. Crowds cheered.
Venizelos was sweeping the polls. 'The best thing for the country.' As
in all companies where politics are discussed, to compensate the
dullness of the subject, one began to feel an illusion of far-sightedness
and worldly wisdom.

Next morning the town was quiet. I was particularly annoyed to find
an antique shop closed and tried to get the concierge to rout up the
missing proprietor. Down the empty street moved a kind of grey Noah's
ark on wheels. At the English tailor's we heard the news. Venizelos had
lost the election. Tsaldaris, the head of the Royalist-Popular party, was
in, but he and all his colleagues had been put in prison. There had been
a revolution in Macedonia. The shops were closing and the proprietors
of travel agencies stood in the doors with the keys in their hands.
Lorries of mud-coloured soldiers passed down the street distributing
handbills. Martial law was proclaimed, newspapers suppressed, groups
of people shot at sight, by order of the Chief of the revolution,
Plastiras. By lunch-time it was accepted that we were under a
dictatorship. All the plats du jour were 'off' and we bawled out the
head waiter. An aeroplane flew over, dropping pamphlets in which
Plastiras described the collapse of parliamentary government. Rumours
collected. Plastiras was a Venizelist. He was going to cancel the
elections and keep Venizelos in office. He was not a Venizelist and was
going to govern by himself. I walked down the University boulevard. It
was warm and sunny. A straggling crowd that was moving about

suddenly thickened and made way for two archaic fire engines, whose hoses were playing over them. The smell of wet earth followed their path through the sunshine. Everybody laughed and teased the soldiers on the engines, who laughed back at them. One could not tell if they were shouting Tsaldaris or Plastiras. In the hotel we received more explanations. Plastiras was in prison. 'It had all been done very quietly.' Venizelos and Tsaldaris had arranged it with the President of the Republic. The soldiers had fraternized. The dictatorship was a wash-out. General Condylis had flown last night to Athens from Salonica. Plastiras had taken him prisoner, but he had escaped and was marching with his army from Thebes on Athens. Tonight there would be a big battle as Condylis wished to avenge Plastira's execution of the Cabinet in 1922.

We went out again. 'Tsaldaris' was being shouted everywhere. There were still crowds in the boulevard, but suddenly down a side street we saw a ragged collection of men marching with staves in their hands. On many of these the olive leaves still remained. Some only carried small untrimmed branches. They looked like a woodcut of Jack Cade's rebellion in a child's history book. It was at this moment that we heard the rattle of machine-guns. Everyone ran giggling into doorways. 'They're only blank, of course,' was said knowingly. Turning into Stadium Street some soldiers rushed up to us pointing down and crying 'Kato, Kato!' The machine-guns began again.

The street, in normal times so straight and dull, became an enormous affair of shadows and relief, of embrasures and exposed spaces. The kiosk at the corner seemed as far away as it would to a baby who could just walk, or a very lame old man. As we ran round the corner volleys seemed to come from every direction. People threw themselves flat on the ground and hid behind trees. The Noah's Ark passed down the end of the street with the snouts of machine-guns thrusting from the wooden windows. We came to a little restaurant where we had dined the day before. The crowd surged on the steps and the doors were barricaded, but when they recognised us we were let in. From the balcony more men with staves could be seen in the falling night. A small cannon boomed at intervals and shook the windows. A man was helped by with a bleeding arm. While one-half of my brain dealt in realities – revolution, street fighting, baptism of fire – the other continued to function as if nothing had happened, and remembering that someone was coming for a cocktail, I insisted on trying to telephone to the hotel that we should be a little late. The wires were cut, but if we went back directly we should still be in time for them. Back on the balcony we saw a crowd collecting at the foot of the University. A man ran up the steps waving something. A machine-gun rattled, the crowd fell apart, and revealed him lying in a growing pool of blood and brains. An ambulance bell sounded and a man with a woman in a mink coat walked down the middle of the street from the other side. We slipped out and made our way round by alleys and crossed the Place de la Constitution in the yellow dusk. We reached the side entrance to the Grande Bretagne. It was heavily barricaded. We knocked and rang, when another crowd of people surged round the corner and up the steps. There was a feeling of real hopelessness and panic. After them, turning elaborately, slid the armoured car. What had seemed comic and antediluvian was now implacable and fatal. The machine-guns pointed straight at us; a fat woman tried to turn us out from behind a pillar where we were, but we shoved her quickly away. The car passed without firing and we got round to the other entrance. Inside all was cheerfulness and commotion; everyone felt important and with a reason for living. We dined in a large party, including several people whom we had avoided for two weeks, and retired upstairs with a gramophone and a bottle of whisky. A business man explained everything. Plastiras was master of the situation. He was a patriot. He would force a coalition between Venizelos and Tsaldaris. The latter's victory was illegal because he had promised the refugees bonuses which he hadn't got. 'Plastiras does not play. He knows his head is at stake. If he fails he will shoot himself. He had eight officers shot who tried to arrest him. General Condylis was locked up. He sent him a telegram signed "Tsaldaris" telling him to fly to Athens. When he landed he took him prisoner. There would be no battle.' It was the best thing that could happen for Greece. The army was with him. The night was dark and cold. Outside a few small tanks patrolled the streets. Machine-guns looked down from the balcony of the palace. The armoured car in previous volleys had chipped bits off the masonry along the front of the hotel. It was quiet and with the cessation of firing people began to feel the anti-climax and grow irritable. One wondered why one was cooped up with the tiresome business man; with the young Frenchman and his crisp platitudes; the clergyman's daughter chorus girl of dubious status, who was explaining why she would never have a lady-dog in the house. Everyone separated, secretly hoping for the roar of Condylis's artillery.

Next morning we were woken by the noise of trams. There were no guns on the palace. Newspapers arrived. The shops were open and nothing remained of the day before but the pool of wet blood by the University, surrounded by gaping students. At a time when Plastiras was supposed to be master of the situation, he had surrendered to the eight generals who commanded the rest of the army for Venizelos.

The dictatorship was over, and had been over since eight o'clock the night before. Plastiras had seized the government with only one regiment; his party had repudiated him. Whether a patriot or a power-grabber he was ridiculous. He had wounded thirty-three people, and killed one and cured two or three discontented pleasure seekers of the curious stoppage of the sensibilities to which they had fallen victims. They, while secretly admitting the futility of the eye-witness, the meaningless and stupidity of all that had happened, knew also that they had tasted the intoxication, and the prestige of action, and were soon rearranging the events of the day on a scale, and in an order, more worthy of the emotions which had been generated by them.

Cyril Connolly, 18 March 1933

The NS's coverage of the Spanish Civil War is now mostly famous, or notorious, for what it didn't *print: George Orwell. Continued debate on the morality of Martin's censorship – and I have no doubt it was wrong – has obscured the quality of what did appear. Communist CLAUD COCKBURN's political analysis of events in Spain was evidently dishonest, but his eyewitness reporting, as here, was superb.*

On the Spanish Front

At the offices of the Cultural Commission they were reading the first leaflets dropped over Madrid by the German planes, threatening 'ruthless bombardment.'

Jose Bergamin, Catholic writer and member of the Commission, said to me: 'To-day, if you come to think of it, is probably our last chance for a long time to come and see some of the finest pictures in the world.' In those first weeks of the war, the picture galleries at least had bloomed. The Cultural Commission of the People's Front, composed of the leading artists, art critics and writers of Spain, had been busy unearthing from steel vaults in the Bank of Spain pictures which for years had lain hidden there serving as bonds, deposited or hoarded by grandee owners.

The list of the newly discovered pictures – now hung in the Prado – by itself reads like the catalogue of some splendid new gallery. The Prado was packed all day with people going to see the new-found treasures. 'This afternoon,' Bergamin went on, 'we shall have to start putting them back in the dark again. They may bomb to-night. Fortunately the Prado cellars are probably bomb proof.'

In the small hours, sirens mounted on motor cars screamed through the darkened streets. Militiamen hammered on bedroom doors, warning everyone to get downstairs. In the lounge of the Hotel Florida people drifted uncertainly about, stumbling over chairs and divans in the darkness. Someone lit a cigarette, and a voice like a pistol shot from the street outside ordered us to be careful with the lights. There was an argument as to whether we should go to the cellar or stay in the lounge. 'I have observed,' said a French lady, 'that Mr So-and-So is staying in this hotel.' She mentioned the agent of a notorious American financial magnate. Mr So-and-So was known to maintain the closest relations with the German Embassy. 'If he goes to the cellar I think we may assume that the raid is intended to be serious.' We agreed to watch out for So-and-So as a barometer of peril. Presently we saw him picking his way towards the cellar. Someone asked him why he did not go to the German Embassy and be really safe. 'The German Embassy,' he said sadly, 'left by plane to-day for Alicante.' We went to the cellar.

The planes were now clearly heard. A bomb screamed through the air and the crash merged abruptly into the agonised screaming of women's voices somewhere far off.

Under the garden trees at the British Embassy, the militia guard played cards. Inside, impoverished gentlewomen, escaping enemy agents who wanted to get British passports, and an assortment of crooks, hung about, most of them insisting on seeing the Chargé d'Affaires immediately.

'And so,' I said to the diplomat, 'when my Spanish friends ask me why the British Government is going on in this way, I don't really know what explanation to give.' That was not quite true. I thought I knew the explanation, but at the back of my mind perhaps still hoped he would give another one.

'Well,' he said, 'we shall have to maintain an attitude of reserve, of course. We shall hope to arrange things with the rebels in a more or less satisfactory manner.'

'You are betting on that?'

'As for me,' he said, beaming and pumping my hand vigorously, 'I have an absolutely clear conscience, I am absolutely neutral. You can assure your Spanish friends of that.'

Morning, afternoon and evening, the recruits gathered round the sergeant instructors asking when the rifles would come. 'To-morrow perhaps.' On the fourth day they gave us dummy rifles. A middle-aged lieutenant, who had fought in the old army in Africa and been cashiered the previous year as a suspected Socialist, explained to me why he thought the newspapers must be making a mistake about the attitude of the British Government on the 'neutrality' question.

'Apart from anything else,' he said, 'it is quite clear to me that the British Government cannot have such an attitude, for I think that it will not be possible for the British to agree to the Germans controlling the mid-Atlantic from here, and Portugal, and the Moroccos. It is impossible.'

'You forget,' I said, 'that you have not a monopoly of traitors in your country. Your General Franco is prepared to give away bits of Spain to foreign powers to help him beat the people of Spain. Our Government is full of similar people who are prepared to open any gate to the enemies of England rather than support a democratic Government in Spain or lead a joint action of the democratic Powers.'

'And the patriots in your country, the democrats and so on. How strong do you estimate them to be?'

'Strong but split,' I said.

'That's bad.'

'One dead, four wounded.' The Sergeant handed to the Captain his report on the accident we had just suffered on the winding road to the front. The lorry in which our platoon was packed and racing had gone fast round a hairpin bend and overturned.

'He was driving too fast,' said the Sergeant.

'He was not,' said the Captain. 'You have to understand, and all the comrades have to understand, that nowadays we can't drive any slower on this road. Before they had all the new planes, yes. Now, you drive slowly along this road and the next thing you know their planes have spotted you. If we lose men in accidents, that isn't the driver's fault.'

'What about our planes?' someone asked. 'Can't they drive them away?'

'Well, Englishman,' said the Captain, laughing and turning to me, 'what about our planes? Are they going to send *us* a present from Portugal for a change?'

The dead man and the four wounded men lay on the roadside in a line together, waiting for a lorry back.

We moved into position on the Sierra. The men we had relieved told us it was a quiet spot. Then, somewhere over on the left, our people took some prisoners whose story indicated the quiet would not last long. The prisoners' story was circulated to the commandants 'for information.' The prisoners said that the big attack was scheduled for the thirteenth of September, but was being held up until the new German planes arrived from over the border.

It began, sure enough, on the sixteenth. The Junkers, with first-class

German pilots and machine gunners aboard, and sometimes – so prisoners told us – a couple of Spaniards for 'look see,' flew low in squadrons, bombing and machine-gunning the line of our riflemen on the hill-tops.

Morning and evening we lay under the rocks, helpless, and trying to keep ready to jump out to meet a wave of infantry attack the moment the planes were gone.

Our water supply was under machine-gun fire, rifle bullets kept coming onto the rock shelter we used as a kitchen, so the eating and drinking was on a limited scale.

Sometimes we were on guard for as much as fifteen hours of the twenty-four. It was uncomfortable because you could neither sit nor stand. You could not sit because you could not see to fire, nor stand because if you stood up you got a bullet in the head. We perched uncomfortably among the rocks, looking across the Guadarrama plain.

One night three men were reported to have slept on duty.

The Captain called a meeting of the platoon, and explained the circumstances. He sat cross-legged in the middle of a circle of men, huddled in thin blankets against the terrible wind of the Sierras, pressed close under the parapets and rocks, with bullets whining intermittently above them.

'You all understand,' he said, 'the gravity of the offence, from every point of view. You are here of your own free will, holding a point which is not simply of significance for us, although we may well die here, nor yet for Madrid and for Spain, but also for civilisation in all the world.' He went on to speak more particularly of the perils brought upon others by a guard who sleeps on duty.

The question was then thrown open to discussion, the words of the speakers being occasionally inaudible as a big shell howled overhead and burst on the hillside behind.

It was proposed that those who had slept and the sergeant responsible for making the rounds of the guards should be shot. The sergeant, a former butcher's boy, who had joined three weeks before and been elected sergeant only ten days ago, spoke, haltingly but with terrible earnest in favour of his own execution. When he had finished he squatted silent, nervously fingering his rifle.

The three guards who had slept – one of them was only sixteen years old and had been a delivery boy in a store in Valencia – spoke against execution, declaring they would never do it again, and suggesting some alternative penalty.

The difficulty was that whenever a 'fatigue' was proposed it was found to be something which everyone was compelled to do anyway owing to the grave danger we were in. One of those who had slept – whom I had already threatened to shoot on the previous night – proposed that 'the Englishman' should be put in charge of all these hard cases. 'We can rely on him to shoot them if necessary,' he said. In the end they went unpunished, and that was the last occasion when there was any sleeping on guard in our platoon.

The battle developed, day in and day out, into a bloody game wherein the poorly armed forces of the democrats sought, by desperate assaults and reckless endeavours, to even out the difference between them and the German air force on the other side. One day we were told that now, indeed, it must be frankly said that the position was hopeless, but that nevertheless retreat could not be contemplated, for it might roll up the whole Sierra front.

'We can only die once,' said the Captain. 'And we have the satisfaction of knowing that we are dying for ourselves and for all free peoples of the world, too. Isn't that so, Englishman?'

There was discussion of the situation. One man said to me: 'Do you believe that if we resist bravely here, fighting until we are every one of us killed, that the time we gain will be of use to the democratic Powers in preparing to come to the help of Spain?' I told them that every hour we gained there would be an hour more gained for these people in England who were fighting day and night with us against the 'neutrality' pact and on behalf of the people of Spain.

'That,' said one of the Assault Guards who was with us, 'is very satisfactory.'

Claud Cockburn, 3 October 1936

All the major 'thirties poets' published in the NS, *as did many of the poets of the Spanish war. STEPHEN SPENDER wrote far more and better on the war than has usually been remembered.*

The Moment Transfixes the Space Which Divides

> *O the watch and the compasses!*
> At five the man fell under the trees
> The watch flew off stopped at a moon
> Of time staring from the dead wrist
> Where no air breathes, hours creep no inches,

Shadows wag over transparent light
And the time and the place are death.

The watch and O the compasses!
He the dead centre, and I their arm
Thrown over mountains and rivers and valleys,
When the clocks struck five and the wrist watch stopped
And nailed to his final loneliness
He lacked my assuaging glance of peace.
And the time and the place are death.

O the watch and O the compasses!
The hour at five, the corpse under the trees,
Distance over mountains rivers and valleys,
The leaden bullet which like a clock
Split open the moment dividing us,
And that space chained to my wrists for ever.
And the time and the place are death.

Stephen Spender, 21 August 1937

Kingsley Martin wrote earlier and better against appeasing Hitler than almost anyone else. J.M. KEYNES, though he later switched to Martin's view, initially wrote better in favour of it.

British Foreign Policy

W.H. Auden's poem, *Spain*, is fit to stand beside great predecessors in its moving, yet serene expression of contemporary feeling towards the heart-rending events of the political world. The theme of the poem lies in the comparison between the secular achievements of the past and the hope which is possible for the future with the horrors of the present and the sacrifices which perhaps it demands from those of this generation who think and feel rightly. Yesterday, all the past. To-morrow, perhaps the future. 'But to-day the struggle,' his refrain runs. Auden conceives of 'the struggle' in terms of immediate war and force, of death and killing:

> To-day the deliberate increase in the chances of death,
> The conscious acceptance of guilt in the necessary murder.

In this he is speaking for many chivalrous hearts. Yet, whilst he teaches us, as a poet should, how we should feel, the object of this article is to question whether he rightly directs how, at this moment at least, we should act.

I view with revulsion the growing tendency to make of the struggle between the two ideologies (or would it be conceded that there are three?) another War of Religion, to believe that the issue can or will be settled by force of arms, and to feel that it is our duty to hasten to any quarter of the world where those of our faith are oppressed. It is only too easy for men to feel like this. The Crusades and the Thirty Years' War actually occurred. But does it seem, looking back, that it was a duty to join in them, or that they settled anything? Assume that the war occurs, and let us suppose, for the sake of argument, that we win. What then? Shall we ourselves be the better for it and for what it will have brought with it? What are we going to do with the defeated? Are we to impose our favourite ideology on them (whatever, by then, it may be) in an up-to-date Peace Treaty, or do we assume that they will adopt it with spontaneous enthusiasm? At best we should be back, it seems to me, exactly where we were. Defeat is complete disaster. Victory, as usual, would be useless, and probably pernicious. It is an illusion to believe that conscious acceptance of guilt in the necessary murder can settle what is mainly a moral issue.

Therefore, and furthermore, I maintain that the claims of Peace are paramount; though this seems to be an out-of-date view in what used to be pacifist circles. It is our duty to prolong peace, hour by hour, day by day, for as long as we can. We do not know what the future will bring, except that it will be quite different from anything we could predict. I have said in another context that it is a disadvantage of 'the long run' that in the long run we are all dead. But I could have said equally well that it is a great advantage of 'the short run' that in the short run we are still alive. Life and history are made up of short runs. If we are at peace in the short run, that is something. The best we can do is to put off disaster, if only in the hope, which is not necessarily a remote one, that something will turn up. While there is peace, there is peace. It is silly and presumptious to say that war is inevitable; for no one can possible know. The only conclusion which is certain is that we cannot avoid war by bringing it on. If, thinking of Spain, someone urges that self-interest does not entitle us to abandon others, I answer that for Spain peace – and to-day, I think, I would add peace on any terms – is her greatest interest. Spain will work out her future in due course. It is not the outcome of the civil war which will settle it. It would be much more plausible to argue that British imperial interests or French security require the defeat of Franco than that the interests of Spaniards require

it. Those who believe in the efficacy of war are misunderstanding the
kind of power we have to influence the future.

But I do not, therefore, claim that war can always be avoided. I do
not need to answer the question whether war is even defensible. The
question does not arise, inasmuch as our knowledge of human nature
tells us that in practice there are circumstances when war on our part,
whether defensible or not, is unavoidable. We are brought, therefore, to
the second aspect of foreign policy. The first duty of foreign policy is to
avoid war. Its second duty is to ensure that, if it occurs, the
circumstances shall be the most favourable possible for our cause. Let
us consider the immediate position from this point of view.

By postponement we gain peace to-day. Have we anything to lose by
it? Our capacity for cuncation is one of our most powerful and
characteristic national weapons. It has been our age-long instrument
against dictators. Since Fabius Maximus there has scarcely been a
stronger case for cuncation than there is to-day. It is maddening and
humiliating to have to take so much lip. We may, conceivably, have to
submit to greater humiliations and worse betrayals than any yet. Those
who applaud war and believe they have something to gain from it have
an inevitable advantage, which cannot possibly be taken from them, in
a game of bluff and in the preliminary manoeuvres; though all the time
they may be running unperceived risks, which one day will catch them
out. But *we* have to look farther ahead; believing that time and chance
are with us, and taking precautions that, *if* we are forced to act, we can
make quite sure. This seems cold and shifty to the poet. Yet I claim the
benefit of the first part of one of Auden's stanzas:

> What's your proposal? To build the just city? I will.
> I agree.

leaving to him the second part:

> Or is it the suicide pact, the romantic
> Death? Very well, I accept.

For consider the immediate political factors staring us in the face. At
the moment Russia is disorganised and France at a disadvantage. Each
is at a low ebb but each needs mainly time. Before long we ourselves
will possess the most predominant sea-power in European waters that
we have ever enjoyed in our history. Meanwhile what is happening to
the brigand powers? One of them is busily engaged in outraging every
creed in turn. If they could find another institution or another
community to insult or injure, they would do so. Both of them are
spending a lot of money on an intensive propaganda to persuade the

rest of the world that they are the enemies of the human race. It is having the desired result, not least in the United States. No one trusts or respects their word. They have not a single friend or sympathiser in the whole world, for I doubt if even Japan thrills greatly to their croonings. Yet even so, all this needs time to sink in, here at home as well as elsewhere. The full abomination is understood to-day in a degree and over an area much greater than a year ago. These tactics are not characteristic of great statesmen and conquerors. They appear to be morbid, pathological, diseased. I gravely doubt their technical efficiency and expect that every sort of idiocy is going on behind the scenes. It is unlikely that those who talk so much nonsense will act quite differently; or that they, who persecute the mind and all its works, will be employing it to the best advantage. It is very probable that, given time, they will over-play their hands, overreach themselves and make a major blunder. It is in the nature of their type of behaviour that this should happen. And if, indeed, the thieves were to have a little more success, nothing is likelier than that they would fall out amongst themselves.

Near the beginning of the Abyssinian affair our Foreign Office was guilty of the gravest and most disastrous error of policy in recent history. It is natural, therefore, to distrust them. But though it has been hateful in its immediate consequences and cruel in some of its details, I am not inclined to criticise the broad outline of Mr Eden's Spanish policy. I should have been afraid if his critics had had a chance to take over from him. The task of cunctator is always a thankless one. To be for ever allowing the brigands yet a little more rope, to be holding up the cup for them to fill yet fuller is not a distinguished office. It is never possible, unfortunately, to estimate a statesman by his results, since we never have for comparison the consequences of the alternative course. But I do not judge his policy to have been inconsistent as yet with the two prime objects stated above.

I bid Auden, therefore, to pass by on the other side. If he will be patient and unheroic, in due course, perhaps, he will be shown (in his own words):

> History the operator, the
> Organiser, Time the refreshing river.

J.M. Keynes, 10 July 1937

NS attitudes to Stalin's Russia wobbled all over the place. Criticism was tempered by MARTIN's belief that Stalin was a crucially necessary ally against Fascism, yet this never wholly *misted vision of the monstrosity of the purges, as shown in this piece on the enigma of the victims' confessions.*

Will Stalin Explain?

According to their confessions Radek, Sokolnikov and the other Old Bolsheviks now on trial for their lives in Moscow have for years been plotting with Trotsky and with Japanese and German Fascists to overthrow the revolutionary regime which they have spent their lives in establishing. Their plan, they tell us, was to seize power for themselves by murdering Stalin and Molotoff; and at the same time to surrender part of Russia's Eastern territory to Japan and the Ukraine to the Germans. Holding that a war with Japan and Germany was inevitable, Radek declares that he and his accomplices arranged to weaken Russia as much as possible. Thousands of railway breakdowns were arranged. Disease germs were to be spread among the populace and acts of sabotage to take place in factories and workshops all over the USSR.

This is a curious story. The various parts of the plot do not seem to hold together, nor is any adequate motive suggested for such a monstrously perverted enterprise. That the remnant of the old Bolshevik guard should have become critical of Stalin and have wished to supersede him is credible enough. That in a dictatorship they may have been driven to underground intrigues is perfectly possible. But no one acquainted with the personalities and the records of Radek and Sokolnikov will readily believe, on the uncorroborated evidence of these confessions alone, that these men have entered into negotiations with Fascists for the destruction of the Socialist Russia. Radek, a master of vituperation and brilliant analyst of foreign affairs, has been the most influential journalist of the regime. We can imagine him capable of many kinds of trickery, but that he should plot to hand over his country to foreign Fascism puts a heavy strain on credulity. Equally difficult is it to cast Sokolnikov for such a role. An unusually able and apparently devoted servant of the USSR, he has been acknowledged as one of the principle architects of Russia's financial stability, and perhaps more than any other Russian, he paved the way, as Ambassador in London, for that improved relationship with the Western democracies which has been the pivot of Stalin's foreign policy.

Supposing, however, that we accept the whole of this story as true. Even so, the present trials in Moscow remain incomprehensible. There are two mysteries: the mystery of the confessions, which are equally mysterious whether we accept them as true or not, and the even greater mystery why such trials should now be publicly staged and such confessions broadcast.

None of the explanations given for the confessions seem even plausible. It is unconvincing to ascribe them to the process of cross-examination in which the confessions or anticipated confessions of one conspirator are used to extort confessions from another. Even supposing that, as a result of this process, all the accused men found it impossible to hide their guilt, how astonishing that no one of them should have followed the example of Dimitroff in Berlin and boldly stood up for himself and defended the conspiracy on the ground of patriotism? In the last trial, when the prisoners grovelled in the dirt and declared themselves miserable sinners, we were told that this strange behaviour was the product of Russian masochistic psychology. We were referred to passages in Dostoevsky and Turgenev for similar examples of self-abasement. On this occasion, however, the prisoners do not grovel nor do they boast. Most of them confess almost with a smile. Radek even goes so far as to joke about his coming execution. Such an attitude in the witness box is equally unexplained by allegations of past torture or threats of future torture. There is no sign of anything of the sort. The prisoners are in good health; they speak freely in court and, with the world listening, declare that no pressure has been brought to bear upon them. Confessions, extorted by torture, would certainly be repudiated in open court by one or other of the prisoners; threats to the families of the accused or of torture at a later stage, which might cow the weaker among them, would certainly not succeed in every case where the accused are as experienced and tough a set of men as these. It is no wonder in these circumstances that some quite intelligent people fall back on almost fantastic speculations. Some have suggested that Kameneff and those who were condemned with him are now living *incognito* and in comfort at a Russian watering place and that the present prisoners anticipate a like fate if they make the right confessions. In this case their trial is merely the Russian equivalent of applying for the Chiltern Hundreds. Others talk of a drug which is supposed so to reduce the resistance power of the victim that after he has been hypnotised under its influence he remains convinced of what he has been told even after the immediate effects of the drug have worn off. We want far more evidence than we at present possess of any drug with such terrible potentialities. The mystery of the confessions is still unsolved.

The second, and politically more important, mystery is why Stalin should have permitted a trial so damaging to the interests of his country. What can be the motive for announcing to Japan and

Germany that Russian factories have been honeycombed with saboteurs, that they may in time of war be put out of action at a minute's notice? Are such declarations calculated to bring Russia support from the Western democracies? The effect inside Russia must surely be equally damaging. We can imagine nothing more likely to undermine confidence inside the USSR than publicly to proclaim that the chief propagandist, whose articles have hounded other men to their death and whose daily declarations have been accepted as the inspired utterances of the Soviet Government, has all the time been a traitor plotting its destruction. Who will now believe in the utterances of Radek's successor? One of the most certain and terrible results of such trials is that it undermines all trust. In whom are the public to have confidence in future? And what must be the effect on public servants waiting in the atmosphere of terror and suspicion engendered by a series of such trials?

We wish that Stalin would explain his reason for putting such a priceless propagandist weapon at the disposal of his enemies in foreign countries. One common assumption is that he is animated by hatred of all the other old associates of Lenin, and in the circumstances comparison is inevitable between events in Russia and the developments of other revolutions where groups have gone on struggling for power long after the revolution was over. But the present trials have more political significance than this. It is clear that we are witnessing the climax of the long struggle between those who supported Stalin's doctrine of 'Socialism in one country' and those who have continued to believe that Trotsky was right in advocating the policy of fomenting world revolution. This struggle reached a new phase at the Seventh Congress where the new policy of the 'united front' and co-operation with democratic forces in foreign countries was decided upon. We may regard this trial as a final effort to eliminate any trace of opposition on this fundamental issue before the new Constitution is put into operation. If this is the root of the matter it still remains curious that Stalin should not realise the damaging effect of such a spectacular method of removing his opponents from positions of influence.

It has always been a central part of Communist theory that the time would come when the bourgeoisie would be so far liquidated and the country so far unified under the happier organisation of Communism that conspiracy, espionage and violence would disappear. Russia has advanced economically beyond the hopes of the most enthusiastic Socialist. It seemed as if the time for relaxation of the political dictatorship had arrived. There were signs of a freer atmosphere as well as an improved standard of life. These trials do not encourage any such optimistic view. To doubt the truth of the confessions is to accuse the

Soviet Government of a disregard for the most elementary principles of justice. But to accept them as they stand is to draw a picture of a regime divided against itself, a regime in which the leaders are at a deadly feud with each other, a regime in which the only way to express discontent is in conspiracy and the only way to suppress conspiracy mass execution. If there is an escape from this dilemma Stalin should tell us what it is.

Kingsley Martin, 10 January 1937

GRAHAM GREENE has been an irregular contributor, but the total bulk of his NS writing is now substantial. Here is one of his earliest and finest pieces, set in the little commuter town of Berkhamsted where he grew up.

Twenty-four Hours in Metroland

The little town always had an air of grit about it, as one came in under the echoing tin railway arch associated with shabby prams and Sunday walks, unwilling returns to Evensong – grit besides the watercress beds and on the panes of the station's private entrance which the local Lord had not used for generations. Now it appeared from the elderly lady's conversation and the furtive appearances in the lamplight that the grit had really worked in. Neither country nor city, a dormitory district – there are things which go on in dormitories. . . .

Sunday evening, and the bells jangling in the town; small groups of youths hovered round the traffic lights, while the Irish servant girls crept out of back doors in the early dark. 'Romans', the elderly lady called them. You couldn't keep them in at night – they would arrive with the milk in a stranger's car from Watford, slipping out in stockinged feet from the villas above the valley. The youths – smarmed and scented hair and bitten cigarettes – greeted them in the dark with careless roughness. There were so many fish in the sea . . . sexual experience had come to them too early and too easily. The London, Midland and Scottish Line waited for everyone.

Up on the hillside the beech trees were in glorious and incredible decay: little green boxes for litter put up by the National Trust had a dainty and doyly effect; and in the inn the radio played continuously. You couldn't escape it: with your soup a dramatised account of the battle of Mons, and with the joint a Methodist church service. Four one-armed men dined together, arranging their seats so that their arms shouldn't clash.

In the morning, mist lay heavy on the Chilterns. Boards marking desirable building lots dripped on short grass where the sheep were washed out. The skeletons of harrows lay unburied on the wet stubble. With visibility shut down to fifty yards you got no sense of a world, of simultaneous existences: each thing was self-contained like an image of private significance, standing for something else – Metroland, loneliness. The door of the Plough Inn chimed when you pushed it, ivory balls clicked and a bystander said, 'They do this at the Crown, Margate' – England's heart beating out in bagatelle towards her eastern extremity; the landlady had a weak heart, and dared not serve food these days in case she went off just like that in the rush. In a small front garden before a red villa a young girl knelt in the damp with an expression abashed and secretive while she sawed through the limbs of a bush, the saw wailing through wet wood, and a woman's angry voice called 'Judy, Judy,' and a dog barked in the poultry farm across the way. A cigarette fumed into ash with no one in sight, only a little shut red door marked Ker Even; 'the leading Cairn Terrier Farm' was noisy on the crest of the down, the dogs like the radio, never ceasing – how does life go on? And at the newsagent's in the market town below the Chiltern ridge there was a shrewd game on sale, very popular locally, called 'Monopoly,' played with dice and counters – 'The object of owning property is to collect rent from opponents stopping there. Rentals are greatly increased by the erection of houses and hotels. ... Players falling on an unoccupied square may raise a loan from the bank, otherwise property will be sold to the highest bidder. ... Players may land in jail.' The soil exacted no service and no love: among the beechwoods a new house was for sale. It had only been lived in a month: the woods and commons were held out by wire. The owners, married last December, were divorced this summer. Neither wanted the house. A handyman swept up the leaves – a losing fight – and lamented the waste. 'Four coats of paint in every room ... I was going to make a pond in that dell – and I was just getting the kitchen garden straight – you can see for yourself.'

Kick these hills and they bleed white. The mist is like an exhalation of the chalk. Beechwoods and gorse and the savage Metro heart behind the Whipsnade wire: elephants turning and turning behind glass on little aesthetic circular platforms like exhibits in a 'modern' shop window, behind them dripping firs as alien as themselves; ostriches suddenly visible at thirty yards, like snakeheads rising out of heaps of dung. A wolf wailing invisibly in the mist, the sun setting at 4.30, the traffic lights out in the High Street and the Irish maids putting the door on the latch. In an hour or two the commuters return to sleep in their Siberian dormitory – an acre of land, a desirable residence for as long as the marriage lasts, no roots, no responsibility for the child on the line. 'The object of owning property.'

Graham Greene, 13 August 1938

MARTIN, as 'Critic', and the NS *campaigned with increasing fury against Nazism. The paper took the horror of Hitler's anti-Semitism seriously earlier than almost anyone else in Britain – but could still in 1938 extract some humour from the situation.*

Reported (on the worst authority) from Germany. A Jew found a starving friend of the same race reading *Der Stürmer*. He expressed his astonishment. His friend replied that he always read *Der Stürmer* to cheer him up. 'Cheer you up!' 'Why, yes, I learn here that the Jews are the most powerful people in the world. The Jews, it seems, control the press and business and finance. They are behind everything, directing all the policy of Europe and planning the overthrow of Hitler. And every Jew over seventy has the virility to violate as many Nordic girls as he wants. Do you wonder that *Der Stürmer* cheers me up?'

Kingsley Martin, 10 December 1938

'SAGITTARIUS' contributed brilliant satirical verse for twenty years. As war grew closer the serious undercurrent, always present, came nearer the surface.

Nerves

I think I'll get a paper,
I think I'd better wait.
I'll hear the news at six o'clock,
That's much more up to date.

It's just like last September,
Absurd how time stands still;

They're bound to make a statement.
I don't suppose they will.

I think I'd better stroll around.
Perhaps it's best to stay.
I think I'll have a whisky neat,
I can't this time of day.

I think I'll have another smoke.
I don't know what to do.
I promised to ring someone up,
I can't remember who.

They say it's been averted.
They say we're on the brink.
I'll wait for the *New Statesman*,
I wonder what they think.

They're shouting. It's a Special.
It's not. It's just street cries.
I think the heat is frightful.
God damn these bloody flies.

I see the nation's keeping cool,
The public calm is fine.
This crisis can't shake England's nerves. ...
It's playing hell with mine.

Sagittarius, 2 September 1939

The outbreak of war found MARTIN's London Diary in sombre mood.

A London Diary

One of the things that one will never forget about these days is the
contrast between the great loveliness of the summer and the pall of
horror accompanying it. On the first night war was declared I looked up
at the captive balloons, silver in the sunset, and thought that it must be
a peace gala that we were celebrating. Even as night fell and the
blackout became complete, London remained peculiarly lovely. The
dark, deserted streets in the moonlight had a mysterious new beauty
and it was not until one sat down behind one's own blackened windows

that one realised that we had entered on a period beginning, as in August, 1914, with a new sense of purpose and comradeship, but with the knowledge that we have in front of us a vista of monotony and tragedy which, whatever our personal views or occupations, will test nerves and endurance to the limit.

Kingsley Martin, 9 September 1939

HENRY NOEL BRAILSFORD is today the most unjustly neglected of all the great British socialist writers. The crisis of spring 1940, with invasion threatening, found him for once writing with rather than against the national current. Even here, though, he asserts the need to retain specifically radical democratic values in emergency – above all those of anti-imperialism.

Survival

Destiny has come to this island with the speed of a bomber diving from the clouds. The British people are fighting for survival. For the first time in our history Mr Churchill made that word the keynote of his address to the Commons as the nation's captain in this struggle. No one was astonished. If there were slow minds that failed to grasp the meaning of our defeat in Norway, they understood what faced us when the German armies swept across the Dutch and Belgian frontiers. Hitler defined his positive purpose in this war in the remarkable proclamation that heralded this invasion: he is fighting for 'the consolidation of Europe' against the two Powers which he accuses of opposing this ideal. He may have forgotten that Henri IV was the first to plan it, and that Napoleon nearly achieved it. There is this to be said for Napoleon: that he recognised the human equality of the peoples whom he forcibly liberated from feudalism. A Nazi 'consolidation' of Europe would mean the subjection of many helot races to one Master-race.

The proclamation of this war-aim warns us of the fate that awaits us, if our defences should collapse. Hitler cannot consolidate Europe under his own sway, unless he can break our will and shatter the military and economic power of the French and ourselves. There can be no compromises or half-measures in such a war. We have to face the possibility of invasion and of a struggle to retain our national existence. Defeat would mean not merely the dissolution of national power; it would mean the utter destruction of our liberties. The restored Holy Roman Empire could not tolerate a free island on its fringes. If we were allowed to retain any measure of nominal independence it would be at the price of assimilating our intellectual and political life to the totalitarian pattern. What is at stake, then, is something incomparably more precious than any imperial power. We are fighting to conserve our values and our traditions, our freedom of thought and our standards of humanity. Ideas are neither immortal nor indestructible. They can live only in the institutions that incarnate them. Freedom must mould the laws as well as the mind of a society, if it is to survive on this earth.

The will of this nation is that our civilisation shall survive. It gave us last week what we ought to have had many months ago, a truly national government. When the unmistakable crisis of destiny faced us, we all realised that as a fighting leader Mr Churchill is the best man available. Five years ago he grasped the meaning of air-power and gave the warning that Mr Baldwin heeded as little as his disastrous successors. He combated the follies of appeasement and understood the necessity of bringing Russia into our coalition. To his capacity for leadership falls the task of improvising amid the struggle the means of defence that his foresight would have given us betimes. We are quit, under him, of the complacency that kept our efforts at half-pressure, for we have faced the fact that the supreme ordeal is actually upon us. We must hold the enemy this summer in the field, or go under.

It is a grim undertaking. After five days of confused and unequal struggle, the Dutch army has laid down its arms. In the air-ports and harbours of the Netherlands German planes and submarines have now their bases. We await with anxious hope the issue of the battle that now rages over the whole width of Belgium. The forces of three nations face the enemy here, but it is clear that he is flinging against them an incredible mass of men and machines. He has set in motion at high speed yet another army on his left, which has crossed the difficult country of the Ardennes to hurl itself on the French lines at Sedan. We do not assume that we can measure even yet the whole scope of the German effort to subjugate Europe in a single campaign. The probability is that Hitler will exploit his superiority in man-power and machinery to attack at many points at once. It is possible that yet another thrust may be attempted across Switzerland in conjunction with an Italian attack, if and when Mussolini decides to act. That brilliant second, clad in shining blackmail, blusters on the verge of a decision. The probability is that we shall be at grips with the Italians from Gibraltar to the Libyan desert before the month is out. Can we, in that event, rely on the neutrality of Spain, exhausted though she be by a ruinous civil war? Sooner or later, if fortune frowns on us, she too may place her strategical key positions at the disposal of the Axis. Finally, it is unlikely, if Italy should attack Jugoslavia, that Rumania can escape partition between Germany and Russia. It has long been our view that nothing could prevent Hitler and Stalin from settling the neglected problems of Eastern Europe by conquest or absorption. Napoleon had the same idea – forcibly to occupy Europe under one rule. He too came near success. He too sought to include this island in his conquest. The results of French domination would have been infinitely less terrible for the human race than Hitler's success would be. Our ancestors faced their peril and survived.

We know our peril now, but we also know our strength. Our fleet meets from the air a new danger, which as yet we cannot certainly measure. We are no longer an island; therefore we can no longer rely on muddling through. The fleet remains, however, a highly competent defence with a powerful air arm working with it. Man for man, gun for gun and staff for staff, we believe that the French land army is still the first in Europe. The air-forces of the Allies are, we know, heavily outnumbered, but there is some reason to accept the view that our fighter planes and pilots are superior to Germany's. On two factors our fate now depends – in France on the strength of the Maginot Line, in England on our ability this summer to make good our numerical inferiority in the air. That problem of industrial organisation has been immensely eased by Labour's entry into the Government. The choice of Mr Bevin and Mr Herbert Morrison to organise man-power and supply should transform the whole attitude of the workers. They serve now under their own leaders, and they too understand that on the work of our engineers, under their own shop-stewards, depends the survival of a working-class free to combine and act for itself. The more sharply we realise that we have got till August or September and no longer to make good our numerical deficiency in the air, the more confidently may we look forward to our future as free men.

Inevitably our attention is now riveted on the visible battle in the air, on the seas, and in the workshops. But our fortunes can still be influenced, even at this late hour, by political sagacity. Under Mr Churchill our chances of winning the maximum of American support are appreciably better. Americans will not measure their help solely by our peril: our imperial record also influences them. We have before us, as we write, some of them painfully frank, editorial comments on our failure to reconcile India. It is a gain that we now have at the India Office a man of Mr Amery's intelligence and courage. He has a simple choice before him. Will he try to coerce the Indian nation, or will he frankly help it to build its own future under its own leaders? The choice must be made in a few days, and over the heads of duller men he must dare to make it.

The most delicate of all our problems of policy is centred in Moscow. About Russia's attitude we dare not write with any degree of assurance. It is arguable that the attitude of the Communist Parties in the Allied countries and in Germany reflects that of the Kremlin. More clearly than in the earlier phases of the war, they are now adopting, though with some verbal reservations, a position that is in effect pro-Nazi. But Kremlin and Comintern do not always time their manoeuvres in step. There is much else to suggest that Stalin's attitude to his quasi-ally is one of extreme suspicious and detachment. Doubtless he was glad to see the Western 'imperialists' weakened. But can he desire a total victory for Germany? The time may have come when he would be willing to check Hitler's success. Mr Churchill may well be able to do in Moscow what Mr Chamberlain neither could nor would have accomplished. But the approach must be made frankly, in the grand manner, and with some regard for the *amour propre* of a Great Power.

For the main purpose unity is now obligatory. Our criticisms of others and of ourselves; our fundamental differences of aim and philosophy – these remain. But for the moment they are irrelevant; united, we have taken our resolution to survive. At stake is all we value in civilisation to-day and all we hope for to-morrow.

Henry Noel Brailsford, 18 May 1940

'SAGITTARIUS', like most journalists, soon became impatient with the reticence of official war news.

No Confirmation

Dense mist on the Channel is lying,
    The jungle is murkier still,
In the desert, where dust-storms are flying,
    Visibility's said to be nil.
Fog over Whitehall's terrific,
    We cannot quite see where we are,
The Japanese claim the Pacific.
    There is no confirmation so far.

We have moved to a stronger position,
    We have shortened our line for a stand,

We are ready to force a decision
    With the whole situation in hand.
Strategic retreat is completed,
    Fierce counter-attacks will begin;
The enemy's claims are repeated.
    Confirmation has not yet come in.

We are mounting a counter-offensive,
    We are holding the enemy back.
He finds it extremely expensive
    When he ventures a full-scale attack.
His lines of supply have been pounded,
    His time-table clearly upset,
He states that our force is surrounded.
    There is no confirmation as yet.

The enemy claims infiltration,
    The action as yet is obscure,
Until we receive confirmation
    Announcements would be premature,
Discount every Axis assertion,
    For ignorance always is bliss;
The Home Front relies on our version.

There is no confirmation of this!

Sagittarius, 14 March 1942

MASS OBSERVATION – the volunteer fact- and opinion-gathering unit founded by Tom Harrisson – pioneered opinion polling and a great deal more. Happily, much of the organisation's work is now being republished. Here, in 1943, its observers look at soldiers' hopes and fears for the peace.

His Private War-aim

In the army, some of the main motives which keep the civilian working and aspiring don't apply at all. There is no security of life, little financial motive. Few soldiers have joined the army as a deliberate calling. Most want to get out as soon as they reasonably, decently can. The main motive for efficiency and fulfilment is to fight the war and get it over. These factors lead to a perpetual underlying impatience, and the process of getting browned off, as evidenced in diaries and personal subjective statements from soldiers, is set going by incidents which, in civilian life, would seem quite small symptoms of a familiar system.

Anything apparently irrelevant to the job in hand annoys the soldier quite disproportionately to the size of the incident. Conscripted into a job he may not like, he only does eagerly those things which he feels necessary to make him efficient. Anything else may become an insult, a further infringement of rights which he has given up in becoming a conscript at all. Elaborate drills, blancoing and polishing, fatigues which appear to be simply a way of filling in time, petty systems of punishment for minor offences or errors, anything else superficially irrelevant to war, set going that mixture of cynicism and subterranean anger which constitutes browned-offness. Privileged action by his superiors, acceptable in civilian life because it is contestable and variable, sometimes puts the soldier into a state of impotent rage which may colour his whole outlook for days or months. There are few conflicting claims on the soldier's attention; he cannot reconcile himself to inequalities by building up his security, home comforts or spending power. One of the results of this narrowed focus is a process of disillusion with established institutions considerably deeper than among civilians. The pattern of the unit's hierarchy is generalised on to army leadership as a whole and it is only a short step for this generalisation to be extended to political leadership.

As the war goes on, and as the end begins to seem in sight, the traditional, largely inevitable impatience of the soldier begins to have more important effects on his personal outlook. An investigation among many specimen units in the army, and among civilians, showed that the army had much less faith in the powers of any existing political party to get things 'right' after the war, than did the civilian population. Only the Communist Party held hopes for soldiers as often as for civilians, and it was only mentioned by a very small minority of each.

Parallel with political disillusion run fears about the insecurity of the post-war world. Members of the forces tend to be rather more optimistic than civilians about a quick end to the war. As a young private put it, at New Year 1943:

> I personally feel that if 1943 does not see the end of this war in sight and a return to 'normal' life I shall lose faith in ever really doing any good for myself. ... For me 1943 is something to look forward to; one has to, or lose faith in things.

Among the home-based, army optimism about the duration is mitigated by background anxiety about being abroad for some time after peace. At the same time the post-war future, with all the insecurities it holds, looms nearer. There are conflicting motifs running through service ideas about the post-war world. The comforts of civvy street assume an exaggerated value; home and civilian life seem like some dream oasis of peace and rest, holding for many virtues which they probably never possessed in peace-time. In the mental background is the hope, though not necessarily the belief, that the end of the war will mean a 'return' to this idealised personal peace.

Cross-cutting the dream of security and personal freedom are realistic doubts about the opportunities which the post-war world will afford. As the war goes on, fear grows, especially among the young, that they will have been out of civvy street too long to pick up where they left off. As one young private put it:

> There's the fear of the war lasting so long that the years of my youth will be past when it's over. Twenty-five now, I might be thirty when it's over, and at thirty one is getting too old for a good many activities, I suppose.

Cynicism about after-the-war is consistently stronger among members of the forces than among civilians. Here are three typical soldier statements:

> Fear that post-war upheavals may again upset my desires of settling down comfortably at home when the war is over. (Lance-Corporal.)
>
> Fear that the post-war world will be unpleasant, contrary to my ideals and temperament, and hostile to liberty and individuality. This is about as strong as an abstract fear of this sort can be, and amounts almost to a certainty. (Private.)
>
> A fear about things in general after the war – that these changes that one hopes for may not come about, that things might be worse instead of better. (Gunner.)

A year ago the soldier's attitude towards the post-war world was considerably more impersonal than this. The impersonal is giving way to the personal. 'This nagging uncertainty is the most disturbing of all,' says an infantry OCTU candidate of his post-war prospects. And a private of twenty-five who was studying architecture before the war:

> I am afraid that the old members will be in reserved jobs and will have all the best positions after the war, and thus nullify the new thought which was making itself patent in architecture in this country in the 'thirties.

The solution to many of these very intelligible worries lies in the method of demobilisation after the war. It is clear from reports that the great majority want to get back to civvy street as quickly as possible after the last all-clear. Despite a realisation that immediate demobilisation would lead to chaos and the very unemployment problem which is one of the main post-war fears at present, the basic feeling is that, whatever may happen to anyone else, 'I personally intend to get back as soon as I conceivably can.' Typical of the more thoughtful private:

> Like 99 per cent of all the forces I am only awaiting the armistice in order to claim an immediate discharge. However, I realise this is foolish.

Many men in the forces feel that, unless intended measures are *pre-announced*, unless efficient propaganda is forthcoming well *before* the armistice, the desire to get out will override considerations of common sense and personal security. Some anticipate serious discontent, if demobilisation is delayed without due preparation of the soldiers' minds for a longish period in uniform after the war is over.

Apart from a greater appreciation of the human tensions involved in the problem, the methods of demobilisation suggested by all Services are very similar. In rough order of frequency these suggested methods are:

> Special corps for training and reconstruction.
> No release except into jobs.
> Army of occupation, police force.
> Priority for men with jobs waiting.
> Priority for key men.
> Priority on compassionate grounds.
> Better conditions for men kept in the services.
> Women to return to the home.
> Reorganisation of industry.

Clearly in a field where the desires even of the more thoughtful tend so nearly to override their better judgment, some form of guidance before the event is most desirable. An army dental officer suggests:

> One fact I consider of paramount importance (both for the war and the peace) and that is the public should be let into the government's confidence about what is to happen to them after the war.

A gunner, who thinks that men should be retrained for their civilian jobs before being released:

> This would need terrific propaganda to get it willingly accepted, but some excuse must be found to prevent people being released wholesale and

haphazardly. I can see a lot of trouble and bitterness being caused over this business.

It is widely felt that the problem of retaining men in the forces once the war is finished will be very difficult. Suggested remedies are mainly concerned with giving the men congenial and constructive activities, in education, in reconstruction work, in training for new trades or retraining in their old. Many feel that concessions will be necessary if slow demobilisation is to take place without trouble. As a private suggests:

Obviously this course [gradual demobilisation] is going to be unpopular with the majority of browned-off Servicemen who will only want to get back to their homes (job or no job) as soon as possible. I suggest that can be alleviated by having men stationed as much as possible near their homes, and giving maximum amount of leave – say the week-end off for everybody – and hope by that means to get the men to regard their continuation in the army as a sort of temporary job away from home.

There is relatively little wishful thinking in the services about the post-war world. Soldiers, sailors and airmen are less inclined to over-optimism than civilians. But the serving male has one great illusion overlaying his general pessimism and cynicism – the illusion that his troubles will be over when he gets back into civvy street. This is his private war-aim, his underlying assumption for post-war peace and security. He hopes that he will be among the first to get back there, though he can realise that it may be some time before he is released. Given the chance, in most cases he would go back immediately the armistice was signed, job or no job.

Mass Observation, 17 July 1943

The African nationalist feeling aroused in 1935 matured rapidly during the world war. HENRY SWANZY, an NS correspondent in Nigeria, surveying the colony's infant press, rightly saw in it a new world 'struggling to be born'.

A Colonial Press

In the middle years of the nineteenth century, the Rev. Henry Townshend set up a printing press. It was at Abeokuta, in West Africa,

home of the Egba-Yorubas; this press had been brought piecemeal
from England. In the true British tradition, he had no idea how the
various pieces went together: but by 1859 there was a 'newspaper for
the Egba and the Yorubas,' three thousand of whom, it is said, could
then read. It was a tiny sheet of eight pages, with English and Yoruba
facing each other across the page, and it cost 120 cowries, about one
penny of our money.

Since that day, Nigeria and West Africa have acquired forty odd
newspapers. There are 22 periodicals and 11 dailies in English, six
periodicals in Yoruba, and one in Hausa, the only Government paper.
Newsprint is scarce, matrices worn, distribution (by lorries along the red
earth roads) scarcely easy. But all the papers bear a resemblance to a
European Press except that they are almost entirely the product of
intellectuals. For they cater for an elite of fifty to sixty thousand
subscribers, nearly all gathered on the coast, and they reach perhaps
half a million more.

The largest and most modern of these papers, wishing to appear on
advertisement lists in England, approached a firm of auditors for this
purpose. It found itself rebuffed. Yet this limitation on the children
of the Rev. Townshend has its advantages, which are not always
recognised. There is the advantage that the big companies do not
consider it worth their while to buy up a paper. There is the advantage
(unconnected with limitation) of the scrupulous non-intervention of the
British Government, whose information officers count their victories in
the inches won for war news. Finally, there is a concealed advantage.
As the result of the lack of a close twentieth-century organisation
generally, even in areas which have known settled capitalist conditions
for well over a century, ideas in West Africa count for more than
interests. Or rather, interests are conveyed by means of ideas which still
have their power of primitive excitement.

This independence also has disadvantages. Though English is freely
accepted as the language of the Press, it is not native to the people, and
they do not always find clear expression easy. Because elbow-grease is a
symbol for hard work, 'to grease one's elbow' is a common expression.
A recent headline read: 'Italy realises war at own doormouth.' A goalie,
after a sequence of passionate sporting prose, saves the ball 'in a
genuflecting position.' For the people have the intoxication of words
possessed by our own Elizabethans. Sometimes there is the same
exuberance – a headline reads, 'Minister of religion overfeeds and
swoons at function.' A Trade Union banner declares: 'The toga of our
inferiority must be laid aside for ever.' A memorial typical of those
which appear in all West African papers begins: 'Who could know that
those bridal festivities were but the prelude to your mournful

obsequies?' But from one fault they are nearly always free: they do not contain the heartlessness of many more technically competent European writers.

But all these minor slips and semi-literate verbosities will pass and the essential humanity that breathes from these tiny papers perhaps remain. Editors and writers, even the reporter from the provinces, describing the narrow ceremonies of West African bourgeois life, which so resemble the style of late Victorian days, are all pioneers; they feel that they are engaged upon a work of renascence, the renascence of Mother Africa. 'I have the happiness to be an African,' a correspondent writes of a squabble between Gold Coasters and the Yoruba traders from Nigeria. Theirs is a literary culture, with language from another culture superimposed on primeval historical experience: but, like African sculpture and dancing, it is alive.

But still, a critic objects, these papers represents the minority of Africans who have passed through Yaba, Achimota, or Fourah Bay, separated in their mental outlook from the rest of their people. It is true, and not true; for they remain African. The situation of the African intelligentsia stems from the same root cause as the situation of Congress India; the literary education. And because, in Africa, their background goes back for many centuries, the intelligentsia are more limited by their environment: even though in the end they may not be so ultimately bound. In May the papers report that a fine of £3 was imposed on a man for throwing the corpse of a smallpox victim into a running stream. In June a Baptist sexton sacrifices a dog on the chapel altar; even though he did fall down dead thereafter. Last spring, a reporter went to a provincial court: 'Ikot Ekbene: Feelings ran high in the police court recently when two witch hunters were arraigned before the magistrate for assaulting their cousin (mistaking him for an owl).' But this barbarism is perhaps less ineradicable than Hinduism in its civilisation.

The papers close their ranks in an effort to cope with the bewildering culture clash which their country is now experiencing. They are as alive to its implications as their most jaundiced critic. A Russian squadron is reported to have been given the name of Pushkin: Pushkin was a negro. A brilliant young doctor's return is publicised: 'West Africa now has seven British doctorates.' A book on draughtsmanship by a young art student in London is praised for its evidence of creativeness. And yet, at the same time, they criticise themselves, even bitterly. Their outlook runs the gamut of the last hundred years. The political organisation, in the coastal towns, is the nebulous Youth Movement, which runs from the Leftist policy in Sierra Leone, through an eclectic Christianity on the Gold Coast, to the straightforward bourgeois nationalism of

Nigeria. They report the Legislative Council, and from time to time
belabour the huge Aunt Sally, the Colonial Government: but equally
they report the endless land disputes and succession struggles of the
'stools,' the countless pocket handkerchief States of the older settled
areas; they report the prostitution and the rack-renting in the towns:
their own weaknesses are daily flayed.

And some at least of these papers attempt to stamp a pattern on
their land. Nnamdi Azikiwe, an Ibo from Onitsha on the Loer Niger,
is a representative leader of this movement, by reason of the violence of
the reactions in his favour or against him. The pattern this 'respectable
son of Africa' attempts to stamp comes from the twentieth century;
partly from America where he was educated, before he founded the
first of the four papers he now controls, the *West African Pilot*, in
1934. In the last nine months, under the pen-name of Zik, he has
written a 'constitutional blueprint' for Nigeria, and a series on post-war
Nigerian economics. He has ransacked the liberal writers of the world,
and treats his country as a modern State. 'Show the light and the people
will find the way,' is his paper's motto: the method is sensational
journalism of the most approved pattern. But he is a man with a head
on his shoulders; he gives his public, mostly the young men, what they
want; and for that, because it is 'lowering,' he is bitterly opposed by
more traditional forces. What they perhaps do not realise is that he is a
born journalist and politician, whose chief aim is clearly shown by his
statement at the end of the 'blueprint': 'Here is a plan, definite and
complete. They asked us what we wanted. Here it is. History will record
that we have made it.' He counts on the immediate effect.

It is Azikiwe's actions that are more instructive to follow perhaps
than his ideas, interesting and encyclopædic though they may be. His
interests do not end with papers, for he controls a sports club, which
goes on goodwill tours through Southern Nigeria: for football, and
perhaps cricket also, are the 'path of national self-consciousness.' His
staff comes from all over southern West Africa: Yoruba, Ibo, Ijaw,
Fanti and Sierra Leonean. Most interesting of all, perhaps, his reporters
attempt to go into areas where self-conscious Ibo and Yoruba of their
type are, to say the least, strangers: through the belt of the tropical
jungle and the mangrove swamps of the river, out into the wide uplands
of Northern Nigeria, where the Moslem culture is still predominant,
under conquering peoples whose relation to the southerners has some,
if not all, of the aspects of the relations of Moslems to Hindus. But this
is a significant step: for, as a young northern *mallam* recently wrote in
the *Pilot*, the north has the land but the south has the money. Zik has
opened subsidiaries on the east coast at Port Harcourt; at Onitsha, his
native place in Iboland; and at Warri for the Benin provinces. But he

wishes to open at Ibadan, the great Yoruba 'meeting place in the fields,' with its population of 380,000; at Jos, the northern centre of the tin-mining on the 'pagan' plateau; and at Kano finally, the historic northern market city and centre of the Hausa. Shortage of newsprint has so far stopped him.

So the fantastic world, alive and kicking in so many directions at once, exists in West Africa to-day: a world more complex perhaps than anything to be found elsewhere except in India: a world surely unforeseen by the Rev. Townshend ninety years ago. The newspapers are the signposts of that world. For me, who have never visited it, Nigeria stands revealed in one March number of the *Pilot*, indeed, in one front page. First, a photograph of the white-robed Sultan of Sokoto, swathed to the eyes like a Tuareg of the desert, whose country marches with his own; below that, an account of the death by ordeal trial of eleven people who had eaten the poisonous esere bean, pounded by a man whose wife had miscarried; and finally, below again, the case of Bessie Amadi, a young Etche girl, found at midnight in the European quarter at Port Harcourt – in pyjamas, said the astonished constable. But she got off, owing to a 'mixture of humour, smartness, and facial expression.'

And this world it is necessary for us to understand. Because by doing so we not only understand the African, from the only real and independent sounding board in the continent to-day. And we not only understand the anguish of two worlds, one dying and one struggling to be born; in part, at least, we also understand ourselves.

Henry Swanzy, 18 September 1943

The wartime British Empire saw also one of the greatest, most thoroughly forgotten tragedies of the twentieth century; the Bengal famine of 1943. British press reporting of the disaster (for which British administrators were substantially to blame) was miserably scant: mass starvation under British rule was bad for wartime morale. The NS was a notable exception, as with this harrowing account from an ANONYMOUS soldier.

Famine

'There's a famine down there,' they told me. Probably people dying and so forth.

I knew that, of course – had read about it in the paper – but on the eve of my move I pigeonholed and forgot the information; the famine would, no doubt, be noticeable if it were real. Anyway, poverty is so ever present in India that forgetting is a protective armour. I left with no more than that half-warning in my head.

On the journey I had too much to do to think of the people or the country. This was a Company move, and I was responsible for 150 Indian troops from the hills, in land as foreign to them as it was to me. They could not speak this language; they had never seen quite this sort of landscape before. Yet, quickly they were bored with it all – the long travelling hours, the awkward changes, the carrying of kit and stores, the rain and the general discomfort.

After a couple of days of slow journeying, we changed trains at a fair-sized junction. Fires were started and food prepared on the platform. I had to make some arrangements, and when I returned the men were all eating. This was the first time I saw the beggars. They were not like other Indian beggars, calling for an anna from a passing train. These people did not ask for money. They wanted food, and they stood there watching the men of their own nation cooking and eating. I counted about 30 of these beggars as they clustered on the railway line between the two platforms; they were of all ages and in one condition; the majority were women; some were blind and all were ill. One old man, tall, and a fine head and straggly beard was being led by a woman; his sightless eyes looked up high over the heads of those squatting on the platform. Some of the beggars were silent and a very few were still; most were watching closely, for occasionally, as a man finished his food, he would walk to the edge and sweep the scraps on to the line. The watchers, who had drawn closer, rushed forward then and scraped in the dirt for the few grains of rice, until they were driven back by a couple of railwaymen. The blind old man, at these times, hearing the movement and the shouts, made a low noise rather like a whine, perhaps an echo of days when he had been a prosperous beggar. For the more romantic of my readers I say with reluctance that this old man had no more dignity than the others. His head was lifted and twisted on a scraggy neck; he was very dirty and his rags revealed no suspicion of former beauty. He was hungry. Like the other beggars he had a small cloth and a tin which he held out for scraps. The men of my Company were rather embarrassed and when I arrived were giving the remains of their food in a hurried way, as though the giving were distasteful. I watched this scene for a short while and then, as more men finished their food and the crowd began to fight among themselves, I stopped this indiscriminate scattering of food and had the scraps placed in a box to be distributed later. But I had forgotten one member of the

Company – the goat. He had been given his ration separately on a small plate. But that day, he was fussy. He had a few mouthfuls, nibbled the rest, turned away, thought again and managed a little more. Then with a rather distant look, deploring the standard of wartime rations, he stalked away. Within ten seconds, a small crowd of men and women were fighting over the remnants of his meal.

We left that place with few regrets and soon after approached our destination. All along the line we met these train beggars – railway stations seem to be the hope of those who can walk from their village. The children were the most pitiful; naked boys and girls with no flesh or large pot-bellies lined the train. Yet they were the least worried, the least intense about their begging. Whether it is the ignorance or the optimism of youth I cannot tell, but it was easy to raise a smile. What they most wanted was the army 'bishcoot.'

Arriving at our destination, we settled in, the Company being split up. My main job was travelling from one platoon to another, making sure they understood their new duties and fixing quarters and ration arrangements.

One day I went into a stationmaster's office to borrow his timetable. I sat facing him, my back to the door, when I heard someone come in and stand beside me. I looked up. He was a tall Indian, not very well dressed, rather the ordinary type of matriculate in the middle twenties that abounds in India. But he spoke excellent English. He stood still and straight and over my shoulder spoke to the stationmaster. 'Excuse me' – courteously, not apologetically – 'there is a man on the platform out there in a dying condition. I thought he was dead, but there is some movement. Is there anything you can do? I will gladly pay the cost.'

The stationmaster did not appear to have heard, and continued to make entries in a large book spread out in front of him. The other waited. After about a minute the stationmaster finished writing, blotted the last words and reached for a small scrap of paper, on which he scribbled a sentence. Without turning his head he shouted:

'Oh, Chowkidar!' – An old man appeared.

'Take this,' the stationmaster said in his language, 'and give it to the policeman on duty.'

Then he turned to the stranger.

'The police will take care of him,' he said

The other turned to go and then stopped.

'Will he be taken to the hospital?' he asked. The stationmaster grew angry.

'The police know what to do,' he said shortly. The tall Indian, still obviously dubious, left the room.

'Do you get many of them?' I asked the stationmaster.

'Two or three a day,' he answered in the same tone, 'We can do nothing.'

About ten minutes later I left and had lunch in the station refreshment room – a plate heaped high with eggs, fish, bread, bacon and beans, costing Rs. 1.8. An hour later, I strolled on to the platform to look for my train.

The dead man was still there. He was lying half in a pool of water, near the edge of the platform on his back, his face uncovered, except for the flies. He was not old, in rags, the skin stretched over his bones. What movement his discoverer had seen had most certainly ceased. I spoke to a naked little boy on the platform – which was full, though no one was paying any attention to the body.

'Is he dead?' I asked.

The child's face lit up and he smiled.

'Oh, yes,' he said, 'he's dead.'

Two days later I came through the same station and stopped again to change trains. About five yards from where the dead man had lain was another body – this time the face was covered. I went to see the stationmaster.

'There's another dead man there,' I told him.

'I know,' he answered as before, 'the sweepers will take it away.' I suppose I looked what I felt, for suddenly his reserve went and he talked rapidly, his English suffering a little.

'What can we do?' he said. 'We can do nothing. Every day they come here and die. Two and three of them. For us there is nothing to do. They get no food in the village that used to support them. Mostly they are people with no land and no family. They suffer the first. The other day, let me tell you something. I was there sitting in my office when an old man and a little girl came right inside, the little girl begging for food. I was about to turn them out, when the old man dropped dead at my feet. Right at my feet. Just dropped dead. What could I do? I gave the little girl some money for food. Before night she was dead also.'

'And I will tell you something,' he added, 'that little girl was the same age as my little girl. That's what I thought. She's the same age as my little girl.'

2 October 1943

*PETER ELSTOB, veteran of the International Brigades and later a fine
military historian, sent this remarkable anonymous vignette from newly
liberated France in 1944.*

Amateur Liberators

My tank broke down in a small village in the Bocage country, and
because of the fluid nature of the fighting we were the only Allied
soldiers there for three days. We had a unique opportunity of seeing a
French village's first reactions to Liberation without the restraint or
artificiality evoked by occupying officialdom.

About nine o'clock there was a bustle of activity as the people began
returning. First they hurried to their shops, surveyed the broken
windows with amusement – there was nothing worse – then hurried to
visit their neighbours. Experiences were exchanged. Everyone, it
seemed, had had a narrow escape or seen something amusing. ... They
came to inspect our tank. Each of them meticulously shook hands with
every one of us before unloosing a torrent of questions about the
campaign which, of course, I was quite unable to answer. I explained
that I was only a corporal and my superiors had not thought it
necessary to consult me on the campaign. But they were quite
convinced that I knew much more and complimented me on my
caution.

Suddenly, someone asked about the Mayor. Immediately a group of
men formed to go and get him. The chemist's wife explained to me:
When the Germans first occupied the village they asked the Mayor to
carry on as before. He agreed to do so as long as his conscience
permitted it. This to the Germans was so much persiflage, and they
didn't take him too seriously. He was 68 when they came, and all went
well for two years, when they asked him to sign a decree of which he
disapproved. He refused and the Germans brought pressure to bear,
but he was quite unshakeable. So they put him in prison where he had
been for two years. He was now to be restored to his position.

They returned with him quite soon. (He looked amazingly well, and
one would never have guessed that he was 72.) He took up his
headquarters in the hotel, and the two gendarmes reported to him
ceremoniously. We had drinks all round.

During lunch two lorry-loads of German prisoners were brought in
and parked for a little while in the market place. A shout went up; the
people poured from their houses running towards the lorries. For a
moment I thought they were going to attack the prisoners, but they

were content to dance around them, shouting abuse and making those insulting signs which they do so well. Someone found a carefully preserved cartoon ridiculing Hitler, and this was quickly passed up to the lorry. A young boy picked it up, looked at it and smiled, then handed it to another prisoner. A third who had been arrogantly ignoring the crowd snatched the cartoon away and dropped it disdainfully to the ground. Then he very deliberately smashed the back of his hand across the face of the one who had smiled.

We were evidently considered to be the representative authorities of the Allies, for we were approached by a succession of visitors. The first were an elderly couple who wanted permission to travel back to visit their son. We sent them back to the nearest military police post. Then came a lady with a quite ravishingly beautiful daughter who completely upset my crew with her friendly smiles. The lady wanted to know if we had any news of her husband, a doctor, who had decided to remain behind in Caen during the bombardment, knowing how badly he would be needed.

Then with great ceremony our friend the gendarme brought to us the leader of the local resistance movement and five others. The leader was a large-boned youth of about 20 with a German bayonet and a brace of revolvers stuck in his belt and the tricolour brassard proudly on his arm. He told me that he had strangled a German soldier for the bayonet. He pulled out a revolver and waved it wildly, saying that he was now going to drag out some *collaborateurs*, some traitors, into the market place.

His second in command, a long, lanky, even younger, youth, was intoxicated with excitement. He was breathing heavily, his eyes rolled behind thick spectacles, and his right nostril twitched most unpleasantly. They both looked cruel brutes, but the underground movement grows in hatred and produces cruelty. They ran down the road brandishing their weapons.

They returned in less than ten minutes pushing three terrified women before them. One was about 65, grey-white hair and the ubiquitous shapeless black dress of the over-middle-age countrywoman; one was about 37 in a smart, colourful dress; and the other a girl of 16 – very *chic*. They were grandmother, mother and daughter. The grandmother fell just in front of us and was jerked roughly to her feet and pushed on. She began limping, and my driver moved forward to her rescue.

My orders had been most explicit. Do not interfere with the French in any way. I held my driver back, explaining that we did not understand what was involved and must not interfere. He was unconvinced. 'Well,' he growled, 'I'd like to see them try that in Liverpool.'

The three women were now the centre of a crowd, and the youth with the twitching nostril climbed on a chair and made a speech. These women, he said, everyone knew as 'Boche lovers.' They were the worst kind of *collaborateurs*; they were traitors to France. It had been decided to mark them so that all Frenchmen everywhere would know them for what they were. He personally would take great delight in cutting their hair off. Scissors were produced, and the youngest was pushed into the chair and he began to cut her long hair close to the scalp.

The bystanders had divided themselves into two groups. The crowd round the women were wild with approval, laughing and clapping as the locks of hair fell to the ground. The other group stood on the far side of the square watching with enthralled disapproval like a censor at a *risqué* play.

The girl was pale and frightened but bore it well. She held her head high and gave the crowd little satisfaction. Only the grandmother could not restrain her tears.

A boy of about fourteen was enjoying this immensely. He caught my eye. 'Good? good?' he asked in English. 'Non,' I replied, '*not* good – *c'est brutal et ce n'est pas juste.*'

It was thought then that I did not understand why this was being done. Several of both crowds took turns explaining the position to me. The grandmother owned a small *pension* at which German officers stayed, and by paying black market prices were fed on the best of the local produce which, because of control, was in short supply to the civilian population. The officers slept with the mother and daughter, paying the mother. About the daughter opinion was divided. Some maintained that the only difference between her and her mother was that she was higher priced. The more charitable said that with her it was purely a matter of '*le cœur.*' But all were agreed that she had been the mistress of a German officer since before she was fourteen.

Out of these explanations the real reason for the hatred of these women emerged. It was not that they had been friendly with the Boche – that was understood if not condoned – but that they had made a lot of money out of their friendship. The price of the mother's favours were variously estimated at 500 to 1,000 francs, and that made these thrifty housewives very angry – that and the fact that because of these women German officers had been well fed while the people were not.

But now many began to criticise the proceedings as hooliganism. If they were guilty of treason they should be tried. Anything else was not the democratic way. One woman reminded the other shrilly that the leader of the resistance was a ne'er-do-well, a waster who had never had a regular job, and during the occupation had done nothing but talk.

By this time the mother and daughter were shorn, their hair cut to a

swastika, and another painted on their foreheads. They were made to
stand on chairs and then paraded around the market square.

Now the grandmother was pushed into the chair, and the self-
appointed barber came forward. I decided that, orders notwithstanding,
I really couldn't allow them to disfigure a woman in her sixties. With
some trepidation I moved into the centre of the circle and as
inoffensively as possible removed the scissors from his hand.

There was a sudden hush, as the crowd expected trouble. The leader
glared at me. Now my French is of the schoolboy variety, but an
explanation seemed necessary.

'Elle est trop vieux,' I said solemnly.

But yes of course she was old, but the sins of the children are the
fault of the parents, and it was his duty to punish her was what I think
he said.

'Non,' I disagreed, and decided that a speech of some kind was
unavoidable, hoping that the quick-witted French would gather my
meaning despite the imperfections. I put it down here as I said it
without any attempt to correct.

'Le guerre,' I began impressively, 'est mal, mais c'est pour les
hommes, ce n'est pas pour les femmes. Les hommes le faisent et il faut
qu'ils souffrent. Alors – vous – vous êtes un homme et vous êtes jeune
et fort. Le Boche – il est jeune et fort aussi.' By this time most of my
audience were smiling, though I suspected more at me than with me. I
struggled on. 'Si vous voulez a combattu les Boche – bien. Il y a
beaucoup des Boches à cinq kilometres au sud – allez là!'

There was a roar of laughter at this in which the leader joined. Then
he clapped me on the shoulder, and we all returned to the hotel for a
drink. Grandmother slipped quietly away.

That night the near-by pocket of Germans mortared the village. Just
before dawn a small boy came running to tell us that there were some
injured in a nearby house. Immediately all the men in the shelter
hurried to the scene. The first mortar had killed four people, among
whom was the young leader of the resistance who had done the hair-
cutting.

This shook the village badly. They were convinced that the Germans
had heard of the hair-cutting episode and had retaliated. I tried my best
to explain the improbability and difficulty of this and to convince them
that it was a coincidence. The men, who, of course, had had military
training, were convinced, but the women remained obdurate.

All that day the mortaring continued. One shell started a fire in a
house on the market square and the village reacted immediately. From
somewhere appeared an ancient hand pump and cistern which was kept
filled by a bucket chain from the fountain in the square. The pump was

manned by men, women and children, while the firemen – and my crew – dashed into the house and staggered out with enormous old pieces of furniture. In the end, as blazing beams were falling, I had to stop my crew, who seemed determined to kill themselves for a hideous chest of drawers.

In the middle of the excitement the two women whose hair had been cut off arrived to join the fire-fighting. They had scarves on their heads, turban fashion, and I thought they looked very smart. There was some awkwardness at their approach; a few people pointedly turned away, a fat shopkeeper said, 'Bonjour, madame,' affably. The majority were undecided about their attitude. A large grizzle-bearded man of about 50 settled the question. He shoved a bucket into Madam's hand with a kindly growl. She moved to the fountain and filled it, passing it to her neighbour. Her daughter took a place in the opposite line, and the chain began again. They had been taken back into the life of the village.

Peter Elstob, 9 September 1944

LEONARD WOOLF's association with both the Nation *and the post-merger* NS *outlasted almost anyone else's. An obituary on Adolf Hitler may seem an eccentric choice from his numerous contributions, but its sentiments seem to me characteristic of the breadth of Woolf's vision and the depth of his passions.*

The Little Man

Reading the obituaries of Adolf Hitler which have appeared since his reported death, one sees that about him personally there is nothing to be said except that he was the modern Little Man, inflated into a world force and then apotheosised. There is some quality of greatness which can be detected in all the 'great men' of action who hitherto had left their mark on history, even though the mark was almost always a curse and the immense evil that they did lived after them and the little, if any, good was interred with their bones. But in the diseased, perverted egotism of the Führer's personality there was not a shred of greatness; there were only exaggerations of littleness, of meanness, vindictiveness, envy, malice, cunning and cruelty. The dreary desert of *Mein Kampf* and of the two volumes of Hitler's speeches reveal a mind remarkable only for its colourless insignificance and its crazy fanaticism; ignorant, stupid and cunning, the author appears to be a kind of depersonalised caricature of all the most despicable qualities of the Little Man.

How did this sub-human, stunted product of the European slum obtain his enormous power in Germany and Europe and become an object of worship in his own country and of admiration and adulation elsewhere? That is one of the most important and puzzling questions which the end of the war and of Hitler raises, for, unless we can answer it correctly, we cannot know what is at the root of the breakdown in our civilisation. To pretend that the answer is to be found in the obsessions of Vansittartism and a double dose of sin in all Germans is to shirk the issue and to comfort oneself with the illusion that, thank God, we are not as other sinners are. The inter-war years were years when dictators sprouted all over Europe, and they were all Little Men, caricatures of human silliness and viciousness. There was the tawdry braggart Mussolini, flattered and courted by British Tory Ministers; there were a bunch of Balkan princelets or kinglets; there was the Greek Metaxas; and the rat-like Caudillo is still with us. They have all been worshipped and hated in their own countries and their power bolstered up by their admirers in the old democracies. Even in England we had the sinister spectacle of the posturing Mosley and his Black-shirt toughs finding followers among 'respectable' people. The Germans are more thorough and carry the logic of stupidity and savagery farther than other European peoples, but the seeds of Hitlerism and its abominations were in the soil of every European nation, and in many besides Germany they flowered and set their poisonous fruit. The flower is the dictatorship of the Little Man and the gangster; the fruit is the rule of everything which is most vile in the slum ideals of capitalist society.

It is not Hitler who has made the bloody desert of our age; it is the desert of our age which made Hitler; and if Adolf Hitler had not come to power in Germany, some other stunted Little Man or crude gangster would have seized power and provided the abominations. There are periods in history when power is so unstable, when the forces and beliefs in civilised society become so disorientated that the winds of chance and force may blow almost anyone, who is ruthless and savage enough, into the dictatorship over a people or even over the world.

One side of civilisation consists in the communal control of power. The Roman Republic, when it disintegrated into the Roman Empire, failed to provide this control, and within a hundred years the civilisation of Julius Cæsar and Virgil was disappearing in the anarchy and barbarism of the Caracallas and Galluses. There was the same failure in the capitalist, middle-class civilisation of Europe in the nineteenth century. We failed to establish communal control of economic power, and that produced the anarchy of the capitalist gangster and the class war; we failed – and are failing once more at San Francisco – to

establish communal control of national power, and that produced the
international anarchy which made the world wars of 1914 and 1939
inevitable. It is in these periods of anarchy that the Caracallas and
Hitlers, the gangsters and the Little Men, find their opportunity and are
transformed by the Legions or the Wehrmacht, by the Hugenbergs and
Neville Chamberlains, into war lords and world rulers.

Another side of civilisation consists in civilised beliefs. In the
economic class war of the nineteenth century and in the international
war of 1914 beliefs and standards which form the basis of civilisation
disintegrated. Democracy, liberty and equality, law, justice and
humanity are not just words or 'machinery'; they are the essential
framework of civilised life. From 1914 onwards the statesmen, writers
and ruling classes in the democracies, upon whom depended the
upholding of these standards, and therefore of civilisation, again and
again betrayed them and compromised with barbarism. Religion and
the Churches had long since done the same. In such circumstances it is
not surprising that Hitler, the depersonalised Little Man, could use the
machinery of modern democracy to appeal to the hatred, the envy, all
the littlenesses of all the other thwarted Little Men. The result can be
seen in Dachau and Buchenwald. And on Thursday, May 3rd, 1945
(not 225 AD, but 1945 AD), *The Times* reported that Mr de Valera
called on the German Minister in Dublin to express his condolence of
Hitler's death. Mr de Valera in the previous week must have seen the
photographs of Dachau and Buchenwald. He is a Roman Catholic and
the head of a State which purports to base its whole policy and actions
upon the Christian religion and the Catholic Church. In Mr de Valera's
condolences we can see the degradation of civilised beliefs and
standards which made Hitler and his Nazi regime possible.

Leonard Woolf, 12 May 1945

*RICHARD CROSSMAN, too, wrote constantly for the NS over four
decades – culminating in a rather unhappy stint in the editor's chair. The
acuity of his intelligence and power of observation are here exercised on
the most horrific of imaginable subjects – though Buchenwald, not an
extermination camp, was far from the lowest circle of hell.*

Buchenwald

I was desperately busy on the morning when the interrogator brought K
into my office. To get rid of them, I asked them both to dinner,

conscious that I was almost certainly in for a wasted evening. We had seen too many, 'Concentration-camp prisoners' – pathetic broken creatures – most of them homeless and stateless. When one had heard their story through, there always came the moment when one had to explain that we could not provide them with visas for England or the States: they must return to a Displaced Persons' Centre and wait.

But the moment we met in the Mess it was obvious that K was different. Fair-haired, slim, about 34, with neat, gold-rimmed glasses and a pleasant Austrian accent, he looked as though his borrowed grey flannel suit belonged to him. In spite of eight years in Buchenwald, he had been able to discard, along with the grotesque grey-and-white prisoner's clothes, the prisoner's mentality. K was not only liberated: he was free.

We started dinner at seven and finished at 3.30 a.m. We talked Buchenwald; and what follows is only a fragment of what K had to tell.

As a young Austrian Catholic, K had had a tough time at first. When he got there in 1938 Buchenwald was composed of criminals, who held all the key positions under the SS; some 2,000 German Communists – the cream of the Party; Jews; gypsies and homosexuals. Each group was distinguished by its own badge, green for criminals, red for politicals, yellow for Jews, and pink for homosexuals. As a political, K was grouped with the Communists, who did not see any particular reason why they should help an Austrian 'crypto-Fascist.'

Somehow K managed to come to terms with three or four Communist intellectuals. 'We had one thing in common – a will to survive. Mine was based on religion, theirs on Marxism. All of us realised there was one thing we could not afford – pity. I remember getting up early one morning to have ten minutes alone. I was sleeping in a three-tiered bunk less than three feet wide with four men on each tier. Privacy was a little difficult. I walked outside the barrack and there were rambler roses in full bloom festooned up the wall. It was five o'clock and dawn was breaking. I wasn't looking where I was going and I stumbled against a body swinging from the gutter and bumping the roses. It was a gypsy who had hung himself by his braces. And do you know, there was a cigarette end drooping from the corner of his mouth.

'Yes, one lived by the will to survive. You remember the winter of 1940? It was our worst winter because they allowed us no parcels. We were beaten if we went to bed in anything except our underclothes. One day we stood for 19 hours on end at attention on the Parade Ground because one prisoner was missing. I saw 19 people fall dead. The SS counted and recounted – and the funny thing was that in the end the silly swine found that no one was missing.

'I had done well. As an intellectual I had no special skill which

would give me a soft job in the jeweller's workshop or the book-
binder's or the shop where the model Viking ships were made for the SS
to give as Christmas presents. I was due for the quarries until a
Communist offered me a job in the smithy a hundred yards away. I
knew nothing about it, but there was a fire there, and he told me to
stand beside it and pull bolts out of a rusty bar and put them back
again. I could see the Jews in the quarry through the windows.

'One day I looked up and saw a Jew crawling on hands and knees
towards the smithy. I watched him. It took him over an hour to do the
hundred yards. I knew what was coming. Finally I heard the scratching
on the door. I moved involuntarily to the door and opened it a foot. I
saw him lying there outside. His nails were bleeding. The next thing I
knew, I was lying on the floor by the fire and my comrade was standing
over me saying "You bloody fool." We picked up the body on our way
home from work and carried it back to the camp.

'You ask me how I, as a Catholic, can tell you that. Because we had
to reserve our pity for useful things – for helping the comrades when we
could really help. I learnt some hard lessons. I hated the Communists'
contempt for the upper-class prisoners. But mostly it was justified.
There were high-grade Civil Servants, important business men and
dignitaries there. In the camp we were all on the level, all dressed the
same. Most people's morale is supported by the corset of their social
prestige and rank and status. Strip those corsets off and they sag. They
lose all self-respect and the proletarians look at them with contempt.
You want examples? Well, the SS gave us a brothel in 1942, fourteen
girls from another camp. The secret Camp Committee decided to put it
out of bounds for all politicals, but some of the upper-class people paid
their two marks and soon they were fighting for the girls and stealing in
order to give them presents. It was the same with the 200 Polish boys.
That was the sort of thing which made the proletarians say that the
bourgeoisie has no self-respect when you take off their corsets.

'How were we organised inside the camp? When the SS got rid of
Commandant Koch – the one whose wife liked men with tattoos,
selected them for her pleasures and then had them skinned to use the
tattooed breast-skins as parchment for lampshades – the new
Commandant was easier to deal with. The Communists got themselves
into all the key positions which had been held by the criminals. There
was a Communist Block Leader in charge of each block; Communists
ran the hospital, the canteen, the kitchen, and, most important of all,
the Labour Office which decided on the movement of prisoners from
camp to camp and the composition of the work commandos. The SS
had to leave most of this work to the German inmates, especially when
the camp grew in size and thousands of foreigners were brought in. The

choice was whether the criminals should have this power or the politicals. Of course, anyone who had it had power of life and death, yes, of life and death. As more and more foreigners came in, the Communists naturally tended to select foreign Communists to head up the barracks. They had an iron discipline. They did many hard things but they saved the camp from total extermination.

'It was funny to see the SS power ebbing away. Partly it was just fatty degeneration. The SS men were shirking military service and were making a good thing out of the camp. They got corrupted by power, emotionally exhausted by beating and killing, and they knew the were losing the war. You won't believe it, but on the day of liberation the Communists and the Russian soldiers were walking about in brand-new SS boots and wind-jackets and many of the SS had only shoes. And all the time the SS were torturing or beating us to death.

'I got a job as secretary to the doctor in charge of the typhus experimental station. I worked in closely with the Communists in the key jobs in the hospital. We were in a strong position because the ordinary SS were terrified of coming near either of our buildings for fear of infection. The two doctors were the only staff provided, and we worked on them pretty successfully. In my section a great deal of experimental work was carried out on the inmates. We produced one good anti-typhus serum, but we reserved that for the inmates and sent one out to the SS division at the front consisting mostly of water.

'It was through our positions in the hospital and experimental stations that we were able to save many people from execution. A party of some fifty British for instance were brought in one day, mostly parachutists from the Maquis. Their morale was OK. They formed a national group like the Russians, and got in contact with the German comrades. One day we got wind that they were all to be executed in a week's time. I talked it over with a Communist in the hospital and we agreed that we might be able to save four. So they held a meeting and selected the four. The rest knew they were for it.

The most difficult problem was the British CO because he was so well known in the camp. The only way to save him was to substitute him for a dying man in the hospital and let him take the dying man's papers. Unfortunately, the only foreign language he knew was French, and he was very tall. And there were no Frenchmen in the hospital. By luck a transport of Frenchmen arrived two or three days before the execution date, many of them down with typhus. But there was only one who would do.

'I shall never forget that time. The Communist who had agreed to do the job kept on saying to me, "One little injection will do the trick. If your man is worth saving we can't be squeamish." But the Englishman and I decided we couldn't murder the man and we hung on till the Frenchman really was dying and the injection would be OK. That was the day before the execution day.

'After the execution we both got the feeling that perhaps the man hadn't been dying after all, and that we really had polished him off. So we've got the address of the Frenchman's wife and we're trying to find her to explain what happened and to offer her compensation.

'Anyway, it all went off all right. After a week in hospital, posing as the dead Frenchman, the Englishman was moved out to a camp where he was less well known. We kept contact with him until liberation. You're surprised that one had scruples about little things like waiting for a man to be really dying before injecting him. But it was those little things which were the faith that kept me going. The Communists, of course, didn't mind about them. For them the end justified the means and there's no doubt it was Communist discipline which saved the camp. In the end we had enough arms in the camp to take over before the Americans arrived.

'It's a queer thing, but in Buchenwald we didn't waste much time hating the SS. They beat us, they butchered us, they exploited us; but our hatred (and our love, too) was reserved for the comrades inside. It was the stool-pigeons and the informers and the men who let us down whom we really hated. The SS was just an Act of God. You didn't hate it, you just accepted it as the established order; or, if you were clever, you worked on it and corrupted it to make life bearable.

'I can see that you still wonder why one troubled to survive. Of course, a lot didn't, especially the non-politicals. But a Concentration Camp is just another form of human existence. After the first shock one accepts it, just as one accepts the front line or the slum. And if you decide to survive and adapt yourself, you live just as fully in Buchenwald as anywhere else; though the chances of death are a good deal higher.

'Like normal people, we had our escapes. We were allowed to receive books. Heavens, how I read in the half-hour available! I shall never read so greedily again. We got the world news from the commandos who mixed with the Germans outside, and I think we were the best informed people in Germany. We used to send directives to comrades outside on propaganda. Then there was the cinema. We had it twice a week, mostly non-political stuff. The SS had a sense of humour. They put the screen in the room where the beating block was kept. We used to watch films of people eating and drinking and sitting in arm-chairs, with the beating block just there behind. But on the whole it helped.'

I shall never forget that dinner party. K with his neat gold-rimmed

glasses, his boyish enjoyment of a good story, seemed not only to have
survived Buchenwald, but to have developed out of it a new steely
ironical philosophy. Perhaps, I thought, as I listened to him, the
fraternity and internecine struggle of Buchenwald, the mixture of
idealism and conspiracy, of self-sacrifice and self-assertion, are a
mirocosm of the moral and political struggle which will face all of us in
the post-war world.

R.H.S. Crossman, 23 June 1945

PART THREE

◆

1945–1960

On the sidewalk Sunday morning   Someone's sneaking round the corner,
Lies a body oozing life.   Is the someone Mac The Knife?—*The Threepenny Opera*

Vicky, 1 February 1958

KINGSLEY MARTIN welcomed the 1945 Labour landslide with a mixture of high hopes and stern warnings, approval and doubt, typical both of his intellectual style and of the paper's general attitude to the Labour Party.

The NS had gained enormously in circulation, prestige and – arguably – influence during the world war. Much of that position was retained over the subsequent years. The collapse of British imperialism saw 'friends' of the NS – people like Nehru or Nyerere who seemed to share the paper's outlook and values – attain power in much of the post-colonial world. The Editor and the paper advocated and welcomed each successive decolonisation, though it remained to be seen just how much of the NS's self-assured metropolitan radicalism might prove to have rested on that very imperial power. At the same time a more acerbic vein of cultural criticism emerged, exemplified in the early writing of Paul Johnson, as contributors probed for the decay they perceived beneath the sheen of 'affluence' in Conservative Britain.

Below is Martin's first reaction to the Labour victory.

'Bold, Decisive and Sensible'

This is what Mr Churchill would call a great 'climacteric' of our history – a moment when hidden forces, long-gathering, break through the crust and present an opportunity of achievement. Such a moment occurred in 1832 when the wave of democratic sentiment, born of the revolutionary movement in France, swept away an obstructive oligarchy and gave power to Reformers. They transformed local and central government, abolished monopolies, and tipped the balance of electoral power in favour of the industrial middle-class. The feudal gentry of Britain resisted, but gave way in time, thereby displaying a wisdom greater than their seventeenth century predecessors who had preferred civil war to admitting the supremacy of Parliament. Again in 1906 a Tory era of reaction and imperialism ended with a great Liberal victory. An able Liberal Government, with a great majority behind it, carried a substantial instalment of social reform, upheld the supremacy of the Commons and curbed the power of the Lords. To-day, once again, the popular forces that ended Divine Right three centuries ago, demanded Parliamentary reform in the 19th century and social services in 1906, have elected a government pledged to a historic task of reform.

For the first time the popular vote demands Socialism. For two generations the notion of deliberately organising social well-being instead of leaving it as the accidental upshot of a competitive struggle has been steadily making headway among industrial workers and professional people. Its victory is complete in 1945, because in addition to a solid vote in industrial areas, many agricultural workers, now effectively organised for the first time, have voted Labour in company with disillusioned service men and women and middle-class electors, who have lost during the war their fear of being on the same side as the horny handed sons of toil. Labour is no longer a class party; it is a national party. It is not revolutionary; it is in itself a popular front, and it is pledged to a practical, constructive, and comprehensible policy.

Those who watched the electorate before polling day, saw the rejoicing when the results were declared and since then studied the details of the majorities will agree that this was no flash-in-the-pan 'agin' the Government' vote. It was a very deliberate vote. The Churchill Government has not been particularly unpopular, and there is no lack of gratitude to Mr Churchill in any section of the community. True, Mr Churchill erred, as no man whose judgment matched his capacity could have erred; no leader in history ever so swiftly and unnecessarily wrote himself down from greatness. True, Labour must thank Lord Beaverbrook for failing to expose any of its real weaknesses and boring the electorate incessantly with dreary nonsense and a disingenuous effort to turn a serious election into a one-man plebiscite. But when all the Tory mistakes are added up and every allowance has been made for the swing of the pendulum, it remains quite clear that this is the most deliberate possible vote for Labour and a policy of democratic Socialism. The Liberals who ran candidates in more than three hundred seats were nearly wiped out. They have finally lost those Western, Scottish and Welsh areas where Liberalism could hope to dominate and their two million voters are thinly scattered. The general verdict is that the voters did not want a minority government. To them, the Liberals seemed divided between disguised Conservatives and Socialists who were too timid to face the logic of their own thinking. The electorate wanted to return to the two-party system, through which alone, under the British Constitution, a positive programme can be carried out. For the same reasons Communist candidates and splinter groups of all kinds were emphatically rejected. In short the country had had enough of the Tories, had learnt to see through scares and irrelevance and wanted a Labour Government in a position to give effect to a practical policy which accords with common sense and present needs.

Reform of Parliament is necessary to speed legislation; Lord

Haldane's *Machinery of Government Report* has remained in the pigeon-holes of Downing Street since the last war. Speed is of the essence of the contract that Labour has made with the people of England. We have a right to demand swift action, and a Labour Government can be aided, as much as any other, by criticism. Criticism, indeed, is more easily come by than discipline in a body of nearly 400 Labour MPs, many of whom have fought all their political life in Opposition. We must strive to end within the Party both Trade Union domineering and irresponsible 'Leftism.' An immediately useful step would be to provide channels through which doubts, criticisms and questions can be regularly expressed to Ministers. As we learnt in 1931 it is easy for a Government, beset with administration problems, to grow out of touch with rank and file opinion. With hundreds of young and able back benchers at their disposal, a wise safeguard would be for Ministers to arrange, as part of the machinery of their Departments, regularly to consult with groups of MPs and others, who have special knowledge and contact with outside opinion.

Mr Morrison, who as campaign organiser had as much as anyone to do with achieving this victory, well summarised what the country demands of the new Government. It must, he said, be 'bold, decisive and sensible.' The adjectives are well chosen. No Government that fails in audacity in this situation is worth six months in office. Only a decisive Government can begin to tackle a situation in which mistakes will often be less damaging than hesitation. It is of the first importance that the new Government should understand the mood of those who elected it.

The public will demand much, but it is in no irresponsible or Utopian mood. It was a quiet, sober election; most of the voters had long made up their minds that they wanted Socialist change and were mainly concerned to assure themselves that the candidates were honest and determined about their programme. Candidates have never before been faced with so many intelligent or searching questions. Those who tried to turn the election into a circus have not done well at this election. Those who showed contempt for the electorate have been rejected; those who respected it were generally chosen. Freak candidates and cheap publicity hunters have usually found short shrift. Youth has been at a premium; the portion of 'pensioners' is now very small indeed on the Government benches. People who wanted the State to organise building, to direct industry and develop the national resources in the public interest were not affected by slogans and red herrings. The supporters of this government want it, as Mr Morrison says, to be 'sensible' as well as bold and decisive. That means that the Government must not be diverted from its constructive job by obstruction or intimidation of the type which did so much damage to Britain in 1931 and which destroyed social democratic governments in France as well as in this country between the two wars. The Government is now armed with ample powers to deal with this kind of sabotage, and the country will expect these to be used if necessary. A sensible government will be one which at once begins to carry out its programme, which refuses to waste time, makes its determination and competence clear to everyone and which, above all, maintains behind it the confidence of its supporters by explaining what difficulties it has to overcome and what it is doing. In a word, it must keep its promises.

Kingsley Martin, 4 August 1945

Of all the fine writers who have edited the 'back half' of the paper, V.S. PRITCHETT is arguably the greatest. His NS literary reviews, especially for the 'Books in General' page, would provide a substantial and splendid anthology on their own. Here he says farewell to another great spirit.

George Orwell

George Orwell was the wintry conscience of a generation which in the 'thirties had heard the call to the rasher assumptions of political faith. He was a kind of saint and, in that character, more likely in politics to chasten his own side than the enemy. His instinctive choice of spiritual and physical discomfort, his habit of going his own way, looked like the crankishness which has often cropped up in the British character; if this were so, it was vagrant rather than puritan. He prided himself on seeing through the rackets, and on conveying the impression of living without the solace or even the need of a single illusion.

There can hardly have been a more belligerent and yet more pessimistic Socialist; indeed his Socialism became anarchism. In corrupt and ever worsening years, he always woke up one miserable hour earlier than anyone else and, suspecting something fishy in the site, broke camp and advanced alone to some tougher position in a bleaker place; and it had often happened that he had been the first to detect an unpleasant truth or to refuse a tempting hypocrisy. Conscience took the Anglo-Indian out of the Burma police, conscience sent the old Etonian among the down and outs in London and Paris, and the degraded victims of the Means Test or slum incompetence in Wigan; it drove him into the Spanish civil war and, inevitably, into one of its unpopular sects, and there Don Quixote saw the poker face of Communism. His was the guilty conscience of the educated and privileged man, one of that regular supply of brilliant recalcitrants which Eton has given us since the days of Fielding; and his conscience could be allayed only by taking upon itself the pain, the misery, the dinginess and the pathetic but hard vulgarities of a stale and hopeless period.

But all this makes only the severe half of George Orwell's character. There were two George Orwells even in name. I see a tall emaciated man with a face scored by the marks of physical suffering. There is the ironic grin of pain at the ends of kind lips, and an expression in the fine eyes that had something of the exalted and obstructive farsightedness one sees in the blind; an expression that will suddenly become gentle, lazily kind and gleaming with workmanlike humour. He would be jogged into remembering mad, comical and often tender things which his indignation had written off; rather like some military man taking time off from a private struggle with the War Office or society in general.

He was an expert in living on the bare necessities and a keen hand at making them barer. There was a sardonic suggestion that he could do this but you could not. He was a handyman. He liked the idea of a bench. I remember once being advised by him to go in for goat-keeping, partly I think because it was a sure road to trouble and semi-starvation; but as he set out the alluring disadvantages, it seemed to dawn on him that he was arguing for some country Arcadia, some Animal Farm, he had once known; goats began to look like escapism and, turning aside as we walked to buy some shag at a struggling Wellsian small trader's shop, he switched the subject sharply to the dangerous Fascist tendencies of the St John's Wood Home Guard who were marching to imaginary battle under the Old School Tie.

As an Old School Tie himself, Orwell had varied one of its traditions and had 'gone native' in his own country. It is often said that he knew nothing about the working classes, and indeed a certain self-righteousness in the respectable working class obviously repelled his independent mind. So many of this contemporaries had 'gone native' in France; he redressed a balance. But he did know that sour, truculent, worrying, vulgar lower class England of people half 'done down,' commercially exploited, culturally degraded, lazy, feckless, mild and kind who had appeared in the novels of Dickens, were to show their heads again in Wells and now stood in danger of having the long Victorian decency knocked out of them by gangster politics.

By 'the people' he did not mean what the politicians mean; but he saw, at least in his Socialist pamphlets, that it was they who would give

English life of the future a raw, muddy but unmistakable and inescapable flavour. His masochism, indeed, extended to culture.

In a way, he deplored this. A classical education had given him a taste for the politician who can quote from Horace; and as was shown in the lovely passages of boyhood reminiscence in *Coming Up For Air*, his imagination was full only in the kind world he had known before 1914. Growing up turned him not exactly into a misanthrope – he was too good-natured and spirited for that – but into one who felt too painfully the ugly pressure of society upon private virtue and happiness. His own literary tastes were fixed – with a discernible trailing of the coat – in that boyish period: Bret Harte, Jules Verne, pioneering stuff, Kipling and boys' books. He wrote the best English appreciation of Dickens of our time. *Animal Farm* has become a favourite book for children. His Burmese novels, though poor in character, turn Kipling upside down. As a reporting pamphleteer, his fast, clear, grey prose carries its hard and sweeping satire perfectly.

He has gone; but in one sense, he always made this impression of the passing traveller who meets one on the station, points out that one is waiting for the wrong train and vanishes. His popularity, after *Animal Farm*, must have disturbed such a lone hand. In *1984*, alas, one can see the deadly pain, which had long been his subject, had seized him completely and obliged him to project a nightmare, as Wells had done in his last days, upon the future.

V.S. Pritchett, 28 January 1956

NORMAN LEWIS sketched, in microcosm, the social transformation and the frustrated hopes sweeping post-war Europe.

Socialism and Don Erminio

At Minozzi's, in the little side street just off the Piazza in Milan, they serve the best risotto in the world. Nine out of ten of Minozzi's regulars, middle-aged or elderly men, disregard their mild scurvy and eat nothing but this highly spiced rice twice a day, and every day. And there, promptly at half-past twelve every day for the last thirty-two years, a little comedy has begun. The curtain rises with the cathedral clock chiming the half-hour and the punctual arrival of Don Erminio Colonna.

Don Erminio is in his sixties; a heavy, sad-faced, silent man possessing a head which is considerably broader at the base than across the temples. With his deep yellow complexion he looks – as indeed do all the other regulars – like an oriental khan. He is described on his identity card as a *rentista*, draws a small income from a few acres somewhere down South which he hasn't seen since childhood, and lives with his sister. Taking the place from which for thirty-two years he has never been absent, except for reasons of sickness, for a single meal, he sticks the enormous napkin provided in the side of his collar, thus with an unconsciously rakish effect revealing his tie and the fact that he is a member of the bourgeois class.

For about five minutes he sits in pleasant anticipation, breaking up a piece of bread and hurling the fragments into his mouth. Each day produces these twin peaks of experience – the midday and evening meals – out of a completely flat plain of boredom. He gazes with unseeing eyes straight ahead of him at a mechanical piano-player, on the music rack of which is a telephone directory. Don Erminio couldn't possibly digest his meal unless sitting exactly in this position and enjoying this prospect. The reason, now forgotten, for choosing the particular table had been a lady cashier whose desk had once stood in the place now occupied by the piano-player. It is 25 years since this lady left the restaurant's employ to get married, and she is now a grandmother.

After five minutes the waiter puts in an appearance and he and Don Erminio settle down to their usual game.

'What's it to be?' the waiter asks. He is quite as willing to play this game as Don Erminio. Serving his customers has become just as much a matter of inviolable ritual to him as the meal itself is to them.

'What soup is there to-day?' Don Erminio asks him. He and the waiter could easily change places and play each other's parts to word perfection.

'Fish soup, *pasta* in broth, minestrone,' the waiter tells him.

Don Erminio hesitates. 'Any rice in broth?'

The waiter thinks about this. There is a moment of delightful suspense. 'Yes,' he finally says. 'We can do you rice in broth.'

'Well, I think I'll have that,' Don Erminio says.

The waiter pretends to note something down and turns slowly away. He does not go, however, awaiting an inevitable question, while Don Erminio unfolds the morning paper. Don Erminio glances at the headlines and his blood pressure goes up a few points. Our poor colonies,' he says. 'They want to squeeze the very blood out of our veins . . . is it cooked first?'

'The blood?' says the waiter, confused. His mind is wandering. It's the first time he has ever been caught out like this.

'No, the rice.'

'The rice ... yes, of course.' Don Erminio grunts with relief.

At this moment the show fish is whisked past on its salver. Minozzi's still has a few fish eaters tucked away in a corner. The show fish is a splendid specimen, chosen only for its looks, with a fine, regular head and a good colour. It bears no relation to what has already been prepared. As usual, Don Erminio follows its passage with a stirring of interest. The waiter says: 'And after the soup – a nice cutlet of hake?'

Don Erminio thinks this over and finally shakes his head, saying as he has done for as long as he can remember, 'No, I think I'll have a risotto.'

'Wine?' asks the waiter.

'A half of Frascati.'

The waiter snaps his book in which nothing has been written and goes away. He is back immediately with the wine; takes out the cork and pours a drop into a glass.

Don Erminio sniffs at the wine and pushes the glass away from him. 'Please smell that,' he says.

'What's wrong with it?' the waiter asks.

'I'm asking you.'

The waiter snatches the bottle away, goes behind a screen and returns with it, seeming, by a manœuvre in which he has acquired incredible skill, to draw out a fresh cork. Don Erminio is satisfied this time, and all the agreeable preliminaries being now at an end, the second stage of the drama, the consumption of the meal itself, begins.

Don Erminio takes about an hour and a half to eat his meal. He eats with utter concentration, wholly absorbed, as if in a solemn rite. Slowly his eyes glaze over; he sees nothing but his emptying plate and beyond it the blurred and slightly wavering outline of the piano player. The onset of digestion brings its unfailing sense of peace that will remain with him, like a faithful companion, during the long hours separating him from dinner.

Now the moment has arrived to dislodge the napkin from his collar, to lean back luxuriously relaxed against the bench's padded upholstery, and there he is with eyes half closed, when suddenly he makes out a dim form sitting at the table opposite him. With some effort he opens his eyes fully and recognises the waiter. There is something faintly alarming about this just as there would be if the officiating priest at the Easter mass in the cathedral were suddenly to light up a cigar. And now Don Erminio notices that there is a peculiar atmosphere in the place. The waiter picks up the note Don Erminio has left as a tip, holds it up to the light and pockets it. 'How was the risotto?'

Don Erminio can't express enthusiasm, but he nods and says, 'Ah.' This is his highest praise.

'And the soup?' asks the waiter. 'Up to standard?'

Don Erminio nods and says 'Ah' again, but bewilderment spreads like a creeping paralysis.

'Good,' the waiter says. 'Glad you enjoyed it, because there won't be any more where that came from.' He takes the cigarette out of his mouth and spits in Don Erminio's own, private spittoon. By this time Don Erminio realises that something terrible has happened.

'You've had your last meal here,' the waiter says. 'We're closing down to-night.'

His tone isn't unkind. He notices that, as usual, Don Erminio's midday bottle of Frascati is half full and reaches over to the next table for a clean glass. 'Don't suppose you'll be wanting this,' he says. '... with your permission.' Don Erminio nods with dazed courtesy, still unable to speak. The waiter gulps down a glass of wine and smacks his lips.

'The cook refused to join the union,' he says. 'So the rest of the kitchen staff announced they were going on strike.'

Don Erminio doesn't see that point. 'There's plenty more kitchen staff to be got, isn't there?'

'Not to work with a non-union cook,' the waiter says, spitting again in Don Erminio's spittoon. 'Any way, Minozzi said he didn't want any trouble with Socialism in his restaurant, so he sold out.' 'And quite right too,' Don Erminio starts to say. Then he remembers the tragedy in which this political obduracy of Minozzi's has involved him.

When he leaves the restaurant Don Erminio is dazed with misery. The whole pattern of his existence has been broken into pieces. He has stuck to his post in Minozzi's through thick and thin. Not even the Allied bombardments ever made him miss a single meal there. With bombs falling all over the place he sat there unmoved, insisting on the rice in the soup being cooked first, turning down the offer of fish, sniffing suspiciously at the wine, piling the risotto on to his knife and thrusting it imperturbably into his mouth. Many times he has been complimented on his example of cool fortitude and determination. They couldn't bomb him out of Minozzi's; but where massed formations of Flying Fortresses failed, Socialism has succeeded.

There is a saddler's shop just down the road from the restaurant, and he goes in. 'What have you got in the way of rope?' he asks. The saddler kicks at a pile in the corner. Don Erminio inspects it without enthusiasm. It is bright yellow hemp twisted up locally by the peasants, and the strands have harsh, glassy edges. He notices a coil of fine-looking white rope which probably has a lot of cotton in its composition. 'That's more the kind of thing I had in mind,' he says. 'Imported, I suppose.' He has always been a snob for the exotic. 'Quite so,' the saddler tells him. 'In hundred metre lengths only.'

Don Erminio's lifetime habit of economy cries out against the purchase of twenty times more than he needs; besides that, how is he going to take a hundred-metre coil away with him when it won't even go into a taxi? 'I'll tell you what,' the saddler suggests. 'I could order a short length specially for you. Have it here by this time to-morrow.' 'Yes, do that,' Don Erminio says. 'Make it ten metres.'

Next day Don Erminio is back at the saddler's. He has just lunched atrociously in a place where the radio bellowed at him right through the meal, while a pair of lovers sat mauling each other at his table, and the waiter, instead of replying to civil questions about the food and wine, shrugged his shoulders and went off without a word. Don Erminio couldn't finish his meal. He asked for his bill and cleared off. However, the specially ordered length of best imported rope has arrived and is already done up in a neat parcel. He is just about to pay when he notices that the customer who is buying a dog collar is none other than the waiter from Minozzi's.

'Just managed to sneak out for a minute,' the waiter says with a grin. 'Didn't see you for lunch to-day.'

'Well, naturally,' Don Erminio says. 'Seeing that the place is closed.'

'Oh, that,' the waiter says. 'No, it's all off. Didn't anybody tell you? Turns out the buyer was a Red, and the boss wouldn't take his money. If he had to compromise his principles, he said, he might as well stay as he was.'

'I honour him,' Don Erminio says, 'but what about the cook?'

'Minozzi persuaded him to join the union,' says the waiter, 'so everything's fine.'

'Is lunch finished?' Don Erminio asks as they walk towards the door.

'Well,' the waiter says, 'in the circumstances we might manage something for you. By the way, you've forgotten your parcel.'

'So I have,' Don Erminio says. He goes back to the counter trying to think up an excuse for not taking the rope. Finally he gives in, pays and picks up his parcel. The fact is, he doesn't want to look ridiculous, and besides that, he thinks, how does anyone these days know what the future holds in store for him. ...

Norman Lewis, 25 February 1950

1956: Hungary was a tragedy, Suez a farce. BRUCE RENTON reported from a doomed Budapest, opening a new era of Soviet repression and NS denunciation of it: no more the equivocations of the thirties. Meanwhile at Westminster J.P.W. MALLALIEU – Labour backbencher, Bevanite, NS regular, cricketer and wit – witnessed the disintegration of a Prime Minister and of an imperial dream.

Budapest

The Feast of the Dead

Bruce Renton writes from Austria: There was a smell of mouldering corpses outside the Hungarian parliament. It was dusk, and the great bridges linking Buda and Pest over the Danube, catching the last rays of an autumn sun, were all one could recognise of the Budapest that was. The population hurried over the rubble in Rakosi St. They crowded round the cars of the western journalists. For the moment they paid no attention to the youths nearby engaged in tommy-gun battles with the last of the AVO secret police troops in the houses. The revolution seemed to have been won. The trophy of an Italian colleague brought home to me the fact that this had been a revolution in the real and full sense of the word: it was the blue-banded hat of an AVO officer. The previous owner was hanging by his feet from the yellow-leaved branches of the trees outside the AVO central barracks on the Pest bank of the Danube.

A strange silence, broken by the whine of stray bullets, fell over the stricken city as the news got round that 200 Russian tanks were moving into positions round the city. At the Hotel Duna a babble of western journalists tried vainly to get through to their capitals. Embassies were burning documents. Columns of rebels responded to Russian tank moves by moving to the outskirts of the city. (One suddenly realised that they could no longer be called 'rebels'; they were Hungarians.)

Budapest that night was a city of candles. From afar it had at times a Scandinavian Christmas air. Candles in the windows of the houses, candles in the cemeteries, candles over the corpses of the freedom fighters stretched out and draped in green, red and white flags in Republic Square, in a great feast of the dead. Boys, solemn and determined, tearless, lit candles on the spot where their fathers had fallen. But the faces of the AVO troops whose bodies were heaped in the square had been crushed and spat on. Scores of cigarette ends had burned them beyond recognition. Parliament Square was silent and deserted, save for a few weeping women who crossed themselves before the candles under the walls of Parliament. A Hungarian officer approached smiling. I told him I wanted to speak to Nagy or Kadar. He was not in the least surprised. Two soldiers, carrying tommy-guns and grinning hopefully, led me through a maze of rich Byzantine corridors. The incredible thing about Hungary's ten days of liberty was the fact that journalists from all over the world, dashing up and down the Budapest-Vienna road, were the unofficial ambassadors of the Hungarian government to the outside world.

The two dirty soldiers, in their Russian uniforms, walking down these golden passages, gave an impression of Russia 1917. After the atmosphere of the streets the warm waiting room was soothing for the nerves, apart from the fact that armed patrols kept passing incongruously across the rich carpets. One of Nagy's assistants spoke fluent English. 'Oh, what a fine paper,' he said when I told him I represented the *New Statesman*. In the next room Nagy was arguing with Soviet ambassador Andropov. The assistant told me that in half an hour's time Nagy intended to declare Hungary a neutral country and ask the UN for protection. 'Russian troops are pouring in from the Ukraine. They are digging in round Budapest. I am very pessimistic. I hope I am safe in telling you this. But you could not communicate it anyway.' There was a swift passing of messages for relatives in the west, a hand-shake, and he advised me to leave Budapest at once.

It seems hopeless to continue this correspondence. As we raced madly back to the Italian legation, shooting in the squares helped us lose ourselves in the now deserted, dark and rubble-covered streets. There was a row with an embassy employee whose baby Fiat 600 we had smashed that day. Several hundred dollars changed hands – almost as if dollars were no longer worth anything. It was a nightmare dash for the road to Vienna. At one point the freedom fighters, with the aid of guns, only just prevented us from driving into the Russian tanks. A youth in a military raincoat, two pistols in his pockets, waved the direction of Vienna with one of them, and shouted after us in the darkness, '*Danke, danke, danke für alles.*' It was a forlorn cry that I took away from Hungary. The freedom fighters jumped out at every corner, poking barrels through the car windows, looking for escaping AVO troops. Their hands shook and they were ready to die or kill. The Russian troops guarding the marshalling yards at Komaron were out in battle array, as we raced along the bank of the Danube with the Czech border on the other side. In the morning those same Russians, who would soon be busy with slaughter, had smiled and waved at us. Not until then had I fully understood the significance of the 'smile policy.'

The Russians were bringing down the curtain with a bang and a massacre. I remembered that when I had first arrived at the Hungarian frontier a week before, and we had all jumped on to a Hungarian lorry which had loaded up with Austrian newspapers at Vienna, it had seemed utterly incredible that this brave, enthusiastic people had freed itself. There had to be a catch somewhere. It was the sight of the red flags burning underneath the walls of Gyor town hall that frightened me. It was the sight of the Hungarian girls carrying away the remains of massive red stars. It was the complete, spontaneous and violent destruction of the Communist regime. It did not make sense. The Russians were bound to react by massing an entire panzer army – and not for Hungary alone. We were all convinced that the tanks which were moving towards the Austrian border from the Pressburg bridge on the Czech frontier were not intended merely for Hungary. In Gyor, the first large town inside Hungary, the people had trampled on each other to snatch the western newspapers from our hands. They had yelled in a wild enthusiasm.

Now in Gyor there was black grief. There was not much time – one could feel it in the air. But we stoppped to say goodbye to our new friends. I went into the house of a young doctor who was a member of the Gyor freedom committee. His family slept on mattresses on the floor, his armchairs were in an advanced state of decomposition. 'The British and the French have betrayed us,' he said. 'To attack Egypt now was to make a dirty bargain of the Hungarian people. The panzers came in from the Ukraine, crossed the frontier after Suez.' I gave him fruit and chocolate. 'If the Russians attack,' he said, 'we shall all die.' He pointed to the round, closed-cropped head of his baby boy, who was eating the first and probably the last banana of his life. 'We can never go back to what we were,' said the doctor. 'He will die, too.'

And as I write, Russian tanks are attacking Gyor.

Bruce Renton, 10 November 1956

Westminster

O What can ail thee, Knight at Arms,
Alone and palely loitering?

The Prime Minister sprawled on the front bench, head thrown back and mouth agape. His eyes, inflamed with sleeplessness, stared into vacancies beyond the roof except when they switched with meaningless intensity to the face of the clock, probed it for a few seconds, then rose again into vacancy. His hands twitched at his horn-rimmed spectacles or mopped themselves in a white handkerchief, but were never still.

The face was grey except where black-ringed caverns surrounded the dying embers of his eyes. The whole personality, if not prostrated, seemed completely withdrawn.

Meanwhile, over his head, there raged an Opposition storm. Selwyn Lloyd was being cross-examined mainly about leaflets dropped on Egypt by British planes and which purported to describe Britain's war aims. He had not seen their content nor authorised their publication. Like one of those citizens who must so infuriate Dr Gallup, he stood at the box and did not know. The Prime Minister looked as though he did not care. By now Mr Anthony Head, a sheaf of papers in his hand, had moved along the bench to the Prime Minister's side. The Prime Minister shot another penetrating glance at the face of the clock and then reverted to the rafters, ignoring his Minister of Defence. Mr Head nudged him, pointing down to the papers in his hand. The Prime Minister put on his spectacles, focused and became alert. Within the minute he was at the despatch box for the first time that afternoon, reading the report that Port Said was negotiating for a surrender and for a cease-fire. The Tory benches exploded behind him and the Prime Minister left the chamber all aglow. It seemed that, against the odds, he had found his faery child.

Next day was different. The surrender was not a surrender and the cease-fire was not a cease-fire. Further, there was Mr Bulganin. The Prime Minister was nowhere to be seen. He was on the 'phone to the Americans, to the United Nations, to the French. He would make a statement at six o'clock. Meanwhile, the corridors were filled with little groups of Conservatives, arguing in whispers. In the chamber, Mr Gaitskell, whose brilliant leadership in this crisis has been as brilliantly supported by Mr Bevan, Mr Griffiths and others, quietly but firmly put question after question at the empty space reserved for the Prime Minister. Mr Butler took notes and then, with that flair of his for getting it all ways without at the same time appearing blatantly dishonest, conveyed the impression that he stood shoulder to shoulder with the Prime Minister, that as Leader of the House he was above all this party mess, and that he entirely agreed with everything Gaitskell had said. There the matter rested until six o'clock, when the Prime Minister entered the chamber, slumped on to the front bench and began his habitual exploration of the ceiling. By now it was generally believed that he would announce a cease-fire in accordance with the United Nations request. That is what he did; and once again the Conservatives, except for some half-dozen members of the Suez group who sat in flushed silence, rose from their seats and cheered; and once again the Prime Minister left the chamber all aglow with his faery child.

The Conservatives had wildly cheered what looked like the success of their Prime Minister's policy. They had also wildly cheered what looked like its certain failure. The Prime Minister looked equally gratified on both occasions. This needs some explanation. It seems that since the crisis broke, the Conservative Party in the House of Commons have been like spectators in the casino at Monte Carlo, taking no part in the play and having no say in the stakes, but just watching someone else gamble with their money. The Prime Minister seems to have taken all the decisions without more than perfunctory consultation even with his Cabinet. All who watched him knew that this was a gigantic gamble. About half believed that it would succeed and about half that it would fail; but in the mounting frenzy of anxiety there were no set groups, urging this course or that. There was only feverishness; and when on Monday it looked as though the gamble might have come off, even those who had been doubtful of its success and, when they had calm moments to think about it, were least enthusiastic about its morality, were overwhelmed with relief. When this relief proved groundless, and they could hear the mounting roar from outside of the middle-class revolt which the gamble had provoked, all except the most extreme Suez group longed for the whole thing to be called off.

But the Prime Minister's performance can only be explained in terms of delusion. Contrary to popular belief he has never been a man of strong principle. He is supposed to have been a leading oppponent of Munich and appeasement. Yet, though he was Minister for League of Nations Affairs when the Hoare-Laval Pact was signed, he sat silent throughout, accepting what was the negation of a League of Nations principle. Having succeeded to the Foreign Secretaryship as a result of this silence, he held on to it, not until disagreement on a great issue forced him to resign, but until Chamberlain's interference in the Foreign Office had reduced him to the position of office boy. It was his pride rather than his principles which provoked his resignation. Since the war he has been continuously under the shadow of the great personality. Over and over again he must have overheard the invidious comparisons made between Sir Winston and himself. When at last he became Prime Minister, he determined to show the world that he, too, was a strong man. He took his chance during the past month. He has probably failed; but the overwhelming burden of taking, on his own account, decisions which have come near to breaking the Anglo-American alliance and the Commonwealth have now made him as incapable of distinguishing between success and failure as it has made him incapable of distinguishing between truth and lies.

No birds sing for him now. The sedge is truly withered. As the Conservative Party shakes his dust out of its eyes, it begins to look for a successor to him – someone who can be considered entirely

uncontaminated by his insanities. Eden may be pitied; but he will not
be forgiven.

J.P.W. Mallalieu, 10 November 1956

*The following article was the pebble which produced the avalanche of
CND. J.B. PRIESTLEY's contributions were usually in somewhat
lighter vein, but this was undoubtedly his finest* NS *hour – and one of the
times the paper made as well as recorded history.*

Britain and the Nuclear Bombs

Two events of this autumn should compel us to reconsider the question
of Britain and the nuclear bombs. The first of these events was Mr
Aneurin Bevan's speech at the Labour Party conference, which seemed
to many of us to slam a door in our faces. It was not dishonest but it
was very much a party conference speech, and its use of terms like
'unilateral' and 'polarisation' lent it a suggestion of the 'Foreign Office
spokesman'. Delegates asked not to confuse 'an emotional spasm' with
'statesmanship' might have retorted that the statesmanship of the last
ten years has produced little else but emotional spasms. And though it
is true, as Mr Bevan argued, that independent action by this country, to
ban nuclear bombs, would involve our foreign minister in many
difficulties, most of us would rather have a bewildered and overworked
Foreign Office than a country about to be turned into a radio-active
cemetery. Getting out of the water may be difficult but it is better than
drowning.

The second event was the successful launching of the Soviet satellite,
followed by an immediate outbreak of what may fairly be called
satellitis, producing a rise in temperature and signs of delirium. In the
poker game, where Britain still sits, nervously fingering a few remaining
chips, like a Treasury official playing with two drunk oil millionaires,
the stakes have been doubled again. Disarmament talks must now take
place in an atmosphere properly belonging to boys' papers and science
fiction, though already charged with far more hysterical competitiveness. If statesmanship is to see us through, it will have to
break the familiar and dubious pattern of the last few years. Perhaps
what we need now, before it is too late, is not statesmanship but
lifemanship.

One 'ultimate weapon', the final deterrent, succeeds another. After the bombs, the inter-continental rockets; and after the rockets, according to the First Lord of the Admiralty, the guided-missile submarine, which will 'carry a guided missile with a nuclear warhead and appear off the coasts of any country in the world with a capability of penetrating to the centre of any continent'. The prospect now is not of countries without navies but of navies without countries. And we have arrived at an insane regress of ultimate weapons that are not ultimate.

But all this is to the good; and we cannot have too much of it, we are told, because no men in their right minds would let loose such powers of destruction. Here is the realistic view. Any criticism of it is presumed to be based on wild idealism. But surely it is the wildest idealism, at the furthest remove from a sober realism, to assume that men will always behave reasonably and in line with their best interests? Yet this is precisely what we are asked to believe, and to stake our all on it.

For that matter, why should it be assumed that the men who create and control such monstrous devices *are* in their right minds? They live in an unhealthy mental climate, an atmosphere dangerous to sanity. They are responsible to no large body of ordinary sensible men and women, who pay for these weapons without ever having ordered them, who have never been asked anywhere yet if they wanted them. When and where have these preparations for nuclear warfare ever been put to the test of public opinion? We cannot even follow the example of the young man in the limerick and ask *Who does what and with which and to whom*? The whole proceedings take place in the stifling secrecy of an expensive lunatic asylum. And as one ultimate weapon after another is added to the pile, the mental climate deteriorates, the atmosphere thickens, and the tension is such that soon something may snap.

The more elaborately involved and hair-triggered the machinery of destruction, the more likely it is that this machinery will be set in motion, if only by accident. Three glasses too many of vodka or bourbon-on-the-rocks, and the wrong button may be pushed. Combine this stock-piling of nuclear weapons with a crazy competitiveness, boastful confidence in public and a mounting fear in private, and what was unthinkable a few years ago now at the best only seems unlikely and very soon may seem inevitable. Then western impatience cries 'Let's get the damned thing over!' and eastern fatalism mutters 'If this has to be, then we must accept it.' And people in general are now in a worse position every year, further away from intervention; they have less and less freedom of action; they are deafened and blinded by propaganda and giant headlines; they are robbed of decision by fear or apathy.

It is possible, as some thinkers hold, that our civilisation is bent on self-destruction, hurriedly planning its own doomsday. This may explain, better than any wearisome recital of plot and counter-plot in terms of world power, the curious and sinister air of somnambulism there is about our major international affairs, the steady drift from bad to worse, the speeches that begin to sound meaningless, the conferences that achieve nothing, all the persons of great consequence who somehow seem like puppets. We have all known people in whom was sown the fatal seed of self-destruction, people who would sit with us making sensible plans and then go off and quietly bring them to nothing, never really looking for anything but death. Our industrial civilisation, behaving in a similar fashion, may be under the same kind of spell, hell-bent on murdering itself. But it is possible that the spell can be broken. If it can, then it will only be by an immensely decisive gesture, a clear act of will. Instead of endless bargaining for a little of this in exchange for a little of that, while all the time the bargainers are being hurried down a road that gets steeper and narrower, somebody will have to say 'I'm through with all this.'

In plain words: now that Britain has told the world she has the H-bomb she should announce as early as possible that she has done with it, that she proposes to reject, in all circumstances, nuclear warfare. This is not pacifism. There is no suggestion here of abandoning the immediate defence of this island. Indeed, it might well be considerably strengthened, reducing the threat of actual invasion, which is the root fear in people's minds, a fear often artfully manipulated for purposes far removed from any defence of hearth and home. (This is of course the exact opposite of the views expressed at the Tory conference by Mr Sandys, who appears to believe that bigger and bigger bombs and rockets in more and more places, if necessary, thousands of miles away, will bring us peace and prosperity.) No, what should be abandoned is the idea of deterrence-by-threat-of-retaliation. There is no real security in it, no decency in it, no faith, hope, nor charity in it.

But let us take a look at our present policy entirely on its own low level. There is no standing still, no stalemates, in this idiot game; one 'ultimate weapon' succeeds another. To stay in the race at all, except in an ignominious position, we risk bankruptcy, the disappearance of the Welfare State, a standard of living that might begin to make Communist propaganda sound more attractive than it does at present. We could in fact be so busy, inspired by the indefatigable Mr Sandys, defending ourselves against Communism somewhere else, a long way off, that we could wake up one morning to hear it knocking on the back door. Indeed, this is Moscow's old *heads-I-win-tails-you-lose* policy.

Here we might do well to consider western world strategy, first grandiloquently proclaimed by Sir Winston in those speeches he made in America just after the war. The Soviet Union was to be held in leash by nuclear power. We had the bomb and they hadn't. The race would be on but the West had a flying start. But Russia was not without physicists, and some German scientists and highly trained technicians had disappeared somewhere in eastern Europe. For the immediate defence of West Germany, the atom bomb threat no doubt served its turn. But was this really sound long-term strategy? It created the unhealthy climate, the poisonous atmosphere of our present time. It set Russians galloping in the nuclear race. It freed them from the immense logistic problems that must be solved if large armies are to be moved everywhere, and from some very tricky problems of morale that would soon appear once the Red Army was a long way from home. It encouraged the support of so-called peoples' and nationalistic and anti-colonial wars, not big enough to be settled by nuclear weapons. In spite of America's ring of advanced air bases, the race had only to be run a little longer to offer Russia at least an equally good set-up, and in comparison with Britain alone, clearly an enormously better set-up.

We are like a man in a poker game who never dare cry 'I'll see you'. The Soviet Union came through the last war because it had vast spaces and a large population and a ruthless disregard of losses, human and material. It still has them. Matched against this overcrowded island with its intricate urban organisation, at the last dreadful pinch – and party dictators made to feel unsure of their power can pinch quicker than most democratic leaders – the other side possesses all the advantages. If there is one country that should never have gambled in this game, it is Britain. Once the table stakes were being raised, the chips piling up, we were out. And though we may have been fooling ourselves, we have not been fooling anybody else.

This answers any gobbling cries about losing our national prestige. We have none, in terms of power. (The world has still respect and admiration for our culture, and we are busy reducing that respect and admiration by starving it. The cost of a few bombs might have made all the difference.) We ended the war high in the world's regard. We could have taken over its moral leadership, spoken and acted for what remained of its conscience; but we chose to act otherwise – with obvious and melancholy consequences both abroad, where in power politics we cut a shabby figure, and at home, where we shrug it all away or go to the theatre to applaud the latest jeers and sneers at Britannia. It has been said we cannot send our ministers naked to the conference table. But the sight of a naked minister might bring to the conference some sense of our human situation. What we do is something much worse: we send them there half-dressed, half-smart, half-tough, half-apologetic, figures inviting contempt. That is why we are so happy and

excited when we can send abroad a good-looking young woman in a
pretty new dress to represent us, playing the only card we feel can take
a trick – the Queen.

It is argued, as it was most vehemently by Mr Bevan at Brighton,
that if we walked out of the nuclear arms race then the world would be
'polarised' between America and the Soviet Union, without any hope of
mediation between the two fixed and bristling camps. 'Just consider for
a moment,' he cried, 'all the little nations running, one here and one
there, one running to Russia, the other to the US, all once more
clustering under the castle wall. ...' But surely this is one of those
'realistic' arguments that are not based on reality. The idea of the Third
Force was rejected by the very party Mr Bevan was addressing. The
world was polarised when, without a single protest from all the noisy
guardians of our national pride, parts of East Anglia ceased to be under
our control and became an American air base. We cannot at one and
the same time be both an independent power, bargaining on equal
terms, and a minor ally or satellite. If there are little nations that do not
run for shelter to the walls of the White House or the Kremlin because
they are happy to accept Britain as their nuclear umbrella, we hear very
little about them. If it is a question of brute power, this argument is
unreal.

It is not entirely stupid, however, because something more than brute
power is involved. There is nothing unreal in the idea of a third nation,
especially one like ours, old and experienced in world affairs, possessing
great political traditions, to which other and smaller nations could look
while the two new giants mutter and glare at each other. But it all
depends what that nation is doing. If it is still in the nuclear gamble,
without being able to control or put an end to the game, then that
nation is useless to others, is frittering away its historical prestige, and
the polarisation, which Mr Bevan sees as the worst result of our
rejection of nuclear warfare, is already an accomplished fact. And if it
is, then we must ask ourselves what we can do to break this polarity,
what course of action on our part might have some hope of changing
the world situation. To continue doing what we are doing will not
change it. Even during the few weeks since Mr Bevan made his speech
the world is becoming more rigidly and dangerously polarised than
ever, just because the Russians have sent a metal football circling the
globe. What then can Britain do to de-polarise the world?

The only move left that can mean anything is to go into reverse,
decisively rejecting nuclear warfare. This gives the world something
quite different from the polarised powers: there is now a country that
can make H-bombs but decides against them. Had Britain taken this
decision some years ago the world would be a safer and saner place

than it is today. But it is still not too late. And such a move will have to be 'unilateral'; doomsday may arrive before the nuclear powers reach any agreement; and it is only a decisive 'unilateral' move than can achieve the moral force it needs to be effective.

It will be a hard decision to take because all habit is against it. Many persons of consequence and their entourages of experts would have to think fresh thoughts. They would have to risk losing friends and not influencing people. For example, so far as they involve nuclear warfare, our commitments to Nato, Seato and the rest, and our obligations to the Commonwealth, would have to be sharply adjusted. Anywhere from Brussels to Brisbane, reproaches would be hurled, backs would be turned. But what else have these countries to suggest, what way out, what hope for man? And if, to save our souls and this planet, we are willing to remain here and take certain risks, why should we falter because we might have complaints from Rhodesia and reproaches from Christchurch, NZ? And it might not be a bad idea if the Nato peoples armed themselves to defend themselves, taking their rifles to the ranges at the week-end, like the Swiss.

American official and service opinion would be dead against us, naturally. The unsinkable (but expendable) aircraft carrier would have gone. Certain Soviet bases allotted to British nuclear attack would have to be included among the targets of the American Strategic Air Service. And so on and so forth. But though service chiefs and their staffs go on examining and marking the maps and planning their logistics, having no alternative but resignation, they are as fantastic and unreal in their way as their political and diplomatic colleagues are in theirs. What is fantastic and unreal is their assumption that they are traditionally occupied with their professional duties, attending in advance to the next war, Number Three in the world series. But what will happen – and one wrong report by a sleepy observer might start it off – will not be anything recognisable as a war, an affair of victories and defeats, something that one side can win or that you can call off when you have had enough. It will be universal catastrophe and apocalypse, the crack of doom into which Communism, western democracy, their way of life and our way of life, may disappear for ever. And it is not hard to believe that this is what some of our contemporaries really desire, that behind their photogenic smiles and cheerful patter nothing exists but the death wish.

We live in the thought of this prospect as if we existed in a permanent smog. All sensible men and women – and this excludes most of those who are in the *VIP-Highest-Priority-Top-Secret-Top-People Class*, men now so conditioned by this atmosphere of power politics, intrigue, secrecy, insane invention, that they are more than half-barmy

– have no illusions about what is happening to us, and know that those responsible have made two bad miscalculations. First, they have prostituted so much science in their preparations for war that they have completely changed the character of what they are doing, without any equivalent change in the policies of and relations between states. Foreign affairs, still conducted as if the mobilisation of a few divisions might settle something, are now backed with push-button arrangements to let loose earthquakes and pestilences and pronounce the death sentences of continents. This leaves us all in a worse dilemma than the sorcerer's apprentice. The second miscalculation assumed that if the odds were only multiplied fast enough, your side would break through because the other side would break down. And because this has not happened, a third illusion is being welcomed, namely, that now, with everything piling up, poker chips flung on the table by the handful, the tension obviously increasing, now at last we are arriving at an acknowledged drawn game, a not-too-stalemate, a cosy balance of power. This could well be the last of our illusions.

The risk of our rejecting nuclear warfare, totally and in all circumstances, is quite clear, all too easy to understand. We lose such bargaining power as we now possess. We have no deterrent to a nuclear threat. We deliberately exchange 'security' for insecurity. (And the fact that some such exchange is recommended by the major religions, in their earlier and non-establishment phases, need not detain us here.) But the risk is clear and the arguments against running it quite irrefutable, only if we refuse, as from the first too many of us here have refused, to take anything but short-term conventional views, only if we will not follow any thought to its conclusion. Our 'hard-headed realism' is neither hard-headed nor realistic just because it insists on our behaving in a new world as if we were still living in an old world, the one that has been replaced.

Britain runs the greatest risk by just mumbling and muddling along, never speaking out, avoiding any decisive creative act. For a world in which our deliberate 'insecurity' would prove to be our undoing is not a world in which real security could be found. As the game gets faster, the competition keener, the unthinkable will turn into the inevitable, the weapons will take command, and the deterrents will not deter. Our bargaining power is slight; the force of our example might be great. The catastrophic antics of our time have behind them men hag-ridden by fear, which explains the neurotic irrationality of it all, the crazy disproportion between means and ends. If we openly challenge this fear, then we might break the wicked spell that all but a few uncertified lunatics desperately wish to see broken, we could begin to restore the world to sanity and lift this nation from its recent ignominy to its former grandeur. Alone, we defied Hitler; and alone we can defy this nuclear madness into which the spirit of Hitler seems to have passed, to poison the world. There may be other chain-reactions besides those leading to destruction; and we might start one. The British of these times, so frequently hiding their decent, kind faces behind masks of sullen apathy or sour, cheap cynicism, often seem to be waiting for something better than party squabbles and appeals to their narrowest self-interest, something great and noble in its intention that would make them feel good again. And this might well be a declaration to the world that after a certain date one power able to engage in nuclear warfare will reject the evil thing for ever.

J.B. Priestley, 2 November 1975

PAUL JOHNSON's long journey across the political map can be traced in the NS *from the fifties to the seventies. All the way, a constant quality has been the incandescent intensity of the* anger *he has directed at the target of the moment. Few writers have so successfully built a style around fury.*

Sex, Snobbery and Sadism

I have just finished what is, without doubt, the nastiest book I have ever read. It is a new novel entitled *Dr No* and the author is Mr Ian Fleming. Echoes of Mr Fleming's fame had reached me before, and I had been repeatedly urged to read his books by literary friends whose judgment I normally respect. When his new novel appeared, therefore, I obtained a copy and started to read. By the time I was a third of the way through, I had to suppress a strong impulse to throw the thing away, and only continued reading because I realised that here was a social phenomenon of some importance.

There are three basic ingredients in *Dr No*, all unhealthy, all thoroughly English: the sadism of a schoolboy bully, the mechanical, two-dimensional sex-longings of a frustrated adolescent, and the crude, snob-cravings of a suburban adult. Mr Fleming has no literary skill, the construction of the book is chaotic, and entire incidents and situations are inserted, and then forgotten, in a haphazard manner. But the three ingredients are manufactured and blended with deliberate, professional precision; Mr Fleming dishes up his recipe with all the calculated accountancy of a Lyons Corner House.

The plot can be briefly described. James Bond, an upper-class Secret Service Agent, is sent by his sadistic superior, M., to Jamaica, to investigate strange incidents on a nearby island. By Page 53, Bond's bodyguard, a faithful and brutal Negro called Quarrel, is already at work, twisting the arms of a Chinese girl to breaking point. She gouges his face with a broken flash-bulb, and in return, he smilingly squeezes the fleshy part of her thumb (described by Fleming as 'the Mount of Venus', because if it is well-developed then the girl is 'good in bed') until she screams. ('She's Love Moun' be sore long after ma face done get healed,' chortles Quarrel.) Next, Bond's mysterious enemies attempt to poison him with cyanide loaded fruit, and then insert a six-inch long venomous centipede in his bed ('Bond could feel it nuzzling at his skin. It was drinking! Drinking the beads of salt sweat!').

Bond visits the island, falls asleep, and on waking sees a beautiful girl, wearing only a leather belt round her waist ('The belt made her nakedness extraordinarily erotic'). Her behind, Bond notices, 'was almost as firm and rounded as a boy's'. The girl tells Bond she was raped at the age of 15 by a savage overseer, who then broke her nose. She revenged herself by dropping a Black Widow spider on his naked stomach while he slept ('He took a week to die'). Bond rejects her urgent invitation to share her sleeping bag. Then the enemy arrives – huge, inhuman Negro-Chinese half-castes, known as Chingroes, under the diabolical direction of Dr No. Quarrel is scorched to death by a flame-thrower, and Bond and the girl are captured.

There follows a vague series of incidents in a sort of luxury hotel, built into the mountain, where Dr No entertains his captives before torturing them. This gives Fleming an opportunity to insert his snob ingredient. A lubricious bathroom scene, in which the girl again attempts to seduce Bond, involves Floris Lime bath-essence, Guerlain bathcubes and 'Guerlain's Sapoceti, *Fleur des Alpes*'. Bond, offered a drink, demands 'a medium vodka dry Martini' ('I would prefer Russian or Polish vodka'). A third attempt by the girl is frustrated only by Bond's succumbing to drugs inserted in the breakfast. At last Dr No appears, 6 ft 6 in tall, and looking like 'a giant venomous worm wrapped in grey tin-foil'. Some years before, his hands had been cut off, but he is equipped with 'articulated steel pincers', which he has a habit of tapping against his contact-lenses, making a metallic noise. He has a polished skull, no eyelashes, and his heart is on the wrong side of his body; he is, needless to say, Chinese (with a German mother). His chief amusement is to subject his captives to prolonged, scientific tortures. ('I am interested in pain. I am also interested in finding out how much the human body can endure.')

Bond contemplates stabbing No's jugular vein with the jagged stem of a broken wine-glass, but reluctantly abandons the idea. The girl is taken off, to be strapped, naked, to the ground and nibbled to death by giant crabs. Bond is put through an ingenious, and fantastically complicated, obstacle course of tortures, devised by No. First come electric shocks. Then an agonising climb up a steel chimney. Then a crawl along a red-hot zinc tube, to face 20 giant Tarantula spiders 'three or four inches long'. Finally Bond is hurled into the sea, where he is met by a 50-foot giant squid (everything is giant in *Dr No* – insects, breasts and gin-and-tonics). Having survived all these, Bond buries No alive under a mountain of bird-dung, rescues the girl and at last has a shot at a jugular vein, this time with a table-knife. He also shoots three Chingroes, one in the head, one in the stomach and one in the neck. The girl's feet get cut up, but they tramp to safety, 'leaving bloody footsteps on the ground'. The story ends with Bond biting the girl in an erotic embrace, which takes place in a special giant sleeping bag.

I have summarised the plot, perhaps at wearisome length, because a bare recital of its details describes, better than I can, how Fleming deliberately and systematically excites, and then satisfies the very worst instincts of his readers. This seems to me far more dangerous than straight pornography. In 1944, George Orwell took issue with a book which in some ways resembles Fleming's novels – *No Orchids for Miss Blandish*. He saw the success of *No Orchids*, published in 1940, as part of a discernible psychological climate, whose other products were Fascism, the Gestapo, mass-bombing and war. But in condemning *No Orchids*, Orwell made two reservations. First, he conceded that it was brilliantly written, and that the acts of cruelty it described sprang from a subtle and integrated, though perverse, view of human nature. Secondly, in contrasting *No Orchids* with *Raffles* – which he judged a healthy and harmless book – he pointed out that *No Orchids* was evil precisely because it lacked the restraint of conventional upper-class values; and this led him to the astonishing but intelligible conclusion that perhaps, after all, snobbery, like hypocrisy, was occasionally useful to society.

What, I wonder, would he have said of *Dr No*? For this novel is badly written to the point of incoherence and none of the 500,000 people who, I am told, are expected to buy it, could conceivably be giving Cape 13s. 6d. to savour its literary merits. Moreover, both its hero and its author are unquestionably members of the Establishment. Bond is an ex-Royal Navy Commander and belongs to Blades, a sort-of super-White's. Mr Fleming was educated at Eton and Sandhurst, and is married to a prominent society hostess, the ex-wife of Lord Rothermere. He is the foreign manager of that austere and respectable newspaper, the *Sunday Times*, owned by an elderly fuddy-duddy called

Lord Kemsley, who once tried to sell a popular tabloid with the slogan (or rather his wife's slogan) of 'clean and clever'. Fleming belongs to the Turf and Boodle's and lists among his hobbies the collection of first editions. He is also the owner of Goldeneye, a house made famous by Sir Anthony Eden's Retreat from Suez. Eden's uneasy slumbers, it will be remembered, were disturbed by (characteristically) giant rats which, after they had been disposed of by his detectives, turned out to be specially tamed ones kept by Mr Fleming.

Orwell, in fact, was wrong. Snobbery is no protection: on the contrary, the social appeal of the dual Bond-Fleming personality has added an additional flavour to his brew of sex and sadism. Fleming's novels are not only successful, like *No Orchids*; they are also smart. The *Daily Express*, pursuing its task of bringing glamour and sophistication to the masses, has serialised the last three. Our curious post-war society, with its obsessive interest in debutantes, its cult of U and non-U, its working-class graduates educated into snobbery by the welfare state, is a soft market for Mr Fleming's poison. Bond's warmest admirers are among the Top People. Of his last adventure, *From Russia, With Love*, his publishers claim, with reason, that it 'won approval from the sternest critics in the world of letters'. *The Times Literary Supplement* found it 'most brilliant', the *Sunday Times* 'highly polished', the *Observer* 'stupendous', the *Spectator* 'rather pleasant'. And this journal, most susceptible of all, described it as 'irresistible'. It has become easier than it was in Orwell's day to make cruelty attractive. We have gone just that much farther down the slope. Recently I read Henri Alleg's horrifying account of his tortures in an Algiers prison; and I have on my desk a documented study of how we treat our prisoners in Cyprus. I am no longer astonished that these things can happen. Indeed, after reflecting on the Fleming phenomenon, they seem to me almost inevitable.

Paul Johnson, 5 April 1958

NS *interest in the clash of Zionism and Arab nationalism in the Middle East had been intense almost from the journal's foundation. Its stance, at least until the mid-seventies, was consistently one of sympathy for the Israeli cause – and especially, naturally enough, for Israeli socialists. None the less NAOMI MITCHISON, in 1956, wrote empathetically of the plight of Palestinian refugees.*

Home Is over the Jordan

To say there are half a million Palestinian refugees in Jordan is only to be out by a few thousands – and who bothers to think about refugees as individuals, anyway? Yes, a few people do: women like Ruth Black at Nablus or Winifred Coate at Zerka. They were there as part of some church organisation, teaching perhaps, or supervising. Then, without warning, a thousand screaming, panicking, terrified people are tumbled out of trucks in front of them and nobody does a thing about it. They start by ringing up the Bishop and distributing milk; they ended by organising industries and housing estates. There is no nonsense about planning permission or sanitary inspectors. Whatever is done is an enormous step up from the hideous squalor of the refugee camps. Nor is there any fuss about whether a refugee is Moslem or Christian, whether he has three or four wives or such small matters of custom; desperate need is met with patient and efficient love and understanding.

Mousa el Alami thinks about refugees as individuals, too. He has an estate between Jericho and the Jordan river, where the land slopes down towards the salt, eroded hillocks by the Dead Sea. Without irrigation nothing was possible; the experts said he would only find brine if he sunk wells. But he had a hunch; his first wells struck sweet water under a clay crust. He has irrigated using sprinklers as well as ditches, grows three crops a year of vegetables, which are expertly washed, graded and packed, also wheat, bananas, oranges and fodder crops. Here he has a hundred Arab refugee boys, to whom he teaches agriculture and also skilled trades, and over a hundred grown-up workers from the Jericho camp. He takes his meals with the boys and knows all their problems and hopes; a boy looks up from his work when Mousa passes and his eyes light with trust and faith.

I saw that. I also saw smashed machinery and incubators, burnt buildings, pillaged desks, empty hen runs. It was done at the end of the last year by rioting refugees. That doesn't make sense until you realise that Mousa has been called an agent of western imperialism and a compromiser with the doctrine of Death to the Jews, as anyone automatically becomes who offers an Arab refugee hope and the future instead of revenge and the past. So people were disappointed that Mousa el Alami was not murdered, since he happened to be away from home. I am glad to say his boys all fought for him and not one has been terrorised into leaving.

Now there is a great deal of potentially good land in Jordan which only needs irrigation; it would get it fast enough in land-hungry Israel! There is even more land in other Arab countries. Saudi Arabia could produce all the capital for the necessary works without anyone being any the worse except the purveyors of solid gold dinner services. Industries could be started in Jordan. At present the main industry is the Arab Legion; every Arab boy seemed to want to join it. No wonder, for it meant good quarters and good treatment, with all the amenities which General Glubb had insisted on – the tree-planted grounds, the club houses, the water supplies and modern buildings, the pipe band and so on, not to speak of the very becoming head-dress. But what is needed is something more productive – and goodness knows, Jordan is short of all kinds of consumer goods.

It should be possible to settle the refugees in the Arab countries, and make them into a productive agricultural and industrial labour force. But is that the right solution? They had a great wrong done to them by the invading Zionists. Yet the Zionists were themselves driven by the even greater wrongs of the gas chambers and the pogroms. Two wrongs, unhappily, do not make a right. And it is this wrong done to the refugees which has made Israel insecure.

It is not the first time in history that such things have happened, and our own hands are anything but clean. The hows and whys of the Palestine story are told very differently on the two sides of this cruellest and craziest of frontiers. The solid weight of misery remains, and still the women in the camps wear the dresses that show they belong to some village which is now perhaps only scattered stones. Their fields that they dream of, where they worked laboriously, tediously and slowly, with no tools but their bare hands and a basket for weeds or stones, are now being far more efficiently cultivated by some kibbutz with modern machinery and decent conditions of labour. Instead of the long black dresses, heavily embroidered on the breast and in stripes, the girls wear jeans or shorts. Instead of walking humbly after the husband, who rides the family donkey, and carrying all the burdens as well as a baby or two, the women work, play and study alongside the men.

Most of the refugees probably come from villages and were deeply attached to the soil, but some came from towns; a few were quite well off. Now they eat their hearts out, year after year, in the mud brick huts of the hideous refugee camps with the continuous stink of open drains and blowing of evil dust. There is no work for them, though some must be finding a little wage somewhere, for the Unwra food only keeps them alive for three weeks out of the month. It is mostly bread. There is an Unwra inquiry going on just now; they can't think why the refugees are still alive.

The children in the horribly overcrowded Unwra schools show a great variety of skin and other diseases. Some people say they are learning Communism. I wouldn't be surprised. There isn't much hope for them in any other doctrine. Or do they suppose that the Arab states really mean to sweep the Jews into the sea and give them back their villages, where they would live, not, of course, on the Israel level – just tolerable by western or Russian standards – but at the old bare subsistence level? Is that their dream? Or is it a more plausible dream, especially for Moslems who like the idea of justice, to do something about evening out standards of living in the Arab world?

Meanwhile, these slum camps have stayed practically unchanged for six years, each of them housing several thousand people in conditions of extreme wretchedness. A lot of babies get born. If one thinks in terms of birth control, the women's answer is that the only thing they can do for their husbands is to bear them sons – daughters don't count – and that while they are pregnant life is made a little less hard for them.

There are also frontier villages in the hills with the frontier line cutting them off from their old lands in the Western plain. Here, one might think, a little mutual good will could work wonders. But there appears to be no official good will, instead a terrifying atmosphere of hate; on one side the word 'Jew' spoken as it must have been in Nazi Germany, on the other 'no good Arab but a dead Arab'. Yet there are plenty of individuals who have had good relations in the past with the almost mythical other side and who realise that, sooner or later, the frontier between Jordan and Israel, with its constant shootings, must cease to exist, because each side needs the other so much and because Jerusalem is the Holy City for everyone.

Is that unofficial good will going to be enough for peace? Enough to stand against Nasser's need to produce Egyptian victories in order that the slowness of progress and the lack of democratic methods within Egypt may be forgiven or unnoticed? Enough to stand against the Big Two (or more) fishing around in the oil for the sardines of power? It seems to me that we have to back that good will wherever we find it. In exchange for peace, it would be worth Israel's while to offer to let some refugees at least go back, to make some frontier adjustments and to arrange some individual compensation. In exchange for even a partial opening of the frontier and possible use of a port, it would be worth Jordan's while to take Unwra money for a big resettlement scheme. And it would be worth the whole world's while to contribute, even if it meant selling fewer cast-off tanks and planes.

Naomi Mitchison, 28 April 1956

C.P. SNOW's lament for the chasm opened between literary and scientific cultures, which aroused fury in certain critical circles, was first voiced in the NS.

The Two Cultures

'It's rather odd,' said G.H. Hardy, one afternoon in the early Thirties, 'but when we hear about "intellectuals" nowadays, it doesn't include people like me and J.J. Thomson and Rutherford.' Hardy was the first mathematician of his generation, J.J. Thomson the first physicist of his; as for Rutherford, he was one of the greatest scientists who have ever lived. Some bright young literary person (I forget the exact context) putting them outside the enclosure reserved for intellectuals seemed to Hardy the best joke for some time. It does not seem quite such a good joke now. The separation between the two cultures has been getting deeper under our eyes; there is now precious little communication between them, little but different kinds of incomprehension and dislike.

The traditional culture, which is, of course, mainly literary, is behaving like a state whose power is rapidly declining – standing on its precarious dignity, spending far too much energy on Alexandrian intricacies, occasionally letting fly in fits of aggressive pique quite beyond its means, too much on the defensive to show any generous imagination to the forces which must inevitably reshape it. Whereas the scientific culture is expansive, not restrictive, confident at the roots, the more confident after its bout of Oppenheimerian self-criticism, certain that history is on its side, impatient, intolerant, creative rather than critical, good-natured and brash. Neither culture knows the virtues of the other; often it seems they deliberately do not want to know. The resentment which the traditional culture feels for the scientific is shaded with fear; from the other side, the resentment is not shaded so much as brimming with irritation. When scientists are faced with an expression of the traditional culture, it tends (to borrow Mr William Cooper's eloquent phrase) to make their feet ache.

It does not need saying that generalisations of this kind are bound to look silly at the edges. There are a good many scientists indistinguishable from literary persons, and vice versa. Even the stereotype generalisations about scientists are misleading without some sort of detail – e.g. the generalisations that scientists as a group stand on the political Left. This is only partly true. A very high proportion of engineers is almost as conservative as doctors; of pure scientists, the same would apply to chemists. It is only among physicists and biologists that one finds the Left in strength. If one compared the whole body of scientists with their opposite numbers of the traditional culture (writers, academics, and so on), the total result might be a few per cent more towards the Left wing, but not more than that. Nevertheless, as a first approximation, the scientific culture is real enough, and so is its difference from the traditional. For anyone like myself, by education a scientist, by calling a writer, at one time moving between groups of scientists and writers in the same evening, the difference has seemed dramatic.

The first thing, impossible to miss, is that scientists are on the up and up; they have the strength of a social force behind them. If they are English, they share the experience common to us all – of being in a country sliding economically downhill – but in addition (and to many of them it seems psychologically more important) they belong to something more than a profession, to something more like a directing class of a new society. In a sense oddly divorced from politics, they are the new men. Even the staidest and most politically conservative of scientific veterans, lurking in dignity in their colleges, have some kind of link with the world to come. They do not hate it as their colleagues do; part of their mind is open to it; almost against their will, there is a residual glimmer of kinship there. The young English scientists may and do curse their luck; increasingly they fret about the rigidities of their universities, about the ossification of the traditional culture which, to the scientists, makes the universities cold and dead; they violently envy their Russian counterparts who have money and equipment without discernible limit, who have the whole field wide open. But still they stay pretty resilient: they are swept on by the same social force. Harwell and Windscale have just as much spirit as Los Alamos and Chalk River: the neat petty bourgeois houses, the tough and clever young, the crowds of children: they are symbols, frontier towns.

There is a touch of the frontier qualities, in fact, about the whole scientific culture. Its tone is, for example, steadily heterosexual. The difference in social manners between Harwell and Hampstead, or as far as that goes between Los Alamos and Greenwich Village, would make an anthropologist blink. About the whole scientific culture, there is an absence – surprising to outsiders – of the feline and oblique. Sometimes it seems that scientists relish speaking the truth, especially when it is unpleasant. The climate of personal relations is singularly bracing, not to say harsh: it strikes bleakly on those unused to it, who suddenly find that the scientists' way of deciding on action is by a full-dress argument, with no regard for sensibilities and no holds barred. No body of people ever believed more in dialectic as the primary method of attaining sense; and if you want a picture of scientists in their off-moments it could be just one of a knock-about argument. Under the argument there glitter egotisms as rapacious as any of ours: but, unlike ours, the egotisms are driven by a common purpose.

How much of the traditional culture gets through to them? The answer is not simple. A good many scientists, including some of the most gifted, have the tastes of literary persons, read the same things, and read as much. Broadly, though, the infiltration is much less. History gets across to a certain extent, in particular social history: the sheer mechanics of living, how men ate, built, travelled, worked, touches a good many scientific imaginations, and so they have fastened on such works as Trevelyan's *Social History*, and Professor Gordon Childe's books. Philosophy the scientific culture views with indifference, especially metaphysics. As Rutherford said cheerfully to Samuel Alexander: 'When you think of all the years you've been talking about those things, Alexander, and what does it all add up to? *Hot air*, nothing but *hot air.*' A bit less exuberantly, that is what contemporary scientists would say. They regard it as a major intellectual virtue, to know what not to think about. They might touch their hats to linguistic analysis, as a relatively honourable way of wasting time; not so to existentialism.

The arts? The only one which is cultivated among scientists is music. It goes both wide and deep; there may possibly be a greater density of musical appreciation than in the traditional culture. In comparison, the graphic arts (except architecture) score little, and poetry not at all. Some novels work their way through, but not as a rule the novels which literary persons set most value on. The two cultures have so few points of contact that the diffusion of novels shows the same sort of delay, and exhibits the same oddities, as though they were getting into translation in a foreign country. It is only fairly recently, for instance, that Graham Greene and Evelyn Waugh have become more than names. And, just as it is rather startling to find that in Italy Bruce Marshall is by a long shot the best-known British novelist, so it jolts one to hear scientists talking with attention of the works of Nevil Shute. In fact, there is a good reason for that: Mr Shute was himself a high-class engineer, and a book like *No Highway* is packed with technical stuff that is not only accurate but often original. Incidentally, there are benefits to be gained from listening to intelligent men, utterly removed from the literary scene and unconcerned as to who's in and who's out. One can pick up such a comment as a scientist once made, that it looked to him as though the current preoccupations of the New Criticism, the extreme concentration on a tiny passage, had made us curiously insensitive to the total flavour of a work, to its cumulative effects, to the epic qualities in literature. But, on the other side of the coin, one is just as likely to listen to three of the most massive intellects in Europe happily discussing the merits of *The Wallet of Kai-Lung*.

When you meet the younger rank-and-file of scientists, it often seems that they do not read at all. The prestige of the traditional culture is high enough for some of them to make a gallant shot at it. Oddly enough, the novelist whose name to them has become a token of esoteric literary excellence is that difficult highbrow Dickens. They approach him in a grim and dutiful spirit as though tackling *Finnegan's Wake*, and feel a sense of achievement if they manage to read a book through. But most young technicians do not fly so high. When you ask them what they read – 'As a married man,' one says, 'I prefer the garden.' Another says: 'I always like just to use my books as tools.' (Difficult to resist speculating what kind of tool a book would make. A sort of hammer? A crude digging instrument?)

That, or something like it, is a measure of the incommunicability of the two cultures. On their side the scientists are losing a great deal. Some of that loss is inevitable: it must and would happen in any society at our technical level. But in this country we make it quite unnecessarily worse by our educational patterns. On the other side, how much does the traditional culture lose by the separation?

I am inclined to think, even more. Not only practically – we are familiar with those arguments by now – but also intellectually and morally. The intellectual loss is a little difficult to appraise. Most scientists would claim that you cannot comprehend the world unless you know the structure of science, in particular of physical science. In a sense, and a perfectly genuine sense, that is true. Not to have read *War and Peace* and *La Cousine Bette* and *La Chartreuse de Parme* is not to be educated; but so is not to have a glimmer of the Second Law of Thermodynamics. Yet that case ought not to be pressed too far. It is more justifiable to say that those without any scientific understanding miss a whole body of experience: they are rather like the tone deaf, from whom all musical experience is cut off and who have to get on without it. The intellectual invasions of science are, however, penetrating deeper. Psycho-analysis once looked like a deep invasion, but that was a false alarm; cybernetics may turn out to be the real thing, driving down into the problems of will and cause and motive. If so, those who do not understand the method will not understand the depths of their own cultures.

But the greatest enrichment the scientific culture could given us is – though it does not originate like that – a moral one. Among scientists, deep-natured men know, as starkly as any men have known, that the individual human condition is tragic; for all its triumphs and joys, the essence of it is loneliness and the end death. But what they will not admit is that, because the individual condition is tragic, therefore the social condition must be tragic, too. Because a man must die, that is no excuse for his dying before his time and after a servile life. The impulse behind the scientists drives them to limit the area of tragedy, to take nothing as tragic that can conceivably lie within men's will. They have nothing but contempt for those representatives of the traditional culture who use a deep insight into man's fate to obscure the social truth – or to do something pettier than obscure the truth, just to hang on to a few perks. Dostoevski sucking up to the Chancellor Pobedonostsev, who thought the only thing wrong with slavery was that there was not enough of it; the political decadence of the *avant garde* of 1914, with Ezra Pound finishing up broadcasting for the Fascists; Claudel agreeing sanctimoniously with the Marshall about the virtue in others' suffering; Faulkner giving sentimental reasons for treating Negroes as a different species. They are all symptoms of the deepest temptation of the clerks – which is to say: 'Because man's condition is tragic, everyone ought to stay in their place, with mine as it happens somewhere near the top.' From that particular temptation, made up of defeat, self-indulgence, and moral vanity, the scientific culture is almost totally immune. It is that kind of moral health of the scientists which, in the last few years, the rest of us have needed most; and of which, because the two cultures scarcely touch, we have been most deprived.

C.P. Snow, 6 October 1956

The NS *had begun prophesying the dangers of a resurgent Fascism almost the moment shooting stopped in 1945. There was an obvious danger of crying wolf too often. As racist violence carved the first of its many scars on post-war British life, in Notting Hill in 1958, CLANCY SIGAL reported that the face of British Fascism was less exotic, less ideological, but no less disturbing than readers might have expected.*

Short Talk with a Fascist Beast

It is a normal evening at the coffee-bar where I'm in the habit of dropping by. The kids are jiving and punching each other around in the juke-box room, an amateur rock-and-roll session is in violent practice upstairs somewhere, and some of us are gathered at the counter sucking Pepsi-Cola through straws. Through the big front window we can see a few of the boys horsing around on their hire-purchased motorbikes. Fat, moonfaced Dave walks in and asks us if we want a ride on his bike and we say no, we'll hang around a while.

Len buys Ginger and Dave and me Pepsis. He's on casual work now, he says, after quitting a warehouse where he moved fridges. 'Keep on casual till they nick me,' he says. I tell Len that I've heard he was up at Notting Hill during the troubles. 'Yeah,' Len replies, 'three nights all in a row'. He is stating a fact, not boasting. 'What were you doing up there?' I ask. 'Hittin' the nigs,' he says.

Dave, off his motorbike, offers that he spent only a single night 'huntin' nigs'. Ginger, who resembles Jimmy Dean and likes being told about it, says, 'Nah, that wasn't the way – all in a mob. Coppers see you. Thing to do, three, four of us, down a side street at night, in a fast car, jump out, do a nig, jump in. That way you can do a dozen blackies a night.'

Len is a lanky, shamble-shouldered bleach-haired boy, with a tall thin blond face and small blank eyes and virtually no upper eyelids. I ask Len if he enjoyed himself during the riots. He says, 'Sure.' I ask him what he did. 'Hit nigs,' he says and shrugs. Did many boys from the café go with him? No, not many. 'It was the Fascists done the work up there,' Len says. How is he so sure? 'I drove around, first night, in a jeep with one of them. A reporter from one of the newspapers gets out of his car and asks us what the trouble is. This Fascist smashed him square in the face, 'e did. Reporter got back in his car and rolled up all the windows.' Dave and Ginger say they chased a few coloured men without much success.

Dave says that his high point came when he led a mob of teen-agers to St Mark's Crescent and pointed a milk bottle at a coloured house. Ginger has no individual exploits to his credit. He wears a brightly coloured Palm Beach shirt and talks like an American radio comedian. He doesn't tell jokes, just maintains a patter of small, pseudo-ironical remarks. They listen while Len speaks of the Fascists. He says that, contrary to public belief, the Fascists still wear the black shirt with the silver lightning insignia. Is he a member of the Union Movement himself? With a quick dart of the long blond head he says no, not a member, only a follower. 'Fascists was active before all the troubles,' he says, 'and now they're gettin' lots of members. Brown shirts started that way, didn't they? I mean, it don't mean just because you start out small that you some day won't be over the whole country, does it?' Dave and Ginger remain neutral in the face of ideology. What Len was doing at Notting Hill was fine with them, but not when he wants to do it in uniform.

I ask Len if it is the uniform that attracts him. He says no, not particularly, it is what the Fascists stand for. 'Riddin' Britain of the nigs,' he says. When I ask him what he has against the 'nigs', Dave and Ginger chime in eagerly. It isn't so much the Indians and Africans they mind. It's the Jamaicans, their word for all West Indians.

Dave says, 'Y'know, when I went in for my national assistance, all they'd give me was two quid after an argument. Crazy Jamaican after me comes out with seven.' How did the Jamaican manage this? Dave says the Jamaican claimed a family back in the islands. Ginger says, 'They come here and they use all our money, lower our standards, that's what they do.' 'Darkies live on two quid a week,' says Ginger, 'eatin' cat food. It's the truth. I seen 'em.' 'Live like pigs,' says Dave.

Len adds, 'An' the way they all walk around, they got no respect. The clothes they wear. I seen one last night, suit the colour of milk, milk mind you, black shoes with a green tassle, and with a girl.' Was the girl white? Len nods. He says, 'Ever see the pants they wear? Big and wide up here, tiny and little at the bottom. Why do they have to dress that way? Crazy pants.' His own trousers are drain-pipe, of a grey tweed material I am not familiar with. Ten minutes later he is to tell me that he had to sleep at a friend's house a week ago because of a row with his old lady over his trousers.

It boils down to this: the West Indians live too high and live like pigs. When I ask them if they do not see a contradiction in this, Len, with the plodding seriousness that is characteristic, says sincerely, after a little confused thought, 'They live in dirt in private and like kings the rest of the time'. He says he used to live in Notting Hill but that a coloured man bought the house and threw them out.

'The coppers,' says Len, 'they was all on the side of the blackies.' Dave and Ginger nod vigorously. I say that the coloured people I have spoken to claim differently. 'Cor,' exclaims Ginger, 'see what we mean? Liars all, the blacks. Can't trust any of 'em.' Do they know any coloured people personally? Vague replies. Len grins slyly, more animation than I usually get from him. 'Yeah, I knew one,' he says. 'Hit him over the head with my shovel.' It happened three weeks ago, at work. 'See what I mean?' says Len. 'I was working on this building site. Driving a dump truck. I got sick, y'know. Out two days. While I was gone this blackie tells the boss he can drive a truck too. When I came back there he is in my cab. I tell him to get down out of my truck and he says no he won't. So me and my mates pull him down and I hit him over the head with my shovel.'

Ginger says, 'What are you gonna do with people who come to take your jobs? How much you willin' to work for, Len?' Len says, 12, 14 quid a week. 'No,' says Ginger, 'I mean, how much *would* you work for?' Len says staunchly, 'I'd work for eight quid.' 'See,' says Ginger. 'Guv'nor knows Len won't work for less than eight, a blackie'll come along who says "six" and he's the one who gets the job.' Len, Dave and Ginger all left school at 15. They are 18 now. Len is a casual labourer,

Dave a public service worker, while Ginger is an assistant to a skilled craftsman.

Dave says, 'Four years.' Ginger says, 'Four almighty years.' Len says, 'Four years is a long time.' The boys are genuinely in awe. Len snaps out of it. 'Four bloody years for *that*? Salmon, that Yid.' When the boys talk it is with a peculiar, rushing, staccato tempo which is the trademark of their group. Dave and Ginger swear the West Indians are lazy, and that the 'guv'nors' prefer them to native-born Englishmen; that they live on nothing a week, and spend all their money on offensive hedonisms, and are worse than savages. Do they resent the West Indians fighting back? 'Bloody well do,' says Dave. 'What right they got comin' to this country, anyway? We get the worst types.' All agree that the coloured immigrants ought to be returned to their source, but if they are not, to serve docilely as fair game for mobs.

Len says, 'On the second day I got me a few. Fell in with this crowd chasing nigs. We saw a nigger conductor on a trolley bus. We chased it. All the people in the bus ran out. But I didn't get to the nig. The mob was in there before me.' I asked Len if he was disappointed. He nods sadly. 'That's all right,' he says. 'Later on, on the corner there was this gang, and they was kicking this blackie on the ground. I ran up and got a few kicks in too.' I asked him if he thought this was fair. 'Yeah, it was fair,' he says. Dave and Ginger leave for a ride on Dave's motorbike. Len and I watch them roar away.

'I hate the niggers,' says Len complacently. I ask him if Mr Justice Salmon's decision will affect his street activities. 'Four years,' Len muses, 'four years is a long time. Nah, I ain't goin' to go in the nick for any nigger.' He says that after the Old Bailey sentences he stopped carrying a flick knife. 'I used to have a gun too,' he says. 'But not now. You know, those coppers at Notting Hill. They'd see us lacing a blackie and they'd stand off, just watchin' us, y'know, and then when we was through they'd come charging through and frisk us for knives, things like that. You had a weapon they'd take you away. But first they'd just stand there and watch.' Even more than Mr Justice Salmon's sentences he resented chasing after a coloured man with a mob, only to be peppered with milk bottles by West Indians on a roof-top. It infuriates him to see coloured men fight back.

'That's why I'm with the Fascists,' he says. 'They're against the blacks. That Salmon, he's a Communist. The Labour Party is Communist too. Like the unions.' His mother and father, he says, are strict Labour supporters. Is he against the Labour Party? 'Nah, I'm for them. They're for y'know – us. I'm for the unions too.' Even though they were dominated by Communists? 'Sure,' he says. 'I like the Communist Party. It's powerful, like.' How can he be for the

Communists when the Fascists hate them?

Len says, 'Well, y'know, I'm for the Fascists when they're against the nigs. But the Fascists is really for the rich people y'know, like the Tories. All for the guv'nors, people like that. But the Communists are very powerful.' I told him the Communist Party of Britain was quite small.

'But,' he says, 'they got Russia behind them.' His voice is full of marvel. 'I admire Russia. Y'know, the people. They're peaceful. They're strong. When they say they'll do a thing, they do it. Not like us. Makes you think: they got a weapon over there can wipe us all out, with one wave of a general's arm. Destroy us completely and totally. Honest, those Russians. When they say they'll do a thing, they do it. Like in Hungary, I pity those people, the Hungarians. But did you see the Russians went in and stopped them. Tanks. Not like us in Cyprus. Our soldiers get shot in the back and what do we do? The Communists is for the small man.'

Dave and Ginger come back in time to hear Len say, 'Them Royals. I'd like to murder them.' Dave and Ginger are profoundly shocked. Dave puts in, 'Nah, why d'you want to say that, Len?' 'Yeah,' says Ginger, 'the Queen's O.K.' Before Len can reply, they quickly wander off to the men's room. They cannot bear to hear Len's reasons. Len puts it to me: 'Would you like havin' all that royalty? Usin' up our money for polo and yachts and goin' round just doin' nothing. It's all for show. We don't need them.' I ask Len if he thinks it will be quiet now at Notting Hill. 'Yeah,' he says, 'it's all over.' A moment later he says, 'As long as the nigs stay there'll be trouble.' Will he be one of the ones to make it? 'No,' he says. 'Well, maybe, you never can tell. Why can't they be just like the Paddies. Just come here and work. They're good workers, those Paddies.'

It's warm in the café, and Len and I stand outside the doorway. I tell Len I hear he writes plays. He smiles shyly. 'Just two,' he says. 'Second one ain't finished. I ...' he shrugs, 'trouble is ... I can't write. It's hard, like.' He is embarrassed. I say that I would like to see one of his plays. He goes into the café and comes out bearing a manuscript. It is crudely typed and enclosed in professional folder-covers. 'I paid to have that done,' he says.

On the street corner, in the glow of the lamp, I read the play. It is about an English pilot who crash-lands his plane in the jungle. Aboard are a judge, a movie star, a headmaster, a company director and a policeman. It becomes necessary for them to eat one another for survival. Only the pilot survives, a young, almost teen-age pilot. When he gets back to England he must stand trial for manslaughter, a martyr. Most of the play is concerned with the pilot conducting his own defence and explaining why he found it necessary to eat parts of the judge, the movie star, the headmaster, the company director and the policeman.

Clancy Sigal, 4 October 1958

PAUL JOHNSON's furious mode again: one of the most enjoyably savage verbal assaults in modern British journalism lands on the Conservative Party at Blackpool.

Rule Like Pigs

More than any other town in England, what matters in Blackpool is people: the vast, vulgar, guzzling, uproarious hordes which swarm in annually from the great industrial towns of the north and midlands. Without people, Blackpool is just an obscene shell of desolate boarding houses and shuttered arcades, an abandoned, ransacked ghost-town waiting for the miracle of Spring. So I found it last week. The Big Dipper was still. Montmartre in Blackpool ('The Show They Tried to Close') was locked-up and silent; so was The Strangest Girl in the World ('It Was All Her Father's Fault'). Along the gigantic promenade a bitter wind whipped up discarded ice-cream papers and the relics of funny hats. At the end of the deserted North Pier, a handful of old men and boys fished pessimistically into an angry sea. 'It's no use', said one of the old men philosophically, 'they've all gone' – as if the fish, too, abandoned Blackpool with the October gales.

But weren't the Tories there? Of course: 10,000 of them, including camp followers; not enough to fill Blackpool, but enough to make it seem inhabited, one would have thought. And yet the ghosts remained unexorcised: in some curious way, the Tory militants, though undoubtedly human beings, are not people. This may seem a perverse remark. The Tories claim to be a national party, above sectional interests, and in a sense they are right. Many millions of Britons, from retired sergeant majors to frail widows living on £2 10s. a week, vote Tory because they think they are voting for England. Tory delegates, when they claim to speak for their country, are not trying to kid anyone, least of all themselves.

During the last ten years, too, the upper-class impedimenta – 'the second magnum and the third cigar, the chauffeur kept waiting at the door till dawn', as Evelyn Waugh put it – have been swept away, or at any rate tidied out of sight. I saw only one Rolls last week, and not a single Brigade tie. True, the platform is still unmistakably Old Etonian, with more than a hint of strawberry leaves (its solitary trade unionist looked as if he had contracted out not merely of the political levy, but of life itself). But in the great body of the hall, it is possible to explore all the myriad ramifications of the British middle class: near-gentry and near-proletarians, provincial barristers with strange accents, military gents with limps acquired in India and the East, bumptious young men from LSE and the anonymous regiment of the minor public schools, young girls training to be air hostesses and gym mistresses, matrons in hand-knitted cardigans, clutching huge, bursting handbags – even a Tory teddy-boy, with Brando cut, check drapes and an exquisite pale-blue tie. Not a party of wealth or privilege, by any means.

But a cross-section of England? Only in a strictly limited sense. The Tory militants offer an image of England, but it is a distorted one: an image of our prejudices and our atavisms, our unreasoning acceptance of unproved truths, because they are comfortable and established, our dislike of controversy, our unwillingness to ask questions when we know the answers may be unpleasant – all the factors which militate against independent intellectual inquiry. Conservatism, in fact, is an authoritarian church of platitudes, a party of proverbs. 'Spare the rod and spoil the child', 'A bird in the hand is worth two in the bush', 'More haste, less speed' – such maxims, which seem incontrovertible until one begins to think about them, evoked roars of approval last week. Indeed, a lady delegate even coined a new one: 'A flogging today may save a hanging tomorrow' – and this went down well, too. This is England, of course, but it is only part of England: the English id, magnified out of all proportion, dominating the whole. The Tories, in short, are atrophied Englishmen, lacking certain moral and intellectual reflexes. They are recognisable, homely – even, on occasions, endearing – but liable to turn very nasty at short notice.

Now the Tory leadership knows this perfectly well, and they are getting some pretty shrewd advice from the Berkeley Square publicity experts on how to handle the problem. Sailing serenely towards their third election victory, they must at all cost make people forget that they still carry a flick-knife. Last week, the Tory catchword was 'civilised'. 'The British,' Lord Hailsham intoned, 'are a highly civilised and very sophisticated people, and we are a very British party.' This being the slogan, the debates required a good deal of stage-managing to make it seem true. Knowing that the old beast had to roar sometime, the platform skilfully threw a few tasty, but safe, morsels into the cage. There was a good howl over Iceland, a screech for Mrs Castle, an ovation for our boys in Cyprus. The flogging debate posed a problem, but the platform dealt with it in masterful fashion. It was pared down to an hour, fixed for a time when most of the nice, savage old ladies are thinking of tea and crumpets, introduced by a singularly dull and dim delegate, and concluded by Mr Butler with such skill that the hall gave him an ovation for his harmless suggestion that, if more corporal punishment were needed, then perhaps it had better be administered by parents.

And, to let off the remaining steam, on Saturday morning Hailsham treated the conference to the most accomplished piece of oratorical demagogy since Nasser's Suez Canal speech, which brought delegates roaring to their feet, but which was confined throughout to such harmless objectives as 'storming the robber castle of Socialism' – whatever that may mean. By lunchtime, with the special trains already lined up at Blackpool Central, and with only Harold's ovation to come, the party managers were breathing well-earned sighs of relief.

But, as they should have known, the flick-knives had to come out sometime; and it happened at the worst possible moment. As the clock ticked towards two, the Winter Garden filled to bursting, and Reg Dixon at the organ regaled the happy, relaxed delegates with tunes from an age when the Union Jack really mattered: 'Daisy, Daisy', 'If You Were the Only Girl in the World', and 'Pack Up Your Troubles'. The Tories, indeed, had already packed up their bags and were waiting only for the ritual genuflection to the leader. The choice greenery and chintz which once separated platform from delegates had been removed, and there sat all the assistant masters beaming benignly, with Dame Florence Elliot, the matron, suitably playing the fool. Promptly, as the clock struck two, the head arrived, the whole school rose and caps were flung high.

Then it happened. As conquering Harold rose to speak, there came a first blast of the trumpet from the gallery, and the old, familiar battle cry of the League of Empire Loyalists. The sheer caddishness of letting off a stink bomb on speech day froze the audience with horror; ample bosoms and manly chests heaved with indignation as the scoundrel was dragged off. By the time the second interruption came, horror had turned to fury: a group of delegates held the intruder's arms while a military gent smashed his fist in his face. The third was flung over his seat, had his face kicked and was dragged out moaning. Another – a middle-aged woman – was punched in the chest and hauled along by the hair by delegates who, forty-eight hours before, had shouted their indignation at attacks on defenceless women. Yet another was dragged, screaming for the police, behind locked doors and detained for some minutes: his bloodstains spotted the stairs. The Old Adam, the secret little Tory hobgoblin, had come out with a vengeance.

In that disturbing little play, *Live Like Pigs*, the author subtly hints that what makes the respectable council estate tenants fear and hate the awful family which has moved in among them is their unconscious realisation that the Sawney family exhibits, in a vastly magnified form, all the degrading instincts which they themselves possess. The Sawneys personify, and finally unleash, the forces of anarchy lying dormant around them. When the outraged housewives storm their house, Col Sawney, peering through the keyhole at the oncoming hordes, cries out in fear 'They're not people, they're bloody *animals!*' Last Saturday; the political Sawneys exposed Conservative civilization for the shabby and dangerous myth that it is. And afterwards, a battered Loyalist, still trembling with shock, told me: 'Communists, Socialist, Liberals – they're nothing by comparison. Them Tories, they're bloody *savages!*'

I left the Winter Gardens as soon as possible, and came upon a scene of strange transformation. While we had been listening to Hailsham and Macmillan, great convoys of coaches had been steadily streaming into Blackpool from all points of the compass, bringing with them joyful, earthy battalions from Stoke and Oldham, from Manchester, Liverpool and Sheffield, from St Helens and Bradford. The Golden Mile was lit up, the pin-tables whirred, Montmartre in Paris was packed, the piers blazed, the Strangest Girl was revealing her charms again. They were only half-day trippers up to see the illuminations, but they were people. As the Tory trains steamed magisterially away, Blackpool came alive again.

Paul Johnson, 18 October 1958

Another long-running New Statesman *campaign was that against the death penalty. Novelist and art critic JOHN BERGER evoked the barbarity of judicial killing more effectively than any more conventional polemic could have done.*

Dear Sir ...

You have now been condemned to death. The following hints are for your guidance during the days or hours that are pending.

(1) Try not to dwell on the past. The dead cannot be brought back to life. Aim at considering the future. The part which you are to play has an important social function. You are to be made an example to others.

(2) Bear in mind that the warders of Her Majesty's prisons are there to help you. It is impossible for you to carry out your appointed task alone and without aid.

(3) The routine of the death cell has been planned on an assessment of your own needs. It has been found that a fixed routine both makes the time go quicker and encourages prisoners to maintain self-respect. It is for this reason that you are asked to wash, shave and keep yourself neat.

(4) Remember that your sentence has a time-honoured tradition behind it. You are in no sense being used as part of an experiment. You are following in the footsteps of thousands of others.

(5) It is hoped that you will ask yourself whether you cannot forgive those responsible for ordering and carrying out your punishment. Do not forget that they have no personal choice in the matter and that on a social and national level there are circumstances in which the taking of life is a legitimate form of self-defence.

(6) Be grateful that you have been tried in the Free World in the 20th century. You have had the benefit of a just trial and have not fallen a victim to mob law based on superstition and propaganda. You can be proud of your trial.

(7) If directly or indirectly you are approached by the press, legal advice is available to you. Publicity does not always serve your interests. Many have found strength in silence.

   Do Not in Any Way Foul or Deface the Walls of Your Cell.

John Berger, 21 May 1960

PART FOUR

◆

1960–1974

WITHDRAWAL SYMPTOMS : TIME FOR A FIX

Horner, 5 February 1971

Kingsley Martin finally left the Statesman *editorship after thirty years in 1960. Some said that he had stayed too long for his or the paper's good, but none the less leaving was intensely painful for him and he left a gap that could not, perhaps, wholly be filled by any successor. Certainly John Freeman never stamped his personality – by all accounts a rather reserved and formal one – on the journal in anything like the same way. Under Freeman, Paul Johnson and Richard Crossman, and despite Johnson's bursts of enthusiasm for such causes as the revolutionary students of May 1968, the* NS *was widely seen to have become more conservative, more staid, more closely tied to the Labour Party and its leaders. Crossman's editorship, in particular, was criticised for excessive preoccupation with Transport House (the then Labour HQ) and Westminster. Circulation fell sharply, though to be fair one should point out that all 'serious' weeklies were losing readers fast at this time.*

Still, the cultural coverage was as rich, varied and exciting as ever, and began to broaden out to include mass media, popular and vernacular cultures in a serious way: and outside contributors could always inject fire, as did the venerable BERTRAND RUSSELL with his appeal for mass civil disobedience against nuclear weapons.

Civil Disobedience

There are two different kinds of conscientious civil disobedience. There is disobedience to a law specifically commanding an action which some people profoundly believe to be wicked. The most important example of this case in our time is conscientious objection. This, however, is not the kind of civil disobedience which is now in question.

The second kind of civil disobedience, which is the one that I wish to consider, is its employment with a view to causing a change in the law or in public policy. In this aspect, it is a means of propaganda, and there are those who consider that it is an undesirable kind. Many, however, of whom I am one, think it to be now necessary.

Many people hold that law-breaking can never be justified in a democracy, though they concede that under any other form of government it may be a duty. The victorious governments, after the Second World War, reprobated, and even punished, Germans for not breaking the law when the law commanded atrocious actions. I do not see any logic which will prove either that a democratic government cannot command atrocious actions or that, if it does, it is wrong to disobey its commands.

Democratic citizens are for the most part busy with their own affairs and cannot study difficult questions with any thoroughness. Their opinions are formed upon such information as is easily accessible, and the Authorities can, and too often do, see to it that such information is misleading. When I speak of the Authorities, I do not think only of the politicians, whether in office or in opposition, but equally their technical advisers, the popular press, broadcasting and television and, in the last resort, the police. These forces are, at present, being used to prevent the democracies of western countries from knowing the truth about nuclear weapons. The examples are so numerous that a small selection must suffice.

I should advise optimists to study the report of the committee of experts appointed by the Ohio State University to consider the likelihood of accidental war, and also the papers by distinguished scientists in the proceedings of Pugwash Conferences. Mr Oskar Morgenstern, a politically orthodox American defence expert, in an article reprinted in *Survival*, Volume II, Number Four, says: 'The probability of thermonuclear war's occurring appears to be significantly larger than the probability of its not occurring.' Sir Charles Snow says: 'Speaking as responsibly as I can, within, at the most, ten years from now, some of these bombs are going off. That is the certainty' (*The Times*, 28 December 1960). The last two include intended as well as accidental wars.

The causes of unintended war are numerous and have already on several occasions very nearly resulted in disaster. The moon, at least once, and flights of geese, repeatedly, have been mistaken for Russian missiles. Nevertheless, not long ago, the Prime Minister, with pontifical dogmatism, announced that there will be no war by accident. Whether he believed what he said, I do not know. If he did, he is ignorant of things which it is his duty to know. If he did not believe what he said, he was guilty of the abominable crime of luring mankind to its extinction by promoting groundless hopes.

Take, again, the question of British unilateralism. There is an entirely sober case to be made for this policy, but the misrepresentations of opponents, who command the main organs of publicty, have made it very difficult to cause this case to be known. For example, the Labour correspondent of one of the supposedly most liberal of the daily papers wrote an article speaking of opposition to unilateralism as 'the voice of sanity'. I wrote a letter in reply, arguing that, on the contrary, sanity was on the side of the unilateralists and hysteria on the side of their opponents. This the newspaper refused to print. Other unilateralists have had similar experiences.

Or consider the question of American bases in Britain. Who knows that within each of them there is a hard kernel consisting of the airmen who can respond to an alert and are so highly trained that they can be in the air within a minute or two? This kernel is kept entirely isolated from the rest of the camp, which is not admitted to it. It has its own mess, dormitories, libraries, cinemas, etc., and there are armed guards to prevent other Americans in the base camp from having access to it. Every month or two, everybody in it, including the Commander, is flown back to America and replaced by a new group. The men in this inner kernel are allowed almost no contact with the other Americans in the base camp and no contact whatever with any of the inhabitants of the neighbourhood.

It seems clear that the whole purpose is to keep the British ignorant and to preserve, among the personnel of the kernel, that purely mechanical response to orders and propaganda for which the whole of their training is designed. Moreover, orders to this group do not come from the Commandant, but direct from Washington. To suppose that at a crisis the British government can have any control over the orders sent from Washington is pure fantasy. It is obvious that at any moment orders might be sent from Washington which would lead to reprisals by the Soviet forces and to the extermination of the population of Britain within an hour.

The situation of these kernel camps seems analogous to that of the Polaris submarines. It will be remembered that the Prime Minister said that there would be consultation between the US and the UK governments before a Polaris missile if fired, and that the truth of his statement was denied by the US government. All this, however, is unknown to the non-political public.

To make known the facts which show that the life of every inhabitant of Britain, old and young, man, woman and child, is at every moment in imminent danger and that this danger is caused by what is mis-named defence and immensely aggravated by every measure which governments pretend will diminish it – to make this known has seemed to some of us an imperative duty which were must pursue with whatever means are at our command. The Campaign for Nuclear Disarmament has done and is doing valuable and very successful work in this direction, but the press is becoming used to its doings and beginning to doubt their news value. It has therefore seemed to some of us necessary to supplement its campaign by such actions as the press is sure to report.

There is another, and perhaps even more important reason, for the practice of civil disobedience in this time of utmost peril. There is a very widespread feeling that the individual is impotent against governments, and that, however bad their policies may be, there is nothing effective that private people can do about it. This is a complete mistake. If all those who disapprove of government policy were to join in massive demonstrations of civil disobedience, they could render governmental folly impossible and compel the so-called statesmen to acquiesce in measures that would make human survival possible. Such a vast movement, inspired by outraged public opinion, is possible; perhaps it is imminent. If you join it, you will be doing something important to preserve your family, friends, compatriots, and the world.

An extraordinarily interesting case which illustrates the power of the Establishment, at any rate in America, is that of Claude Eatherly, who dropped the bomb on Hiroshima. His case also illustrates that in the modern world it often happens that only by breaking the law can a man escape from committing atrocious crimes. He was not told what the bomb would do and was utterly horrified when he discovered the consequences of his act. He has devoted himself throughout many years to various kinds of civil disobedience with a view to calling attention to the atrocity of nuclear weapons and to expiating the sense of guilt which, if he did not act, would weigh him down. The Authorities have decided that he is to be considered mad, and a board of remarkably conformist psychiatrists have endorsed that official view. Eatherly is repentant and certified; Truman is unrepentant and uncertified. I have seen a number of Eatherly's statements explaining his motives. These statements are entirely sane. But such is the power of mendacious publicity that almost everyone, including myself, believed that he had become a lunatic.

In our topsy-turvy world those who have power of life and death over the whole human species are able to persuade almost the whole population of the countries which nominally enjoy freedom of the press and of publicity that any man who considers the preservation of human life a thing of value must be mad. I shall not be surprised if my last years are spent in a lunatic asylum – where I shall enjoy the company of all who are capable of feelings of humanity.

Bertrand Russell, 17 February 1961

*The Beats formed probably the last Western subcultural movement
which was not specifically a youth culture, and which was based around
literature more than music. The splendid American jazz critic RALPH J.
GLEASON, later to be born again as a psychedelic rock enthusiast,
mourned their passing.*

Begone, Dull Beats

A full U.S. Grant beard, luxurious and flecked with grey, provided Bill
the Beatnik with a supplementary income during his several years in
San Francisco's North Beach neighbourhood, home of the original
Beats.

Photographed – for a fee – by a tourist against the wall of the Co-
Existence Bagel Shop, the Coffee Gallery or any telephone pole on
Grant Avenue, Bill was the living symbol of modern American urban
dissent, proof positive to the folks back home that the tourist had seen
a Beatnik in the flesh.

Last year Bill went to Veterans' Hospital for repairs. He came back
to the Beach this spring, his beard a hospital casualty. But it didn't
matter really because, for Bill, North Beach is now a strange and lonely
land. The tourists still throng the streets, but the regulars have gone like
the ferries from the Bay. 'What happened? Everybody's split.' Bill
complained on his first night back On the Scene: 'All the joints are
closed. Where's everybody?' Now beardless. Bill is no longer even in
demand as a model. 'There's nothing to do but sit in somebody's car
and dig the tourists,' he says resignedly.

Bill's dilemma symbolises what has happened to North Beach,
locale of Beat Generation literature from Kerouac and Ginsberg to *The
Connection.* The Beatnik in his native form has all but disappeared
from its alleys and cafés, like the Model T Ford from the roads of the
US. When you see a Model T now, it's owned by a vintage car club
member. Any surviving Beatnik on the Beach belongs to the
entrepreneurial minority, making a living off the tourists, selling sandals
or running guided tours for Little Old Ladies from Dubuque. Or they
are amateur Beats, fleeing part-time a dull office.

The situation illustrates a sort of Gresham's Law of sociology which
was once articulated by a New Orleans madame named Countess Willi
Piazza. Some 40 years ago she dramatised a not entirely different
amateur-professional dichotomy when she remarked: 'The country club
girls are ruining my business.' Madame Piazza's territory of non-
conformity, Storyville, and Beatnik-land met the same fate. They
attracted too much publicity and too many amateurs – and the cops

closed them down. The week-end commuters to Bohemia and the tourists increased in strength until the San Francisco police reacted. North Beach, like Storyville, had, in the words of the Beat hipsters, 'blown its cool'.

The great diaspora began like chunks of ice slipping away from an iceberg entering warm waters, a few at a time and then a grand rush. They went to Big Sur, to Monterey, down the coast to Santa Monica and Venice: westward. They moved to other neighbourhoods in San Francisco – the Fillmore, Potrero and Russian Hills. They went up-coast to Bolinas and inland to the Sierra. Mostly they went to New York.

Kerouac and Ginsberg had already left by the time the tourists and the amateurs took over (though both returned for brief visits in 1960). Bob Kaufman, known as Bomkauf and author of the Abominist Manifesto, went to New York; Pierre deLattre, the Beatnik priest, whose Bread-and-Wine Mission was a landmark but is now a laundromat ('Pierre got tired of being a housemother to the Beats, on call any hour of the night'), went to the country to write a novel. Grant Avenue now is as dark and lonesome at night as any neighbourhood street. The Cassandra (Zen soup – 20 cents) is a record store; The Place is an art-goods shop; the Coffee Gallery is open only occasionally ('They have events now,' an old timer says disgustedly); the Co-Existence Bagel Shop is a sandals-and-jewellery shop, and the Jazz Cellar is dark and empty.

The end was really heralded when the whole of Grant Avenue burst into brief flame last year with a series of tourist traps. The Surplus Store added berets and turtleneck sweaters to its staples of sweatshirts, blue jeans and GI clothing. A leather-goods shop offered 'sandals for beatnik dogs'. Henri Lenoir hired Hube-the-Cube Leslie, one of the authentic originals, who in recent years had existed at survival level by serving as a human guinea-pig at hospital laboratories, to sit in the window of the Café Vesuvio, an earnest of the café's authenticity.

The City Lights Bookstore, owned by poet-businessman Lawrence Ferlinghetti, and featuring an extraordinary collection of paper-back books and magazines, began to remain open to two and three o'clock in the morning. 'The tourists buy books all night,' says Shig Mauro, whose corduroy jacket and full beard behind the counter fit the late-night bookstore mood.

The Place, which originated Blabbermouth Night, where the customers could rise and speak at will, was the first to topple. Leo Kerkorian, the owner, recalls it as 'the kind of a joint where I had a bartender once took off his pants and worked all night with no pants. Some places he couldn't do that but in my place it was all right.'

The Co-Existence Bagel Shop lasted until this winter when, under continual police harassment (once a cop even ripped down a poem from the window), its proprietor, Jay Hoppe, universally known as Jay Bagel, gave up. Jay Bagel is only one of the colourful names of Beats. Others are Reverend Bob, Dr Fric-Frac, Linda Lovely, Barbara Nookie, Mad Marie, Lady Joan, Big Rose, Groover Wailin', Taylor Maid and The Wig.

'I'm tired of dealing with a psychopathic police department,' Hoppe said when he closed the Bagel Shop and left town. Hoppe also credits the police with being the basic cause of the others leaving. 'Bob Kaufman gave up when he was arrested on his birthday,' Hoppe says. 'Everybody got tired of being rousted by the cops. In New York City, San Francisco poets are treated like visiting celebrities.'

But the tourists still come; and Bill the Beatnik, a vestigial remnant of a departed era, alternates between parked cars in the day and the window of the grocery store on Broadway, across from the Expense Account Row of restaurants, at night. 'They got TV in here,' he says, 'and I can watch it with one eye and catch the Passing Parade with the other. But it's not like it was. All the old-timers are gone and the cops never bother the tourists.'

Ralph J. Gleason, 2 June 1961

Literate football stars are like hens' teeth. Witty ones are like roosters' dentures. DANNY BLANCHFLOWER, regular NS sports columnist for several years, was crowing all the way to the dentist. Here he reflects on the origins of soccer.

The Skull Game

Once upon a time some whiskered gentlemen in top-hats and hansom-cabs flitted through the gaslit streets of London on their way to a rather important meeting at a tavern in Lincoln's Inn Fields. It was on Monday, 26 October 1863, to be exact, and they met to form the Football Association. Now, as part of the centenary celebrations, a couple of official FA publications tell the whole story. In *100 Years of Soccer in Pictures* the camera's eye recalls the long trousers, the big boots, the changing landscapes and faces and fashions. Thrown in under the caption 'Some Important Events' is a running glossary of bits of information such as that in 1873 the Cup Final had a morning kick-

off to allow the teams to see the Boat Race, while in 1890 the FA ruled
that football on skates was not contrary to the laws. In *A Century of
Soccer* Terence Delaney covers a lot of old ground tracking the early
beginnings of the game and some aspects of its growth and influence
around the world. But perhaps you haven't heard that it might have
been the Roman soldiers who first brought the game here or that faint
evidence traces it back to the ancient Chinese dynasties or that it might
all have started with cave-men kicking human skulls around. Anyway it
certainly took a pace forward with the arrival of the public school
system in England. Each school fashioned its own rules and style to suit
its surroundings – confined cloisters or open fields. But when the
different partisans gathered at the universities they found the need for a
common set of rules. And so in time this led to the Football
Association.

Terence Delaney, an aspiring lover of the game, flatters the rare
evidence and fact with much speculation. But nobody could deny him
the liberty because the game is wrapped in illusion and exaggeration.
The mysterious magnetism of a bounding ball ... as I leafed through the
pages of these books I continually found my imagination wandering.
Every Saturday afternoon a crowd begins to gather. It trickles, then
swells, throbbing expectantly as it crocodiles through clicking turnstiles.
It is a passionate crowd with something to care for, a crowd that knows
the feelings of anguish and joy. They want their team to win because its
winning is evidence of their own prowess, it demonstrates their vitality,
upholds their beliefs and proves their judgment. If cricket is a
conservative's game, then soccer is for socialists. And perhaps the day
will come when the *News of the World* will carry on its front page a
picture of Harold Wilson in soccer togs. This is the game of the working
classes. Perhaps that is why it has such strong support all over the
world. It is a simple game, though the skills are intricate. Its actions are
clearly defined and easy to appreciate, though the patterns it assumes
are utterly complex. There are countless permutations of movement.
The whole spectacle is like a gigantic kaleidoscope: the ball is the
magnet and the two teams are the revolving particles. Every shuffle is
fraught with human error, with uncertainty and excitement. Each game,
related to other games in other towns, is a sequel in a series of
melodramas, all part of one greater drama. How do you sum up a
hundred years of that?

One Thursday night at a mental institution somewhere in Scotland
the staff had a meeting. The inmates were getting completely out of
hand. One of the staff suggested a new game, which he called football.
They tried it the following day, picking two teams from the inmates,
and it was a success. So fascinating was the game that the staff wanted

to play it themselves. Saturday was their half-day so they chose teams. But what to do with the patients? They decided to rope them in to watch. The match took place that Saturday afternoon and the lunatics stood around and gave vent to their feelings. And that's the way it's been ever since.

Danny Blanchflower, 25 October 1963

John F. Kennedy seemed to epitomise much of what the early sixties NS felt itself to stand for. However illusory the image thus projected of the President who took the US into Vietnam, the Bay of Pigs and the Cuban Missile Crisis, KARL MEYER's elegy for what might have been remains moving.

History as Tragedy

John F. Kennedy died a mortal on Friday and was already a legend when he was buried on Monday in a ceremony that strangely mixed tenderness and dignity. The princes and presidents lent pomp to the final rites and the demeanour of his widow was, as one reporter wrote, like that of a queen in classic tragedy. But what made the funeral unbearably moving was the uncounted tens of thousands of young people who came from afar as if by invisible command to Washington. At freezing dawn on Monday, they formed most of a line far more than a mile long of those waiting to pass the President's coffin in the dimly lit dome of the Capitol. Until one stood with them, it was impossible fully to grasp what President Kennedy meant to the generation for which he spoke.

For four days, beginning on Friday, television carried nothing but news about Mr Kennedy's death, and for once without commercial interruptions. As from another world, there were glimpses of Dallas and that city's slack-jawed police, then the funeral itself, endless panel discussions, and throughout the tolling of bells and the muffled beat of drums. Friends sought each other's warmth; floors were littered with newspapers; there was a mingled sense of incredulity, indignation and remorse as most of us became aware in Washington how much we had taken for granted the singular man in the White House.

So soon afterwards, how can one pick up the fragments and make of them a meaningful pattern? Yet surely there is one – the theme of

violence, both domestic and international. The circumstances of his
death were ironic enough – a sniper's bullet at high noon, fired by a
madman, brought down a President who sought to make sanity and
realism the core of his political philosophy. But even more ironic, the
murder of this gifted man may make it possible for his far less imposing
successor to approach unexpected greatness by carrying out the
Kennedy programme.

JFK: Nunc Dimittis

He came in with a snowstorm, and the setting was flawlessly right on
Inauguration Day, 20 January 1961. There was no premonition of
tragedy, but rather a sense of rebirth in a capital mantled in beauty as
the oldest President yielded power to the youngest man ever elected
Chief Executive of the United States. More than a change of
administrations, it was a change of generations, a change of outlook –
and most immediately apparent, a change of style. When John
Fitzgerald Kennedy was sworn in, he appeared to fulfil Robert Frost's
augury that an age of poetry and power was commencing in
Washington. But the poetry is now hushed, and the promise of power
wisely used is now an unfinished chapter in a volume entitled. 'Let Us
Begin ...' None of us suspected that in retrospect the Inaugural snow
would seem as a shroud.

It is too early to fix Mr Kennedy's place in history because so much
of what he initiated was left for others to complete. But two of his
achievements seem likely to take root. He was not a man given to easy
commitments, but before his death he embarked on two major ventures
– for the first time in this century, he placed the power and might of his
office behind a dispossessed race whose second-class status demeaned
all citizens; at the same time, he took the world to the precipice of a
war but followed his unexampled personal triumph by deeds intended
to eliminate the risk of a holocaust through madness or miscalculation.
The special pathos of his death is that he seemed on the verge of
broadening his commitment.

Something else, however, is irretrievably lost – the brilliance of his
presence, the glow of his style. To Americans like myself who were
near to his age, he renewed our pride in our country and gave a dignity
to the political calling. If we fretted at his failures and reproached him
for his excessive caution, it was because he seemed more a brother than
father, and because we judged him in terms of his capacity for greater
things. His unfailing wit, which he could turn on himself, his literacy,
his physical grace and his sense of history were part of a harmonious
whole. By virtue of television, and his superb performance at press

conferences, he became in life an intensely personal figure to millions; in death he leaves a mournful void.

A prodigious reader, he cherished not only learning, but the learned. His ideal of government seemed to be half academy, half precinct-headquarters. He opened the White House to anybody who could impart a ferment and his good humour as a host was legend. His favourite biography was Lord David Cecil's *Melbourne*, and the choice tells a good deal about the strengths and weaknesses of his self-definition. Like the urbane Whigs of Melbourne's age, he blended a studied detachment, broad if conventional interest in the arts, moderate liberalism, family pride and belief in reason. It is savage irony that this child of the Enlightenment was cut down by the very fanaticism that he sought to contain. The cause for which he stood remains in doubt, and the last page of his biography must be written with what Virgil called the tears of things.

Karl E. Meyer, 29 November 1963

If there were to be a competition for the most ferocious, and funniest, NS *attack on Toryism, MALCOLM MUGGERIDGE would be contending closely against Johnson and Mallalieu.*

Thirteen Years Soft

Looking back on 13 years of Conservative rule, now, as we must all hope, drawing to its close, and on the men – Churchill, Eden, Macmillan, Home – who have ruled over us since October 1951, there is little that is memorable in the record, except the Suez fiasco and the Profumo scandal; two episodes which they, certainly, would prefer should be forgotten. How, one wonders, did they employ their time?

Baldwin used to disconcert the more earnest among his supporters by sitting for hours and hours on the government front bench, apparently dozing or turning over the pages of a magazine. Churchill's mental powers were already seriously impaired when he came to form his postwar government. In conversation, one of his visitors told me, he was liable to confuse the 1939–45 war with with 1914–18 one. Macmillan, one gathers, was always surprisingly available. Visitors would find him sitting ruminatively before an empty desk. Certainly, he never lacked time for one of those meandering historical disquisitions which so tried the patience of his colleagues, and reduced Americans to a condition of frenzied boredom (Thus Kennedy, at the Bermuda Conference, in desperation was reduced to passing a note to one of his aides, telling him at all costs to intercept Macmillan's relentless flow.) Even Home, who as far as paperwork is concerned is what French schoolmasters call a *retardataire*, has been able to absent himself from Downing Street for a good proportion of his short period of office without, apparently, suffering any ill consequences. There seems to have been no particular need for him.

Few can have supposed, when Churchill formed his 1951 government, that it represented anything but a transient arrangement. The majority was tenuous; the names of the ministers, as they were announced in little batches, were far from reassuring, especially when it became clear that Churchill was hankering after a revival of his wartime overlord arrangement, with outsiders like Lord Leathers supervising the work of the regular politicians. Stories abounded of how incomprehensible appointments were made (for instance, Manningham-Buller's as Solicitor-General) because Churchill forgot faces and muddled up names. Men called to Downing Street found themselves addressed as someone else, and some, though they served in his ministry, never did succeed in establishing in the mind of the Prime Minister who they actually were.

Both in the manner of its formation and in its conduct of affairs, this government was a shambles such as has rarely, if ever, existed before. It has largely escaped criticism because of the Churchill legend. Like an Anglican clergyman turning to the altar and intoning: 'Now to God the Father ...' on completion of his sermon, it is part of the Conservative ritual to proclaim at some point in a discourse that Churchill is the greatest living Englishman. If he is the greatest living Englishman, clearly he cannot, on the record of his postwar administration, have been one of the worst of modern Prime Ministers.

After the war, the Conservatives were stuck with Churchill, and in private groaned over the weight of the burden. They never liked him, and when he led them to overwhelming defeat in 1945 their dislike and distrust, submerged in the war years under mountains of sycophancy and adulation, came to the surface again. As Leader of the Opposition he gave them little joy. In the only private conversation I ever had with Eden, in 1951, he remarked bitterly that Churchill might yet keep Labour in office a little longer.

For the Conservatives, getting Churchill out once he had formed his postwar government was a major operation. He wanted at all costs to go on having the diversion of his dispatch boxes – his toys, as he called them. The Conservative party-machinemen, however ardently they longed for him to go, could not admit as much in public. The choicest and largest collection of abusive communications I received when I was editor of *Punch* was as a result of a cartoon suggesting that Churchill was unfit to go on being Prime Minister – a proposition taken for granted in the conversation of most of his colleagues, as well as at most Conservative dinner-tables.

In assiduously hanging on, Churchill was helped by the fact that his chosen successor was Eden, who was disliked by quite a few Conservatives and despised by many more. This may have been why Churchill was so strong for Eden to be accepted as his successor, even though, in private, he seldom troubled to hide his poor opinion of him. He may well have calculated that, if the alternative to him was Eden, he might reasonably expect to remain in office for the maximum possible time; no one was going to turn him out to put Eden in. If this was his calculation, it proved in the end mistaken. Eden, then in possession of his faculties such as they were, was preferred to Churchill with his in disarray. In the end, Churchill was told in the bluntest and most brutal terms that he had to go. In the context of British politics, it must almost have been like getting rid of Stalin. Nor would it surprise me if, as with Stalin, a mood of de-Churchillisation of the Conservative Party were, in due course, to set in. Indeed, there are signs of it already.

At long last Eden's moment came, and he moved into Downing Street, the previous incumbent having been given a big send-off on the occasion of his 80th birthday. It must be maddening for Eden today to reflect that if, instead of embarking on his fatuous Suez adventure, he had followed the normal Conservative routine and just done nothing about anything, he would probably be Prime Minister today and about to go to the country for yet another renewal of his mandate.

Precisely why he should not have run true to form is still a matter of dispute. I suspect myself that the basic reason was a desire to demonstrate that, contrary to the prevailing opinion, he too, could be a man of destiny – like Churchill, send for his chiefs-of-staff in the middle of the night, study maps, initiate campaigns, and even on occasion defy the White House. Descriptions I have heard of his conduct of the dismal affair of Suez convey an impression of a grisly parody of Churchillian war leadership; of a benzadrine Napoleon and pinchbeck Foreign Office Machiavelli all in one.

Alas, the poor fellow was ill-suited for such desperate courses, and, if a recent work (*Dulles Over Suez* by Professor Herman Finer) is to be believed, burst into a flood of weeping when President Eisenhower rebuked him on the transatlantic telephone. In a matter of months he succeeded in reducing his country to a laughing-stock throughout the world, his government to impotence, his party to confusion, and himself to a condition of nervous prostration, accentuated by excessive doses of sedatives, pep-pills and John Foster Dulles.

The lesson was not lost on his successor, Harold Macmillan. No Conservative Prime Minister, it is safe to predict, will ever again act in defiance of an American President or Secretary of State, or even of the CIA. Nor will one ever again recommend large-scale military operations in defence of imperial interests or positions. To guard against any such possibility the empire has been dismantled. 'I was not appointed to be His Majesty's principal Secretary of State,' Churchill remarked in one of his grandiloquent moods, 'to preside over the dissolution of his empire.' This, had he but known it, was precisely what he had been appointed for. Conservative ladies still sing 'Land of Hope and Glory' at their rallies, without. I should suppose, reflecting that under successive Conservative governments our bounds have been set narrower still and narrower.

Macmillan's choice came as a surprise. Churchill, for some impish reason of his own, or perhaps mistaking Macmillan for Sir John Anderson, sent him first to the Ministry of Housing. One saw him in those days disconsolate in gumboots. Nonetheless, with the expert assistance of Mr Marples, houses were duly built – at a price. Eden, to keep him away from the Foreign Office, sent him to the Treasury. There, initially, he was an ardent supporter of the Suez operation, though subsequently, according to Randolph Churchill's account, one of the decisive voices in calling it off.

After the Suez debauch, Macmillan was a sorely needed prairie oyster. The Conservatives swallowed him, and lo! their shakes subsided, their eyeballs again fitted into the sockets, and those pink elephants which Eden had summoned up mercifully disappeared from view. Telling the Wogs where they got off was all very well at garden fêtes, or at meetings in country schoolrooms across a table adorned with a Union Jack; but for Eden – of all people – to carry matters to the point of actually moving troops about! And then petrol-rationing! And the pound shaky! That would not do at all. What a relief, when Eden mercifully disappeared into the shadows, to be confronted by this genial Scottish publisher, with crofter origins and ducal connections and enough relatives in and around parliament to form a family government, down to the under-secretaries!

Eden had ruled out the field of battle as a sphere of operations for Conservative Prime Ministers, but there remained diplomacy. It was in pursuit of distinction in this field that Macmillan put on his white fur hat and undertook his hilarious visit to Mr Krushchev in Moscow. No one who accompanied him (as I did) is likely to forget the experience; particularly the visit to a collective farm, with Macmillan in a grouse-moor outfit which he had brought with him for such outdoor occasions; and his speech at Kiev, when he recalled how in the 12th century a Ukrainian princess had married into our English royal family, and was not this a happy augury for relations between our two peoples?

With the collapse of the subsequent Summit Conference in Paris, Macmillan had one more try; this time to get into the Common Market. It, too, was a failure, thanks to De Gaulle, who had old scores to settle, dating back to the time when Macmillan was Resident Minister in North Africa. In those far-off days Macmillan had imprudently followed Churchill's example, and treated De Gaulle with lofty condescension. It was a mistake. Condescension, as Talleyrand once remarked of treason, is all a matter of timing.

Summitless in Westminster, and excluded from the Common Market, there seemed no reason why Macmillan should not drift quietly along until in the fullness of time the Garter and an earldom rewarded him for the years of non-endeavour on his country's behalf. It was not to be. Eden came to grief because of a fatal itch to do something about Nasser; Macmillan because of an equally fatal propensity to do nothing about Profumo. The Suez Canal, Lady Eden bitterly complained, had flowed through her drawing-room at Number 10; the flood of rumour and innuendo about ministerial improprieties, it would seem, flowed everywhere else in the kingdom except through Number 10. Eden had to go because he tried, inappropriately and belatedly, to behave like a Kipling short story; Macmillan because he confused trollops with Trollope.

After Suez, the Conservatives were bewildered and in disarray; after the Profumo affair, angry and embittered. In the choosing of a new leader, the pushing and shoving to get to the front took place for once on stage instead of, as is the usual procedure, in the wings. It was not an edifying spectacle, and the resultant choice – a disclaiming 14th earl (truly today whoever would keep his earldom must lose it) – was scarcely calculated to restore morale and win an election.

Yet perhaps the Conservatives chose more wisely than they knew in preferring Home to Butler; Bertie Wooster to Jeeves. As in a game of strip-poker, they have shed everything, down to the jockstrap – empire gone, and Kenyatta and Nkrumah necessarily preferred to Dr Verwoerd and Mr Ian Smith; Britannia no longer ruling the waves, or even Holy Loch; admirals without ships, and missiles from over the water; Conservative freedom too circumscribed to be even mentioned. Better, in such circumstances, a 14th earl who thinks he is fully clothed than wily old Rab prancing about in the nude.

The real harm of this 13 years of Conservative government has been that it has offered the country no sort of purpose, not even a misguided one. It has been a time of political, economic and moral free-wheeling, with the encouragement of every sort of soft indulgence, from betting and bingo to the Beatles. Nothing was said or done by those in authority which could possibly seem worthy of remembering hereafter; they all things common did and mean on that unmemorable scene. The records set up have been in road accidents, hire-purchase, juvenile delinquency and telly-viewing. It is the politics of the trough, into which we, the electorate, are invited to bury our snouts for another five years.

Malcolm Muggeridge, 16 October 1964

The division between the political front half and the literary back part has existed throughout the Statesman*'s history. Often it seems artificial and impoverishing – there are too many people who claim, at least, only to read one or the other. Yet much of* NS*'s best writing has straddled the two, as does CONOR CRUISE O'BRIEN's fine essay on Yeats, and even more* should *do so.*

Yeats and Fascism

What Rough Beast

In the spring and summer of 1933, the fascism of the Irish Blueshirts looked to many people like a possible winner and in this phase Yeats was with the Blueshirts. But the autumn and winter of 1933/34, the government's energetic measures – described by Yeats as 'panic measures' – made it clear that De Valera was no Von Papen. O'Duffy, failing to devise anything effective in reply, revealed that he was no Hitler. The blue began to fade, and Yeats's interest in it faded proportionately.

Commenting on a mildly anti-Blueshirt anecdote in a letter of Yeats, Professor Jeffares says:

> This ironic attitude to the Blueshirts reveals the true Yeats, detached and merely playing with his thoughts, except for the intervals when he wanted to achieve complete directness and accuracy.

The date of the anecdote in question is February 1934, by which date the Blueshirts were beginning to look a little silly. The thoughts Yeats had 'played with' in the days when they had looked possibly formidable were less 'detached'. I cannot see on what grounds we are to regard the Yeats who began to sneer at the Blueshirts when they proved a flop as being more 'real' than the Yeats who was excited about them when he thought they might win. It was the same Yeats, strongly drawn to fascism, but no lover of hopeless causes.

In April 1934 he was still advocating 'force, marching men' to 'break the reign of the mob', but professing, somewhat disingenuously, that 'no such party' as would undertake this work had yet appeared. By August 1934 – when the party for which he had in fact written the songs was on the verge of public disintegration – he had found that that party 'neither could nor would' do what he proposed for it. This, it will be noted, does not amount to a disavowal of the programme of 'force marching men' to 'break the reign of the mob'. The irony and detachment of the poem 'The Church and the State' belong to the period after the final break-up of the Blueshirt movement.

Comment on the question of Yeats's attitude to fascism has been bedevilled by the assumption that a great poet must be, even in politics, 'a nice guy'. If this be assumed then it follows that, as Yeats obviously was a great poet, he cannot *really* have favoured fascism, which is obviously not a nice cause. Thus the critic or biographer is led to postulate a 'true Yeats', so that Yeats's recorded words and actions of fascist character must have been perpetrated by some bogus person with the same name and outward appearance. If one drops the assumption, about poets having always to be nice in politics, then the puzzle disappears, and we see, I believe, that Yeats the man was as near to being a fascist as his situation and the conditions of his own country permitted. His unstinted admiration had gone to Kevin O'Higgins, the most ruthless 'strong man' of his time in Ireland, and he linked his admiration explicitly to his rejoicing at the rise of fascism in Europe – and this at the very beginning, within a few weeks of the March on Rome. Ten years later, after Hitler had moved to the centre of the political stage in Europe, Yeats was trying to create a movement in Ireland which would be overtly fascist in language, costume, behaviour and intent. He turned his back on this movement when it began to fail, not before. Would the irony and detachment of this phase of disillusion have lasted if a more effective fascist leader and movement had later emerged? One may doubt it. Many in Germany who were 'disillusioned' by the failure of the Kapp putsch and the beer-cellar putsch were speedily 'reillusioned' when Hitler succeeded – and 'disillusioned' again when he lost the war.

Post-war writers, touching with embarrassment on Yeats's pro-fascist opinions, have tended to treat these as a curious aberration of an idealistic but ill-informed poet. In fact, such opinions were quite usual in the Irish Protestant middle class to which Yeats belonged (as well as in other middle classes) in the Twenties and Thirties. The *Irish Times*, spokesman of that class, aroused no protest from its readers when it hailed Hitler (4 March 1933) as 'Europe's standard bearer against Muscovite terrorism', and its references to Mussolini were as consistently admiring as those to Soviet Russia were consistently damning. But the limiting factor on the pro-fascist tendencies of the *Irish Times* and the Irish protestant middle class generally was the pull of loyalty to Britain – a factor which did not apply, or applied only with great ambivalence, in the case of Yeats. Mr T.R. Henn is quite right when he says that Yeats was 'not alone in believing at that moment of history, that the discipline of fascist theory might impose order upon a disintegrating world'. I cannot follow Mr Henn, however, to his conclusion that 'nothing could be further from Yeats's mind' than fascism's 'violent and suppressive practice'. 'Force, marching men' and the victory in civil war of 'the skilful, riding their machines as did the feudal knights their armoured horses' (*On the Boiler*) surely belong to the domain of violent and suppressive practice.

Just as one school is led to claim that the pro-fascist Yeats was not the 'true' Yeats, so another tries to believe that the fascism to which Yeats was drawn was not a 'true' fascism. Several critics have assured us that he was drawn not really to fascism but to some idealised aristocracy of 18th-century stamp. 'In all fairness,' writes Dr Vivian Mercier, 'we should allow that his views were closer to Hamilton's or even to Jefferson's than they were to Mussolini's.' As far as political theory is concerned this is probably correct – although the name of Swift would seem more relevant than those of Hamilton or Jefferson. But it ignores one important reality: that Yeats was interested in contemporary politics and that he was a contemporary, not of Swift's or Jefferson's, but of Mussolini's. He had, in any case, the assurance of his friend Ezra Pound that the Duce was translating Jeffersonian ideas into 20th century terms. He would certainly have preferred something more strictly aristocratic than fascism, but since he was living in the 20th century he was attracted to fascism as the best available form of anti-democratic theory and practice.

George Orwell, though critical, and up to a point percipient, about Yeats's tendencies, thought that Yeats misunderstood what an authoritarian society would be like. Such a society, Orwell pointed out, 'will not be ruled by noblemen with Van Dyck faces, but by anonymous millionaires, shiny-bottomed bureaucrats and murderous gangsters'. This implies a degree of innocence in Yeats which cannot reasonably be postulated. O'Higgins and O'Duffy were not Duke Ercole and Guidobaldo, and Yeats had considerable experience of practical politics, both in the Nineties and in the early Twenties. 'In the last 40 years,' wrote J.M. Hone in the year of Yeats's death, 'there was never a

period in which his countrymen did not regard him as a public figure.'
When he thought of rule by an elite, it was a possible elite, resembling
in many ways the nominated members of the Senate in which he had
sat. Its membership – bankers, organisers, ex-officers – would
correspond roughly to what Orwell, in more emotive language,
describes. Nor should it be assumed – as Orwell with his 'murderous
gangsters' seems to imply – that the sensitive nature of the poet would
necessarily be revolted by the methods of rule of an authoritarian state.
Yeats – unlike, say, his brother, or Lady Gregory – was not, in politics,
a very squeamish person. 'Seventy-seven executions' did not repel him;
on the contrary, they made him admire O'Higgins all the more. At least
one of his associates of the early Thirties might have been described as
a 'murderous gangster'.

It is true that neither Yeats nor anyone else during Yeats's lifetime
knew what horrors fascism would be capable of. But the many who,
like Yeats, were drawn to fascism at this time knew, and seemed to
have little difficulty in accepting, or at least making allowances for,
much of what had already been done and continued to be done. 'The
Prussian police,' wrote the *Irish Times* in an editorial of February 1933,
'have been authorised by Herr Hitler's Minister to shoot communists ...
on sight.' The same editorial ended with the words: 'Naturally the
earlier phases of this renascence are crude, but Germany is finding her
feet after a long period of political ineptitude.'

Yeats read the newspapers; he also read, as Hone records, several
books on Fascist Italy and Nazi Germany. If, then, he was attracted to
the dominant movements in these countries, and if he supported a
movement in his own country whose resemblances to these Continental
movements he liked to stress, it cannot be contended that he did so in
ignorance of such 'crude' practices as the *Irish Times* described. It is
true that the Blueshirts did not even try to go to anything like the
lengths of their Continental models. It is also true that, unlike the case
of their models, the communists whom the Blueshirts were fighting
were, in Ireland, largely imaginary.

Some writers – notably Professor D.T. Torchiana in his well-
documented study *W.B. Yeats, Jonathan Swift and Liberty* – have
insisted that, in spite of Yeats's authoritarian and fascist leanings, he
was essentially a friend of liberty. 'Both Swift and Yeats,' Torchiana
concludes, 'served human liberty.' The senses in which this is true for
Yeats are important but clearly limited. He defended the liberty of the
artist, consistently. In politics, true to his duality, he defended the
liberty of Ireland against English domination, and the liberty of his own
caste – and sometimes, by extension, of others – against clerical
domination. Often these liberties overlapped, and the cause of artist

and aristocrat became the same; often his resistance to 'clerical' authoritarianism makes him appear a liberal. But his objection to clerical authoritarianism is not the liberal's objection to *all* authoritarianism. On the contrary, he favours 'a despotism of the educated classes' and in the search for this is drawn towards fascism. It is true that fascism was not in reality a despotism of the educated classes but it was a form of despotism to which the educated classes in the Twenties and Thirties showed a disposition proportionate to the apparent threat, in their country, of communism or 'anarchy'. In assessing Yeats's pro-fascist opinions, there is no need to regard these as so extraordinary that he must either not have been himself or not have known what he was about.

Yet, in challenging the assumption that Yeats's pro-fascism was either not 'truly Yeats' or not 'truly pro-fascist', one must not overlook the intermittent character of his pro-fascism and of all his political activity. If his pro-fascism was real, his irony and caution were real too, and his phases of detachment not less real than his phases of political commitment. The long phase of nationalist commitment (1887–1903) was followed by a long phase (1903–1916) of detachment from almost all practical politics (except those to which the theatre exposed him), by a critique of Irish nationalist politics, and by the formation of an aristocratic attitude which did not find practical political expression until after 1916 when he re-entered Irish politics on the right, in the Free State Senate. After clerical pressures had made the Senate uncongenial to him and had extruded him from it, he withdrew again from active politics (1928–33), only returning when a situation propitious to fascism seemed to present itself. When O'Duffy's Irish fascists failed ignominiously he turned away from politics again, though not forever: in the last two years of his life politics flared up again. And always, in the long phases of withdrawal, he tended to write of all politics with a kind of contempt, a plague-on-both-your-houses air. ('Contempt for politics' is of course a characteristic conservative stance.)

Yeats's 'manic' phases of political activity were no less real or important than the 'depressive' phases which followed them. And the options of the 'manic' phases were not haphazard or middle-of-the-road. They were either anti-English or – in Irish politics – aristocratic and, from the time fascism had appeared, distinctly pro-fascist. At the end, in the last two years, as we shall see, these two elements were beginning to combine.

It was Yeats's misfortune as a politician, and his good fortune as a poet, that his political opportunities or temptations were few and far between. Irish politics in their normal run have not, since the introduction of universal suffrage, been receptive to poets, aristocrats or Protestants. It is only in rare conjunctures, times of great national stress and division, that an Irish party is likely to find room for such exotics, for, in such times, men welcome an ally with a name and voice. Such moments of excitement and emotion, which offered opportunities, were also the moments which most stirred the poet. Such times were the Parnell split of 1891 and the Sinn Fein split of 1920/22. The abortive fascist movement of 1933 seemed to be, but was not, the opening of another profound fissure in Irish political life.

In the first two cases, the world of Irish politics proved, when 'normalcy' had returned, no place for the poet. In the third case the poet retired from a political movement which had lost momentum. It is fairly safe to say that, if it had succeeded, it would have dropped him or forced him out: not through any great aversion on his part from thugs in coloured shirts, but because an Irish fascism, to have any chance of staying in power, would necessarily have to become an intensely clerical fascism. In fact, the successor movement to the Blueshirts – the Christian Front – was a noisily Catholic clerical-fascist movement. This was a kind of fascism – perhaps the only kind – which Yeats could not accept, or tolerate, since his authoritarian view of life derived ultimately from his concept of the caste to which he belonged, and the distinguishing mark of that caste was its Protestantism.

In the political writings of his last two years the two elements in his politics – the 'Irish' and the 'Protestant' elements – entered into a new set of relations. The 'Irish' element became more vocal than it had been since 1916 and the 'Protestant' element was obliged to break finally with the traditional right wing in Irish politics. Anti-English feeling, long dormant in Yeats, became increasingly pronounced in the period 1937/9. A series of poems – 'Roger Casement', 'The Ghost of Roger Casement', 'The O'Rahilly', 'Come Gather Round Me Parnellites' – both expressed and did much to rekindle the old pride in Irish nationalism which the cynicism that followed the Civil War had dulled. The Casement poems especially had a powerful anti-English charge:

> O what has made that sudden noise?
> What on the threshold stands?
> It never crossed the sea because
> John Bull and the sea are friends;
> But this is not the old sea
> Nor this the old seashore.
> What gave that roar of mockery,
> That roar in the sea's roar?

The ghost of Roger Casement
Is beating on the door.

No Irishman, reading these lines on the eve of the Second World War, had forgotten that Casement had been hanged, as well as 'morally assassinated', for trying, in 1916, to bring help to Ireland from Germany. And some Irishmen, at least, must have reflected that if the sea was no longer the old sea, which had been friends with John Bull, the reason for this might be that the nation from which Casement had tried to bring help now possessed a powerful air force. Potentially, 'The Ghost of Roger Casement' was as explosive as *Cathleen ni Houlihan.*

Just at this time Yeats was writing to Ethel Mannin that, while he liked neither side in Spain, and did not want to see his old leader O'Duffy – now fighting for Franco – return to Ireland with enhanced prestige to 'the Catholic front', he was attracted by the thought that a fascist victory would weaken England.

> I am an old Fenian and I think the old Fenian in me would rejoice if a fascist nation or government controlled Spain because that would weaken the British empire, force England to be civil to India and loosen the hand of English finance in the far East of which I hear occasionally. But this is mere instinct. A thing I would never act on. Then I have a horror of modern politics – I see nothing but the manipulation of popular enthusiasm by false news – a horror that has been deepened in these last weeks by the Casement business. My ballad on that subject has had success ...

The success of the ballad was mainly among those who had been Yeats's political enemies and against whom he had conspired – De Valera's party. It was in De Valera's paper, the *Irish Press*, that the ballad appeared. There were adequate reasons for a degree of reconciliation between Yeats and his former foes. First, from Yeats's point of view, the events of the early Thirties had shown that, if there was a 'strong man' in Irish politics it was not O'Duffy but De Valera. Second, five years of De Valera's government had dissipated the theory – once cherished by Yeats's former political friends – that De Valera meant communism. Third, De Valera was the main barrier against what Yeats then saw – with considerable justice – as a rising tide of clericalist power, a tide which threatened all that Yeats had built in Ireland:

> I am convinced that if the Spanish war goes on or if [it] ceases and O'Duffy's volunteers return heroes, my 'pagan' institutions, the Theatre, the Academy, will be fighting for their lives against combined Gaelic and Catholic bigotry. A friar or monk has already threatened us with mob violence.

In the same letter, Yeats noted how De Valera had carried in Parliament, against a pro-Franco opposition, a measure to stop Irish volunteers from going to Spain.

The fourth reason for a rapprochement with De Valera's party is more complex. Just as Yeats's own mind was hopelessly divided about the Spanish War – the authoritarian and Anglophobe in him desiring a Franco victory, the Irish anti-clerical dreading the results – so the party of his former friends was also in confusion. But their confusion was almost the mirror-image, the inversion, of his. They wanted, or said they wanted, a Franco victory, on Catholic grounds. But also, as the party of the Anglo-Irish treaty, the 'Commonwealth Party', they contained the most 'pro-British' elements in Irish life: the people who, in the event of Britain's going to war, would try to see to it that Ireland came in on Britain's side.

De Valera at this time was engaged, with the Chamberlain government, in the negotiations which led to the return of the Irish ports, which the Treaty had retained under British control. Without the return of these ports Ireland's neutrality in the coming war, which it was De Valera's policy to ensure, would scarcely have been practical politics. Yeats – who, as Frank O'Connor has told us, in his last years admired and defended De Valera – put his name and influence explicitly behind the recovery of the ports; implicitly but clearly behind a policy of neutrality.

From the point of view of De Valera's party, Yeats's tentative overtures – for such, I believe, they were – would have presented some advantages. The patriotic poems undoubtedly struck a genuinely responsive note among most Irish people: their appearance in De Valera's newspaper was helpful, especially at this time, in Ireland; the prestige – by now great – of Yeats's name in England would be helpful there in relation to the ports and to neutrality. Yet, while there were reasons on both sides for some degree of rapprochement, it may be doubted whether this would ever have become close or warm. Irish political life between the wars had been too bitter for that. De Valera's memory has not the reputation of being short or inaccurate. Yeats's activities in 1922/23 and in 1933 would have been quite fresh in De Valera's mind. It is believed also that he had read, with distaste and distress, the lines:

> Had De Valera eaten Parnell's heart
> No loose-lipped demagogue had won the day,
> No civil rancour torn the land apart.

Real reconciliation had to wait for the next generation. After the war Yeats's son, Michael, joined De Valera's party and became a senator.

The two main currents in Yeats's active politics – his Anglophobe Irish
nationalism and his authoritarianism – necessarily converged in the
years immediately before the war, thrusting him in the direction of
desiring the victory of the fascist powers. The doctrine of John O'Leary,
to whose school Yeats always claimed to belong, was Tone's doctrine:
that 'England's difficulty is Ireland's opportunity.' The caution and
scepticism which were also permanent features of Yeats's personality,
worked, together with his repulsion from Irish clerical fascism, to
prevent him from being carried too far by Tone and O'Leary. But an
underlying wish found voice at this time, when the prestige and
authority of England were lower than they had been for centuries, in an
increasingly anti-English tone, in verse and prose and in his
conversation. This did not happen without a violent inner struggle. 'The
"Irishry",' he wrote in *A General Introduction for My Work* (1937),

> have preserved their ancient 'deposit' through wars which, during the 16th
> and 17th centuries, became wars of extermination; no people, Lecky said at
> the opening of his *Ireland in the 18th Century*, have undergone greater
> persecution nor did that persecution altogether cease up to our own day. No
> people hate as we do in whom that past is always alive, there are moments
> when hatred poisons my life and I accuse myself of effeminacy because I
> have not given it adequate expression. It is not enough to have put it into the
> mouth of a rambling peasant poet. Then I remind myself that though mine is
> the first English marriage I know of in the direct line, all my family names are
> English and that I owe my soul to Shakespeare, to Spenser and to Blake,
> perhaps to William Morris, and to the English language in which I think,
> speak and write, that everything I love has come to me through English; my
> hatred tortures me with love, my love with hate. I am like the Tibetan monk
> who dreams at his initiation that he is eaten by a wild beast and learns on
> waking that he himself is eater and eaten. This is Irish hatred and solitude,
> the hatred of human life that made Swift write *Gulliver* and the epitaph upon
> his tomb, that can still make us wag between extremes and doubt our sanity.

On the Boiler, written the following year, assumes – without however
being altogether explicit about it – that the fascist powers are winning
and England is in contemptible decline. 'The fascist countries,' he
writes in the section 'Tomorrow's Revolution', 'know that civilisation
has reached a crisis, and found their eloquence upon that knowledge.'
The only fault he has to find with them is that 'perhaps from dread of
attack' they encourage large families. He assumes in 'Ireland after the
Revolution' that 'some tragic crisis shall so alter Europe and all opinion
that the Irish government will teach the great majority of its
schoolchildren nothing but' – a list of manual and menial occupations
follows.

At the time when this was written, the 'tragic crisis' many expected was that which was to lead Pétain's France to adopt somewhat similar educational policies. It is hard to resist the conclusion that Yeats, when writing this, expected, and hoped, that Ireland 'after the revolution' would be a sort of satellite of a fascist-dominated Europe. As regards England his contempt, in this year of Munich, is unqualified and savage. After saying some hard things about King George V he concludes 'Ireland after the Revolution' with the words:

> The Irish mind has still, in country rapscallion or in Bernard Shaw, an ancient cold, explosive detonating impartiality. The English mind, excited by its newspaper proprietors and its schoolmasters, has turned into a bed-hot harlot.

Dorothy Wellesley, who was troubled by his increasingly anti-British attitude in the last years of his life, made a shrewd comment:

> Why then in the 20th century and when the Irish are freed from their oppressors the English, does he despise and dislike us increasingly? Because he dislikes the stuffed lion and admires the ranting, roaring oppressors.

During Yeats's life the English government gave him a Civil List pension and offered him a knighthood which he refused. The Athenaeum Club gave him the signal honour of a special election. Since his death, the British Council has presented him to the world as one of England's glories. There is therefore some irony in the thought that there was something in him that would have taken considerable pleasure – though not without a respectful backward glance at Shakespeare – in seeing England occupied by the Nazis, the Royal Family exiled, and the Mother of Parliaments torn down. Meanwhile in Ireland one would have expected to see him at least a cautious participant, or ornament, in a collaborationist regime. It is probably fortunate for his future reputation, and especially his standing with the British Council, that he died in January 1939 before the political momentum of his last years could carry him any farther than *On the Boiler*.

How can those of us who loathe such politics continue, not merely to admire but to love the poetry, and perhaps most of all the poems with a political bearing? An important part of the answer is supplied by the poet himself in a note on 'Leda and the Swan':

> I wrote 'Leda and the Swan' because the editor of a political review asked me for a poem. I thought 'After the individualist, demagogic movement founded by Hobbes [*sic*] and popularised by the Encyclopaedists and the French

revolution, we have a soil so exhausted that it cannot grow that crop again for centuries.' Then I thought 'Nothing is now possible but some movement from above preceded by some violent annunciation.' My fancy began to play with Leda and the Swan for metaphor, and I began this poem; but as I wrote, bird and lady took such possession of the scene that all politics went out of it, and my friend tells me that his 'conservative readers would misunderstand the poem'.

They would have been puzzled, certainly.

Very little seems to be known – and perhaps little can be known – of how this process of transformation works. How can that patter of Mussolini prose 'produce' such a poem? How can that political ugly duckling be turned into this glorious Swan? It is in a sense like the transmutation, in 'Easter 1916', of those whom Yeats had thought of as commonplace people:

> All changed, changed utterly:
> A terrible beauty is born.

Is the connection then between the politics and the poetry only trivial and superficial? There is, I think, a deeper connection: if the political prose and the poetry are thought of, not as 'substance' and 'metaphor', or 'content' and 'style', but as cognate expressions of a fundamental force, anterior to both politics and poetry.

The force was, I suggest, Yeats's profound and tragic intuitive – and intelligent – awareness, in his maturity and old age, of what the First World War had set loose, of what was already moving towards Hitler and the Second World War. That he is conscious of the danger a letter shows as early as 1923: 'Unless Europe takes to war again and starts new telepathic streams of violence and cruelty.' But the poetry is already responding to the telepathic streams as early as 1920, when he wrote 'The Second Coming':

> Things fall apart; the centre cannot hold;
> Mere anarchy is loosed upon the world.

Years afterwards, just before the Spanish War, he drew Ethel Mannin's attention to this poem:

> If you have my poems by you look up a poem called 'The Second Coming', It was written more than 16 or 17 years ago and foretold what is happening. I have written of the same thing again and again since.

The words 'violence', 'hatred' and 'fanaticism' became keywords in Yeats's poetry. He often uses them in condemnation of the Left in Irish politics – the politics of Constance Markievicz and of Maud Gonne. But he is also increasingly conscious of these same forces on himself:

> I carry from my mother's womb
> A fanatic heart.

The 'fanatic heart', an unusual capacity for hatred and an unusual experience of it, probably made him more sensitive and more responsive to the 'telepathic waves' coming from Europe than other writers in English seem to have been. The forces in him that responded to the hatred, cruelty and violence welling up in Europe produced the prophetic image of 'The Second Coming' and the last part of 'Nineteen Hundred and Nineteen'.

It may be objected that 'Nineteen Hundred and Nineteen' and 'The Second Coming' were written not about the coming of fascism but about the Anglo-Irish War and the Black and Tans. The distinction is less than absolute: the Black and Tans were in fact an early manifestation of an outlook and methods which the Nazis were later to perfect. The *Freikorps* on the Polish-German border were at this time trying to do exactly what the Black and Tans were doing in Ireland and the *Freikorps* were the direct and proudly acknowledged predecessors of Hitler's Nazis. There is even a direct link between the Black and Tans and the Nazis in the person of Lord Haw-Haw, who fought for the British government in the first movement and was hanged by it for his work in the second. Bruno Brehm, one of Hitler's novelists, made the assassination by Irish revolutionaries of Sir Henry Wilson – the principal exponent of intensified Black and Tan measures in Ireland – symbolic of the tragic confrontation of hero and submen. Wilson was to the Irish as Hitler was to Jews and Bolsheviks.

In a *General Introduction to My Work* Yeats made specific the connection between his own hatred and what was happening in Europe:

> When I stand upon O'Connell Bridge in the half-light and notice that discordant architecture, all those electric signs, where modern heterogeneity has taken physical form, a vague hatred comes up out of my own dark and I am certain that wherever in Europe there are minds strong enough to lead others the same vague hatred arises; in four or five or in less generations this hatred will have issued in violence and imposed some kind of rule of kindred. I cannot know the nature of that rule, for its opposite fills the light; all I can do to bring it nearer is to intensify my hatred.

By the time the *General Introduction* was written, fascist power and 'rule of kindred' were already in full swing: the length of time – 'four or

five generations' – is odd and perhaps calculated: it brings to mind the
retrospective 'commentaries' on the songs for O'Duffy. The paragraph
itself may be taken as a kind of retrospective commentary on 'The
Second Coming'.

In 'The Second Coming' the poet, perhaps from the foretaste of the
Black and Tans, augured the still more terrible things that were to
come. The sort of 'premonitory' intuition present in 'The Second
Coming' and in other poems necessarily affected Yeats in his ordinary
life as well as in his poetry. Yeats the manager, the senator, the
politician, stands in a diplomatic relation to these intimations of power.
His references to fascism, though sometimes mildly critical, are never
hostile, almost always respectful, often admiring, and this especially in
years of fascist victories: 1922, 1933 and 1938. Some reasons for this
have already been suggested; it might be added that for Yeats a
bandwagon had the same high degree of attraction that it has for other
political mortals:

> Processions that lack high stilts have nothing that catches the eye.

If a Marxist, believing that history is going in a given direction, thinks it
right to give it a good shove in the way it is going, it is natural enough
that one who, like Yeats, feels that it is going in the opposite direction
should accompany it that way with, if not a shove, at last a cautious tilt.

In the poetry, however, the raw intimations of what is impending –
the 'telepathic waves of violence and fear' – make themselves known,
not in the form of calculated practical deductions, but in the attempt to
reveal, through metaphoric insight, what is actually happening and
even, in a broad sense, what is about to happen. The poet, like the lady is

> so caught up,
> So mastered by the brute blood of the air,

that he does indeed take on the knowledge of what is happening with
the power to make it known. The political man had his cautious
understanding with fascism, the diplomatic relation to a great force; the
poet conveyed the nature of the force, the dimension of the tragedy.
The impurities of this long and extraordinary life went into its devious
and sometimes sinister political theories and activities. The purity and
integrity – including the truth about politics as Yeats apprehended it –
are in the poetry concentrated in metaphors of such power that they
thrust aside all calculated intent: bird and lady take possession of the
scene.

Conor Cruise O'Brien, 26 February 1965

The most consistently stimulating material in the mid-sixties Statesman,
it seems to me, appeared in the 'Centrepiece' column. Here is MERVYN
JONES on negative and positive aspects of the era's supposed sexual
revolution.

Long Back and Sides

More and more men, young men especially, are wearing their hair long.
Not simply or negligently long, either, but cultivated in a variety of
styles. Barbers – or rather hairdressers, as they call themselves if they
draw this kind of clientèle – say that long-haired men spend as much
time and money in establishments devoted to the art as women. All this
is disturbing to the type of Englishman for whom 'Short back and sides'
is a principle as morally binding, in a small way, as 'For Queen and
country'. He is right to be disturbed, to feel the ground shifting under
his feet. The psychological and social implications of long hair are
worth more than a passing thought.

Long hair has been with us for a considerable time; it might be more
correct to say that it was never entirely extirpated. It caused some
anxiety in the 1890s, and more in the 1920s. Until recently, however, it
could be dismissed with a simple explanation: long-haired men were,
actually or unconsciously, homosexuals. They were observed to be
unconventional in their dress, delicate in their manners, interested in
the arts, and inclined to close friendships with other men of similar
tastes and appearance. The case was held to be proved.

This theory no longer convinces. For one thing, the numbers are
becoming so great that – despite Lord Arran's statistics and Sir Cyril
Osborne's warnings – it is incredible that there can be quite so many
homosexuals. Then, long hair is now found among all social classes. It is
really a sign of that blurring of class lines which is the most hopeful
aspect of modern England, and it is favoured by young men who
identify themselves by generation and outlook more than by class. But
it is rather more acceptable in the factory than in the office (in the
south, at least): rather more in evidence on the streets of Bermondsey
than of Mayfair. This makes quite a dent in the theory, for the short-
back-and-sides man believes tenaciously that proletarians cannot be
homosexuals, perhaps because they don't come from public schools.
But what finally knocks the theory on the head is the fact, not to be
denied however wrong or puzzling it may seem, that long-haired men
are interested in women – and women are interested in long-haired
men.

By the standards of the short-back-and-sides man, the long-haired

man is unmanly in behaviour as well as appearance. He gives open
expression to his emotions – on occasion to distress or even fear. In
relation to a woman he asserts neither superior strength, superior
wisdom, nor the right to command. Discarding the traditional pose of
impregnable silence, he is willing to talk to her, which includes listening
to her. Indeed he loves not only to talk but to gossip and chatter. In
short, he is altogether remiss in demonstrating his masculinity. No
matter – the girls love it.

Here it may be remarked that literature is for once lagging behind
life. The accepted attitude of the male is ruthless: aggressive before the
female is annexed, possessive or at least protective afterwards. In one
modern play after another – *Look Back in Anger, The Knack, Saved,
The Homecoming* – this behaviour is carried to extreme lengths. And
yet, in my observation at least, the young male of the 1960s does not
conduct himself according to these obsolete precepts, and would be an
also-ran in the sex race if he did. Can it be that the long reign of the
cave-man is over?

Let us look at the matter from the viewpoint of the young woman of
today. She can please herself as to whom she sleeps with, whom she
marries, and whether at a given age she sleeps with anyone or marries
anyone at all. This is incompletely true, and truer in some environments
and some parts of the country than others, but it is more of a truth than
it has been. There is no longer a prospective partner to whom she must
yield herself in order to gain social or parental approval. The cave-man
routine was a device whereby the woman could yield without any
strong inclination, excusing herself on the plea that male insistence left
her no option. (Of course, she was glad after it happened – in plays
written by men.) But once the pressure is off, a woman has no reason
to be bullied into submission. She prefers to be patiently and
courteously wooed.

Since she can pick and choose, she expects a man to attract her by
some kind of adornment, such as long hair. He must take a bit of
trouble; being of the approved type is no longer enough. Moreover, the
right to choice implies a taste for variety (which men have always been
able to indulge). With its range of style, long hair is the passport to
variety, just as short hair is the badge of uniformity. This naturally
disturbs the short-back-and-sides man, unsure of individuality in his
own person and afraid of it in others. It is relevant that armies, prisons
and strict schools insist on the uniform short haircut; also that cropped
hair is the rule in nations where conformity is valued – Germany,
Russia and America.

But this is not all. Women nowadays are aware, more or less clearly,
that they have somehow been cheated over this sex-equality business.

They have been fighting for equality for over a century, and on paper they have won victory after victory. They can be professors, cabinet ministers and all that. What this means, however, is that they are equal to men in the male sphere – the sphere of work, property ownership and public affairs. It is no longer a male preserve, but it remains a male sphere run according to male rules. Wherever a woman goes, she has to conform to standards, methods and values which she has had no part in shaping, which existed before she was allowed on the scene, and which she has not succeeded in altering in any essential respect. You get served in a pub in a certain way, you sue for justice in a certain way, you get a bill through parliament in a certain way. In no case is it the way that a woman would have devised, or that makes much sense to her.

Thus, women are in the position of working-class students at Oxbridge. No matter whether they form 10 per cent or 50 per cent of the college roll, Oxbridge remains an upper-class institution. Similarly, while women as individuals have gained equal status in a male world, they have not succeeded in making it any less male.

When a woman reflects on her hollow triumphs, it begins to strike her where she – and her mother and grandmother – have gone wrong. Of course! Rebelling against the ancient idea (not so ancient really, and more tightly imposed in the 19th century than in most periods of history) that men and women are utterly different and ought not to meet on equal terms, she has followed the strategy of becoming like a man. She has put on the judicial wig and the academic mortar-board; she has squeezed her breasts into police and army tunics; where no uniform is prescribed, she has adopted an office suit, complete with shirt and tie, like a man's office suit. She has accepted at face value the whole rigmarole of hierarchies, promotions by seniority, committees and commissions, honours and titles.

The falsity of this progress has become more obvious as the victories have been chalked up: for, while it was once a serious matter that a woman could not be a doctor or a barrister, it is pretty pathetic to be reduced to worrying about when the first woman will capture some ludicrous position like Black Rod or President of the Oxford Union. Nor is this the worst of it. The masculinity to which she has conformed is not masculinity itself, but the distorted form dominant at the time when her struggle began. Becoming like a man has meant becoming like a hidebound, authoritarian, unimaginative, emotionally stunted man – a short-back-and-sides man.

And what ought she to have been doing all this time? That is dawning on her too. *Of course!* If she wanted genuine equality, and at the same time a more civilised and rational world, the right course was to see to it that men became like women. This is not nearly so unlikely a proposition as it seems to the short-back-and-sides man, who imagines that he is the only type of man known to history. It is not very long – about two centuries – since men dressed gaudily, used scent and powder, wore rings on all their fingers, followed fashion in their walk and their manner of speech, gossiped freely, wept when they were moved (even by a play or a novel), and in general unbuttoned their emotional selves without the constraint that later descended on them. They did not behave like this in all-male clubs, to be sure. They did not spend their time in such clubs; they lived with women, as men are now coming to do again.

We need men like this in our time. Womanly men, like women, have sometimes been foolish or thoughtless, but they have never done much harm. It is the manly men who have waged wars, conquered colonies, established harsh criminal codes, exalted competition above mutual aid, left the poor to starve (formerly at home and now all over the world) and finally made weapons that can destroy the lot of us. They have done these things because they had not, or would not allow themselves, the imagination that engenders compassion – because, in short, they could not weep.

The short-back-and-sides man, who is also the plays-must-be-censored man and the deterrence-means-peace-man, is not going to give up easily. He has a weight of accepted prejudices on his side, and even accepted English usage: 'effeminate' is a pejorative term, which has no equivalent to describe the 'masculate' woman. But I believe his day is almost done, because he has the girls against him. They have got his number at last. They go for the men with the long hair.

Mervyn Jones, 3 June 1966

Apparently delighting in being called the rudest man in London, COLIN MACINNES was also one of the sharpest writers. Could anyone else so thoroughly damn British myopia, hypocrisy, racism, stuffiness and muddle as he does, and still remain so peculiarly affirmative about the country?

Decolonial Delusions

On returning recently to London Airport, I was confronted, at Immigration, with the three alternative entrances – British, Aliens and Commonwealth. Believing that Britain *is* a member of the

Commonwealth, I made the experiment of joining the queue of Maltese and Pakistanis. On arrival at the desk I was told, as I expected, that as a Briton I was not a Commonwealth citizen, and I kept everybody waiting trying to prove to the official that I was.

This absurd exercise is one proof among so many that we have a thoroughly muddled attitude towards the nations of our former empire. Thus, in relation to the tottering Commonwealth, the Right regards it either as an interfering fraud or, if romantics, as an echo of our empire that has vanished. The Left sees it as a means of belabouring the Right (because the Left supposes itself more attuned to the spirit of 'developing' nations), and as an opportunity for gracefully bestowing bounty from empty coffers.

The fact is, I think, that we have not yet adjusted ourselves to the reality that, internationally, we are basically alone. It would seem that to shake off an empire in two decades is far more disturbing to the shaker than the shaken. Ex-colonial nations have their problems, heaven knows, but these are chiefly economic, and largely confined to their single country. Our own seem far greater, since they are largely psychological, and our troubled thoughts range over the whole globe. We do not yet *feel* that the empire has vanished forever, or realise that the Commonwealth is in no sense a substitute for it. Failing to accept our manifestly reduced status, we still cling to a number of what one might call 'decolonial delusions'. For example: '*We may have lost an empire, but we have profoundly marked the countries that we governed.*'

Except for the English language, some lingering law, medicine and eccentricities like cricket, red pillar boxes and driving on the left, the cultural lives of the nations we governed remain unaltered by our passing presence. The reason we never had any cultural impact on the people of our former empire is that, except for rare scholars, we never took the slightest interest in *their* culture. We overlaid on their ancient lives a superficial superstructure of colonial habits which, with our departure, has simply vanished. The only exception I can see to this is in the case of the West Indies, which were largely a British creation, but whose culture is now rapidly evolving away from ours. As for white nations we peopled, like Australia, our direct influence ended, in any real sense, when the umbilical cord was finally severed during World War II. It is correct to think of a past *impact* on such nations; but the present impact – political, economic or cultural – is shrinking.

As for the English language, our most useful contribution, there is no longer one English, but at least seven: English English, North American, Caribbean, African, Indian, Australasian and what one might call 'international' English – the speech of congresses and air pilots. None of the six beside our own belongs any more to English

English, or is influenced by it. As to our laws, their effect is now
residual and in many nations they are being radically changed.

'*We may have lost power in the world, but we continue to exercise a
profound moral influence on the peoples we once ruled.*' Words fail me
to refute this pathetic claptrap, heard so often from the mouths of
politicians of all parties. No one outside England believes this for a
moment – they don't even 'disbelieve' it, it just doesn't occur to them.
Every time I hear this said my heart sinks, for to suppose a 'moral
influence' betrays immense moral arrogance. If anyone doubts this, let
him ask an Egyptian what was our moral influence after Suez, an Israeli
after we fled from Palestine, an African after a year of shilly-shallying
over Rhodesia, an Indian after our support for the Vietnam war, or a
New Zealander after tackling our own racial problem far less effectively
than he has – and so on.

'*We have opened our doors to hundreds of thousands from the former
colonial territories.*' What happened here was that, thinking we could
transform the Commonwealth into a pseudo-empire, we maintained at
first the old imperial structure of (relatively) free movement, imagining
that few (except for such as students and businessmen) would take us at
our word. When hordes arrived, we did nothing whatever for years to
welcome them, then suddenly realised they were here for good,
panicked, clamped down controls, and talked about deportations.
Meanwhile, though preserving an outwardly correct attitude to the
strangers (except for such happenings as Notting Hill in '58), we
received a low-paid largely manual labour force for jobs we were too
idle or distainful to do, did little officially to encourage equal
integration and waited more than 15 years before appointing a
government body with minor powers to look into racial adjustment.

'*Our queen remains a symbol of surviving unity with our former
colonies.*' Phrased like this – as it usually is – the thought reveals the
fossilation of our decolonial thinking. In the first place, an increasing
number of these countries are now republics, while among those of
which she still is queen, she is not *our* queen at all, but theirs. As for
the queen being 'Head of the Commonwealth', this means to us that we
still emotionally rule, and to the ex-colonial nations, nothing whatever.
'They will welcome her (or sometimes not, as in Canada) just as they
would Jacqueline Kennedy, but it stops right there: they have no sense
of 'allegiance' whatever.

'*The Commonwealth, shorn of the tares of empire (such as they
were), provides an international forum of the highest order.*' No one
except ourselves believes this any longer. For the ex-colonial countries,
the Commonwealth is a convenience to be used or ignored according
to whatever economic-political advantages it may afford. If

'Commonwealth unity' conflicts with national interest, this interest will come first every time – as will even regional interests, alliances, or status in the UN. The key failure of Commonwealth effectiveness was its total inability to halt the India-Pakistani war. And our antics over Rhodesia are an excellent illustration of the decolonial delusion that government can be exercised without responsibility, sacrifice and power. If I were a white Rhodesian (which God forbid), I would certainly have called Britain's bluff; and if I were an African Rhodesian, my very first question would be why we spent £60 millions failing to suppress Mau Mau, and yet left a legal governor in Salisbury without even a guardsman in his sentry-box.

'*Although our role east of Suez has diminished, we owe it to the Commonwealth, our allies and ourselves to maintain a military presence there.*' This I believe to be the most deadly delusion of all; for one has only to ask oneself how *effective* such forces would be in the case of any actual conflict. That we should still think Singapore worth a penny or a soldier, after what happened to it during World War II (when we were immensely more powerful than now), seems to me lunacy. That we should begin all over again in Aden the dismal experience of failing to suppress terrorism, as in Cyprus, and be driven to committing it ourselves, fills one with gloom. That we should imagine oil can only be bought by propping up potentates in the Persian Gulf, while our competitors buy it merrily without having an expensive soldier in sight, seems quite extraordinary. This whole futile operation is immensely costly, and earns us the hatred and suspicion of countless people whose enmity we would not otherwise arouse. As to the argument that we are pleasing the Americans by sitting under-manned and -equipped on kegs of oriental dynamite, one answer among many is that the Americans, not being – one hopes – idiots must know how futile our military intervention would be in any actual crisis. This was one of the many lessons of the Suez war, and we haven't yet learned it.

One cannot say all this, and believe it, without being assailed by two sorts of Englishman. Many of the Right consider that to abandon supposed responsibilities left to us by the fallen empire is to betray a cowardly retreat from glory. Well, the glory has gone anyway (if it ever existed), and it is surely not cowardly to recognise a potential fight you can never hope to win. The equivalent illusion of the Left is to suppose that now Mr Wilson, and not Mr Macmillan, is in charge of our post-imperial destinies, Mr Wilson will see that we behave abroad in a nicer, more 'progressive' way. But there are situations – such as that in Aden – in which it is impossible to behave in such a manner. A further Left illusion is that ex-colonial peoples love the Labour party more than they do the Conservatives: they don't, they see them both as Britons.

So what should we be doing? First and foremost, we must get into our heads that the longer we hang on to bits and pieces of surviving colonial territory, we are letting ourselves in for hatreds, deaths of our own men, and grievous financial burdens whose only purpose can be to soothe our idiotic vanity. As for freed nations, it is essential that, if the Commonwealth is not to disintegrate in rancour and mockery, we recognise these nations absolutely as equals, and indeed realise that some of these countries, like India, are much larger than we in population and area, and others, like Canada, potentially richer. Thus conceived, the Commonwealth could still be of value since any international, multi-racial forum for discussion rather than quarrels can be so. But we must free ourselves from the notion that is the *British* Commonwealth.

Colin MacInnes, 16 December 1966

I love The Unquiet Grave. *I also greatly admire TOM NAIRN's writing and, I think, understand completely why Palinurus (himself, as Cyril Connolly, once an NS regular) makes him so cross. If the Statesman can manage to contain both sensibilities, why can't the reader?*

The Old Sensibility

Palinurus has risen from the grave. Aïe! Dripping with nostalgia, as full as ever of sage musings on the agony of life, the groaning old cadaver now confronts and tempts another generation, this time in the shape of a Penguin Modern Classic. So, thanks to Penguins, Cyril Connolly has again been given the chance to realise the ambition he described one sultry day in the France of 1937, at the beginning of his other book *Enemies of Promise*. That was the day when '... after lunch (omelette, Vichy, peaches) ... between the dissipated bedridden morning and the dangerous night', he pondered the problem of how to write a book which would 'hold good for 10 years afterwards'. The task seemed to be getting harder and harder, he noticed with gloom.

Nevertheless, with this edition *The Unquiet Grave* has lasted 23 years. It was written during the war, in the time its author could spare from editing the literary monthly *Horizon,* and appeared in a private *Horizon* edition in December 1944. The success of the book was remarkable, and unexpected, it had clearly touched a sensitive chord in

the literary public: the following year it was republished by Hamish
Hamilton, and it has been re-issued several times since then.

Does it still 'hold good' in 1967? Perhaps it does – but surely in a
sense unrecognisably different from the one Connolly had in mind,
digesting those peaches 30 years ago. He wanted to produce an
exquisite personal philosophy, an 'affirmation of the values of
humanism'. What survives is more like a monument to a bygone
culture-world. A few weeks ago I discussed here some aspects of the
'new sensibility' in the arts preached by Susan Sontag. Palinurus by
contrast represents a form of the old sensibility, with a vengeance. *The
Unquiet Grave* is like a mini-scale Albert Memorial to Literature, and
especially to the older literary intelligentsia of this country.

The pseudonym of Palinurus came from Virgil's *Aeneid.* Palinurus
was the pilot of Aeneas's fleet on the voyage back to Italy, and tumbled
overboard one night after falling asleep at the helm, to be washed
ashore three days later and torn to pieces by the savage inhabitants of
Lucania. Not having had a decent burial, he was forced to spend the
next 100 years pining away on the banks of the Styx. To Connolly, he
stood for 'the core of melancholy and guilt that works destruction on us
from within', and also for 'a certain will-to-failure or repugnance-to-
success, a desire to give up at the last moment or urge towards
loneliness, isolation and obscurity'. Palinurus must have really wanted
to fall overboard, in other words. Out of his unquiet grave, this shade
reminisces and philosophises at us over 150 pages, characteristically
described as 'a word-cycle in three or four rhythms; art, love, nature
and religion'. In fact, it is a philosophical-cum-personal journal, loaded
with quotes from and references to other, mainly French writers. The
tone is one of heavy melancholy.

'Life is a maze in which we take the wrong turning before we have
learnt to walk. ...' Consequently, life is haunted by sinking feelings of
ennui and angst – 'Christmas Eve: 'Dégouté de tout. Midwinter cafard
... sensation of what is lost: lost love, lost youth, lost Paris – remorse
and folly. Aïe!' The plight of the intellectual is frequently touched
upon: 'Civilisation is maintained by a very few people in a small
number of places. ... The civilised are those who get more out of life
than the uncivilised, and for this we are not likely to be forgiven.'
Nature is in it as well: 'Why do sole and turbot borrow the colours and
even the contours of the sea-bottom? Out of self-protection? No,
out of self-disgust.' One of the best cures for angst, besides a cottage in
the Dordogne, is – 'Art (Renoir landscapes), the true escape into
Timelessness'.

The climactic wisdom pressed from this simmering tub of after-
dinner musings comes in the last section. *La Clé des Chants*

(... suggests Grandville's *la clé des champs* ...) where one is sagely counselled to

> reconcile fanaticism with serenity. ... For nothing can be accomplished without fanaticism and without serenity nothing can be enjoyed ... we must select the Illusion which appeals to our temperament and embrace it with passion, if we want to be happy. This is the farewell autumn precept with which Palinurus takes leave of his fast-fading nightmare. *J'ai cueilli ce brin de bruyère.*

Like the dead world of Literature as a whole. *The Unquiet Grave* is haunted by a ghost. And the ghost is reality itself, the lost authentic origin of the labyrinth. It was written in the aftermath of an unhappy love affair, and the author describes its central impulse (in the introduction to this edition) as 'a signal of distress from one human being to another ... which went unanswered'. In another, much more famous phrase, Connolly once said: 'It is closing time in the gardens of the West, and from now on an artist will be judged only by the resonance of his solitude and the quality of his despair.' He wrote this in the editorial of the last number of *Horizon* to appear, in December 1949, only five or six years after *The Unquiet Grave* came out. Here one does glimpse the solitude and despair, movingly, here and there, in a phrase or an intonation. But the feelings have no resonance, the quality of the despair is utterly drowned in the literary stew-pot. The particular wounds of one time and place, given face and history, are transformed into drooling pseudo-wisdom: 'We love but once, for once only are we perfectly equipped for loving. ... And on how that first true love-affair will shape depends the patterns of our lives.' Now and then the manner hardens into self-regarding paroxysms of bad taste:

> Ah, see how on lonely airfield and hill petrol station the images of Freud and Frazer are wreathed in flowers! From Wabash to Humber the girls are launching their fast perishing gardens of Adonis far out to the stream: with sacred rumbas and boogie-woogies the Id is being honoured in all the Hangars, the Priestess intones long passages of the liturgy to which it is most partial.

From the very first words of the book ('The more books we read, the clearer it becomes that the true function of a writer is to produce a masterpiece.') we are ushered into the presence of Literature. The self-conscious literary stance blots out experience with extraordinary completeness, mangling the simplest notions into dreary and precious convolutions of style.

Probably the excess derives in part from *The Unquiet Grave's* being a war book – like many others, not a book about the war, but a spiritual retreat from it to reaffirm the values and standards the war seemed to be menacing. And here, the standards are those of a world where life existed for Literature, and Literature was the carefully-tended garden of the sensitive (and privileged) few. Art did not merely have autonomy, a life of its own; it was separated by walls from the rest, a precious acre of *Timelessness*. The genteel narcissism of this cultural existence perpetuated itself through the familiar cycle established in the 19th century: avant-garde creation, meaningless to most but appreciated by the most discerning of the few, then acceptance and canonisation in the literary pantheon as the new style another avant-garde would have to break with. The tensions of this cycle were balanced by the supposedly permanent Platonic standards governing it, the values of *the* tradition of Literature, possession of which was the meaning of culture. To these values there corresponded an equally permanent and changeless reality of human nature and feeling.

So, Palinurus was worried (realistically) by the problem of writing anything that would hold good for 10 years. Yet he chose naturally to write in this personal-philosophical genre whose assumption is precisely that of total, basic constancy in human experience – so that the 'truths' of life and love can be disclosed in any piece of living, if one analyses it finely enough. The maximum of generalisation from the minimum of data joins one to the great minds of the literary past, in an armchair contemplation of the verities. He felt at the mercy of time and change, yet wrote as if through Literature time could be automatically transcended. This contradiction did not affect the past great minds so abundantly quoted in *The Unquiet Grave* (Pascal, Sainte-Beuve, Chamfort) because they lived in a more stable universe. Today, it can only generate falsity, and has made this the deadest of the literary genres.

The obvious temptation of the book arises from the same source, and explains how it has held thousands of adolescent imaginations enthralled across the years. In our quicksands, it offers an easy vision of certainties, a stance of Tiresian knowingness, a cultured life-style to identify with. This is actually as phoney as the certainties. In *Horizon*, again looking back over the history of the review, this arch-druid of Literature was to remark bitterly, about this same world:

> London, of course, is a particularly disheartening centre from which to operate ... one is continually reminded of that sterile, embittered, traditional literary society which has killed so many finer things than a review of literature and art.

The Unquiet Grave is killed by something else besides this general literary mystique. A second dimension of illusion – more especially

English – comes from the idea of France found in it. The daydream of
the culture-garden required a French décor. Connolly says he wanted
to express how, during the war, 'as a European, he was acutely aware
of being cut off from France'. But what France? 'Tout mon mal vient
de Paris. There befell the original sin and the original ecstasy; there
were the holy places – the Cross-Roads and the Island. Quai Bourbon,
Rue de Vaugirard, Quai d'Anjou.' This is a dream-France, an unknown
land of nostalgia where one imagines oneself

> Peeling off the kilometres to the tune of *Blue Skies*, sizzling down the long
> black liquid reaches of Nationale Sept, the plane-trees going sha-sha-sha
> through the open window, the windscreen yellowing with crushed midges, she
> with the Michelin beside me, a handkerchief binding her hair.

Twenty years after closing time, take a trip back into the gardens of
the West with *The Unquiet Grave.* Those in the Eng. Lit. Departments
of many universities will need no reminder. But where it is needed, the
trip will show one that Literature really is dead. And what it died of.

Tom Nairn, 28 April 1967

If Kennedy's death marked the shattering of New Statesman*ish hopes
for the USA which, in retrospect, look naive, few anticipated the depths
of the violent night into which American society voyaged during the
1960s. To a still startling extent, the atmosphere of the British Left was
to be defined in response to events in the US and in its semi-colonies:
pre-eminently Vietnam. NORA SAYRE witnessed the bringing of
Vietnam back to sweet home Chicago, in 1968.*

On the Battlefield

Such blood: released from bruised and broken veins, from foreheads,
scalps and mouths, from eyesockets, shattered wrists and skulls. Broad
bloodstreaks on the pavements showed where bodies had been dragged.
We all bleed inwardly from the particular atrocities we witnessed. I saw
seven policemen clubbing one girl – long after she had fallen; a row of
sitting singers whose heads were cracked open by a charge of running
cops; a photographer's camera smashed thoroughly into his eyes. Each
day, scores staggered bleeding through the streets and parks, reeling or
dropping, their faces glistening with vaseline – for Mace. Gas rinses
your lungs with the lash of iodine and vinegar; your own breath burns

your throat. Outside the Hilton, a nice little old lady patted a rebel on the chest, murmuring 'knock the socks off them'. Then she and I were suddenly hurled against the wall when 100 policemen seized their blue wooden barricades to ram the crowd (mainly onlookers and press) against the building with such force that many next to me, including the old lady, were thrust through plate-glass windows. People sobbed with pain as their ribs snapped from being crushed against each other. (I still have ribs, thanks to an unknown man's magnificently fat, soft back. All praise to fat power.) Soon a line of stick-whipping cops swung in on us. Voiceless from gas, I feebly waved my credentials, and the warrior who was about to hit me said: 'Oops, press.' He let me limp into the hotel, where people were being pummelled into the red carpet, while free Pepsi was offered on the sidelines.

Since delegates, McCarthy workers, newsmen, and spectators were thrashed along with the demonstrators, many learned what blacks have always known; that the democracy of savagery makes no distinctions – everyone's guilty for his mere presence or existence. The Chicago police made niggers of us all: rubble with no protection or defence. In future, we can easily share the ghettos' fate: without uncoiling any imagination. Later, I watched beatings and gassings from a second-floor McCarthy room. Twelve policemen surged in, slammed the windows, drew the curtains and told us to turn away and watch the TV set, where Humphrey was starting to speak – 'and that's an order'. The Chicago cops, whose trucks advise 'Reach out and grab the greatest summer ever', direct traffic as though they were flogging invisible bodies. Seasoned Chicago reporters said that they're extremely afraid of the local blacks. Hence they took a special revenge on the marchers, primarily because the police failed to subdue last April's ghetto riots. Yet even Humphrey has defended them, and a recent poll suggests that 71.4 per cent of queried citizens 'find police actions justified'.

Thus it's delicate to determine what the protest accomplished. True, the world, the press and all free minds throbbed with a communal concussion. But, as James Reston noted, the young, the poor, the black and the intelligent 'have the fewest votes', and the demonstrations were probably deplored by the voting majority. Still, 'voting with bodies' wasn't bootless. Tom Hayden: 'We are coming to Chicago to vomit on "the politics of joy".' Indeed they did, and the image was distilled by a stinkbomb at the Hilton, which smelled as though dozens of gorges had risen. The motto is: 'There can be no peace in the US until there is peace in Vietnam' – and there won't be. At a Black Panther rally, young white revolutionaries vowed 'to joint the blacks – by putting ourselves in the same crisis that blacks are in'. And certainly a whole new collaboration is accelerating. A black militant replied: 'The

strongest weapon we have is all of us. United black-white opposition.'
Undoubtedly new militants were created; some liberals became radicals,
some dissenters became revolutionaries. The most triumphant moral
point came from Dick Gregory: 'Had there been a bunch of young
people who challenged Hitler the way you challenged Mayor Daley,
there might be a whole lot of Jews alive today.'

After that statement, one's pride in the throng kept dilating. (In this
journal, J.B. Priestley wrote that 'A mob tends to behave like the worst
person in it' – which is often true. But the Chicago crowd reflected its
best members – who were also the majority.) The aims are so simple:
peace, liberation for blacks, a radically new America where property is
less valuable than human life. These goals must be repeated, because
the tactics confuse older (often sympathetic) people. The movement
seethes with such contradictions about method and leadership that,
when Humphrey said it was 'programmed', one only wished that he
were right.

A few leaders are lavishly irresponsible: they excite the most naive –
hippies and teenagers – who don't know that the mild term 'personal
risk' can mean getting killed or maimed. These gentle waifs, plus a few
glittering hysterics, usually rush to the front; at moments, one feared
that they would be used as fodder. SDS – which decided that 'mass
confrontations don't effect constituencies' – didn't demonstrate;
instead, it worked to organise and protect the marchers. SDS 'does not
believe that a bop on the head is more educative than a pamphlet'. But
some mobilisation workers generate a tension that splits bones instead
of hairs. Different leaders springing to the microphones instructed the
crowd to be cool, to get hot, that they were helpless, that they were
powerful, to go home, to gather, to disperse in small groups, to mass for
a huge non-violent march – in which other leaders warned that they'd
be trapped. (And they were.) Many marchers were too inexperienced
to choose clearly. Obviously, the need for organisation is as desperate
as the ache for peace.

One comes lurching out of these vast flesh-packs with a reeking
dilemma about 'violence' – which is now a suitcase-word for
assassinations, student protests, ghetto riots, mugging, and nut crimes.
For the Right, these are indistinguishable. For SDS, violence means
wrecking Selective Services files or bombing a draft board – at night,
when no one's there to be hurt. 'We're not non-violent; we'd like to
take over the city. But we can't. So we'll use long-range political
organisation. We're ready to use force but ... does it achieve that end?'
For others, 'revolution is a form of self-defence ... since our society is
already founded on force.'

Meanwhile, for one who has never accepted violence and has always believed in working through the political process, Dick Gregory's words keep echoing, underlining the realisation that the threat of black violence has become an excellent tool for Negroes. Yet how do you draw a dotted line between street fights and killing, between 'good' and 'bad' violence? Any brand of violence is contagious, as this land of assassination knows. However, since madness now seems to be the country's most pungent odour, more people may become violent merely to get attention, merely to be heard. Many of us are wrestling with evaluations of the fact of force. If violence in the US could result in peace in Vietnam, then I would support it – with a ravaging disgust at a society which forces one to make such a choice. I haven't the physical courage to fight in the streets, but I bless those who do. A Chicago clergyman was sympathetic; he said that the church hasn't yet decided its own position: 'Since no social change occurs without violence.' Certainly, the new revolutionaries cannot remould America on their own. (And, at moments, some sound like the general who said that he had to destroy a Vietnamese village in order to save it.) But their power could be a partial fuel for change – if a right-wing renaissance doesn't stifle us all. That possibility hums in every wire of the mind. Chicago taught us what law and order can mean. After all, these protestors were not violent. The streets were dangerous because of the police.

Nora Sayre, 6 September 1968

The political charge of DOUGLAS DUNN's 'Backwaters' was quiet, but devastating.

Backwaters

They are silent places, dilapidated cities
Obscure to the nation, their names spoken of
In the capital with distinct pejorative overtones.

For some, places mean coming to or going from,
Comedians and singers with their suitcases
Packed with signed photographs of themselves;

Business-men in sharp suits, come to buy and sell,
Still seeking their paradise of transactions,
The bottomless market, where the mugs live.

For others, places are sites for existence,

Where the roads slow down and come to a stop
Outside where it's good to be, particular places,

Where the instantly recognised people live,
The buses are a familiar colour and the life is
Utterly civilian.

And for a very few, places are merely the dumps
They end up in, backwaters, silent places,
The cheapest rooms of the cheapest towns.

These darker streets, like the bad days in our lives,
Are where the stutterers hide, the ugly and clubfooted,
The radically nervous who are hurt by crowds.

They love the sunlight at street corners
And the tough young men walking out of it,
And the police patrol. Poverty makes fools of them.

They have done so little they are hardly aware of themselves.
Unmissed, pensioned, at the far end of all achievements,
In their kiln-baked rooms, they are permanent.

Douglas Dunn, 3 October 1969

CORINNA ADAM observed the first-ever national conference of the contemporary British women's movement, in Oxford in 1970. She was at least as much irritated as exhilarated, but could not doubt the future significance of what she saw.

Sisters versus Comrades

'Those people who feel the need to paint slogans on the wall must also please feel the need to wash them off again by tomorrow morning,' said one of the organisers at last weekend's Women's Conference at Oxford. 'Because if they don't, the cleaners will have to do it, and we shall be contributing to the exploitation of another group of women.' The half-dozen young Maoists in front of me fidgeted nervously on their seats, obviously longing to get up and shout that washing off slogans was counter-revolutionary, but in difficulty because of the cleaners being working-class and therefore good. Now if only the cleaners themselves had painted the slogans. ... But of course they hadn't. And that, in a sense, was symbolic of the whole conference.

It reflected, as any such occasion is bound to do, the contradiction always present in women's movements: the question whether they are part of existing political and ideological structures, or something separate and essentially different. (See the way Women's Liberation Movement is always comparing itself — wrongly — with blacks.) Crudely put, it resolves itself into the question whether you believe men are the oppressors, or capitalism; or, if you believe both are, which you think is worse. Women in women's movements, since they are rarely right wing, tend to be torn between being sisters and being comrades.

The slogan-painting was an example of this. As far as one could tell, it had been done by revolutionaries — yet the slogans said things like 'Phalluses are Fascist' and 'End Penal Servitude'. The Oxford police are certainly quick to get the point of a smutty pun; the second slogan was judged to be offensive when the paint was scarcely dry. Come to that, there were some pretty offensive notices put up by men, quite probably male trade unionists, on Ruskin College noticeboard. Facetious invitations to 'share a bed on an equal basis'; witticisms like 'Emancipation makes you blind'. So that despite the countervailing influence of the men volunteers running the crèche next door, one entered the conference in the correct militant state of mind.

It was called to bring together as many as possible of the new women's groups which have sprouted up over the past few years, though any individual who wanted could also attend. (Male organisations, please follow.) So apart from a few trades unionists, and some seasoned ladies who wanted to form a Woman's Party (overwhelmingly defeated, I'm glad to say), this was essentially a meeting between the extreme Left and the Women's Liberation Movement. The International Socialists were there, and the International Marxist Group, and people from the CP (Marxist-Leninist) and so forth, confronting women from the Workshops, as the WL calls its local groups. It was interesting, if depressing, to be reminded how women always have subservient roles in even the most supposedly progressive organisations. As one girl put it: 'At least this is something we've done ourselves; we've called it, we've organised it, we've made a start in breaking down female passivity. Because usually we're the ones who sew the banners, and duplicate the broadsheets, while the men decide where the demo's going to be held.' (Indeed a man at the conference was heard to remark to a friend, after leaving a room where the IS women had been meeting: 'I've just been telling our girls what to say.') And there were cheers for the women, who, when it was suggested that a session be cut short so that we could go and join the student sit-in in the Clarendon, said 'But if we do that we're just going back to our supportive role. It's typical. We've got ourselves here to meet other women, and all we want to do is rush off and help a lot of men with *their* political activity.'

Fair enough. But unfortunately for those who believe in women-only organisations, it became more and more clear as the meeting progressed that it was precisely those women who had been involved in male-dominated organisations, like trades unions or political parties, who had something to say and knew how to say it. WL puts a premium on amateurishness which is no help at all on large-scale occasions: and if women are to be liberated, large-scale occasions there will have to be. It is a deliberate policy, because it is thought to help people who are shy, isolated, unsure of themselves. Their magazine, *Shrew*, prints every contribution it receives, in order to build up people's self-confidence, and be different from the competitive, masculine outside world. But it also seems to me to mean that women *are* taking their inferiority for granted ('not done well, but you are surprised to find it done at all'). It also makes it even more difficult for WL to fulfil its stated aim of reaching working-class women, who place no premium on amateurishness whatsoever.

This is not, of course, true of all WL groups — any more than the contrary picture usually presented of them, as terrifying harpies. Even the groups which do just provide therapy for lonely middle-class mothers are doing a useful, if limited, job. There was, nevertheless, something rather shocking about the posture adopted by a lot of the young women at this conference; an apolitical stance betraying a refusal to think. It was only shocking given the occasion: in a democracy one has, of course the right *not* to be interested in politics. But this conference was supposed to be about the oppression of all women; and yet a typical attitude was that of a 'captive wife', who had made a speech about the dreadful boredom of housework, and then said: 'When I hear about my oppression being the result of capitalism I just don't listen — it has nothing to do with *me*.'

There was a curious lack of interest in concrete proposals — such as how to fight the equal pay battle to make sure it does not prove another factor actually limiting women's freedom. There was a sad failure to get beyond contemplating what they delicately referred to – when men were present — as their 'guts' and think about other women, worse off than themselves. For instance, in an excellent paper given on delinquent women it was pointed out how many are in jail for social security fraud. This usually consists of failing to inform the authorities when a man is living temporarily in the house, which one is supposed to do because he is automatically assumed to be providing support. As the speaker put it: 'They are in jail for the offence of refusing to become a prostitute.' One might suppose that at such a conference, there would be some discussion about changing the law: but no. An American woman said hysterically: 'Just as all black prisoners in the United States are political prisoners, so all women prisoners are political prisoners,' and this ludicrous statement was applauded.

Female chauvinism at its worst: a mirror-image of the feminists' most bitter complaint against men. Still, it was all a beginning: and the mere sensation of being with hundreds of other women who were, at least, angry about their position in society, was a pleasant one — even for those of us who (as one WL member said angrily to me) are supposed to have 'made it in a man's world and therefore lost all sympathy'.

Corinna Adam, 6 March 1970

SAMUEL BECKETT, the incredible shrinking man, offered some cheerful thoughts in 1970.

Lessness

Ruins true refuge long last towards which so many false time out of mind. All sides endlessness earth sky as one no sound no stir. Grey face two pale blue little body heart beating only upright. Blacked out fallen open four walls over backwards true refuge issueless.

Scattered ruins same grey as the sand ash grey true refuge. Four square all light sheer white blank planes all gone from mind. Never was but grey air timeless no sound figment the passing light. No sound no stir ash grey sky mirrored earth mirrored sky. Never but this changelessness dream the passing hour.

He will curse God again as in the blessed days face to the open sky the passing deluge. Little body grey face features slit and little holes two pale blue. Blank planes sheer white eye calm long last all gone from mind.

Figment light never was but grey air timeless no sound. Blank planes touch close sheer white all gone from mind. Little body ash grey locked rigid heart beating face to endlessness. On him will rain again as in the blessed days of blue the passing cloud. Four square true refuge long last four walls over backwards no sound.

Grey sky no cloud no sound no stir earth ash grey sand. Little body same grey as the earth sky ruins only upright. Ash grey all sides earth sky as one all sides endlessness.

He will stir in the sand there will be stir in the sky the air the sand. Never but in dream the happy dream only one time to serve. Little body little block heart beating ash grey only upright. Earth sky as one all sides endlessness little body only upright. In the sand no hold one step more in the endlessness he will make it. No sound not a breath same grey all sides earth sky body ruins.

Slow black with ruin true refuge four walls over backwards no sound. Legs a single block arms fast to sides little body face to endlessness. Never but in vanished dream the passing hour long short. Only upright little body grey smooth no relief a few holes. One step in the ruins in the sand on his back in the endlessness he will make it. Never but dream the days and nights made of dreams of other nights better days. He will live again the space of a step it will be day and night over him the endlessness.

In four split asunder over backwards true refuge issueless scattered ruins. Little body little block genitals overrun arse a single block grey crack overrun. True refuge long last issueless scattered down over four walls backwards no sound. All sides endlessness earth sky as one no stir not a breath. Blank planes sheer white calm eye light of reason all gone from mind. Scattered ruins ash grey all sides true refuge long last issueless.

Ash grey little body only upright heart beating face to endlessness. Old love new love as in the blessed days unhappiness will reign again. Earth sand same grey as the air sky ruins body fine ash grey sand. Light refuge sheer white blank planes all gone from mind. Flatness endless little body only upright same grey all sides earth sky body ruins. Face to white calm touch close eye calm long last all gone from mind. One step more one alone all alone in the sand no hold he will make it.

Blacked out fallen open true refuge issueless towards which so many false time out of mind. Never but silence such that in imagination this wild laughter these cries. Head through calm eye all light white calm all gone from mind. Figment dawn dispeller of figments and the other called dusk.

He will go on his back face to the sky open again over him the ruins the sand the endlessness. Grey air timeless earth sky as one same grey as the ruins flatness endless. It will be day and night again over him the endlessness the air heart will beat again. True refuge long last scattered ruins same grey as the sand.

Face to calm eye touch close all calm all white all gone from mind. Never but imagined the blue in a wild imagining the blue celeste of poesy. Little void mighty light four square all white blank planes all gone from mind. Never was but grey air timeless no stir not a breath. Heart beating little body only upright grey face features overrun two pale blue. Light white touch close head through calm eye light of reason all gone from mind.

Little body same grey as the earth sky ruins only upright. No sound not a breath same grey all sides earth sky body ruins. Blacked out fallen open four walls over backwards true refuge issueless.

No sound no stir ash grey sky mirrored earth mirrored sky. Grey air timeless earth sky as one same grey as the ruins flatness endless. In the sand no hold one step more in the endlessness he will make it. It will be day and night again over him the endlessness the air heart will beat again.

Figment light never was but grey air timeless no sound. All sides endlessness earth sky as one no stir not a breath. On him will rain again as in the blessed days of blue the passing cloud. Grey sky no cloud no sound no stir earth ash grey sand.

Little void mighty light four square all white blank planes all gone from mind. Flatness endless little body only upright same grey all sides earth sky body ruins. Scattered ruins same grey as the sand ash grey true refuge. Four square true refuge long last four walls over backwards no sound. Never but this changelessness dream the passing hour. Never was but grey air timeless no sound figment the passing light.

In four split asunder over backwards true refuge issueless scattered ruins. He will live again the space of a step it will be day and night again over him the endlessness. Face to white calm touch close eye calm long last all gone from mind. Grey face two pale blue little body heart beating only upright. He will go on his back face to the sky open again over him the ruins the sand the endlessness. Earth sand same grey as the air sky ruins body fine ash grey sand. Blank planes touch close sheer white all gone from mind.

Heart beating little body only upright grey face features overrun two pale blue. Only upright little body grey smooth no relief a few holes. Never but dream the days and nights made of dreams of other nights better days. He will stir in the sand there will be stir in the sky the air the sand. One step in the ruins in the sand on his back in the endlessness he will make it. Never but silence such that in imagination this wild laughter these cries.

True refuge long last scattered ruins same grey as the sand. Never was but grey air timeless no stir not a breath. Blank planes sheer white calm eye light of reason all gone from mind. Never but in vanished dream the passing hour long short. Four square all light sheer white blank planes all gone from mind.

Blacked out fallen open true refuge issueless towards which so many false time out of mind. Head through calm eye all light white calm all gone from mind. Old love new love as in the blessed days unhappiness will reign again. Ash grey all sides earth sky as one all sides endlessness. Scattered ruins ash grey all sides true refuge long last issueless. Never but in dream the happy dream only one time to serve. Little body grey face features slit and little holes two pale blue.

Ruins true refuge long last towards which so many false time out of mind. Never but imagined the blue in a wild imagining the blue celeste of poesy. Light white touch close head through calm eye light of reason all gone from mind.

Slow black with ruin true refuge four walls over backwards no sound. Earth sky as one all sides endlessness little body only upright. One step more one alone all alone in the sand no hold he will make it. Ash grey little body only upright heart beating face to endlessness. Light refuge sheer white blank planes all gone from mind. All sides endlessness earth sky as one no sound no stir.

Legs a single block arms fast to sides little body face to endlessness. True refuge long last issueless scattered down four walls over backwards no sound. Blank planes sheer white eye calm long last all gone from mind. He will curse God again as in the blessed days face to the open sky the passing deluge. Face to calm eye touch close all calm all white all gone from mind.

Little body little block heart beating ash grey only upright. Little body ash grey locked rigid heart beating face to endlessness. Little body little block genitals overrun arse a single block grey crack overrun. Figment dawn dispeller of figments and the other called dusk.

Samuel Beckett, 1 May 1970
© *John Calder Ltd*

If J. K. GALBRAITH had been a Brit, he'd have been a natural New Statesman, combining as he does some of the qualities of Keynes and of Kingsley Martin. In a guest appearance he compared the fortunes of British and US radicals, and warned of the coming crisis of Keynesianism.

The Left in Britain and the US

The British Labour Party and the liberal-Left in the United States – those recently celebrated by the peculiar eloquence of Vice-President Agnew as the Radic-Libs – have one indubitable characteristic in common: both are out of office. Beyond that, comparisons become more disputable and, on some matters, to one side or the other, odious. The political Left in Britain is roughly conterminous with a political party. In the United States it is a part of a party which for historical reasons (as well as for no reasons at all) includes nominally its most implacable political enemies, the ante-bellum and even prehistoric Southern wing. These Democrats are united only in laying claim to the same party name. (A new moderate generation of Southern Democrats seeking election with black votes is emerging.) In the North, liberals share party participation with those whose political interest is ethnic or habitual or devoted to scraping together a modest livelihood.

The Labour Party proudly calls itself socialist without, always, insisting too strenuously on the associated socialism. In the United States even if a measure can reasonably be described as socialist it is thought better not to arouse the resulting storm. The word socialism remains synonymous with political extremism.

There are other differences. Although the defeat of the Wilson government is variously explained, foreign policy was not central to its failure, I did not much applaud Labour policy in these last years. The natural alliance of a Labour and socialist government on Vietnam was not with the supporters of the war in the United States, whatever the conveniences. It was with those in the United States who were opposing this cruel and deeply foolish mistake.

But my personal doubts about such socialist eccentricities did not, I would gather, bulk large in the mind of the British voter. Clearly they were not decisive in the recent election. In economics, the parallels between the American and the British experience become very much closer. Subject only to secondary differences, we are making the same mistakes, evading the same truths and suffering the same resulting misfortune.

The truth we evade is that the age of Keynesian economics is now

over: the macroeconomic revolution in fiscal and monetary
management which we owe to Keynes has run afoul of the
microeconomic revolution in trade union and corporate power. In
consequence there is no way within the Keynesian modalities to
reconcile adequately high employment with reasonably stable prices. It
is possible to combine a politically unacceptable level of unemployment
with a socially damaging rate of inflation. This is now being
accomplished in the United States – and with no great effort. Mr Nixon
has inadequate economists. But, save in their relentless predictions of
lower prices and more jobs, they are *not bad* in any inspired way.

The reason for the Keynesian failure is that at any near approach to
full employment, unions can seek and win wage increases much in
excess of productivity gains. They can do so because, in the market that
sustains such a level of employment, corporations can retrieve the wage
increase and something more. They have won the market power that
protects them from precisely this risk. Then, public employees (for very
good reasons now the most militant of workers in both the US and
Britain) must act to remain abreast. Their employer cannot, so easily,
pass on the cost. But eventually government too has to yield and thus it
also becomes part of the inflationary process. Only an intolerable level
of unemployment (and idle plant capacity) arrests the inflationary
process. And the threat of such unemployment is sufficient to cause
government to ease fiscal and monetary restraint lest the lesser evil of
much inflation and moderate employment give way to the greater evil
of greater unemployment and slightly less inflation. This is how matters
stand in both the United States and Britain. Conservatives in both
countries have a recourse: they think that because they uphold free
enterprise, free enterprise will surely uphold them.

The secondary differences in the position of the Left in the two
countries are not altogether slight. In the United States the unions,
some ritual protest to the contrary, will probably accept wage and price
control in preference to the alternatives. (I use the hard words here: I
doubt that we make the policy more acceptable by using such
euphemisms as guide-posts, wage-price restraints or even incomes
policy.) Our unions must, of course, be assured that the control is real
and fair, i.e. that it will stabilise living costs and allow for productivity
gains. But given this they will (in my view) go along. Nor is the political
community averse. Knowing that Mr Nixon would not necessarily
welcome the help, the Democrats in Congress have authorised controls.
In the United States most influential opposition comes, in fact, from the
economic establishment. A diminishing but still a large number of those
who speak and write on economic matters continue to protect their
vested interest in that they have always taught or believed. They have

always taught and believed that markets (including those where prices are fixed by corporations and wages established as between strong unions and strong employers) are sacrosanct. It's the free market – however odd that thought. They have also always taught and believed that, with John Maynard Keynes, economists' work was done. No difficult problems remained. No task in economic management arose that could not be resolved by properly learned gentlemen, suitably equipped with figures and charts discussing taxation, expenditure and interest rates around a large well-polished table. In Britain the situation is different: both the economists and the unions are hostile.

But the fact remains. There can be no economic policy tolerable to the Left that does not involve wage and price controls. Without such controls there can be no policy that combines adequate employment with reasonable price stability. And there can be no attempt to achieve this result which does not disemploy the most vulnerable workers vulnerable businessmen and the neediest consumers and would-be houseowners. It is too bad that this is so; whoever arranged things with such atrocious disrespect for socialist or liberal convenience is open to grave criticism. But so it is.

A very good reason for wage and price control is that not otherwise can we preserve a civilised balance between the public and the private sectors of the economy. If monetary and fiscal policy are carrying (even though ineffectively) the whole burden of inflation control in an inflationary context then the public sector will always be subject to recurrent attack. It is the part of total expenditure to which Chancellors and budget directors have access. And borrowing by states, cities or local authorities will be vulnerable to tightening money rates – as the capital expenditures of large corporations from earnings are not.

Here I sense another parallel: neither in the United States nor Britain is the vulnerability of the public sector to neo-Keynesian policy sufficiently appreciated on the Left. In the depression years, when expansion was sought, the instruments were increased public expenditure and lower money rates. Keynesian policy thus favoured the public sector. In the age of chronic inflation, by contrast, the policy strongly favours the private sector.

An American coming even briefly to England cannot but sense how much better British socialism, as compared with American liberalism, has supported the public sector since World War II. One could argue that, in consequence of the better balance between public and private services, the British standard of living is, in its general yield of satisfaction, now higher than that of the United States. Few things to me are so discouraging as the reluctance of the American Left to face up to the costs of modern government. The modern metropolis in particular, is an incredibly expensive thing. Unless its price is paid modern urban life is not even tolerable, much less agreeable. There are, I've long thought, few problems in New York City which would not be solved by doubling the city budget. There is none which will be solved by the present liberal device, which is to use sociology as a substitute for higher taxes. No matter how well we understand Harlem its problems will only be solved by better housing, more police, better street-cleaning, better schools, better parks, better and better-supervised recreation, more day nurseries and all the rest. And all will cost money. On these matters the British Left (and to be fair also the British Right) is a geological age in advance of the United States.

I turn now to a problem – more precisely a number of closely related problems – to which British socialists and American liberals have the same reaction. Both either decline to recognise them or, recognising them, they wish these questions would go away.

Modern industrial society achieves its not inconsiderable technical performace by massive organisation – and by imposing the needs and values of organisation upon the society. It persuades its participants to accept its goals and its work disciplines. It persuades the public to accept its products – to believe that the things it produces are the *sine qua non* of contentment and happiness. It exists in close association with the equally massive bureaucracies of the modern state. All of this adds up to the industrial life style – an acceptance of the goals of organisation, of the need to maximise income and consumption in accordance with its persuasion, of a public bureaucracy that reflects the interests and serves the needs of organisation. The older Left in both Britain and America has accepted this life style. It has sought to remedy defects in the functioning of the industrial system – in the level of output and the efficiency at which it operates, to a degree in the way it distributes its income, ineffectively in its predisposition to inflation. It has supported it with the educational establishment, technical research and public facilities that it required. Where, as in the case of Rolls-Royce or Lockheed, it encounters financial difficulty it goes along in the rescue operation. It has not, in the past, expressed doubt about either the purposes or the disciplines of the system itself. Until recently in the United States the Left has accepted the highly symbiotic relationship of the industrial system with the Pentagon.

But increasingly doubts are being expressed – are becoming part of the political context. This is especially but not uniquely so in the United States.

The most frequently asked questions concern the effect on the environment. Most people are still hoping that this is an essentially regulatory and cosmetic problem – one that better industrial zoning, better control of industrial effluent, better design of the internal combustion engine, the internalising of external diseconomies, will solve. Do these things and we can continue to emphasise economic growth as before. But others are sensing a larger problem. That is whether the established purposes of the industrial system, in particular its preoccupation with steadily increasing consumption, can be indefinitely sustained.

But the purposes of the system are being questioned in a more specific way. This is by younger people, many though not all of the university generation that the industrial system has itself called into being. They no longer automatically accept its values. They question its working disciplines – the notion that you work hard and competitively five days a week (or more) to maximise consumption in the other two. Somewhat selectively – more on clothing than electronics – they have come to reject the persuasion which sustains its consumption.

The massive industrial and associated public bureaucracy which we have artificed in the last half century will be the next great concern of the Left both in Britain and the United States. The problems it poses are new but they are also real. We must recognise that modern industrial organisation pursues purposes that are its own. In the past, broadly speaking, the Left has facilitated, humanised and on occasion restrained these purposes. Increasingly now it must call them into question. Certainly it must maintain sympathetic communication with those who do.

Specifically it must ask if environmental damage to air, water, countryside is merely a technical fault of the system. Or is it inherent in industrial growth and thus in industrial purpose? I think the latter. And thus I believe that the Left must balance the need for more private consumption against the claims of public amenity. The Right is certainly not going to do so. And the Left must ask if the seeming indifference and impersonality of great industrial bureaucracy – the kind of thing which has given rise to Naderism in the United States – is not also inherent in great organisation. And the Left must surely begin to wonder about the urgency of consumption which depends as much as does ours on persuasion – or advertising. Are we to be endlessly a party to this exercise in illusion?

And it must ask whether, merely because something must be invented, we must have it. Is the case for technological progress so strong that we must have even what makes life more unpleasant? The bearing of this on supersonic travel will be evident. And we must inquire increasingly about the curious unevenness of our blessings in a society that emphasises growth – the unevenness as between the automobile industry which has high virtuosity in persuasion and industries like housing or mass transport where the persuasive power is low. We can no longer evade these problems by saying that they reflect consumer choice. They do not. They reflect persuasion by producing organisations in their own interest.

All of this adds up to questions about a life style itself – about a life style that emphasises increased consumption, that accepts that it will be producer-influenced if not producer guided, that accepts the maximisation of income to maximise such consumption; and which accepts whatever organisation of whatever impersonality or even arrogance that serves this result.

I am a poorly reformed Calvinist, I have been disturbed in the last couple of years at how easily student distress whatever its origins comes to focus on the oldest of student grievances, which is the need to work. On the whole I applaud man's emancipation from physical toil; his liberation from mental effort seems to me premature. I also have serious misgivings on the matter of drugs. Perhaps the serious ones expand consciousness; it's my impression that they serve mostly to dull it. Hemingway and his generation thought they had found in alcohol a deeper form of self-release, a more profound form of self-expression. I never believed that either. I think it was merely an improved excuse for getting drunk.

But we must respect the instinct of a younger generation when it raises questions, which an older generation of radicals does not wish to face, about the purposes of the economic system. And perhaps some of the aberrations of the young are a reaction, not only to the purposes of economic society, but to the unwillingness of an older generation to face the evidence before its own eyes.

I do not doubt that the need to face the purposes of the economic system is more urgent in the United States than in Britain. But let me warn against the oldest of the British devices for evading thought on such matters. That is to say: 'I can see how this kind of problem bugs the Americans but, of course, we are a good deal less rich than they are.' I do not think that the question of life style – of artificially stimulated and competitive consumption, of strenuous maximisation of income to maintain it, of massive organisation which commands this behaviour – can any longer be evaded in any Western industrial country. There is no better way for the present Left to become obsolete than to suppose, as now, that its only function is to facilitate and moderate the industrial process, but never ask to what end.

John Kenneth Galbraith, 4 December 1970

The NS*'s involvement in battle against the philistinism of British obscenity laws was long-standing and honourable: compare the list of defence witnesses at the* Lady Chatterley *trial with a list of* Statesman *contributors.* Oz *and its countercultural connections were less congenial to the then rather middle-aged ethos of the journal, but there could be no doubt where its sympathies lay. JONATHAN DIMBLEBY reports.*

The Oz Trial

'It is some time', intoned His Honour Judge Argylle as the *Oz* trial entered its fourth week, 'since I have had to remind people that this is not a theatre but a court of law.' The reminder was timely if vain. A few days later one of the hundreds of American tourists who had tramped noisily in and out of the proceedings was overheard to ask: 'Are they running this thing right through the tourist season?'

At that level it was great entertainment. In the dock stood the prisoners: Richard Neville, Jim Anderson and Felix Dennis, hair close around their shoulders, dressed in long flowing robes or dungarees and brightly coloured teeshirts with the words 'University of Wishful Thinking' emblazoned across the front. Facing them from on high, the Judge, equally bizarre in his black robes and tight white wig. We watch him closely – a soft pale pink face, pince-nez covering rarely blinking eyes, an occasional neat smile, a dry distant voice: middle-aged. On his right, down in the well of the court sits Detective-Inspector Luff whose zeal has enabled this event to take place. For nearly three years he has tirelessly pursued the accused: advising, admonishing, raiding and seizing. Now, his duty performed, he relaxes amid piles of the offending *Oz*, turning occasionally behind him with some whispered information for the prosecution counsel Mr Brian Leary. In this airless ritualistic atmosphere Luff is unmistakably an outsider: dark-suited, club-tied, well-slicked black hair, suede shoes, a face roughened by the outside back-street world of the Vice Squad.

Mr Leary for the Crown is slim, dapper, sharp-featured, his voice well trained in the arts of moral outrage and silky sarcasm. At his side defending: John Mortimer QC, playwright. A shaggy yellowing wig fails to hide shaggier hair; his waistcoat is ill-fitting. A man of sharp wit, he has an air of world-weary tolerance.

As the court processed through its days of debate it was easy to forget what everyone in the courtroom knew: that the three *Oz* editors were liable to be sent to prison for publishing what was eventually found to be an obscene magazine.

By the end the jury had spent some five weeks hearing an assorted collection of sociologists, psychologists, writers and teachers inform them that this School Kids issue of *Oz* could not possibly have any harmful effect on young people. These 'persons with progressive opinions', as Mr Leary disapprovingly described them, parade an impressive if repetitive wealth of experience. John Mortimer gently extracts their knowledge. Richard Neville, conducting his own defence with daily increasing expertise, playing the game the law's way, seeks deeper moral support. 'Is it true that the authorities are likely to be out of touch with what young people think?' 'Is open discussion healthy?' 'Why don't university authorities "moralise" about drugs and promiscuity?' The answer comes exquisitely: 'It would be a completely mindless thing to do.'

The prosecution has a hard time of it. One detects, though, a pattern. First the witness's social (and thereby moral?) standing.

Mr Leary: 'Dr Klein, we know you are a doctor; what we don't know is whether you're Miss or Mrs?'

Dr Klein: 'Miss.'

Mr Leary: 'So you have no children?'

Dr Klein: 'No.'

Mr Leary (slowly): 'I see.'

He rubs his hands, pauses and glances significantly at his jury sitting opposite.

Then comes the cross examination proper. The prosecution is nothing if not thorough. Each witness is taken slowly through the magazine stopping at length to examine some dozen drawings and strip cartoons, a paragraph here and there, and the small ads. The cartoons vary. Some are crude, some silly, some funny: often sexually explicit, usually fantastic. The magazine had been compiled by around 20 teenagers at the invitation of the three defendants. The prosecution allows no detail to escape. Where is that hand? At what? That cane – what is it doing? What does this word signify? That smile? That gesture? The witnesses pore hopelessly over the pages, desperately trying to recall their first-year undergraduate skills at textual analysis: the concentrated stares of the jury diffuse into blankness: a policeman resumes his reading of *Reveille*: an exasperated witness bursts out: 'But to go through it inch by inch, line by line ... is judging it at an absurd level.'

Rupert Bear rubs the point home. In *Oz* 28 the little bear is provided with a massive phallus and a girl friend, the virgin Gypsy Granny. They have intercourse. The cartoon is absurd by itself: it did not need the memorable exchange between the prosecution and the psychologist Michael Scofield.

Mr Leary: 'What sort of age is Rupert Bear to your mind?' Mr
Scofield intimates that his mind had never considered the question
before. Mr Leary offers assistance: 'He's a young bear isn't he, he goes
to school ...' and then with sudden vehemence: 'children can identify
with the young bear, isn't that the truth?' Utterly incredulous Scofield
expostulates: 'What, children identify with a *bear*?' The public gallery,
watching from above, explodes with mirth and two friends of *Oz* are
escorted away.

The inch by inch analysis completed, the witnesses almost to a man
unyielding; the prosecution shifted its ground, fortifying itself behind
some general unstated but only too visible moral principles from which
it advanced armed with the General Question – so simple, so lethal: is
it a good thing that children discuss drugs, take part in group sex ... is
it a good thing? Or, similarly: 'Have you ever come across
pornography?' It depends, as the witness points out, what you mean by
pornography. The question, the Crown retorts, is really very simple. He
sighs and the Judge steps in: 'The answer is either "Yes", or "No" or "I
don't know".' The statement has depressingly ruthless overtones. Do
we really seek the truth, the whole truth and nothing but the truth by
these means?

Witness: 'I don't know because I don't know what the Court means
by pornography.'

Judge: 'I am recording that answer as: "I don't know because I don't
understand the question".' (Later Mr Leary offers us a definition:
something is pornographic '... if it is there to present sensuality in an
attractive light'.)

Sometimes the Judge partakes of the general question, too: 'Do you
think prostitution is a good thing or a bad thing?' 'It depends. ...' His
Honour puts down his pen with a flourish of irritation. Why won't they
answer simple questions? Have they *no* morality? Judge Argylle's skill
with the pen is soon renowned. To note or not to note – his choice is
made decisively; no one (least of all the jury) can fail to detect what in
his view is significant, and more important, *in*significant.

In his closing address to the jury Mr Leary expressed the hope that
they had found the trial interesting, informative, and intelligent. It was
certainly revealing; not least for the fact that the prosecution
conspicuously ignored the bulk of the magazine – some 21 pages of
youthful anti-authoritarian political writing. According to the Crown,
neither 'politics', nor what the kids thought of 'the pigs' were relevant
in what was merely a criminal trial. Quite so. But as the trial wore on
despite repeated protestations of this kind, it emerged that, like politics
and sport, quite plainly politics and morals *do* mix, indeed are
inextricably entangled.

When Felix Dennis gave evidence, pale-faced, leaning heavily on the witness box, few could have missed the antagonism concentrated in the few feet separating him from Mr Leary. He was taken through the production history of *Oz*.

Mr Leary: 'How did the sex get in?'

Dennis: 'I'm not sure what you mean.'

Judge (sighing): 'Take as long as you like. The question has five simple single-syllable words.'

And then onto the small ads. One advertises an 'exclusive private male "Gaye" guest house'. Does it not, Mr Leary wonders: 'pander to the lusts of homosexuals'.

Dennis: 'I find that question repulsive. Would you re-phrase it?'

Judge (with irritation): 'No. Answer it.'

Mr Leary seemed to have doubts about Felix Dennis's integrity. Surely the witness knew, if he were to be honest with himself, that *Oz* 28 was both indecent and obscene before it came out? Dennis made it clear he knew nothing of the sort.

Mr Leary (heavily sarcastic): 'Is there *anything* you consider indecent?' Suddenly the court-room tensed. Felix Dennis looks as if he will lose control, but sits down heavily, and pausing between each word, quietly and with contempt, says: 'There are a great many things I find indecent, Mr Leary.' Moments like that were rare. Suddenly the tiresome details of *Oz* 28, the pictures, the drawings, the swear words, the slang, the small-ads, event the children, fade from thought. Here is the confrontation that matters: one morality set resolutely against another; an 'alternative' challenging the Establishment. And in case any of us should have been in doubt about this, Mr Leary made it quite clear in his closing address. The alternative society, represented by the defendants consisted of those '. . . drop-outs who expected the state to provide for them – and by the state I mean nothing more than you and me – those of us who are fools enough to work.'

'Remember,' learned counsel continued, 'morality is essential to the well-being of a community like ours. It is up to you members of the jury to set the standard.'

There was perhaps little else for them to do. After five weeks they had heard one policeman (Luff) and one hostile teenager (Vivien Berger who was originally indicted as a co-producer of *Oz* 28) called on behalf of the prosecution, and more than a dozen defence 'experts' all of whom has testified at great length that *Oz* could do no harm. Perhaps fundamental questions like: 'What is corruption? and depravity? and indecency? and how are people corrupted? and by what?' are not susceptible to an easy 'yes, no or I don't know' formula so favoured by the criminal law. As a result, the witnesses were all but ignored.

The Judge's summing-up was stunning. Suddenly the defence witnesses became 'so-called defence experts', some of whom, members of the jury: 'you may think reached the position ... where they either had to admit they were wrong or tell a lie.' If *Oz* was a window on the hippie world – 'well, windows sometimes need cleaning, don't they?' As he finished with a witness, he would toss his copy of *Oz* disdainfully down onto the table, and with it, one felt, the case for the defence. It was a distressing and perhaps crucial exercise. For after constant 'exposure to' (a favourite expression of Mr Leary's) 'fucking in the streets', 'masturbation', 'deviation', 'lesbianism', 'corruption', and 'cannabis', this middle-aged group of British householders – the jury – was asked quite simply 'to set the standard'. What an invitation.

Jonathan Dimbleby, 30 July 1971

Maybe the brightest young star of the early seventies NS was JAMES FENTON. His capacity for running close to serious trouble was considerable, his skill at evoking the resultant circumstances equally so. He seems to have enjoyed Cambodia more than Belfast, but both were as hair-raising as Fenton's prematurely shiny crown would admit.

Under a Misapprehension

A man called Kolly Kibber goes down to Brighton and becomes convinced he is about to be murdered? Ridiculous. I gave up the book after a few pages and began to go over my code of conduct at arrival in Belfast. Above all, be vigilant, circumspect and discreet. Do not, if you value your life, be found talking to children. At some point, I told myself, you will find yourself in an impossible hole. Don't panic, and don't try to be clever.

The first time I visted Belfast, for instance, I set out to find my IRA contacts and walked straight into trouble. I was going down a desolated street early on a Sunday morning when I became aware of an army barricade at the other end. Half way along the street, deciding to try a different route, I turned around and, in a slight access of nerves, lit a cigarette. Immediately I was challenged by the armed soldier at the post. With fatal presence of mind, I explained that I was looking for a street adjacent to my actual destination. What I did not know was that the street I mentioned had been levelled to the ground months before. There was no possible reason, on a cold November morning, to be visiting it, and the Protestant vigilante who was with the soldier found my explanations, shouted down the empty road, most unsatisfactory. Immediately afterwards I learnt to my cost about not talking to children.

On this occasion, however, I was determined not to do or say anything silly. One afternoon I took a two-shilling taxi (there is an improvised local service which performs roughly what Lord Curzon expected of a bus) up to Andersonstown, in order to join one of the prongs of the PD march. I arrived a little early, nobody was around, and in order to while away the time I entered a local pub. There was no space to sit in the public bar, so after one drink I went round to the lounge and sat at a table alone. Within a couple of minutes I was joined by three youths of about 17, who as they sat down appeared to be mumbling something for me to hear. I think I indicated in my polite way that, yes, the table was free and they were welcome to join me. Then I noticed that they all appeared to be carrying something bulky under their coats. Finally I caught what they were saying, which was 'Put your hands on the table, and don't try anything clever'.

There is a passage in a Nancy Mitford novel which impressed me a long time ago, where some young girls are asking an older relative what it is like having babies. The woman replies that between times one entirely forgets the feeling, but that, just before the birth pangs begin, an extraordinarily vivid memory comes flooding back and one begins cursing oneself for ever having let it happen again. By which time it is too late. Well, we sat there huddled over the table, and as the physiological changes of fear began to manifest themselves throughout my body I said to myself: 'You stupid, bloody fool! You nana! You've really done it this time, haven't you?' My knees were knocking against their knees, their knees knocked against my knees, we all sat there terrified out of our wits and before I could say 'You are the Provisional IRA and I claim my five pounds' one of them whispered: 'We are the Provisional IRA and watch out because we've got a gun on you.'

I didn't, on reflection, believe them about the gun, but that wasn't really the main point. What worried me, after they had failed to believe my reasons for drinking first in the public bar and then in the lounge, and when they were unconvinced by my press card, was the fact that my pockets were full of documents relating to arms searches. This was difficult to explain away. 'Look,' I said, 'if I was an army or RUC spy, as you claim, would I have come in here with so little identification but carrying all these figures?' They replied that they had seen much worse cases than this. So we sat there, and during the half hour that followed, while someone went to check what they should do, they bought me drinks and gave me cigarettes like a man about to be shot. I had to behave naturally, although everyone in the lounge clearly knew what was going on. This was why it did not matter whether they had a gun.

The irony of the situation was that when I told the truth about my general attitude to the IRA nobody believed me. Gradually, therefore, as garrulousness and stout began to tell, I began questioning them and criticising the politics of the Provisionals. They in turn asked me about life in England, and I must say the Catholic church should congratulate itself on having produced such a set of high-minded bigots. Our first clash came over the question of drugs. 'You must admit,' they said, 'that in Ireland the working people have put an end to all that.' Later, after I had been taken by car to another part of Andersonstown and made to sit in an upstairs room (on the floor, for fear of the ubiquitous army surveillance), I asked them about their ultimate political aims. Suppose, I said, the IRA won tomorrow, and a United Irish state under their political domination was set up, what would they do with their success? How would they change society? The most articulate of the youths thought for a moment and simply replied: 'I suppose we would just clean up the dirt.'

Is it right to judge a movement by its young recruits? Clearly not, though the complete lack of political direction in my captors' minds was to a large extent a reflection of their leadership. Their main concern was to avoid appearing like bandits: after the initial histrionics, as I was passed from hand to hand to more senior officers, and as the contents of my pockets were scrutinised with blank incomprehension, every propriety was observed. My money for instance was carefully counted out and returned to me in full. Every time a single guard was left in the room he would apologise personally for their having to put me to such trouble. I was given continual assurances that there was no connection between the IRA and the recent spate of assassinations, and that I was not about to become another statistic. It was very comforting, and built up into a picture of an organisation desperately striving for some kind of respectability. When I was finally identified and independently vouched for, three hours after the original incident, we shook hands and parted on the best of terms.

But I kicked myself all the way back to the hotel for having behaved like a carefree man in a quite embattled town. And I had forgotten to ask what would have happened to me had I in fact been a spy. To calm myself, I ran a hot bath and settled down with a book. A man called Kolly Kibber had gone down to Brighton and was becoming convinced that he was about to be murdered. Somehow I knew I was not going to get very far with this one.

James Fenton, 23 February 1973

In Search of Cambodia's War

From time to time, as evening draws in on Phnom Penh and the sound
of the mortars is carried through the dusk, like interference on a radio,
one comes across men who are afraid to go home. The army, they
explain, is looking for them. 'So you do not wish to fight for your
country?' 'I do not wish to die, monsieur.' And where yesterday they
would refer to the enemy as the VC, today the war is a question of
Khmer fighting Khmer, where yesterday the patriotic phrases fell easily
from their lips today they are philosophical. Suppose, I asked one man
who was expressing contempt for such faint hearts, suppose it was not a
question of fighting *pour la patrie* but for Lon Nol and the generals –
would you still be prepared to die? That, he replied, is a question I have
been asking myself very often recently, and I have not yet found the
answer.

A common expression for draft evasion is 'going into the forest for a
few days'. Unfortunately in the vicinity of the capital there are not
many forests available: it lies in a plain of rice fields and it is at present
surrounded by enemy troops and water. But there are still a couple of
provinces in Cambodia where a man may go to forget. This summer's
siege of Phnom Penh turned Battambang into a resort for the families
of the powerful and rich. Fifty miles away, on the Thai border and in
the foothills of the Cardamom Mountains, lies Pailin. Both towns were
annexed by Siam under the Japanese occupation, and both are rich –
Battambang lies in the most fertile agricultural area in the country,
Pailin has sapphires and rubies. It is the latter town which exerts the
more powerful influence on the imaginations of the poor.

Getting there is like going on a pilgrimage. Somebody in Battambang
has amassed a fleet of 40 white Peugeot station wagons, which set out
each morning in a convoy of lorries, buses and assorted curious
vehicles, all under army supervision. For the first part of the journey the
cars – 11 passengers in each – make good progress along a reasonable
road. Then it is time to eat. Cambodians, particularly the soldiers, do
not like going into danger on an empty stomach. 'Why are you not
eating?' a soldier asked me. I replied that I was not hungry. 'Are you
afraid of the VC?' 'No.' 'But they are savages. Did you know that the
VC have been bombing Phnom Penh with B-52s?' 'No I did not.'

Afterwards the road is slow and potholed. I had been told that the
soldiers extort protection money from the passengers along the way, but
what I saw was rather a system of tipping. One threw down a loaf or a
handful of fish for one's protectors, and the average tip was five riel,
that is to say five sevenths of a penny on the official exchange rate. (For
a black-market figure the rates given below may be approximately

halved.) Shots are heard from the forest as the hills begin. Shots are fired in return, but into the air with a shrug, as if to call a bluff. We stop again for oranges and coconut water. The road is not mined, but the enemy have dug two trenches across it – trenches of archaeological precision which delay our progress for hours. Eight hours after setting out we arrived in Pailin.

'I am poverty, monsieur.' That, it occurred to me, is neither French nor true, and surveying my would-be guide I wondered whether to correct his grammar or give him the lie. He was neatly dressed in a drill shirt and long trousers, well pressed, with a natty bush hat, and I assumed that he was one of those of whom I had heard: at home there would be a television (picking up the Thai network) and all mod cons. In his pocket he would have a pouch of sapphires, and probably in two minutes he would try to sell me some hopeless gem at a fraudulent rate. Still, I was alone in a strange town. I asked him if he would show me the pagoda.

Later, having spent almost all my time with him, and having supped on a thin fish-and-gherkin gruel at his hut, I realised that he knew what he was talking about. He really *was* poverty. Recently arrived from Battambang with two brothers and a friend in order to seek his fortune, he had so far found nothing. The basic wage for a miner is 100 riel (14p) a day. The big money comes from the finds, which are shared with the proprietor of the mine of a 50/50 basis. Presumably, since work on the mines is divided between diggers of mud and sifters, there is a further sharing among groups of friends when a stone is found. The possibilities for wealth are certainly there, but the sums in question are pretty modest. Cheerful my guide certainly was. In this country, where happiness (not its pursuit – the thing itself) is written into the constitution, together with liberty, equality and progress, everybody insists on being happy. In his English exercise book I saw he had written the sentence: 'No one need be despair as long as he breathes.'

'Things,' said an army captain who came up to my table in Pailin's one restaurant, 'are not very well organised here.' And bringing a plastic wallet out of his pocket he selected two fair-sized rubies from a large collection and pressed them into my hand. 'When you get back to England, please send me a postcard,' he said, leaving. He was right about the organisation. Before 1970 the wealth of Pailin was nationalised to the extent that all the gems had to be exported through the state monopoly firm, Sonexpieror. But the Lon Nol government is consistent in its attitude to business. Instead of keeping a tighter grip on this useful dollar earner, they relaxed all restraints. Sonexpieror became a trading company like any other, competing at a disadvantage against the Thai businessmen nipping across the borders, who nowadays smuggle out nearly all the gems. The loss of revenue to the Cambodian government may be computed in millions of dollars. (Incidentally, not far away the Khmer Rouge have their own mine, said to be ten times larger than Pailin's. Here the Thai traders come as well, trading guns for rubies.)

On 9 October, Mr In Tam gave a reception in honour of the third anniversary of the republic, and the Palais du Gouvernement was filled with politicians, diplomats and journalists. A double cordon of soldiers from the prime-ministerial bodyguard provided our protection in the vast opensided building, and as the drink flowed the level of conversation reached an abyss. ('Fenton, ah yes, there was a Harry Fenton in the Philippines before the war.') Tiring of this, I wandered out onto the balcony, thinking naively that I might be able to offer one of the soldiers a drink. Naively, I say, because when I got there I found that most of the soldiers had a triple Scotch at their elbows; but cigarettes and refills were welcome and we began to talk. Below us, on the grass, a group of children had penetrated the outer cordon and were stretching out their hands for food. Across the Mekong 'my friendly artillery' was pursuing an energetic campaign against the communists. We discussed at length whether London was a finer city than Phnom Penh, and I found it impossible to make up my mind.

For the first weeks it was scenes of that kind which typified the war for me. When later I commented sternly upon the behaviour of the bodyguard, one Cambodian replied: 'They behave like that because there is a war on. In peacetime they would never get away with it.' This is true. Because there is a war on, you do not take off your shoes on entering the Pagoda – you sling your hammock there and eat your rice in the hollow space under the very statue of the Buddha. Because there is a war on, you go up to the front with a herd of duck inside your APC, or a live chicken in your rucksack. The shrines of faith are destroyed, the mores of village life suspended, and discipline is very much an empirical affair. I am not saying that the soldiers do not obey orders – merely that it is a far cry from here to the Combined Cadet Force. Once, in the past month, I met a truly conscientious type. It was on a quite deserted road, in an area where there had been no serious fighting for weeks. I stepped off the Honda, paused tactfully while he donned his helmet, gun, grenades and all, and received his salute in the manner of a kindly field marshal on a flying visit.

But where was the war? For weeks I had searched for it with a diligence stopping short only of the suicidal. The artillery looked magnificent, as it gave the covering fire which used to be supplied by the B-52s. And the APCs would set off across the beautiful fields and disappear into the undergrowth. And then ... nothing. 'Alors, mon général,' I said, returning to the field HQ after a morning of such waiting, 'il n'y a pas des ennemis.' He gave a shrug and invited me to lunch. An awning had been set up beside the ruined house, and a clean tablecloth, napkins and cutlery laid out. There were 20 dishes to choose from, snails, chicken, beef all freshly cooked, and the only drink was brandy and soda. The soldiers stood around, bringing more ice as it became necessary, and twirling napkins all the time to ward off the flies. It was like dining among a group of morris dancers, excepting that they didn't kick.

My difficulties in finding the war were not exceptional. For the past month, while the rain has been sporadic and the water going down, it has been something of a cat-and-mouse game. The road to Kompong Som, for instance, which is the important supply route from the sea, has been shut, opened, shut and opened again. In some areas the army has regained ground, and they are quite optimistic. The communists seem to have a real shortage of ammunition, although they use what they have well. When things become hot, they simply up and leave. It is very difficult to catch a glimpse of them. One journalist, a seasoned Vietnam veteran, told me that in the three months he had been here he had seen just one dead one. On Highway Three I was driving out with a photographer when we met a crowd of panic-stricken civilians retreating from the front. I stopped one man on a motorbike who told me that the enemy had crossed the river with a large cannon and that a VC girl with hair down to her waist, whom he had seen, had been shooting at them. We asked him, since our driver would go no further, to take us up to the front. He assented happily and when we got there we found a scene of utter calm. The password for this month has been 'Aucun incident significatif'.

Which is why, perhaps, some curious local developments have been reported. On the same road, for instance, there was a small ceasefire. According to the UPI and AP reporters who arrived there before the front line was sealed off by the high command, it happened like this. The Khmer Rouge captain got on the radio to his opposite number (not an uncommon practice, even during earnest fighting) and asked whether there were many Americans on the other side. It was explained that the Americans had gone home (not entirely true). Then, he said, he didn't want to kill more Khmers. On either side, one soldier was sent out to the river's edge, and each, to prove he was unarmed, stripped naked. Afterwards both units emerged unarmed and lined the river bank. The Khmer Rouge had a drum. They began dancing and singing humorous songs. The ceasefire lasted more than a week.

On only one occasion I have felt panic coming on. It was during a boxing match in Phnom Penh's large covered stadium (one of the prestige buildings dating from the days of Sihanouk). The place was packed beyond capacity but the contestants were not very good. They seem more interested in avoiding each other than attacking, and my attention wandered to a little scene taking place a few yards from me. One soldier had somehow managed to upset another's chair, and a space was being cleared around the argument. Suddenly I looked up and saw the whole crowd running towards the exit. My first thought was that they were getting out before the national anthem, my second, as the rush came down on me, that the building was falling down, my third, as I began to run, that there was a bomb scare. It was indeed a bomb scare. The crowd, attentive to this small scene, was terrified that one of the soldiers would throw a grenade at the other. Incidents of this kind, I was told, were fairly common, and if you saw an angry soldier you should take to your heels. During August, when things were admittedly a little tense, a soldier threw a grenade at a taxi which failed to stop for him – a trick I must remember when I get back to London.

Apart from such mishaps, Phnom Penh is a comparatively safe place. Terrorist activity runs at a rate of about one incident a week. Mostly the targets are market stalls and cinema crowds – very bloody but not much publicised. So during the first part of my stay I lived in a state of lunatic happiness, loving the people, the place and the novelty of this elusive war. I cannot claim that I found it unreal – I knew what it was, and I liked it. I never found the war, but in the end it found me, and now I feel slightly differently – blooded, you might say, although I have only a strained muscle to show for it, and not enough to justify an attractive limp.

Towards the end of the month the Khmer Rouge moved across the Tonle Sap river and occupied a stretch of road about 20 kilometres to the north of the capital. I was curious about this manoeuvre, since I knew that the river was wide (about twice as wide as the Thames at Greenwich), and the road, with villages on either side, afforded a space of dry land about 100 yards wide most of the way. Since the government has a monopoly of naval vessels, there would be no eastward escape by daylight across the river. To the west indeed there lay Khmer Rouge territory, but to reach it you would have to cross several kilometres of flooded terrain.

It must have been a very quiet infiltration. Two days later, going with the troops along the previously occupied territory, we came across a motor-bike with the swollen bodies of two government officers lying beside it, hideously destroyed. They had probably set out on the morning after the operation had begun, and had become the victims of the first shot fired – a B40. Further on, we reached the army position which had been isolated during the operation, and beyond we were able to see the enemy who were still left on the road. First, across the river, a sampan tried to put out to come and evacuate the remaining men, but a gunboat made it turn back. Next, on the west side, another sampan with about four men visible on board was making for the hills, and was immediately fired on from our position.

It was then that I was told of our danger. The pagoda in which we were based was well within the range of enemy mortar, and as soon as we fired on the escapers they would attempt to put us out of action. We lay flat, and shortly afterwards a mortar landed, seriously wounding a pregnant woman who had been sitting in the infirmary. The mortar had been aimed slightly wide of the position of our gun, but this could easily be rectified. Shortly afterwards we heard another launched, and hid in a different area. Something fell, but there was no explosion. We heard shouting and looked out. Behing the hut in which we were hiding, under a tree, a young joker was pulling up his trousers and gesticulating wildly. Six feet away from him the mortar had landed, buried itself in the earth up to its fins and failed to go off. He had been having a shit at the time. Enough, as someone said later, to give you constipation for a week.

But this was not the blooding to which I have referred. The day before, further back down the road, I had witnessed the beginning of the enemy retreat. Since coming to Cambodia I had been expecting something to happen which I would recognise and say 'So *that* is what war is like', but nothing had, and after a while I gave up expecting it. Either I was in the wrong country or there was no such thing. Here however from the start each element had a familiar quality – perhaps something I had read or dreamt of had prepared me. A few yards ahead of us, a burning building marked the enemy front line. Firing was sporadic, but the wind was blowing in our direction and it occurred to me that we might simply be forced by fire back down the road. Along the river came two boats filled with women and children, and as they got nearer a low sound, a sort of moaning in chorus, reached the bank. They were the wounded and afraid – but how had they managed to leave the enemy position?

Then quite suddenly it appeared that all was over, and a group of soldiers and civilians set out to go into the village. I went with them, and was shown the civilian dead. An old man lay on his bed. He must have been shot while sitting in the lotus position, and had simply toppled backwards, his legs still entwined and a polythene bag full of cigarettes at his side. The soldiers moved from house to house, tying up the pigs and looting whatever they fancied. My first looting, I thought, and what a genteel phenomenon it is. When you loot your countryman's wine, you do not swig it from the bottle. You take out his small glasses, set out his table and chair on the verandah and drink it at a decent pace. We passed the freshly dug position of the enemy front line, with the remains of their meals laid out as in the *Mary Celeste*. Then, as I was wandering ahead a little, the captain restrained me and said that beyond a certain fence things were not too safe. Wait ten minutes and we would proceed.

Ten minutes later the soldiers began to move past the fence where I had been standing, and immediately the firing began. We hid behind trees, with weak smiles. Then we crouched on the ground, looking serious. Then as the APCs on the road began firing and the noise of the shooting began to fill every space around us, we made for the river bank and lay very low. I felt a fool, not being able to tell what direction the shots were coming from and what the different noises were. Besides the heavier sounds, which I reckoned (wrongly) must be ours, what was the sudden sharp sound which seemed to take place above one's head, all around, like fireworks at a regatta? At least I thought, I am not afraid. Prudent, but keeping my head. I noticed my heartbeat – how at the beginning of each burst of gunfire it would go fast, and then regulate itself. It was exactly what I had learned in psychology – the whole organism, brain and reflexes, was coping admirably. It would anticipate heavy fire, something in the brain would attenuate the signal, and yet at the same time the slightest unfamiliar sound would be seized upon. I would turn my head as a hen ran past, or a frog slithered down the bank beside me. I was coping. I was quite pleased.

But there is a time factor to fear. It infiltrates the mind in the shape of a strong desire for something else. I wanted a shower (normally I hate showers). My shirt was filthy (something that rarely worries me). I would have to get back before the curfew (not true – and besides it was only three o'clock). I had run out of cigarettes and I wondered whether my driver was afraid. This was the first stage.

'When we meet a bear in the woods and run, we are afraid because we run: we do not run because we are afraid,' said William James, and whatever precisely he meant by it, and whether it was philosophically correct, this is just what happened in the second stage. A decorative young man, in a white, broadbrimmed polystyrene hat came down the path in a state of some commotion. Then a soldier tapped me on the back, saying 'Vietcong arrivent'. People were pointing to the other side of the river, but I could see nothing there to merit attention, and this worried me. We began to retreat, ducking through the undergrowth and wading through the shallows, and I began to feel my legs give way with fear. On the path, which we were studiously avoiding, a wounded soldier came limping by. He had taken off his trousers to apply a camouflaged compression bandage to the back of his leg, and as he passed me he fired an angry Parthian shot, a volley of automatic fire from his M16, into the water. I jumped. Had the whim taken him otherwise, or his aim failed, he might have directed the bullets at me. That was the third stage – a real, if momentary fright. The pain was driving him wild and he was beginning to wander and stagger. So I did what under the circumstances was probably the least advisable thing for both of us – I hitched him up and carried him from the field of battle. He had given me the perfect opportunity to make my excuses and leave.

In the first advanced position I saw here, a transistor radio was playing Handel's *Music for the Royal Fireworks*. The soldiers were snoozing in hammocks or tucking into large meals. I thought – how relaxed and unafraid. Now I shall interpret these things differently, having learnt that a sharp appetite may be a prelude to terror. On the day after the initiation I have described, examining the enemy positions which had been vacated the night before, I came upon an enamel plate with the remains of a meal neatly set upon an improvised tripod of twigs. Such fastidiousness, in the front line! 'But I do not wish to die, monsieur.'

James Fenton, 9 November 1973

Trotsky once said that if one had to face the choice, it was better to be a victim than an executioner. He didn't stick by the principle, of course – though at the end he was both. The agonies of the Left in the post-war era were most often those of seeing their supposed friends become butchers, from Hungary to Cambodia. When they were the victims, though, it didn't seem to feel any less painful. The great GABRIEL GARCIA MARQUEZ reports the bloody end of Chile's socialist experiment.

Why Allende Had to Die

It was toward the end of 1969 that three generals from the Pentagon dined with five Chilean military officers in a house in the suburbs of Washington. The host was then Lieutenant-Colonel Gerardo López Angulo, assistant air attaché of the Chilean Military Mission to the United States, and the Chilean guests were his colleagues from the other branches of service. The dinner was in honour of the new director of the Chilean Air Force Academy, General Carlos Toro Mazote, who had arrived the day before on a study mission. The eight officers dined on fruit salad, roast veal, and peas, and drank the warm-hearted wines of their distant homeland to the south where birds glittered on the beaches while Washington wallowed in snow, and they talked mostly in English about the only thing that seemed to interest Chileans in those days: the approaching presidential elections of the following September. Over dessert, one of the Pentagon generals asked what the Chilean army would do if the candidate of the Left, someone like Salvador Allende, were elected. General Toro Mazote replied: 'We'll take Moneda Palace in half an hour, even if we have to burn it down.'

One of the guests was General Ernesto Baeza, now Director of National Security in Chile, the one who led the attack on the presidential palace during the coup last September and gave the order to burn it. Two of his subordinates in those earlier days were to become famous in the same operation: General Augusto Pinochet, President of the military junta, and General Javier Palacios. Also at the table was Air Force Brigadier General Sergio Figueroa Gutiérrez, now Minister of Public Works and the intimate friend of another member of the military junta, Air Force General Gustavo Leigh, who ordered the rocket bombing of the presidential palace. The last guest was Admiral Arturo Troncoso, now naval governer of Valparaiso, who carried out the bloody purge of progressive naval officers and was one of those who launched the military uprising of 11 September.

That dinner proved to be a historic meeting between the Pentagon and high officers of the Chilean military services. On other successive meetings, in Washington and Santiago, a contingency plan was agreed upon, according to which those Chilean military men who were bound most closely, heart and soul, to United States interests would sieze power in the event of Allende's Popular Unity Party victory in the elections.

The plan was conceived cold-bloodedly, as a simple military operation, and was not a consequence of pressure brought to bear by International Telephone and Telegraph. It was spawned by much deeper reasons of world politics. On the North American side, the organisation set in motion was the Defence Intelligence Agency of the Pentagon, but the one in actual charge was the Naval Intelligence Agency, under the higher political direction of the CIA, and the National Security Council. It was quite the normal thing to put the navy and not the army in charge of the project, for the Chilean coup was to coincide with Operation Unitas, which was the name given to the joint manoeuvres of American and Chilean naval units in the Pacific. These manoeuvres were held at the end of each September, the same month as the elections, and the appearance of land and in the skies of Chile of all manner of war equipment and men well trained in the arts and sciences of death was natural.

During that period Henry Kissinger had said in private to a group of Chileans: 'I am not interested in, nor do I know anything about, the southern portion of the world from the Pyrenees on down.' By that time the contingency plan had been completed to its smallest details, and it is impossible to suppose that Kissinger or President Nixon himself was not aware of it.

Chile is a narrow country, some 2,660 miles long and an average of 119 wide, and with 10 million exuberant inhabitants, almost three million of whom live in the metropolitan area of Santiago, the capital. The country's greatness is not derived from the number of virtues it possesses but, rather, from its many singularities. The only thing it produces with any absolute seriousness is copper ore, but that ore is the best in the world, and its volume of production is surpassed only by that of the United States and the Soviet Union. It also produces wine as good as the European varieties, but not much of it is exported. Its per capita income of $650 ranks among the highest in Latin America, but, traditionally, almost half the gross national product has been accounted for by fewer than 300,000 people. In 1932 Chile became the first socialist republic in the Americas and, with the enthusiastic support of the workers, the government attempted the nationalisation of copper and coal. The experiment lasted only for 13 days. Chile has an earth tremor on the average of once every two days and a devastating earthquake every presidential term. The least apocalyptic of geologists think of Chile not as a country of the mainland, but as a cornice of the Andes in a misty sea, and believe that the whole of its national territory is condemned to disappear in some future cataclysm.

Chileans are very much like their country in a certain way. They are the most pleasant people on the continent, they like being alive, and they know how to live in the best way possible and even a little more; but they have a dangerous tendency toward scepticism and intellectual speculation. A Chilean once told me on a Monday that 'no Chilean believes tomorrow is Tuesday', and he didn't believe it either. Still, even with that deep-seated incredulity, or thanks to it, perhaps, the Chileans have attained a degree of natural civilisation, a political maturity and a level of culture that sets them apart from the rest of the region. Of the three Nobel Prizes in literature that Latin America has won, two have gone to Chileans, one of whom, Pablo Neruda, was the greatest poet of this century.

Henry Kissinger may have known this when he said that he knew nothing about the southern part of the world. In any case, United States intelligence agencies knew a great deal more. In 1965, without Chile's permission, the nation became the staging centre and a recruiting locale for a fantastic social and political espionage operation: Project Camelot.

This was to have been a secret investigation which would have precise questionnaires put to people of all social levels, all professions and trades, even in the farthest reaches of a number of Latin American nations, in order to establish in a scientific way the degree of political development and the social tendencies of various social groups. The questionnaire destined for the military contained the same question that the Chilean officers would hear again at the dinner in Washington: what will their position be if communism comes to power? It was a wily query.

Chile had long been a favoured area for research by North American social scientists. The age and strength of its popular movement, the tenacity and intelligence of its leaders, and the economic and social conditions themselves afforded a glimpse of the country's destiny. One didn't require the findings of a Project Camelot to venture the belief that Chile was a prime candidate to be the second socialist republic in Latin America after Cuba. The aim of the United States, therefore, was not simply to prevent the government of Salvador Allende from coming to power in order to protect American investments. The larger aim was to repeat the most fruitful operation that imperialism has ever helped bring off in Latin America: Brazil.

On 4 September 1970, as had been foreseen, the socialist and Freemason physician Salvador Allende was elected President of the republic. The contingency plan was not put into effect, however. The most widespread explanation is also the most ludicrous: someone made a mistake in the Pentagon and requested 200 visas for a purported navy chorus, which, in reality, was to be made up of specialists in government overthrow; however, there were several admirals among them who couldn't sing a single note. That gaffe, it is to be supposed determined the postponement of the adventure. The truth is that the project had been evaluated in depth: other American agencies, particularly the CIA, and the American ambassador to Chile felt that the contingency plan was too strictly a military operation and did not take current political and social conditions in Chile into account.

Indeed, the Popular Unity victory did not bring on the social panic US intelligence had expected. On the contrary, the new government's independence in international affairs and its decisiveness in economic matters immediately created an atmosphere of social celebration. During the first year, 47 industrial firms were nationalised along with most of the banking system. Agrarian reform saw the expropriation and incorporation into communal property of six million acres of land formerly held by the large landowners. The inflationary process was slowed, full employment was attained, and wages received a cash rise of 30 per cent.

The previous government, headed by the Christian Democrat Eduardo Frei, had begun steps toward nationalising copper, though he called it Chileanisation. All the plan did was to buy up 51 per cent of US-held mining properties, and for the mine of El Teniente alone it paid a sum greater than the total book value of that facility. Popular Unity, with a single legal Act supported in Congress by all of the nation's political parties, recovered for the nation all copper deposits worked by the subsidiaries of American companies Anaconda and Kennecott. Without indemnification: the government having calculated that the two companies over 15 years had made a profit in excess of $800m.

The petite bourgeoisie and the middle class, the two great social forces which might have supported a military coup at that moment, were beginning to enjoy unforeseen advantages, and not at the expense of the proletariat, as had always been the case, but, rather, at the expense of the financial oligarchy and foreign capital. The armed forces, as a social group, have the same origins and ambitions as the middle class, so they had no motive, not even an alibi, to back the tiny group of coup-minded officers. Aware of that reality, the Christian Democrats not only did not support the barracks plot at that time, but resolutely opposed it, for they knew it was unpopular among their own rank and file.

Their objective was something else again: to use any means possible to impair the good health of the government so as to win two-thirds of the seats in Congress in the March 1973 elections. With such a majority they could vote the constitutional removal of the President of the republic.

The Christian Democrats make up a huge organisation cutting across class lines, with an authentic popular base among the modern industrial proletariat, the small and middle rural landowners, and the petite bourgeoisie and middle class of the cities. Popular Unity, while also inter-class in its makeup, was the expression of workers of the less-favoured proletariat – the agricultural proletariat – and the lower-middle class of the cities.

The Christian Democrats, allied with the extreme right-wing National Party, controlled the Congress and the courts; Popular Unity controlled the executive. The polarisation of these two parties was to be, in fact, the polarisation of the country. Curiously, the Catholic Eduardo Frei, who doesn't believe in Marxism, was the one who took best advantage of the class struggle, the one who stimulated it and brought it to a head, with an aim to unhinge the government and plunge the country into the abyss of demoralisation and economic disaster.

The economic blockade by the United States, because of expropriation without indemnification, did the rest. All kinds of goods are manufactured in Chile, from automobiles to toothpaste, but this industrial base has a false identity: in the 160 most important firms, 60 per cent of the capital was foreign and 80 per cent of the basic materials came from abroad. In addition, the country needed $300m. a year in order to import consumer goods and another $450m. to pay the interest on its foreign debt. But Chile's urgent needs were extraordinary and went much deeper. The jolly ladies of the bourgeoisie, under the pretext of protesting rationing, galloping inflation, and the demands made by the poor, took to the streets, beating their empty pots and pans. It wasn't by chance, quite the contrary; it was very significant that that street spectacle of silver foxes and flowered hats took place on the same afternoon that Fidel Castro was ending a 30-day visit that had brought an earthquake of social mobilisation of government supporters.

President Allende understood then, and he said so, that the people held the government but they did not hold the power. The phrase was more bitter than it seemed, and also more alarming, for inside himself Allende carried a legalist germ that held the seed of his own destruction: a man who fought to the death in defence of legality, he would have been capable of walking out of Moneda Palace with his head held high if the Congress had removed him from office within the bounds of the constitution.

The Italian journalist and politician Rossana Rossanda, who visited Allende during that period, found him aged, tense and full of gloomy premonitions as he talked to her from the yellow cretonne couch where, seven months later, his riddled body was to lie, the face crushed in by a rifle butt. Then, on the eve of the March 1973 elections, in which his destiny was at stake, he would have been content with 36 per cent of the vote for Popular Unity. And yet, in spite of runaway inflation, stern rationing, and the pot-and-pan concert of the merry wives of the upper-class districts, he received 44 per cent. It was such a spectacular and decisive victory that when Allende was alone in his office with his friend and confidant, the journalist Augusto Olivares, he closed the door and danced a *cueca* all by himself.

For the Christian Democrats it was proof that the process of social justice set in motion by the Popular Unity Party could not be turned back by legal means, but they lacked the vision to measure the consequences of the actions they then undertook. For the United States the election was a much more serious warning and went beyond the simple interests of expropriated firms. It was an inadmissable precedent for peaceful progress and social change for the peoples of the world, particularly those of France and Italy, where present conditions make an attempt at an experiment along the lines of Chile possible. All forces of internal and external reaction came together to form a compact bloc.

The truck owners' strike was the final blow. Because of the wild geography of the country, the Chilean economy is at the mercy of its transport. To paralyse trucking is to paralyse the country. It was easy for the opposition to coordinate the strike, for the trucker's guild was one of the groups most affected by the scarcity of replacement parts and, in addition, it found itself threatened by the Government's small pilot programme for providing adequate state trucking services in the extreme south of the nation. The stoppage lasted until the very end without a single moment of relief because it was financed with cash from outside. 'The CIA flooded the country with dollars to support the strike by the bosses, and that foreign capital found its way down into the formation of a black market,' Pablo Neruda wrote a friend in Europe. One week before the coup, oil, milk and bread had run out.

During the last days of Popular Unity, with the economy unhinged and the country on the verge of civil war, the manoeuvring of the government and the opposition centred on the hope of changing the balance of power in the armed forces in favour of one or the other. The final move was hallucinatory in its perfection: 48 hours before the coup, the opposition managed to disqualify all high officers supporting Salvadore Allende and to promote in their places, one by one, in a series of inconceivable gambits, all of the officers who had been present at the dinner in Washington.

At that moment, however, the political chess game had got out of the control of its players. Dragged along by an irreversible dialectic, they themselves ended up as pawns in a much larger game of chess, one much more complex and politically more important than any mere scheme hatched in conjunction by imperialism and the reaction against the government of the people. It was a terrifying class confrontation that was slipping out of the hands of the very people who had provoked it, a cruel and fierce scramble by counterpoised interests, and the final outcome had to be a social cataclysm without precedent in the history of the Americas.

A military coup under those conditions could not be bloodless. Allende knew it. The Chilean armed forces, contrary to what we have been led to believe, have intervened in politics every time that their class interests have seemed threatened, and they have done so with an inordinately repressive ferocity. The two constitutions which the country has had in the past hundred years were imposed by force of arms, and the recent military coup has been the sixth uprising in a period of 50 years.

The blood lust of the Chilean army is part of its birthright, coming from that terrible school of hand-to-hand combat against the Auracanian Indians, a struggle which lasted 300 years. One of its forerunners boasted in 1620 of having killed more than 2,000 people with his own hand in a single action. Joaquín Edwards Bello relates in his chronicles that during an epidemic of exanthematic typhus the army dragged sick people out of their houses and killed them in a poison bath in order to put an end to the plague. During a seven-month civil war in 1891, 10,000 died in a series of gory encounters. The Peruvians assert that during the occupation of Lima in the War of the Pacific, Chilean soldiers sacked the library of Don Ricardo Palma, taking the books not for reading, but for wiping their backsides.

Popular movements have been suppressed with the same brutality. After the Valparaiso earthquake of 1906, naval forces wiped out the longshoremen's organisation of 8,000 workers. In Iquique, at the beginning of the century, demonstrating strikers tried to take refuge from the troops and were machine-gunned: within ten minutes there were 2,000 dead. On 2 April 1957, the army broke up a civil disturbance in the commercial centre of Santiago and the number of victims was never established because the government sneaked the bodies away. During a strike at the El Salvador mine during the government of Eduardo Frei, a military patrol opened fire on a demonstration to break it up and killed six people, among them some children and a pregnant woman. The post commander was an obscure 52-year-old general, the father of five children, a geography teacher, and the author of several books on military subjects: Augusto Pinochet.

The myth of the legalism and the gentleness of that brutal army was invented by the Chilean bourgeoisie in their own interest. Popular Unity kept it alive with the hope of changing the class makeup of the higher cadres in its favour. But Salvador Allende felt more secure among the Carabineros, an armed force that was popular and peasant in its origins and that was under the direct command of the President of the republic. Indeed, the junta had to go six places down the seniority list of the force before it found a senior officer who would support the coup. The younger officers dug themselves in at the junior officers' school in Santiago and held out for four days until they were wiped out.

That was the best-known battle of the secret war that broke out inside military posts on the eve of the coup. Officers who refused to support the coup and those who failed to carry out the orders for repression were murdered without pity by the instigators. Entire regiments mutinied, both in Santiago and in the provinces, and they were suppressed without mercy, with their leaders massacred as a lesson for the troops. The commandant of the armoured units in Viña del Mar, Colonel Cantuarias, was machine-gunned by his subordinates. A long time will pass before the number of victims of that internal butchery will ever be known, for the bodies were removed from military posts in garbage trucks and buried secretly. All in all, only some 50 senior officers could be trusted to head troops that had been purged beforehand.

The story of the intrigue has to be pasted together from many sources, some reliable, some not. Any number of foreign agents seem to have taken part in the coup. Clandestine sources in Chile tell us that the bombing of Moneda Palace – the technical precision of which startled the experts – was actually carried out by a team of American aerial acrobats who had entered the country under the screen of Operation Unitas to perform in a flying circus on the coming 18 September, National Independence Day. There is also evidence that numerous members of secret police forces from neighbouring countries were infiltrated across the Bolivian border and remained in hiding until the day of the coup, when they unleashed their bloody persecution of political refugees from other countries of Latin America.

Brazil, the homeland of the head guerillas, had taken charge of those services. Two years earlier she had brought off the reactionary coup in Bolivia which meant the loss of substantial support for Chile and facilitated the infiltration of all manner and means of subversion. Part of the loans made to Brazil by the United States was secretly transferred to Bolivia to finance subversion in Chile. In 1972 a US military advisory group made a trip to La Paz, the aim of which has not been revealed. Perhaps it was only coincidential, however, that a short time after that visit, movements of troops and equipment took place on the frontier with Chile, giving the Chilean military yet another opportunity to bolster their internal position and carry out transfer of personnel and promotions in the chain of command that were favourable to the imminent coup. Finally, on 11 September, while Operation Unitas was going forward, the original plan drawn up at the dinner in Washington was carried out, three years behind schedule but precisely as it had been conceived: not as a conventional barracks coup, but as a devastating operation of war.

It had to be that way for it was not simply a matter of overthrowing a regime but one of implanting the hell-dark seeds brought from Brazil, until in Chile there would be no trace of the political and social structure which had made Popular Unity possible. The harshest phase, unfortunately, had only just begun.

In that final battle, with the country at the mercy of uncontrolled and unforeseen forces of subversion, Salvador Allende was still bound by legality. The most dramatic contradiction of his life was being at the same time the congenital foe of violence and a passionate revolutionary. He believed that he had resolved the contradiction with the hypothesis that conditions in Chile would permit a peaceful evolution toward socialism under bourgeois legality. Experience taught him too late that a system cannot be changed by a government without power.

That belated disillusionment must have been the force that impelled him to resist to the death, defending the flaming ruins of a house that was not his own, a sombre mansion that an Italian architect had built to be a mint and which ended up as a refuge for presidents without power. He resisted for six hours with a sub-machine gun that Fidel Castro had given him and was the first weapon that Salvador Allende had ever fired. Around four o'clock in the afternoon Major-General Javier Palacios managed to reach the second floor with his adjutant, Captain Gallardo, and a group of officers. There, in the midst of the fake Louis XV chairs, the Chinese dragon vases, and the Rugendas paintings in the red parlour, Salvador Allende was waiting for them. He was in shirt sleeves, wearing a miner's helmet and no tie, his clothing stained with blood. He was holding the sub-machine gun, but he had run low on ammunition.

Allende knew General Palacios well. A few days before he had told Augusto Olivares that this was a dangerous man with close connections to the American Embassy. As soon as he saw him appear on the stairs, Allende shouted at him: 'Traitor!' and shot him in the hand.

According to the story of a witness who asked me not to give his name, the President died in an exchange of shots with that gang. Then all the other officers, in a caste-bound ritual, fired on the body. Finally, a non-commissioned officer smashed in his face with the butt of his rifle. A photograph exists: Juan Enrique Lira, a photographer for the newspaper *El Mercurio* took it. He was the only one allowed to photograph the body. It was so disfigured that when they showed the body in its coffin to Señora Hortensia Allende, his wife, they would not let her uncover the face.

He would have been 64 years old next July. His greatest virtue was following through, but fate could grant him only that rare and tragic greatness of dying in armed defence of the anachronistic booby of the bourgeois law, defending a Supreme Court of Justice which had repudiated him but would legitimise his murderers, defending a miserable Congress which had declared him illegitimate but which was to bend complacently before the will of the usurpers, defending the freedom of opposition parties which had sold their souls to fascism, defending the whole moth-eaten paraphernalia of a shitty system which he had proposed abolishing, but without a shot being fired. The drama took place in Chile, to the greater woe of the Chileans, but it will pass into history as something that has happened to us all, children of this age, and it will remain in our lives forever.

Gabriel García Márquez, 15 March 1974

ROBERT LOWELL, self-torturing archetype of the tragic poet, the patrician radical, the holy fool – a man who attracts this kind of cliché as surely as his own work avoids it – rarely published in British periodicals. 'History', one of his finest late poems, appeared in the NS *in 1973.*

History

History has to live with what was here,
clutching and close to fumbling all we had –
it is so dull and gruesome how we die,
unlike writing, life never finishes.
Abel was finished; death is not remote,
a flash-in-the-pan electrifies the skeptic,
his cows crowding like skulls against high-voltage wire,
his baby crying all night like a new machine.
As in our Bibles, white-faced, predatory,
the beautiful, mist-drunken hunter's moon ascends –
a child could give it a face: two holes, two holes,
my eyes, my mouth, between them a skull's no-nose –
O there's a terrifying innocence in my face
drenched with the silver salvage of the mornfrost.

Robert Lowell, 15 June 1973

In 'Farewell, Grosvenor Square', with Labour precariously back in office and direct action left politics in decline, PETER SEDGWICK drew up a provisional balance sheet for a political era.

Farewell, Grosvenor Square

The story of the British Left from the 1956 split in the Communist Party up till the growth and disintegration of the Vietnam Solidarity movement is the record of a political adolescence. And who can review his own adolescence without an embarrassed blush or an amused smile at follies recognised as such too late? Not all of it will have been folly, of course: but even what was ardent and delightful is now revealed as without issue, harbouring from the outset the contradictions that would dissolve or defeat its hope. *Where have all the flowers gone?* sang the marchers; and, in pacific elegy, *Where have all the soldiers gone?* And now, a few years later, where have all the marchers gone?

A generous but possible estimate of the largest CND march, the one from Aldermaston and Wethersfield into Trafalgar Square at Easter 1961, is of a final turnout of 100,000 participants. The great Vietnam solidarity demo of October 1968 took the whole width of Central London's streets under marchers' control; the press scare about impending violence and the known record of the Metropolitan Police on these occasions meant that nobody could have come on the march without a realistic fear of trouble on the way; and the occasion drew, at a fair approximation, 100,000 participants. But it was not the previous 100,000 grown up by seven and a half years. In terms of personnel, the demonstrating Left of Britain simply did not cumulate.

The only *dramatis personae* who can be identified as recurring from the scenes of the Left in the late Fifties right along to the Sixties *and* the Seventies consist of two sorts of people: militant trade unionists and active (usually Marxist and usually card-carrying) revolutionaries.

If the movements have gone, and if both the leaderships and the ranks which staffed them have nearly all vanished from political activity, can anything be said for the effectiveness of the British independent Left over 1956 to 1968? We did create some precedents: we broke the ice of an age dominated by a concept that was then on everybody's lips: apathy. *Out of Apathy* was the title of the first New Left Book.

The contrast from then to now is evident in the very nature of a demonstration. People simply gawped and gaped at the first public CND marchers; we were external to the public upon the pavements, and for much of the time conscious that we would be viewed and judged as an alien force. And now there is simply no longer a public which is exterior to demonstration and visible mass action. Everybody is within the constituency of possible political crowds: demonstration has demonstrated its own necessity so demonstratively that we have the counter-demonstration and even the counter-counter-one: those who started the long trek to the Nuclear Weapons Research Establishment in 1958 have a lot to answer for.

The first New Left of Britain, that formed by the collision and fusion of the two world-wide shock waves of Suez and Hungary, entered the Campaign for Nuclear Disarmament and perished with the first form which it found. Invisible within the great marches that wound around and through the metropolis, there lay a conscious general staff for a wider social transformation, a small mobile headquarters not for this action, nor for the next engagement, but the total war that is the politics of socialism. Peggy Duff (the organising secretary of the Campaign for its entire active phase) concludes that 'in one way, CND did them [the New Left] no good. It swallowed them up as a political force in Britain.'

As an initial rallying point CND was wonderful: but as a training ground for a permanent commitment to radical politics, it was a dreadful failure. The sophisticated militants from the New Left embroiled themselves in high diplomacy or counter-electoral strategy around the Labour Party, they remained glued to foreign policy, they refused to educate the ranks of the Campaign either in general socialist theory or in the sordid practicalities of mass action around immediate bread and butter questions. And, truth to tell, the CND rankers did not want to be educated like this: 'There were too many people in CND who disliked and distrusted politics and too few with the will or the capacity to transform the movement into a different and more political entity.' Thus, once again, Peggy Duff, who in her memoirs of CND points to the 'escapism' of foreign-policy campaigns which 'can wrap themselves up in their single issues and in the purity of their pacifist concerns, ignoring the essential links between repression and arms, between imperialisms and the arms race, between liberation, revolution, and peace'.

While its grass-roots success and the sheer creativity of many of its participants remain unparalleled before or since in British politics, the basic model of the anti-nuclear campaign was that of the pressure group trying to right a specific injustice, like the campaign to abolish hanging before it, and the campaign to abolish the slave trade before that, and the anti-abortion lobby of recent years. CND could not even shift its concerns and resources towards action on the Indochina war, although a moral fervour which takes to the streets in opposing the

possible annihilation of London but remains paralysed in the face of the
actual obliteration of Vietnam is surely rather suspect. And the very
conception of single-issue activity in which the Campaign was rooted
reflects an over-intellectual, over-ideologised vision of influence and
power. The rest of politics does not stand still while you push on the
question that you have selected as the supreme topic. Issues are levers
which take persons and movements another step on in their
development (or in their death) and which, once used for that purpose,
must be left to go rusty.

The Vietnam campaigners were for their own part quite receptive to
the generalisation of their politics beyond its initial entry-point. The
year of the NLF's Tet offensive was also that of France's semi-
revolution of workers and students, of Prague's liberalising Springtime
and Stalinising autumn: at home yet another flock of starry-eyed social
democrats were learning the bitter truths of Labourism's betrayal,
looking for the real meaning of the words that had been tarnished by
Wilson, and for other words with fresh meanings. Gone was the old
liberal campaign's desperate concern to be unsullied, to keep faith with
the vicars and the MPs: after all, there were now no vicars or MPs
around.

It was not often that the orbits of working-class planet and student
comet came near one another in this phase. But in future years the link
between foreign and trade union issues, demonstrator and striker, high-
minded altruist and class-conscious egoist would cease to be a matter of
verbal advocacy and analysis and become a part of common experience
in the labour and socialist movement. Lenin's vision of the Russian
revolution was that it depended on a link – the *smychka*, he called it –
between the working class and the poorer peasantry. The British Left
had in its attitude towards students and graduates something of
Bolshevism's ambivalence towards the peasantry, at once part of the
toiling masses and a layer of the petty bourgeoisie, even conceivably a
mainstay of capitalism; but, along with the ambiguity and uncertainty,
came a determination that the worker-student *symchka* must be
maintained.

The development of the *symchka* in Britain was certainly not a
synchronous process whereby campus and factory ignited in
simultaneous combustion. Industrial unrest proceeded under its own
momentum: days lost in strikes and lockouts per 100 union members
moved to 113 in 1968–72 (from 30 in 1960–67 and 38 in 1952–59);
the percentage of union members involved in stoppages followed a
straight progression, from 8 per cent in 1952–59 through 12 per cent in
1960–67 to 16 per cent in 1968–72, at approximately the proportion of
strikers among the organised work-force during the peak of militancy in

this century from 1901 to 1925. The number of workers per dispute is also climbing, and the duration of strikes is getting longer: the epoch of the short, sharp stoppage in which a small key section of highly organised and strategically placed workers won a quick victory as a precedent for themselves and for others is now clearly over. (These conclusions are extracted from a table of strike trends to appear in the forthcoming book by John Westergaard and Henrietta Resler, *Class in Contemporary Britain.*)

But the style and manner of militancy increasingly partook of a new experimentalism and confidence, particularly in the rise of the factory occupation as a form of pressure against redundancies – over 100 of these seizures occurred between March 1971 and mid-1974 – and in the avalanche upheavals, here one moment and gone without trace the next, that shook hitherto backward industries and dormant sections of workers in this period.

The exuberance of this working-class revolt, its insistence on expanding within its local base and squeezing the opportunities there to the full, followed closely on a wider cultural revolution of protest and Your Own Thing, manifested as much in May events in France and in the hippie-politics alliance in the United States as in any happenings nearer home. As the worker movement summated locally and nationally to the grand climax of direct action that liberated five dockers from Pentonville, shattered the Tories' intransigence before the miners and reduced Heath's bluster of early 1974 to a deflated departure from office, the student movement lost its heroic altruism and abstraction: students now fought their own battles not those of others, no longer for the great liberal causes but for the gritty indispensables of everyday existence: higher grants, lower rents, payment for postgraduates, union recognition, fair academic assessment.

Just as the euphoria of the old student-based radicalism had been the harbinger of an expansive buoyancy in the demands of workers, employees and tenants, so the new bread and butter militancy of the NUS and its local affiliates bespoke a necessary change in priorities: with inflation rampant and the job market cut, the traditions of rebellion that had been constructed in the clouds had to find their proof, or else their refutation, here on earth. More recently, while the experienced structures of organised manual labour have held back, it is the white-collar and professional sections of trade unions, the teachers, local government workers, nurses and hospital staff who have been able to make a similar movement from new, sometimes barely existent traditions of organisation to a forthright challenge against *de facto* wage cuts and attendant worsenings of the conditions of toil. Who can afford, nowadays, to be noble?

On the whole, among activists and former activists the experience of
the Fifties and Sixties seems to have produced a permanent inoculation
agains any involvement in the Labour Party. There is no chance that
the militants will extend their endorsement of Labour to any greater
loyalty than the act of voting for Wilson on the mainly negative grounds
of knocking the Tories and the Liberals. Transport House may regard
this indifference of revolutionaries as no loss: but the revolutionary Left
has come to fulfil the role laid down prophetically for the older New
Left by E.P. Thompson: 'The bureaucracy will hold the machine: but
the New Left will hold the passes between it and the younger
generation.' A positive social-democratic revival has been blocked off,
not least through the antics of Wilson and his minions both in office
and in opposition, but also because alternative socialist traditions have
been revitalised, have in fact become available for masses of people,
especially those with any inkling of enthusiasm, to flirt with, perhaps
even to embrace wholeheartedly.

Even the odd Labour minister is not immune from the temptations
of dalliance with ideas whose very attractiveness stems from their long
serious relationship with socialism's steadies. For there is every reason
to believe that Mr Benn really is taken by the charms of workers'
control and militant-gradualist perspective on socialist advance drawn
variously from the late Robert Owen, the late G.D.H. Cole and the late
Salvador Allende. The sectarian Left are quite wrong to see Bennery as
yet another of Mr Wilson's many rubber faces: Mr Wilson, no less than
Mr Jenkins and Mr Rees-Mogg, detests Benn's New Left language and
is worried by it. There is a long, definite and traceable genealogy of
anti-capitalist politics and prescriptions for industry, running from the
early Utopian Socialists through the Marxists and the Industrial
Unionists and the Syndicalists into the Guild Socialists, latterly bandied
around the Trotskyist and academic Left, preserved in formalin in the
documentation and discussion of the Institute for Workers' Control,
diluted in half-measures and conference rhetoric by Jack Jones, Hugh
Scanlon and other high union officers, whom the Institute imagines to
be its allies, mixed in with rival programmes for the codetermination of
private industry by joint boards of trade unionists and capitalists and
served up as such in official Labour Party policy, adulterated further (in
order to appease business fears of anything approaching socialism) by
the fraction of the Labour Party – a distinctly unrepresentative sample
of its members – that actually runs the Government, and then
postponed indefinitely for any actual legislation because of the crowded
Commons timetable, the minority status of the Labour Government,
and, irrespective of other circumstances, the independence of the
Parliamentary Party.

Benn's expansionary proposals for nationalisation are the surfacing of a Left undercurrent in this confused tradition, a timely resuscitation of reformist socialism of a type which would have been recognisable in most of the parties of the Second International before a neo-capitalist or a technocratic liberalism became their dominant creed. Benn is not a solitary swallow: apart from the other ministers and under-secretaries with a left social-democrat disposition there is the intriguing emergence of the Labour Party's National Executive Committee as the Second Consul of the new Wilson Administration, vetting, vetoing and consulting its own sub-committees and those of the TUC whenever a promise of future legislation is to be drafted. The bonds between an incumbent Labour government and the extra-parliamentary institutions of Labour have never been as close as now: and, in the context of the anti-capitalist politics of some of the watchdogs both inside and outside the Government, we can speak of Labour's own New Left as a force to be reckoned with.

But, having reckoned with it, we must at once discount it. The bourgeoisie may tremble, or make a show of trembling, before the name of Benn: as Trotsky commented when Hitler went into hysterics on hearing speculation that the exiled man of October might prove to be the real victor of World War II, 'They fear revolution, and give it a man's name.' In the case of Benn they have given it a veritable misnomer, for the Government's proposals for a National Enterprise Board are not more than a continuation of the programme for a State Holding Company outlined in the 1969 NEC document *Labour's Economic Strategy*, where the new institution is explicitly modelled 'along the lines of the Italian IRI', the state-enterprise conglomerate founded under Mussolini and developed under Christian Democracy without any noticeable butchery of business leaders. The moderate programmatic shift leftwards was the very least that could occur given the deterioration of the economy and private capital's failure to invest: the complacency of the Gaitskell-Crosland-Jenkins-Jay programme *Industry and Society*, which stated that 'the Labour Party recognises that, under increasingly professional managements, large firms are as a whole serving the nation well' and proposed that the state should become an equity stockholder (not a manager) in private industry to give the community 'the opportunity of participating in the almost automatic capital gains of industry', would nowadays be impossible.

The party's movement towards industrial statism was a halting, fumbling response to the storm warnings of coming economic collapse signalled in the payments crises of the first Wilson government. It did not proceed from any mobilisation of the Left within the constituencies or union delegations. For there was no recurrence of the Bevanite Left revolt during the 1964–70 government, nor in the opposition period afterwards. In betraying the party's hopes, the Wilson cabinet also ravaged its flesh and poisoned its circulation as droves of constituency workers moved out of activity in disillusionment. It is useless now for the left ministers and union leaders to consecrate to the old cults of socialism a party whose fabric is still in fundamental human and ideological disrepair.

The middle-class New Left has finished. Labour's New Left will not begin. What then of socialism's future, in a Britain now leading the deceleration of the world capitalist economy in the same spirit of stoicism with which it long ago presided over the system's more expansionary destinies? The politics of liberal enthusiasm and of social-democratic reform have elapsed. Class politics, in this heartland of enmity founded on industrial division, remains as ever, has indeed become more powerful. The rank and file movement of workers in industry and public service was long advocated by International Socialists and others as a means both of organising against employer and state tactics and of supplanting the weak and bureaucratised leaderships of trade unions. This movement has now begun to make a serious appearance. For many years a revolutionary political organisation like IS could function only in a propagandist or narrowly servicing relation to the active elements of trade unionism.

Fifteen years ago one sold the organisation's paper outside the meetings called by larger, grander bodies and built an essentially morale-boosting local group for isolated and highly theoretical revolutionaries. The Liverpool group at this time, for example, included a garrulous french-polisher, a couple of dropouts from the ILP, a mathematics lecturer, and an affable joiner of immense hostile intransigence against any involvement in the Labour Party, who once denounced Stan Newens, then a comrade of the same sectarian persuasion, as 'basically a social democrat'; the joiner's name, by the way, was Eric Heffer.

Five years ago one lobbied any conceivable trade union activist to buy Tony Cliff's exposé of productivity deals, *The Employers' Offensive*, became a specialist in bonus schemes and manning agreements, and tried to integrate worker-recruits into an IS ambience whose meetings were dominated at worst by gurus, groupies, hairies or routinist hacks, and at best by keen young folk without a regular industrial base. A good many trade unionists survived the ordeal, infiltrating a structure that was supposed to be ready to receive them but in practice had to undergo its own transformation, with the establishment of factory branches and a constant pressure from head office to face outwards, before it could start to become a workers' organisation. Rank and file work in industry is now open to socialist revolutionaries as never since the Twenties.

The last era of the independent Left, from 1956 to roughly 1970, can be termed the Age of Minorities. The strength of a radical demonstration, whether numbered in hundreds or in scores of thousands, reflected the ingathering of local weaknesses, tiny powerless groups who in their own terrain were unable to win the mass of people around them except perhaps in the temporary euphoria of one college or one workshop. The great mobilisations of the Sixties were compounded as an assemblage of these manifold minorities; the Left seemed to be everywhere precisely because it enjoyed a stable mass support nowhere; its quick local industrial victories during the boom epoch of labour shortage and wage drift risked a certain thinness in the loyalty of workers to stewards and ensured that a nationwide solidarity of strikers in any industry would be rare, an untested weapon. When the test came, in the wave of redundancies and productivity deals that purged the economy in the late Sixties, or in the outburst of worker racism around Powell's speeches, the stewards and the left militants usually found themselves isolated under fire, dazed by the enemy's capacity to hit deep into their shop-floor base.

The middle-class Left in its various campaigns swung from action to inertia, paying the price of the exhausted forerunner but leaving a residue of cadres for future contests. In the coming era of mass unemployment, general job insecurity and inflation-led cuts in real wages, the defensive traditions of the Age of Minorities must be junked as so much garbage, and recycled. The ground formerly occupied by middle-class radicalism and working-class Labourism lies naked to all-comers, susceptible to any new thrust that emerges after the collapse of old party loyalties, open to the opportune probings of the Nationalists and Liberals, to the temptations of the fascisms whether latent or blatant, and to the activity of a realistic and courageous Marxism. For revolutionary socialists it now has to be the Age of Majorities: the majorities which have to be won, in factory after factory, workplace after workplace, in every cell of social and economic organisation, to ensure that the workers, be they of the blue collar or the white, do not have to bear across their own hides the lash of capital's retrenchment.

There are, in general, no specific 'transitional demands' for the present period of working-class consciousness. Any demand which unites workers and takes them forward together is to that extent transitional. Some of these demands are roughly foreseeable but by no means all. Nobody knew, for example, that the abolition of pay-beds would become the marshalling point of direct action among health service workers. The requirements of an Age of Majorities mean that every socialist must engage, as the first call on his or her time and energy, in mass work within a real rank and file. This is, incidentally, one more reason why the committed revolutionary or radical will be unable to support the Labour Party in any other way beyond attendance at the polling booth: if he has his priorities right, he will simply have no time for electoral canvassing. The acquisition of active, campaigning roles by socialists within a local constituency should ideally present few difficulties. In theory that is what militant socialism is all about. But practically the transition is likely to be somewhat painful. We have all fled from the tasks of the socialist campaigner into the peculiar satisfactions of the prophet or the administrator, the minimal shop steward or the archetypal student leader, the paper-selling wanderer or the paper-reading follower: these postures are so much less demanding, so much more fulfilling in the short term, than the role of the active ferment among a group of people who see us every working day, know us by name and face and will call us to account for every word and action.

The socialist must join the worker's movement as a trade unionist in his own right, with card, rule-book and box of anti-management tricks, undergoing the same problems of skill and morale in leadership as those he is addressing. His politics must be open: not regurgitated by the yard into every resolution with a practical content, but visible to everyone, displayed on his lapel rather than tucked away behind it. The crowning aim of the Age of Majorities is to construct, within the working class, a majority of conscious socialists. Every act, every demand in revolutionary mass work must be subordinated to that first and final aim.

The road that runs from the capturing of active minorities to the securing of real majorities has very few signposts. Most of those that we have show us, as Rosa Luxemburg remarked, the way *not* to go. But it is clear that the way forward lies through a sharpening polarisation of society, whose coming is not the creation of socialists – even though it forms their greatest opportunity – but the product of an anarchic social system based on competitive profit. The extremisms are now on the agenda, and the middle position of moderation has to balance itself more and more precariously in relation to those extremes, and to become somewhat more extreme itself, on both the Left and the Right. It is important that we should not be deterred or gulled by the threat of right-wing violence, whether from the state or from extra-parliamentary quarters. No process of radicalisation has ever taken place in any crisis without a corresponding threat of radical Rightism.

But it would be wrong to raise the perspective of a repetition of the Thirties. The forces of the Left are far better organised and more powerful than in the Thirties. Europe entered the decades of fascism in the grip of the massacre's nightmares following World War I, its petty bourgeoisies inflamed by despair, its labour movements crushed or worn down in a contracting market. The working class of this country has no memory of any major defeat. Its organisation into trade unions has proceeded, in a heavy impetus of expansion and amalgamation, without respite, since 1940. While the horizons of its economic expectations are still narrower than those of American and Continental labour, its appetites are zestful, its confidence unimpaired. The organised workers have at present little to fear from any counter-movement of the individualist middle classes, since the former professions are themselves now enrolled in trade unions with militant habits and a TUC alignment.

Even from the universities the worst that the workers can fear is from the dons, for in the event of a re-run of 1926 the students of the present day will not be seen driving the trams but harassing the scabs. And the labour movement has new regiments of its own whom it has scarcely begun to muster, whom indeed it has often caused to turn back from its recruiting offices because it was known the reception there would be frosty: the blacks, the Asians, the migrants from Europe, and the women. In the impending polarisation these millions can be won to a socialist mass movement. The relaxation of manners and rules among younger people has produced an anti-authoritarian complex which, while far from constituting an arm of socialist militancy, produces a numerous reserve of benevolent neutrals for any future punch-ups with established authority. For the moment the proper response to a hint of military take-over or paramilitary violence is to say: how very interesting and very salutary if they try anything on. Let them just dare.

But such a response should be only momentary. To engage in a public mental rehearsal of the scenarios of civil confrontation is merely to repeat the follies of the retired Blimps, who delight in the drafting of contingency plans as a recompense for the fact that nobody any more is offering them actual contingencies to deal with. Contingencies there indeed are, and scenarios, but they contain well-tried actors with familiar faces: government, employers, TUC, top union officials, the Special Patrol Group of the Metropolitan Police, the established political parties. Both the pace and the scope of the developing social confrontation in Britain are virtually unknown quantities.

If the resources of the British Left are stronger than in the Thirties, it is because then they were pitiful, infinitesimal. Today the forces of capital and of labour both suffer from a discrepancy between their state of organisation and their state of morale: but the contradiction is slanted in an opposite direction within the two camps. The centralised organisation and planning capacity of the ruling class and its state compensates for their loss of political conviction, economic confidence and general *savoir faire*. By contrast, the working class is buoyant and potentially highly assertive: but its organisation is in fairly poor shape, and its leadership appalling both in structure and in staffing. The national trade union bureaucracies of both Left and Right are vying in contest for the lowest public profile: with the exception of the passively conducted miners' strike just before the election of Wilson, no major section of manual workers has engaged in a really serious action since the great upheavals of 1972.

The unions' honeymoon with the Labour Government is a heartless repetition of the first fling of 1964–7; observers stationed around the bridal suite of the Hotel Social Compact so far report little evidence of action, not even the noise of smashing crockery. This is an epoch of a million looming redundancies, soaring home costs, and washed-out wages, when bacon and beef were first appreciated as delicacies. Further down the hierarchy of labour, several hundred thousand shop stewards are looking at their pay-conscious workmates, at their quiescent union supporters and at their own thumbs, nabbing a threshold agreement if they can get one but without any lead for the new possibilities that now arise with the repeal of the Industrial Relations Act and the end of Tory incomes policy.

On the political Left, the membership of the Communist Party of Great Britain slumbers on, counting left MPs as it snores, its parliamentary dreams only temporarily disturbed by the sad news of the crushing of an identical electoral strategy in Chile. The more recent news of the Portuguese Communist Party's entanglement with the military regime has set off no qualms whatever in Britain's Communists. Short of an escalated pre-revolutionary situation, a 1917 of Imperial Russia or 1936 of Republican Spain, which can at present be ruled out from any working perspectives, the expansion which any Marxist organisation can envisage in its activities and recruitment must be modest by comparison with the seriousness of its goals. Boiled down to the proportions of immediately realisable possibility, the revolutionary work in the Age of Minorities means increasing the nucleus of politically minded workers in a pit or depot from around two to around six; selling *Chingari*, the socialist monthly produced in Urdu and Punjabi, to those Asians who are confident enough to take its programme to heart; building a trade union base in a shift of 60 women without previous experience of organisation; winning a vote in a union committee for firm policies against wage restraint; systematically working over a street on a council estate, finding the few workers there who will be already predisposed towards socialist attitudes, and to forming a political, not simply a sociable, relation with them; in a hostile workshop, with management keen to fire trouble makers and a frightened or apathetic labour force, it will mean finding one other person with whom to discuss the next step, without risking exposure by breaking cover.

There will also be the big jobs and the central occasions, the industry-wide gathering of stewards, the physical cordon against fascist marchers, the delegate conference of revolutionaries waging a fraternal polemic on perspectives, taking the decisions and dispersing to implement them. But the Age of Majorities, unlike that of the minorities without a base, consists for the most part of a cellular, even molecular chain-building. It is the march of the spermatozoa into the eggs, the duplication, over and over again, of specialised cells, the use of tiny living templates for the growth of a new organism.

If this process does not sound spectacular, we should remember that it has been already enough to start the beginnings of a generation: a generation whose growth in power and numbers must become accelerated in the struggle of the next decade if the working-class movement is not to experience a terrible retrogression.

Peter Sedgwick, 13 September 1974

PART FIVE

1974–1987

Lowry, 19 September 1986

The French philosopher Louis Althusser, popular in Left academic circles in the mid-seventies, used to refer portentously to certain works of Marx as those of 'the break'. For British politics, 1974–9 were the years of the break. The post-war consensus unravelled beneath the uncomprehending gaze of an immobilised Labour government, while a renewed Conservatism waited to scoop the benefits of mounting discontent. Since then, the climate for the Left, and for the New Statesman, *has grown ever colder. There have been exciting new departures – the explosion of investigative journalism under Bruce Page, the renewal of the peace movement (first rallied, like the original CND, from the pages of the* NS), *discovery of the liberatory politics of feminism, a return to Kingsley's argumentative, opinion-moulding role under John Lloyd and now Stuart Weir. The dominant single theme, however, has been searching reappraisal of the idea of socialism itself, in the recognition that the British radical tradition also has undergone an historic rupture.*

The break came, too, for former NS *Editor PAUL JOHNSON. At the time of the following article, he still asserted that his disgust at the state of the Labour movement arose from a desire to rescue the Left from drowning in trade unionism's dirty bathwater. Soon thereafter he decided that baby, bathtub and all must go along with the water.*

The Rise of the Know-Nothing Left

The biggest change that has overcome the British socialist movement in my time has been the disintegration of Labour's intellectual Left. The outstanding personalities who epitomised, galvanised and led it are dead and have never been replaced. I am thinking, for instance, of G.D.H. Cole, whose activities covered the whole spectrum of working-class activism and whose voluminous writings constituted a *summa theologica* of left-wing theory and practice; of R.H. Tawney, who placed the modern Left firmly in a long historical context and who endowed its philosophising with enormous intellectual and literary distinction; of R.H.S. Crossman, who brought the bracing austerities of reason into the grossest skulduggeries of practical politics; and, above all, of Aneurin Bevan. The majesty of Bevan's contribution lay in the fact that he transcended classes and categories – a working man with the instincts and capacities of a philosopher-king, a man of action with a passion for reflection, a romantic devoted to the pursuit of pure reason, and an egalitarian obsessed by excellence. Around these, and other, great planets swam many scores of satellites, collectively constituting a huge left-wing galaxy of talent and intelligence.

And where do we find the left wing of the party today? Without a struggle, with complacency, almost with eagerness, it has delivered itself, body, mind and soul, into the arms of the trade union movement. There is a savage irony in this unprecedented betrayal, this unthinking *trahison des clercs*. For Labour's intellectual Left had always, and with justice, feared the arrogant bosses of the TUC, with their faith in the big battalions and the zombie-weight of collective numbers, their contempt for the individual conscience, their invincible materialism, their blind and exclusive class-consciousness, their rejection of theory for pragmatism, their intolerance and their envious loathing of outstanding intellects. The whole of Cole's life was devoted to demonstrating, among other propositions, that trade union organisation was not enough, that there was a salient place for the middle-class intelligentsia in the socialist movement, and an essential role for didacticism. What Labour lacked, argued Tawney, was what he termed 'the hegemonic way of thinking': it concentrated on the basic trade union aim of sectional gains for its own members instead of trying to create a new moral world.

Bevan, though a trade unionist, never regarded trade unionism as a substitute for socialism – in some ways he thought it an enemy, indeed a part of the capitalist system. He fought bitterly against the attempts by the TUC to determine Labour policy in conference and to usurp the political role in government. He believed passionately that Parliament was the instrument of strategic change, and its control the political object of social democracy – he would have resisted at all costs the brutal threat of a syndicalist takeover. Crossman put the anti-union case a little more crudely: what invalidated the TUC claim to control Labour was its sheer lack of brains and talent. Hence his notorious article pointing out that only five trade union MPs were fit to participate in a Labour ministry. For this heinous heresy he was dragged before the inquisition and, just as Galileo was forced to recant his heliocentric theory, Dick was made to pay public homage to the dazzling genius of his trade union 'friends'. Afterwards, he said to me: 'There was only one thing wrong with my article – I should have written three, not five.'

In those days, it was a dismally common event to see a left-winger stretched on the rack of trade union power. Intellectuals from Stafford

Cripps to Bertrand Russell were the victims of drumhead courts-martial conducted by the union satraps. Yet today the leaders of what is hilariously termed the Left look to the unions as the fountain-head of all wisdom and socialist virtue. Mr Michael Foot, a Minister of the Crown, will not stir an inch unless he has the previous approval of the TUC General Council. Mr Eric Heffer, Foot's *doppelgänger* and cheerleader on the back benches, regards any criticism of British trade unionism as a compound of high treason and the Sin Against the Holy Syndicalist Ghost. Did this gigantic U-turn come about because the trade union bosses have undergone a cataclysmic change of heart and transformed their whole philosophy of life and politics? Not a bit of it. It is true that the general secretaries of the biggest unions no longer, as in Deakin's day, pull the strings from behind a curtain, but prefer to strut upon the stage of power themselves. It is true, also, that they inspire more genuine fear than they did 20 years ago, as their crazy juggernaut lurches over the crushed bodies of political opponents. In other respects, however, their metaphysic has not altered: it is still a relentless drive to power by the use of force and threats.

The union leaders still regard money as the sole criterion of success and (to them) social progress. They are prime victims of what Tawney, in *Equality*, called 'the reverence for riches, the *lues Anglicana*, the hereditary disease of the English nation'. Blind to the long term, to the complexities of the economic process, to the well-being and rights of other human beings – blind, in fact, to what Tawney called 'fellowship', to him the very core of the socialist ethic – they see the whole of the political struggle in immediate cash terms. The other day one of them said he would not hesitate to bring the entire publicly-owned steel industry to a halt, and throw perhaps hundreds of thousands of his 'comrades' out of work, unless he was offered 'more money on the table', as he put it. Asked if he would heed the activities of the government conciliation service, he said he was not going to take advice from those he contemptuously referred to as 'college boys'.

Indeed, one of the startling characteristics of modern British trade union activists is their systematic dislike for intellectual and cultural eminence and their hostility towards higher education. Here a great and deplorable shift in attitudes has taken place since the 19th century. To me, the saddest newspaper report of recent years was a survey of the miners' clubs of South Wales, which revealed that their large, and often rare and valuable, libraries of political books and pamphlets had been sold off to dealers in order to clear space for jukeboxes, pin-tables and strip-shows. Part of the price the left wing of the Labour Party has paid for its alliance with the trade union bosses has been the enforced adoption of a resolutely anti-intellectual stance. If miners prefer strip-shows to self-education, the argument runs, then so be it: the fact that the collective working masses express such a preference *in itself* invests the choice with moral worth. Anyone who argues the contrary is 'an elitist'.

'Elitist', in fact, has become the prime term of abuse on the syndicalist Left; it heads the list of convenient clichés which are brought on parade whenever the Eric Heffers put pen to paper, or give tongue. It is a useful bit of verbiage to be hurled at those who, by any stretch of the imagination, can be accused of criticising wage-inflation, strikes, aggressive picketing, the Shrewsbury jailbirds, the divinity of Hugh Scanlon, 'free collective bargaining', differentials, overmanning and other central articles of syndicalist theology. And equally, anyone who pays attention to quality, who insists on the paramountcy of reason, who does not believe the masses are always right or that the lowest common denominator is the best, and who considers there are more things in heaven and earth than are dreamt of in the philosophy of a Mick McGahey or an Arthur Scargill – well, he or she can be dismissed as an elitist too. Crossman, Tawney, Cole, above all Bevan, would have been given short shrift today – elitists, the lot of them.

It says a great deal for the power of the syndicalist Left in the councils of the Government, and even in the immediate entourage of Harold Wilson (who, secretly, is one of the outstanding elitists of our time), that anti-elitism has, to some extent, become official government policy, at any rate in the sphere of higher education. Our universities used to be autonomous, and for all practical purposes exempt from state control or guidance – a very elitist and reprehensible state of affairs! But all this is now being changed as the financial cuts begin to bite and the University Grants Committee progressively takes up its role as the Government's instrument of supervision. Earlier this year, Reg Prentice, one of Harold's innumerable Education Ministers, sneeringly told the universities to 'live off their fat' and, if necessary, 'sell their art treasures'. Prentice, of course, has come and gone, being succeeded by one of the faceless Freds; direction of the anti-elitist policy has now devolved on the Prime Minister's personal academic henchman, Lord Crowther-Hunt. In an earlier incarnation he was Dr Norman Hunt, an assiduous gatherer of Westminster anecdotage – Robert McKenzie writ small, you might say – with a fashionable prole accent, who made himself useful to Harold Wilson and other Labour magnificos. His reward has been a peerage and ministerial charge of higher education, where he politely tells the vice-chancellors that they must conform to the Government's 'manpower planning' needs or go to the financial wall.

The new anti-elitist spirit in the realms of higher education both complements and echoes the alliance between the trade unions and Labour's know-nothing Left. Away with the ivory towers! To hell with expensive research which ordinary people can't understand, and will probably come to nothing anyway. The job of a university is to turn out field-grey regiments of 'socially relevant' people, with the right egalitarian ideas, the capacity to learn by heart the latest fashionable slogans, and to march, shout, scream, howl and picket as and when required. Degradation of the universities, of course, would fit in neatly with the syndicalisation of the Labour Party, since the ideal student – according to the anti-elitists – is one who conforms as closely as possible, mentally, emotionally and culturally, to a trade union militant. The operation is part of an uncoordinated but nevertheless impressive effort to proletarianise the educated classes, and to smash to bits what are venomously referred to as 'middle-class values' (such as honesty, truthfulness, respect for reason, dislike of lawbreaking, hatred of violence, and so forth).

It is by no means confined to students. At a recent conference of local authority education officials, a former headmaster and university vice-chancellor had the temerity to attempt a half-hearted defence of elitism and was promptly denounced, by a yobbo from Glamorgan, as 'an educational fascist'. But students are the prime targets of the anti-elitists because they can be so easily organised into Rentamobs by Labour's syndicalists and their allies (and future masters) even further to the Left. As all totalitarian rulers have discovered, once you have hacked away the logical and rational foundations on which the edifice of civilisation rests, it is comparatively easy to invert the process of ratiocination, dress up the results in verbiage, and sell them to thousands of apparently well-educated people.

A typical example of anti-elitist Newspeak is a dissenting minority report of a Yale Committee on Freedom of Expression, appointed after left-wing students smashed up a meeting addressed by William Shockley in 1974. The overwhelming majority of the Yale academics concluded that disruption of a speech should be regarded as an offence against the university, and one which could lead to expulsion. The dissentient, speaking for the Left, argued that free speech was both undesirable and impossible until there had been 'liberation from, and increased self-consciousness of, the social and irrational factors that condition knowledge and preform the means and structures of language'. Hidden in this ugly gobbet of verbiage is the thoroughly totalitarian idea that the meanings not merely of words but of moral concepts must be recast to conform to political expediency – the very essence of Newspeak. The example is American; but there are plenty of parallels over here, not always expressed quite so naively as by the Essex student leaders who refused even to discuss an 'independent report' on their activities, for which they had clamoured, on the grounds that 'reason is an ideological weapon with which bourgeois academics are especially well armed'!

When reason ceases to be the objective means by which civilised men settle their differences and becomes a mere class 'weapon', then clearly the anti-elitists are making considerable progress. How long will it be before the books are burning again, and the triumph of the 'Common Man', that figment of violent and irrational imaginations, is celebrated by another *kristalnacht*? Already, at the extreme fringe of the syndicalist Left, the aggrosocialists are taking over public meetings, with their ideological flick knives and their doctrinaire coshes. Not long ago, hearing and seeing a group of students and trade unionists giving the Nazi salute, and shouting 'Sieg heil!' at some very stolid-looking policemen, I shut my eyes for a few seconds, and tried to detect the redeeming note of irony in their rhythmical chanting. For the life of me, I could not find it. What differentiated these mindless and violent youths from Hitler's well-drilled thugs? Merely, I fear, the chance of time and place, a turn of the fickle wheel of fortune. Unreason and thuggery are always the enemies, whatever labels they carry; for labels are so easily removed and changed. I remember Adlai Stevenson – an elitist if ever there was one – saying wearily: 'Eggheads of the world, unite, you have nothing to lose but your yokes.' Perhaps it is time for the elitists to stand up for themselves – there may not be so few of us, either – and start the long business of rescuing the Labour Left from the know-nothings and the half-wits.

Paul Johnson, 26 September 1975

The long agony of Northern Ireland dragged through the seventies – and now most of the eighties. FENTON put his balding head (about which it is cruel to feed his evident self-consciousness) back into the lion's mouth of Crossmaglen.

Christmas in Cross

'So you're going to Comanche country,' said a Protestant lady in Belfast. Crossmaglen has become something of a byword recently. And not only recently. At the end of the Crossmaglen conspiracy trial, on 28 March 1883, Mr Justice Lawson said: 'This unfortunate district of Crossmaglen has been to my own knowledge – having been in this circuit for the last 14 years – always a stain on the fair province of Ulster.' That was after 12 men had been found guilty, during a notorious trial, of belonging to a murderous fraternity known as the Patriotic Brotherhood. Today, what has seized the public imagination? Surely it is the notion that, in South Armagh, Britain is at war: there are military operations, soldiers are surrounded and killed, it is a hostile country.

We drove through the dark from Newry, and I confess to a certain quickening of the pulse as the headlights picked out the signposts, the road deteriorated and we approached the town. At one point we passed a crater blown by a mine. Further on, the military checkpoint. In the main square a crowd of children were assembled for the turning on of the Christmas tree. Santa Claus drawn along on a cart, was making the rounds of Crossmaglen. Arriving at the tree, he stood up and said: 'I now declare this Christmas tree officially – er – open.' Somebody in the Gents' lavatory flicked the relevant switch.

Yet another journalist! Everyone I met expressed the same dismay at the attention the town had received from press and television. They were not bandits or Comanches, they insisted indignantly. They were misrepresented. They were simply keen on going their own way, and not being mucked around by army and press. There was Dutch television in town. There had been a series of reporters, who had seemed perfectly friendly on the spot, but had gone off and told the wildest stories about what was happening. 'Crossmaglen, town of hate.' In vain did one protest one's utter reasonableness. They'd heard that one before.

'And the thing is,' said one woman, 'it's not as if the place was intimidated by the Provisionals. I've lived here for a long time and I don't know one member of the Provisional IRA. There are youths who sell the paper, of course, but not active members of the Provos.' And it was pointed out, as has recently been pointed out to Airey Neave and the other members of the Conservative Party's own Provisional Wing, that there had not been one internee from Cross. There had been no sectarian murders there, and no civilian casualties (this was before last weekend's pub bombing). Nor any IRA funerals. Indeed one began to wonder, from the way they talked, what on earth all the fuss was about.

I was having one of these sorts of conversation with a highly respectable lady in a pub when the soldiers came in. It was instructive to see the way in which her manner changed. The pub went silent. The soldiers singled out two youths and began to question them. Then more

soldiers came round the bar. They were being friendly – it was pathetic
– they made cheery little remarks, which floated in the air for a
moment, like soap bubbles, and then burst. One girl began imitating a
soldier behind his back. A black soldier came up to the bar, made a
joke, and went away. At this point the highly respectable lady leaned
forward and told me a highly unrespectable story about black men,
which I shall not repeat.

I thought at the time, how strange these British soldiers are. They
really seemed like foreigners to me – sad, isolated members of an
occupying army, coming from ... where? I'd almost forgotten whose
they were.

The next day, after breakfast, I wondered what I should do in order
to avoid indulging in the obnoxious art of journalism. There was a
signpost marked 'Horned Cairn, Ancient Monument, 2 Miles', and I
thought that would do. I walked out into 'Comanche country' through a
mist so thick that it seemed to congeal. The dripping trees were
festooned with lichen. There were black branches and twigs. But the
Horned Cairn appeared to have been a practical joke.

Returning from my walk, and slightly relieved that I had not met
anyone, since I would have been hard put to explain that I had been
looking for a horned cairn (whatever that is), I came back into the
square. A sort of military operation was in progress, with soldiers
fanning out on either side, guns at the ready. I thought the best thing to
do was walk straight through. A soldier stopped me and asked for
identification. 'Where do you come from?' he said.

This is always a difficult one for me. After a moment's thought I
said: 'London. Where do *you* come from?' He smiled for a moment,
and also looked confused. Then he collected himself. He was a rather
small man. 'I'm asking the questions,' he said. During this time, an
officer with one of those tiny Instamatics was taking my photograph.
Then the soldier let me go.

As I walked away, I could hear the officer – and this gave the scene
an eerie quality – speaking into his walkie-talkie: 'Says his name's
James Fenton ... dark hair ... wearing a long coat ... conspicuous ...
he's growing a beard. ...' I realised I must look a terrible mess. I hadn't
shaved for days, and the mist had drenched what remains of my hair.
Not surprisingly, the soldier called me back, and I was questioned by
the officer.

He was the sort of man you see on the television after there's been
an outrage – the trained army PR man. When he was satisfied as to my
identity, he began a little speech. As I could see, he said, there was no
tricolour flying over the town. It was a tragedy that the whole place was
being intimidated by a handful of terrorists. Well, they weren't even

real terrorists, really, they were just common criminals. Etc., etc.

It was reasonable PR, I suppose, but it was just too late. The officer had made one mistake, if he wanted a sympathetic hearing, and that was – he had taken my photo. I don't mind identity checks, I quite enjoy a frisk, but when soldiers start sneaking snapshots I begin to object. If you think *I'm* being unreasonable, consider how it must feel when these sort of things happen to you every day.

'What is the army doing in Cross?' asked one inhabitant, with cogent simplicity. They are not protecting the inhabitants against anything. There are five Protestant families, who take care to play a full role in the community. The army are here, defusing bombs, booby-traps and mines which are placed here because ... because the army's here. 'It seems like a terrible waste of manpower,' he said.

The army do two things which inevitably earn them the dislike of the population: they have to escort the police on their rare visits to the town (when the RUC come, a notice is pinned up on the approach road saying 'Police in Town', so that all those who have not paid their road tax, etc. can give the place a wide berth) and they carry out a continual census and close scrutiny of the inhabitants. I was told that this questioning can often be brutal and humiliating – but even if it were not, it could hardly be expected to win the hearts and minds of the locals. When a soldier asks you your name, and then says, 'Oh yes, you're the brother of so-and-so, and your family comes from such-and-such' – are you pleased that he knows so much about you? Of course you aren't.

Crossmaglen is unusual in that it is near the border, and therefore has stronger links with the Republic than most other northern towns. A large proportion of its population go to work in Dundalk (there is one factory in Cross, which makes Newcel toilet paper), the nearest markets are in the Republic, and there is a strong cultural tradition, which is Irish. It would be odd, then, if some sort of Republicanism did not flourish. I asked one woman whether all the problems of Cross would not simply disappear if the border was redrawn. 'Well, I don't think so at all,' she retorted indignantly. 'What we want is a 32-country Republic. And that's what we're fighting for.'

Which brings one straight back to the question of Ireland as a whole, if it is or can ever be a whole. A Protestant friend reacted strongly against what he called the romantic notion of the Protestant – the idea that the Prods are really Irish 'at heart', and that once the border went, the problem would simply sort itself out. Certainly things look very clear cut in Crossmaglen, clearer, perhaps, than anywhere else in Ireland. And it may be that the Republicans are simply blind to the existence of a million Protestants in the North – that they simply 'look straight through them'. My only point is a very simple one, but it is, I think, topical. The British public looks at incidents in places like Crossmaglen; it sees that the army is at war; it feels the war is not worth it; it begins to want out. British politicians, the army and the police are embarrassed. They evade the issue, dubbing the Republicans mere criminals and bandits. The impression is given that, with a few more Sir Robert Marks, the whole matter could be cleared up in no time. We are told that the Provisionals were against the ending of internment because it would undermine their appeal. And yet the Republicanism of Crossmaglen has nothing at all to do with internment. It does however have a lot to do with the presence of the army, and the presence of the border.

Poor old army. I watched them in Newry, escorting the Wolfe Tone Accordion Band (tiny little majorettes in red and green) who in turn were escorting the local Santa to the Milestone Supermarket. And they were obviously trying to be very nice. I also watched them in Belfast, where they stood on guard around the Christmas tree at the council's open-air concert. The band struck up (tactlessly I thought) a Beatles tune – 'Get back to where you once belonged.'

James Fenton, 26 December 1975

The connections between Fenton's theme and that of Ulster poet TOM PAULIN should, I hope, be obvious enough.

The Impossible Pictures

In this parable of vengeance
There is a grey newsreel
Being shown inside my head.

Its subject is that pointless
Reflection – what might have happened
If this had never been the case?

What happens is that Lenin's brother
(Alexsandr Ulyanov)
Is being led to execution.

He carries a small book
Wrapped in a piece of cloth.
Is it the bible or a text

His brother will be forced to write?
He twists it in his hands.
I think he is frightened.

I am wrong, because suddenly
He strikes an officer on the face –
His gestures now are a jerking

Clockwork anachronism.
He is goosestepped to the scaffold.
The frozen yard of the prison

Is like this dawn of rain showers
And heavy lorries, a gull mewling
In its dream of the Atlantic.

Ah, I say, this is Ireland
And my own place, myself.
I see a Georgian rectory

Square in the salt winds
Above a broken coast,
And the gulls scattering

Their cold cries: I know
That every revenge is nature,
Always on time, like the waves.

Tom Paulin, 1 December 1978

A rising tempo of industrial and civil unrest in the late 1970s met the response of an ever more heavy-handed policing. Civil libertarians voiced increasing concern about police behaviour – but few got quite such intimate opportunity for observation as did DENIS MACSHANE.

Picked Up on the Picket Line

In the past month I have been arrested twice by the police. The first time was at the back entrance to Mr George Ward's Grunwick factory by Dollis Hill tube station. The second was 250 miles further north outside Lord Gibson's *Northern Echo* building in Darlington where 108 members of my union, the NUJ, are on strike.

Three weeks ago a report on Grunwick in the *Sunday Times* claimed that it was currently fashionable to get oneself arrested on a picket line. It may be for some, not for me. I hated being arrested. Whoever typed out those fatuous words had clearly never heard the extraordinary depressing and lonely sound of a cell door clanging shut behind him. Yes, the door really does clang, a heavy metal bong as a hundredweight of steel slams into its frame. And the jailers still carry their long cell keys on big rings of metal just like in the John Wayne pictures. But the cells, at least at Wembley and Darlington police stations, don't have bars on the windows. They don't have windows at all. Just four inch square slabs of reinforced opaque glass like the ones you walk over on streets. They let in some light but a glimpse of sky would have been welcome.

Nor could the man who wrote that 'Insight' report in the *Sunday Times* have experienced the smell from the open lavatory inside the cell. The second time around, in Darlington, I quickly adjusted to it, but there is no pleasure, and less fashion, in the smell of a badly run public lavatory. Nor either in the messy indignity of being finger-printed. I had thought – and again how the cinema and TV is responsible for all ideas of police procedures – it was simply a matter of a dainty dab of thumb and first finger on an ink pad and then on to paper. Not so. Every finger, even the pinkie, is carefully rolled in ink and then held firmly down on to a printed form. Finally the palms are covered in ink and an imprint taken (I wonder if there are amateur palm readers in the police who are let loose on all those palm prints – 'I see a tall dark stranger who will take you away'). Your hands end up covered in glutinous black ink. 'You journalists ought to be used to it,' quipped the finger-print man in Darlington. 'After all, it's the same as printer's ink.'

The awful thing is that until those two arrests, although I've been too close as a reporter to the police in action to swallow the 'aren't they all wonderful' line, I have always kept firmly within the law. My only previous brush with criminality was a speeding conviction six years ago, and that for doing 37 m.p.h. in a Fiat 500. Princess Anne probably goes faster on horseback.

The sergeant who arrested me at Grunwick was quite adamant that I had destroyed my career. 'Fucking rabble. That's all you are. Fucking rabble,' he kept repeating as we entered the green police coach designated for arrestees. I couldn't work out a riposte as the arm-lock he had effected around my neck in the 40 yards between picket line scrum and the police coach had left me quite breathless.

'Fucking rabble,' he said again as he pushed me into a seat and sat down heavily beside me. 'You probably don't know it but having this on your record will ruin you, you little cunt.' It was only as I recovered my breath that I realised my right foot was hurting considerably. Trying to move it I found out why. A large police boot was placed firmly on it.

'Excuse me, sergeant. You're on my foot. Could I have it back.'

'Am I?' he said, looking down. 'Oh dear. So I am.' He lifted his boot and slammed it down again on my foot. 'What a pity.'

This particular exercise was interrupted when a young man, a complete stranger, knocked on the side of the bus window and asked if I was all right. I gave him a name to contact when my sergeant leant across me and snapped the window shut. That wasn't enough however and as the man kept talking to me the sergeant leapt out of the bus.

'Right, cunt. You're coming inside.'

'What for?' said the stranger.

'Obstructing the police,' said the sergeant, as he hustled my would-be samaritan into the coach. As peace settled I took out a pen to click into action when he snatched it from me.

'Give me that back,' I said, perhaps a shade peremptorily given my circumstances.

'No way, cunt,' he said. 'This is now one pen, prisoner's property.'

'Come on, I'm only going to write with it.'

He looked at the pen, a pricey Parker ball-point and as I made a half-hearted reach for it held it between his hands and snapped it in half.

'Oh dear. One broken pen, prisoner's property.'

At Wembley police station he led me off the coach with a peculiarly painful rigid arm lock. It wasn't his local nick and someone had to point the way to the charge room. The way there was down a sloping corridor. 'You're fucking lucky there aren't any stairs to fall down, aren't you?' Perhaps I was. I hope he was kidding, though.

In Darlington the police hardly swore at all. The nearest thing to an oath was a muttered 'Anarchy, anarchy' from a sadfaced Inspector watching the parade of local reporters and sub-editors being charged. Some 40 odd people have been arrested on the Darlington picket line, not as impressive a total as the Grunwick arrests but given the relative size of the picket line – the Darlington journalists have been lucky to get more than 70 pickets for their mass turn-out – the Durham Constabulary must feel that they have done much better, proportionately, than their brothers in the Met.

The inside of the cell was as miserable as at Wembley. My first companion was even more depressed than I was. He was a local court reporter and knew all the police by their first names. What was worse, his girl-friend, to whom he was engaged, was a policewoman; and he worried over her career prospects. The next one in was one of Darlington's most respected journalists and clearly in full possession of that ratlike cunning that Nick Tomalin once wrote was an essential quality for successful reporters. As the cell door shut he reached into his socks – shoes, belts and ties had to be left outside and pulled out cigarettes and matches. He had heard from pickets arrested the previous week that the police wouldn't let you have a smoke – so in the ride from the *Northern Echo* to the police station he had carefully transferred cigarettes and matches to inside his socks.

It was a small victory in a rotten night. The cell was then livened up by a drunk picked up for fighting outside a kebab house. He was markedly scornful of the sheepish, shamefaced journalists confronting him and regaled us with tales of times past spent inside a police cell. He also explained what the initials ACAB scrawled everywhere on the cell walls stood for.

'All coppers are bastards,' he told us as he lurched to the cell door to shout more abuse at a policeman passing down the corridor.

Dennis MacShane, 15 July 1977

Paul Johnson's rapid progress toward the political Right eventually drew an extended response in the pages of the NS. *ROBIN BLACKBURN's polemical ferocity almost matches Johnson's own, but the essay is important primarily because of the wider issues it raises about the politics of the 'New Right'.*

A Fabian at the End of His Tether

The belligerent looking gent at the bus stop, on the train, in the bar makes some obnoxious remark about Africans, trade union militants or the link between the crime rate and socialism. Do you give battle for the sake of the bystanders? If the gent in question wears a three-piece suit, carries a stick and is doing a passable imitation of Evelyn Waugh in his later years, then the line of least resistance might seem attractive.

From May 1975 Paul Johnson unloosed a series of extraordinarily vicious attacks, first on the trade unions and the Labour Party, and then on an ever widening range of targets from the ecology movement to modern art, from the philosophy of Herbert Marcuse to the Notting Hill Gate carnival. Johnson identified the Left as responsible for an insidious assault on civilisation, paradoxically combining chaos and collectivism; his recommended solutions, no less paradoxically, combined re-affirmation of the individual with calls for a stern restoration of law and order. Johnson's central preoccupation has been, and remains, the sinister totalitarian threat represented by organised labour. Johnson soon established himself as by far the most authoritative interpreter of the Left so far as the Tory press was concerned: articles that first appeared in this journal were reprinted in their entirety by the *Daily Mail* or the *Telegraph*. The readers of these papers were insistently reminded that Johnson was a former editor of the *New Statesman*, an intimate of leading Labour politicians, and someone who had been 'one of the Labour Party's most brilliant and influential crusaders'. If a man with these credentials declared that the Labour Party had become a Marxist-fascist Party, then surely he must know what he is talking about?

The impression created by Johnson's confident harangues can scarcely have been dented by the few, isolated attempts to rebut them. Too often those who responded to Johnson would preface their remarks by tributes to him as a 'master of polemic' whose sallies were 'adventurous, learned and deeply funny', or would nervously concede: 'There is much in the detail of Johnson's argument with which it is difficult to disagree.' But this obligatory politeness had no effect on the recipient, unless it was to encourage him to further outrages. Clearly in the matter of Paul Johnson the Left had special responsibilities which it did not discharge. If his polemics are, in fact, vilely abusive, his learning shallow, and his details frequently false or deranged, then this must be pointed out without equivocation. Otherwise we become, in effect, silent accomplices of the master polemicist.

Here are some representative samples of the Johnson polemical technique:

> It is astonishing that the British Labour movement, whose original aim was to civilise industrial society, should repudiate this tradition, turn again to the dark past and harbour the thugs. Nor will the men of violence be content with the mere patronage of Labour. They are on the march. Violence feeds on its triumphs over the law. Labour's leaders may think the beastliness of a picket line is acceptable. But violence is an evil continuum which begins with inflammatory verbal pursuit of the class war, continues with Grunwick and the lawless use of union power ... and then – as we may well fear – rapidly accelerates into full-blooded terrorism, with firearms, explosives and an utter contempt for human life. This is where the Labour Party is heading. It has already embraced corporatism, which ultimately must mean the end of parliamentary democracy. But corporatism *plus* violence is infinitely worse. It is fascism: left-wing fascism maybe, Marxist-fascism if you like, but still fascism all the same. ('Farewell to the Labour Party', NS 9 September 1977)

Indeed Johnson was so pre-occupied by the fascism of the Labour movement that he entirely discounted the ominous activities of the National Front in 1977-8. The establishment of the Anti-Nazi League brought out Johnson's visceral hostility to left-wing antiracism. He chose the *News of the World* for the following comment on 12 March 1978:

> Most sensible people in this country are not unduly disturbed by the activities of the National Front. Some Labour Party propagandists are trying, for their own political purposes, to present the Front as a potential Hitlerian menace – unless we all join in an anti-racist crusade to oppose it. ... Much more serious in my view is the antidemocratic threat posed by the extreme Left. ... The great problem this country faces is not race, but crime – and especially violent crime ... many senior policeman feel they are fighting a losing battle, and that the forces of disorder are gradually gaining the upper hand. It is against this background that the extreme Left flourishes. ... At one level the assault is generalised: judges, like policemen, are presented as the administrators of a biased, capitalist legal system, heavily weighted in favour of the bourgeoisie. But at another, and more dangerous, level there are violent verbal attacks on particular judges over particular decisions. ... Unfortunately the habit of criticising judges on political grounds is by no means confined to the extreme Left. Members of the present Cabinet have been known to do it. ... Radical dons preach that judges are essentially political figures, and that in many cases there is no obligation to obey the law. Herein lies the real strength and danger of the extreme Left. ... Membership is no bar to academic or civil service promotion, or to access to the media.

The bullying tone, the toboggan slide from one real or supposed fact to another, the construction of an identikit Public Enemy, the invitation to red-baiting, are all hall-marks of the Johnson polemic. But perhaps the chief selling point in Johnsonian bombast is his talent for the flashy phrase, the slogan that neatly abbreviates reflection: 'violence is an evil continuum', 'left-wing fascism' and so forth. When Johnson takes up a case every resource of calculated and colourful hyperbole will be exploited to distract the critical faculties and induce acceptance of Johnson's terms of debate. The reader may feel that Johnson goes too far but the striking pattern he imposes on a diverse, or even unrelated, set of facts leaves an enduring after-image. Johnson likes large subjects and has no hesitation in making large pronouncements upon them. This type of punditry is typically conducted from such a lofty vantage point that it can dispense with the hard-earned techniques of the reporter or the researcher. But though much expense is thereby saved, a heavy toll is taken by the pundit's *deformation professionnelle*, a failure to distinguish between the reality of one's hopes and fears and that of the outside world.

The striking effects of Johnson's prose are achieved by the repeated invocation of a few key terms which are never themselves explained or investigated. One such term is 'violence' and its derivatives. So far as Johnson is concerned violence does not consist in physical assaults upon the person, but simply in words or behaviour of which he disapproves. From the passages quoted above it is already clear that he sees little difference between violent words and violent acts. Violence is not that which produces, or tends to produce, actual bodily harm but rather violations of what Johnson regards as right and proper: the laws of the state and the laws of the market. In Johnson's imagination violence is a disembodied fury menacing all order and civilisation. He never troubles to situate it socially within the modern world, with its harsh inequalities and lip-service to freedom and justice. The fetishised abstraction of violence in Johnson's denunciations is simply the inverse of its claimed authenticity and expressiveness in the writings of those, like Fanon and Sorel, who celebrate it. Used in this fashion, the world is designed to arouse emotion while subduing reason.

For Johnson the main purveyors of violence, in his chosen sense, are terrorists, demonstrators, pickets, and the left-wing press. Thus Johnson shares the terrorist delusions that terrorism is something other than an utterly puny and insignificant phenomenon when compared with the concentrated means of violence at the disposal of the modern state. Johnson is content that President Suharto, who climbed to power over the bodies of half a million Indonesians and who is responsible for the holocaust in East Timor, should be an honoured guest of the Queen and Margaret Thatcher. On the other hand he will condemn those on the Left who drew attention to such unwelcome facts:

> The papers [of the far left] abound with stories of murder and massacre of workers abroad, of police violence at home; they are as it were political horror comics. ... Attention is constantly drawn to papers published by other, related causes such as homosexuality, women's lib, black power; one such, called *Flame*, is said to be 'burning now' (NS 11 February 1977)

His sensibility offended by the violent language of the Left, Johnson is now prepared to use the debauched and sadistic publications of Rupert Murdoch to launch his campaigns against that motley alliance of trade unionists, left-wing thugs, homosexuals, women and blacks, who threaten civilisation as we know it. These people are recklessly smeared with the charge of terrorism and violence as a means of distracting attention from the true sources of wretchedness and tyranny in the modern world, especially the West. Johnson's definition of violence is nicely calculated to stimulate and titillate the jaded palate of the readers of the yellow press but to render literally invisible the victims of poverty, avoidable disease, starvation, aerial bombardment, torture, or racialism.

According to Johnson, 'it is a fact that collectivism and violence always go together.' For this reason Johnson has no difficulty in concluding that: 'With its doctrine of class-warfare, and its anti-individualist cult of violence, the new Labour Left is ... strongly corporatist and directly related to the main body of Marxist-fascist ideology' (NS 11 February 1977). If violence represents all that Johnson fears and hates, and would like others to fear and hate, then individualism is the recommended antidote. Johnson does not see that, once the sense of human community is lost, then the individuals who count will be a constantly narrowing circle. Johnson's discovery of individualism is the occasion for stealthy self-congratulation: 'I have come to appreciate, for the first time in my life, the overwhelming strength of my own attachment to the individual spirit.' For Johnson the individual is almost entirely antithetical to the collective. Indeed it is because the individual is single, spare and isolated that he or she requires the protection of an external agency: the spiritual protection supplied by the Church, the physical protection supplied by the state. The idea of 'an association in which the free development of each is the condition for the free development of all' (Marx) is incomprehensible to Johnson. For Johnson every man is an island, entire unto himself, who would be diminished or threatened by being joined to the main. In his book *The Offshore Islanders* Johnson quotes Donne's famous lines: 'For every man alone thinks that he hath got/To be a Phoenix, and that then can be/None of that kind of which he is but he.' But Johnson, the would-be Phoenix, truncates the quotation in mid-line, at that word (p. 205).

Johnson's plea for the individual would be more impressive if he made any effort to identify the forces which currently menace civic freedoms: but his unremitting tirades focus monotonously on trade unions with never a mention of the ways in which the new powers of the police, the secretive bureaucracy of the civil service, the concentrated ownership of the media or the vast power of the multi-nationals trespass upon the freedom of individuals. Johnson claims that his philosophy of individualism is drawn from the writings of Hobbes and Locke. In fact their 'possessive individualist' doctrines embodied only a highly restricted series of individual rights and freedoms, available, if at all, only to the propertied classes. While Hobbes endowed the monarch with absolutist powers, Locke was prepared to condone, and profit from, the slave trade. Yet if their theories did contain insight, this would certainly include the notion that rights should not be divorced from economic power and responsibility. In the modern world economic forces are far more social and co-operative in nature than in the time of Hobbes and Locke; unless these forces are socially and co-operatively controlled the extension of political rights to the mass of the population is pathetically inadequate and incomplete. Johnson proclaims the virtues of Hobbesian and Lockean individualism without ever considering the successive attempts that have been made to transcend its narrow framework, from the writers of the Scottish historical school to the magisterial opening chapters of Talcott Parsons's *The Structure of Social Action*. Although Johnson once called himself a socialist, he also ignores the socialist critique of individualism to be found in Marx and William Morris, C.B. MacPherson and Herbert Marcuse.

Johnson sought, in *Enemies of Society* (1977), to supply a philosophical foundation to the alarmist turn of his political interventions. The book largely consists of hit-and-run attacks on a series of peripheral or second-rate thinkers whom Johnson regards as responsible for the most dangerous trends in the modern world. Johnson's selection of targets (Teilhard de Chardin, Ivan Illich, Marshall McLuhan, etc.) seems to have been largely determined by the fashions of yesteryear. Marcuse is awarded a few pages on the basis of the publicity he received at the time of the student revolt. Quite apart from the fact that Marcuse's best writings are unmentioned, the portentous gravity of his Marcuse-critique is undermined by a failure accurately to render the concepts employed in the works he is attacking – thus Marcuse's notion of 'repressive tolerance' is referred to as 'oppressive permissiveness'. Though Johnson is worried by the growth of Marxism in Britain, he does not refer to the products of the Anglo-Marxism which have developed in the 60s and 70s. Johnson is a historian yet he chooses not to comment on Hobsbawm, Thompson, Raymond Williams or Perry Anderson.

The positive poles of reference in *Enemies of Society* are science, which must be *trusted*, truth, which must conform to Christian principles, and art, which must encourage the 'common certitudes', presumably lay versions of 'Christian truth' and fideistic science. Johnson's forays into science and the arts are not happy. The scientist whose achievements he seems to rate most highly is Eysenck, who is presented as the Galileo *de nos jours*. Otherwise Johnson seeks to confound the entire ecological critique by an appeal for confidence in scientists, as if scientists were not themselves divided over such questions.

Johnson feels that he has glimpsed the awful predicament of modern culture on his theatre-going expeditions to London's West End. The work of Pinter and Stoppard reflects the moral wasteland inhabited by the modern artist. Goya is commended as an artist with a much sounder grasp of the 'common certitudes'. His painting *The Third of May 1808* is particularly praised on the grounds that 'It is quite clear what the painting portrays ... we are not disorientated' (p. 222). Johnson even claims that 'There is no doubt from the picture where Goya's sympathies lay ...' Johnson is, it seems, unaware that this painting has a companion, *The Second of May 1808*, in which the roles of victim and executioner are reversed, introducing a critical element of ambivalence. Both paintings were sufficiently disturbing of the 'common certitudes' of 19th century Spain – they portray the revolt of the Madrid *populacho* – to have been stowed away in the Prado reserves for 40 years.

Readers of this journal have recently been reminded of the central importance attributed by Johnson to Christian values and Christian truth. Johnson is an enthusiastic supporter of the new direction in which Pope John Paul II is taking the Church. He passionately believes that Christianity must nourish national, popular roots. He is filled with foreboding by the spread of secularism in our society, and especially within the ranks of the labour movement. We will not consider the strictly religious aspect of Johnson's concern here but focus instead on his more relevant and interesting theses on British history. This will also throw some light, we hope, on the evolution of Johnson's own politics and on how he came to make the transition from being a reactionary radical to being a radical reactionary.

The chief ingredients of Johnson's philosophy have not changed much over the years, though their respective proportions certainly have. In a sincere tribute to the spirit of England-for-all Johnson attempts to synthesise in his own person the contending trends of the ruling class Britain of his youth. Up until about 1974 his reflexes and prejudices made up the following cocktail: three parts Fabian tonic water, one part Colonel Blimp's home brewed gin, a dash of French vermouth and a tincture of Chester-Bellocian bitters. According to report both Kingsley Martin – already prejudiced against Johnson's Catholicism – and Leonard Woolf thought this a weird and unstable concoction and insisted that his appointment as editor of the *New Statesman* in 1965 would remain provisional for a six-month trial period. Around 1974 the proportion of the various liquids was drastically changed with the Colonel's home-brew drowning the tonic water, and the French vermouth replaced by a toxic twist of monetarist lemon.

According to legend Johnson experienced a conversion to socialism when he saw a French policeman beat up a female student on one of the demonstrations against General Ridgeway in the 1950s. Johnson long entertained the conviction that the Gaullist state was fascist, a view that one might not unfairly describe as an early example of intellectual laziness and impressionism when confronted with the unfamiliar. In the 1950s Johnson was as ready to attack the British as the French state. In his first book *The Suez War* he vividly denounced that adventure as a possibly fatal blow to the British political system, placing it on a path 'marked with ministerial lies and corruption, with deceit and evasion in high places, with increasing public cynicism, with ever-failing faith in democratic institutions'. The British state was in any case 'faulty, illogical and archaic'; Suez had destroyed the public confidence which alone lent it authority and stirred up 'hidden depths of race hatred and violence.' But even at this period Johnson's indictment was garnished with loyal declarations and patriotic conceit. The worst aspect of the affair was that it could no longer be said that 'the world's moral centre of gravity was in Westminster'. For Johnson Suez was not the death rattle of British colonialism but a break with 'a century of British foreign policy in which the maintenance of the balance of power and the rights of individual nations had been our principal concerns' (p. 143).

Johnson's most ample statement of England's national destiny came with the publication of *The Offshore Islanders*, published in 1972, two years after he left the editorship of the *New Statesman.* Of his various books it is the most revealing, since he cares much more for English history than for philosophical or theological disputation.

Johnson's history of England is suffused by a besotted love of country and an eager identification with the great men and women who best express 'English genius'. The English first showed their sturdy taste for independence when they threw off the Roman yoke in the fifth century. In the eighth century the man we know as the Venerable Bede distilled the essence of Englishness in his Yorkshire monastery and this precious heritage has been handed virtually intact to succeeding generations. Central to that heritage was Bede's 'deep, if gentle and unassertive, strain of patriotism and racial pride'. Johnson, whose full name is Paul Bede Johnson, writes that the English saint was the author of 'perhaps the most remarkable work of the entire Dark Ages; in some ways ... a finer piece of scientific history than anything produced in the ancient world'. The purpose of this inflated claim is to add greater force to Bede's most notable political discovery: 'Bede understood that the strength of Old English society rested on the ability of church and state to work together in closest harmony. ... And of course Bede was right. England was the first society to create a strong and civilised central authority on a permanent basis; it lies at the root of

LINES OF DISSENT

such felicity as this country has enjoyed throughout its history' (p. 39).

In Johnson's view the unique virtues of Old English society – 'a fortunate marriage between geography and race' – persist down to the most recent times and largely explain why the English became the 'chosen race' leading humanity out of the darkness and misery of the pre-capitalist era. One could describe Johnson's style of historiography as 1066 and all that, but this would be somewhat paradoxical since the Norman Conquest itself is entirely subsumed in a chapter entitled: 'Unity, Stability, Continuity (600–1154)'. For Johnson the decisive figures in English history are those who have contributed to strengthening and perfecting the 'strong and civilised central authority' and who have understood the need for a judicious balance of temporal and spiritual power. Among them are King Alfred, William I, Queen Elizabeth I, Cromwell, William Pitt the Younger and Gladstone. The villains in Johnson's story are usually alien interlopers, such as that Scottish King James I, who flaunted his homosexuality, or the Puritans who were an 'alien import' who not only 'believed in a doctrinaire religion imposed by force' but also 'oozed hypocrisy'. 'Fortunately Elizabeth was quite capable of dealing with such men. ... She killed only four of them; but a good number were gaoled, and on the whole she held the movement in check' (p. 162). It is with a barely suppressed sob that Johnson records the passing of Elizabeth: 'When she said she loved the people of England – and they are not a people whom anyone can easily love – she meant it' (p. 176).

This, and many another maudlin passage, inspire the thought that the book might better have been called *This England.* Yet there is a radical theme running through the work, a late flowering of one type of Fabian radicalism. Johnson favours all those reforms which enable England to retain the place that is rightfully hers, as the most advanced and civilised nation on earth. The introduction of needed reforms requires not popular turbulence but the dedication of an enlightened elite. Johnson salutes the revolution of 1640 as a great moment of national regeneration. The Putney debates are praised for embracing 'every major political concept known to us today ... through five continents' (pp. 171–2). The despised Puritans are denied any significant role whatever in this achievement.

The concluding sections of *The Offshore Islanders* suggested that England had again drifted into the sort of impasse she faced in the early 17th century. The integrity of her institutions was threatened from within by the heterodox ideas of the student revolt and from without by the imposition of a new alien yoke, that of the Treaty of Rome. During the long years of empire the English wasted their substance on adventures in foreign lands instead of cultivating their own genius.

Continuity and stability were purchased at too high a price, the price of chronic institutional stagnation and national decline. All the country's best energies were suffocated by an intense corporate spirit. The army, the City, the civil service, the trade unions, the universities, even Parliament itself, were 'organised' along the lines of a private club, with an attendant mass of restrictive practices, corporate privileges and secretive procedures for making and carrying out decisions. 'Thus the true reformer will appear in the guise of Henry II, breaking down the castle and stockades of the private franchises; or like Edward I, he will ask, *Quo Warranto*, by what warrant, right or authority any group claims and exercises privileges above the common folk. ... The levelling of institutional inequalities is the key to the gospel of improvement' (pp. 424–5). In an earlier passage Johnson has made it clear that Parliament itself is not exempt from this egalitarian imperative: 'Parliament is the custodian not so much of liberty as of the existing distribution of property' (p. 213).

It might seem that Johnson, given his radical aim of national regeneration, should rather have looked to some new popular movement than to a reforming monarch. But at no point does Johnson display sympathy for unruly behaviour on the part of the 'common folk'. Given the ugly sectarian bigotry of English crowds from Titus Oates to Lord George Gordon this is understandable. But Johnson's distrust of the populace is so pervasive that it leads him to misconstrue some major episodes of popular unrest. Johnson complains that such reformers as Jeremy Bentham ran into stiff popular opposition when they proposed measures of penal reform, and that it was only in government circles that they were well received. Johnson omits to point out that Bentham, possessed of a strongly individualist psychology, was advocating a prison system in which all prisoners would be subjected to months, if necessary years, of total isolation, and would be incarcerated in cells that could be inspected from a central point at any time. Prisoners were to wear masks to prevent them from making signs to one another during the exercise period and were only to be permitted to speak to the chaplain. The first attempts to construct prisons along the lines of a 'Panopticon' were (as shown in Michael Ignatieff's remarkable study *A Just Measure of Pain*) intensely unpopular and their more extreme features were eventually modified in consequence.

If the 'common folk' cannot better themselves, to whom is the task to be entrusted? At this point there are echoes of Beatrice Webb's 'elite of unassuming experts.' According to Johnson national redemption must be sought through 'an elite, classless because drawn from all classes, providing, in Gladstone's words, "a natural leadership, based on free assent"''. 'In an earlier gloss on what Gladstone meant by 'natural leadership' Johnson explained: 'Englishmen born to wealth and privileges have a special duty to society, to supply the defects of a mass-democracy which arise from the political consequences of inequalities which no human wisdom can finally eliminate' (p. 314).

At the time he completed *The Offshore Islanders* which, despite its entirely mythopoeic approach to its subject, remains his most substantial attempt to explain his ideas to date, Johnson was still unclear about the true path to national salvation. But it is clear that he had already identified the necessity for soliciting a vital contribution from those 'born to wealth and privileges'. By 1972 Johnson was a Fabian at the end of his tether. The events of 1974 snapped his emotional ties to the labour movement, preparing the way for the extraordinary exercises in union-baiting of 1975. Insurgent miners, revolting students, lawless Labour councillors at Clay Cross and elsewhere, seemed like a nightmare to the man who wanted radical change within a context of reinforced law and order. In 1970 Johnson voted Labour, so he informed NS readers, because 'the solid ranks of Labour men and women (in the House of Commons) sitting behind their ministers' were 'an absolute and cast iron defence against adventurism' (NS 19 June 1970). By 1975 Labour offered no such cast-iron guarantee.

In the Fabian tradition there was always a profound ambivalence. On the one hand there was a genuine interest in socialist theory, a preparedness to undertake painstaking research, an eventual decision to throw in their lot with the labour movement rather than the ruling class. But at the same time there was about them an invincible insularity and philistinism that rendered them incapable of learning anything from the great debates among continental social democrats; a fear that the sub-human Morlochs might emerge from the lower depths and threaten civilisation; and a longing for respectability that led to the most abject accommodation to the local political Establishment. Fabian socialism was too often simply a collectivist version of Bentham's utilitarianism. With Johnson the elitist and nationalist component of Fabianism, which had always been considerable, broke free and found more suitable moorings in the Tory party. Fabian elitism only really made sense so long as the activists in the labour movement were resigned to a thoroughly subordinate and impotent role. With the 'revolt on the shop floor', flying mass pickets, conferences of the TGWU at which the General Secretary could lose the vote, demands for re-selection of MPs, all this changed. The Fabian elitist had then to decide either to attempt to put the genie back in the bottle, like the Labour 'moderates', or to depart, like Johnson. This is not to say that the Fabian tradition is wholly negative. It is interesting to recall that even such an irreconcilable foe of the bourgeois order as Trotsky advised British Marxists to organise themselves openly, along Fabian lines, to carry their message within the British labour movement instead of standing apart in doctrinaire isolation or burrowing away as entrist moles frightened of the daylight. This is even better advice today, as Labour is shaking off Fabian tutelage and the Paul Johnsons are at last consummating their frustrated love affair with Britain's 'natural leaders'.

As we saw at the beginning, Johnson's overriding obsession is with the power of the trade unions. He never pauses to reflect that the trade union movement itself is sustained by the dedication of a great multitude of *individuals*, and that it represents a decisive proportion of those who create social wealth while themselves struggling to exist, and to feed their families, on considerably less than a take home pay of £100 a week. Trade unions seek, but do not usually obtain, some control over hiring and firing, and over conditions of work. For Paul Johnson this is colossal impertinence and a menacing threat to the rights of the individual. The vastly larger powers of those who own and control industry, or run the public corporations, are entirely natural, right and proper so far as Johnson is concerned. Thousands can be sacked or declared redundant, whole regions or industries condemned to decay, vital natural resources laid waste for commercial profit, all without Johnson noticing any infringement on individual liberty. Socialists scarcely need to be informed that there can be unlovely aspects to trade union power: trade union officialdom can be timid toward employers and arrogant to the membership, trade union militants can meanly pursue a sectional interest. But the power of general secretaries or shop stewards, which ultimately derives only from their members, is certainly different in kind from the utterly arbitrary and secretive power wielded by the directors of large companies and the heads of the civil service. Moreover, Johnson's assault on the narrow selfishness of trade unions would carry more conviction if he did not reserve his most virulent prose for those socialists who seek to introduce within them a more ample vision of social co-operation and workers' control. Whatever the failings of British trade unionism today they are less pronounced than in the days of Bevin or Carron, for which Johnson is nostalgic.

In January 1974 Johnson wrote an article in the *Evening News* advising Heath to throw in the towel and calling on the miners to come to England's rescue. This seems to have been his last gesture in favour of organised labour; on all the evidence it seems to have been prompted more by a feeling that might was apt to be right than by any conviction of the justice of the miners' claim. Henceforth he saw national salvation wholly in terms of destroying, not releasing, the potential of the organised producers. In his view a draconian new labour law was needed because 'powerful men who conspire together to squeeze the community are gangsters' (*Evening Standard,* May 1975). So that Paul Johnson can sleep safely at nights the whole of society must be turned into a vast 'Panopticon', with no communication or association permitted unless it meets with the approval of 'senior police officers'. To give us all a sense of purpose, an intolerant and insular sense of Englishness must be promoted which denies all that is most positive in our national history: the mingling or coexistence of the most diverse cultural strains, the making of the English working class, the cosmopolitan legacy of a country that was both the centre of empire and a place of refuge for the heterodox and persecuted.

It would be easy, employing a familiar Johnsonian trope, to portray him as Benito Johnson, the journalistic prophet of a national socialist England. Yet this would be to misunderstand the project of Johnson and of his new patrons. There is not a trace of anti-capitalist demagogy in Johnson's current polemics: given the weakness of genuine socialist anti-capitalism in this country, if compared with Italy or Germany after the First World War, one could say that demagogic anti-capitalism is quite unnecessary to defenders of the established order. The ideological problem today is to kindle some positive enthusiasm for capitalism while persuading the mass of people to forgo the consumer goods, and social services, which have in the past compensated the labouring population for the tyranny and emptiness of a life spent as a appendage of someone else's machine. Capitalism today desperately needs romance and poetry; British capitalism further needs a propagandist who can plausibly represent the levelling of social conquests and popular liberties as a crusade of national regeneration. These are the roles that Johnson now attempts to fulfil. He would like to see Margaret Thatcher assume the mantle of Good Queen Bess, defy the continental powers, shoot a few puritans, outlaw their congregations, and encourage the natural leaders of the island race to restore England's glory.

Robin Blackburn, 14 December 1979

The 'Martian poets' or 'metaphor men' of the 1970s aroused some puzzlement and even mockery from critics – but the poem by CRAIG RAINE which gave the movement (if there ever was a movement, which I doubt) its name more than bears rereading.

A Martian Sends a Postcard Home

Caxtons are mechanical birds with many wings
and some are treasured for their markings –

they cause the eyes to melt
or the body to shriek without pain.

I have never seen one fly, but
sometimes they perch on the hand.

Mist is when the sky is tired of flight
and rests its soft machine on ground:

then the world is dim and bookish
like engravings under tissue paper.

Rain is when the earth is television.
It has the property of making colours darker.

Model T is a room with the lock inside –
A key is turned to free the world

for movement, so quick there is a film
to watch for anything missed.

But time is tied to the wrist
or kept in a box, ticking with impatience.

In homes, a haunted apparatus sleeps,
that snores when you pick it up.

If the ghost cries, they carry it
to their lips and soothe it to sleep

with sounds. And yet, they wake it up
deliberately, by tickling with a finger.

Only the young are allowed to suffer
openly. Adults go to a punishment room

with water but nothing to eat.
They lock the door and suffer the noises

alone. No-one is exempt
and everyone's pain has a different smell.

At night, when all the colours die,
They hide in pairs

and read about themselves –
in colour, with their eyelids shut.

Craig Raine, 23/30 December 1977

Monarchy-bashing is a sport with far too few adherents on the British Left. Realisation is now slowly dawning that a politics which isn't prepared to criticise the survivals of feudalism cannot be taken very seriously in its assault on more contemporary oppressions – but why has this renewed interest in republicanism taken so long? The NS *has often been a* partial *exception: Kingsley Martin published one of the few sustained radical critiques of the Crown's continued constitutional role, whilst Paul Johnson was scathing about royal tax-fiddles. Over the last decade the overdue attack has been renewed. Here CHRISTOPHER HITCHENS has a go at Prince Charles, while PIERS BRENDON generalises the critique and urges a new republicanism.*

A Man Born To Be ...

The British Royal Family is a rather uninspiring and dowdy crew of people; indeed its general dullness is part of the protective colouring which has helped it to avoid being identified with the last quarter-century of national decline. There are four living ex-Prime Ministers to whom nobody really gives the time of day, and a bevy of leaders and institutions publicly discredited and exposed. Yet the monarchy seems to most people a thing apart from civil society, which is probably why it is almost the last surviving specimen of its kind.

How much longer can this go on? In the case of the present Queen, the great thing has been continuity. She is the last of the imperial British monarchs, and provides a link with an age slightly more confident than our own. After all, as the *New Statesman* put it shortly before the Jubilee:

In 1952, the Tories had just got back to office after the Attlee years; Churchill had made his famous address to Congress, Monty was at NATO

HQ, Stalin ruled Russia, Chiang's men were fighting a rearguard action against the Chinese Communists on the Burma frontier. Virtually the whole of Africa was still partitioned among the colonial powers, and the British authorities had just informed the UN that they did not see their way to abolishing flogging in the mandated territories.

How different, how very different. ... At this moment, it is the full-time job of a large number of courtiers to groom a successor to Elizabeth II; a successor more suited to the sleazy, corrupt, confined and corporate society we have become, or to 'the exciting challenge of the last quarter of the twentieth century', as they would and do put it.

Anthony Holden was granted a fairly close look at the young king in the making, and My Lord Weidenfeld of Chelsea makes an ideal publisher for the result (*Charles Prince of Wales*, Weidenfeld & Nicolson, £6.95). The lineaments of the new-style monarchy start to become apparent very early on:

> Royal links with industry, for instance, are traditional. The Queen's Awards for Export are only the most familiar of a number of devices of moral encouragement. ... In his early thirties, Prince Charles has begun to extend those links into the virgin royal territory of the trade unions, as befits the times; in 1979 he attended the annual conference of the Iron and Steel Trades Federation, carefully selected as one of the few unions which had then submitted to the Callaghan Government's pay policy.

Above politics, too, don't you see. And a slight change of tempo from the boring harangues about 'getting your finger out' from his wholly unacceptable father.

Selected sweetheart trade unions apart, the Prince is not lost for contacts in the boardroom either. His choice of entourage reflects this imperative. Holden tells us that:

> Perhaps the most significant appointment, however, was that in 1978 of a thirty-five-year-old diplomat, Oliver Everett, to be assistant private secretary. Everett's bird-like appearance belies his athletic prowess, notably as a polo-player of even more accomplishment than his master [there's glory for you]; more important, he has organised such initiatives as the Prince of Wales's tour of British industry under the auspices of the National Economic Development Office.

In the same spirit of buccaneering enterprise, the Prince leases his rich oyster-beds on the River Helston in Cornwall to Mac Fisheries Ltd, who thereby subcontract and market about a million oysters a year. This decision shows his up-to-dateness in the matter of his Cornish dukedom – his right to a tithe of 300 puffins from the Isles of Scilly would look foolishly behind the times if exercised.

Towards his Welsh subjects the Prince is hardly less generous and go-ahead. We learn that:

> Visiting Expo '70 in Tokyo, he met the president of the Sony electronics conglomerate, and learned of their plans to build a plant somewhere in Western Europe. 'Why not try Wales?' suggested its Prince, less than a year after his investiture at Caernarvon. Two years later, Prince Charles was able to open the new Sony plant in Bridgend, Glamorgan. ...

Where they could certainly do with the work. At home, abroad, there is the same unsleeping salesmanship – the head of PR for Great Britain Incorporated. South America? No problem:

> By fortunate timing, his presence in Brazil coincided with the finalisation of a huge investment by British banks in a steel-mill complex near Rio, expected to yield a profit of some £11 million. A little delicate blurring at the edges, and the Prince could be said to have 'clinched' the deal. As his ten day trip had cost the British taxpayer some £11,000, it showed an equally neat 1,000–1 return on investment.

And no doubt a vote of thanks from the board of GB Inc., who can't afford to pass up any *coups* however small.

Not that Prince Charles is indifferent to the greater issues. We are assured that while in Brazil he expressed a private desire to be informed about the human rights situation. His personal library and reading habits are also scrutinised by Holden, who reveals that 'E.F. Schumacher's *Small Is Beautiful* is something of a bible, but he will fall asleep over a novel'. (This last, even though 'anything by Alexander Solzhenitsyn' is considered absorbing. One imagines him ordering his Solzhenitsyn by the yard, though it's difficult to picture him asking the bookseller to leave the soporific old novels out.)

So it is hardly a surprise to discover that 'his religious convictions were first encouraged by the Rt Rev. Robert Woods, when Dean of Windsor and Chaplain to the Queen'. Now Bishop of Worcester, Woods is gratified to find the Prince 'unassailed by doubts'. Not bad for a boy of more than thirty years of age. But of course, this must not be allowed to degenerate into mere blandness. There are twentieth century challenges out there just waiting to be met. 'As the future head of the Anglican Church he is anxious to use his position to encourage *rapprochement* with Rome.' Well, he would, wouldn't he? Anything else would look hidebound and, well, traditional.

Even more indicative of the new-style bourgeois monarchy is the

retinue of private secretaries as described here. First there was
Squadron Leader David Checketts, written up in true Seventies style as
'an urbane, grammar-school educated public relations man with a
distinguished RAF record'. When he was felt to be too old and
conventional for the growing boy, he 'returned to more lucrative full-
time public relations work'. His replacement, the Hon. Edward
Adeane, is a man much in tune with the times:

> To work for the Prince, he gave up a lucrative [that word again] practice as a
> libel barrister, with such disparate clients as Lady Falkender and the Tory
> Party, *The Times* and *Playboy* magazine.

Adeane went to Eton and Cambridge all right, but there is nothing
fuddy-duddy about *him*. Any more than there is about the Hon. John
Baring, chairman of the merchant bank, who looks after the new and
dynamic financing of the Duchy of Cornwall. Hardly perceptible, but
definite after a second and third glance, here is the gradual process by
which the monarchy is being steered into the post-imperial age. Even the
royal choice of friends and companions has to be trimmed. The
Nicholas Soames lot, for instance, are written off as 'upper-class twits'.
'The Prince these days', says Holden, 'favours more substantial figures,
such as his barrister friend Richard Beckett, who serves on the
committee of one of his trusts, and Hywel Jones, a socialist economist
who shared his staircase at Cambridge.' A socialist, of course, among
one's friends would be *de rigueur*. (Though Holden comments matter-of-
factly that the royal parents have 'orthodox conservative attitudes' to
which Charles 'reverted' after being talked out of joining the University
Labour Club by none other than Lord Butler.)

Sometimes the description of his efforts with his 'circle' are
downright laughable. Torn between his kinship with the well-born and
his need to appear democratic and modern, Charles causes sentences
like this to be written about him, and his chums the Tollemaches
(Timothy and Alexandra):

> Though heir to the Tollemache and Cobbold brewery fortune, the fifth Baron
> has recently felt obliged to open Helmingham's gardens to the public.

There was none of that sort of foolishness when Edward was waiting to
become king.

Then of course there is showbiz, an essential means of com-
municating with the aspirations of modern youth, etc., and one
which previous princes have properly scorned. Not so our boy, whose
friend Norton Knatchbull (chip off the Mountbatten block) has

occasionally persuaded him to wear promotional T-shirts from films he has worked on – notably *A Bridge Too Far*. His phrase for his better-favoured younger brother Andrew is 'the one with the Robert Redford looks'. He likes *The Goodies* and *Monty Python*, and still affects to find *The Goons* funny. In touch, in touch, always in touch. It must be hell, but it must be done.

To the Left, the monarchy has often seemed an irrelevant issue – either a tedious anomaly to be mocked or an occasional target for criticism concerning luxurious expense. This philistinism is a big mistake. First, the Palace still retains considerable political reserve influence, through the Royal Prerogative and through other influences more informal. We learn from Holden of a lunch where 'The Prince of Wales reckoned he got the better of the PM in one or two exchanges on the small print of Cabinet memoranda'. Oh he did, did he? The Prime Minister was James Callaghan, so it probably wasn't difficult to win the argument. But the point is the access of the Royal Family to the secrets which the voters never know, and the resulting manoeuvrability which this confers on them.

At times, in the recent past, this has been important. We know how vital it was to Harold Wilson, in his disastrous foot-dragging over Rhodesia in 1965, to keep the confidence of the Palace at every step. We know how the Palace and the prerogative helped to foist Sir Alec Douglas-Home on the country as Prime Minister, and we know how nearly they foisted the Marquess of Salisbury (just imagine it) on us instead. True, many of these backstairs deals involve the Queen's staff of advisers and retainers, but their power, too, deserves to be reckoned with.

Then there is the ideological element. If nothing else, Jubilee year demonstrated to many radicals that the monarchy still has a vast claim on the popular imagination. It is, of course, only to be expected that the very apex of our system should be an absurdity – in historic terms, constitutional terms, or even showbiz ones. But it is a great mistake to underestimate its subliminal effect on the country, and on the formation of opinion.

It is in this dimension – the ideological one – that the re-shaping of the present Prince of Wales is taking place. His advisers know that the pomp and circumstances cannot be jettisoned – indeed, events like the Investiture show that they often feel it needs beefing up. But they also know that it will not do on its own; that the next monarch will have to make his way in the world and that his subjects will have to be conditioned for it. Through every page in Holden's book shines the fact that the Prince is short on intelligence, imagination or charm. Very well then, Prince of mediocrity.

The boy has been through every hoop that can be devised for him – and apparently has no doubts or complaints. He has piloted a plane and made a parachute jump. He has commanded a Royal Navy vessel though he has never (unlike his Uncle Dickie) heard a shot fired in anger. He has been around the world, and yet according to Holden *he was seized with jealousy while having dinner with Sir James Goldsmith.*

Perhaps this is what we have come to – a king in the making, programmed to respond to that kind of success, regretting its apparent decline in Britain and determined to do his bit. A king who knows a few social democrats by their Christian names; a king who has more or less acceptable packages of opinion on everything from racial harmony to ecumenicism. A king fit to be on the board in his own right. A king in the image of Peter Jay; with relatives slightly better connected.

Christopher Hitchens, 21/28 December 1979

Totem and Taboo

George III, as we know, should never have occurred. Nor, in the opinion of *The Times*, should George IV. Its obituary notice in 1830 branded him an 'inveterate voluptuary' and pronounced, 'There never was an individual less regretted by his fellow creatures.' William IV came off little better: 'His late Majesty, though at times a jovial and, for a king, an honest man, was a weak, ignorant, commonplace sort of person.'

But Queen Victoria, despite unpopularity in girlhood and early widowhood, made the monarchy what it is today. She did so as a result of two innate traits – fertility and longevity – and one acquired characteristic – respectability, otherwise known as Balmorality. After about 1875 the throne was so secure that it could not even be shaken by press reports that there was nothing between Edward Prince of Wales and Lily Langtry – not even a sheet.

Actually 'fat vulgar dreadful Edward', as Henry James called him, had quite involuntarily helped to destroy the growing republican movement – by the drastic expedient of almost dying from enteric fever in 1871. The prince's illness provoked such an outburst of sovereign sympathy that no subsequent grossness on his part could quash it. A few dissidents might fling their barbs – Marx liked to quote Cobbett's sardonic contrast between the *Royal* Mint and the *National* Debt.

But British loyalty to royalty has waxed ever since, just as orthodox religion, for which it is a secular substitute, has waned. Like the Pope himself, the monarch has lost in power but gained in prestige. And

those inclined to approach the throne without due reverence are liable
to be visited with all sorts of reprisals. Malcolm Muggeridge was
banned from appearing on the BBC and sent used pieces of lavatory
paper through the post. Lord Altrincham was disowned by the
Observer, to which he contributed regularly, and, almost thirty years
later, little seems to have changed – the *Observer* commissioned me to
write an earlier version of this article and eventually declined to print it.

Recently, by even seeming to censure the Queen, Enoch Powell
managed to erode his populist power base and to make himself even
more of a parliamentary pariah then before. However desirable this
effect, its cause raises two serious questions. Can our national life be
regarded as healthy when at its centre there exists an institution the
criticism of which amounts to blasphemy? And should the case against
the monarchy be heard, not necessarily because it will convince (reason
being powerless against faith) but at any rate in order to strike a blow
against the tyranny of conventional opinion? The answers, I submit, are
respectively no and yes.

The monarchy is doubtless as much proof against fact as against
argument, yet considered objectively the record of the past 100 years
has been a lamentable one. From the tea-time adulteries of Edward
VII's time to the Rod and Koo follies of today, the royals have scarcely
set a flawless example of conventional propriety. More seriously, they
seem to have exercised their vestigial influence in a wholly reactionary
direction. Victoria's intrigues with Disraeli and her aversion to the 'mad
unpatriotic ravings' of Mr Gladstone are well known. Edward VII did
all he could to prevent the Liberal government of 1906 from employing
radical men or adopting radical measures. George V's support for
General Haig during the First World War, at a time when Lloyd
George was trying to get rid of him, was ill-judged to say the least.

During the Second World War Churchill was much embarrassed by
the Duke of Windsor's pro-Nazi antics. George VI's insistence that
'India must be governed' was hardly calculated to help Attlee's
government. Queen Elizabeth preferred the conservative Macmillan, a
hard-liner over Suez, to the liberal Butler when Eden resigned in 1956.
In its observance of stuffy etiquette and its fondness for landed
aristocrats, the present court harks back to that of Queen Victoria, who
once said 'a democratic monarchy is what she will never belong to'. The
royal 'we' has been replaced by the royal 'one' ('one is not amused'),
but not much else is new.

It is impossible to say how much influence is wielded by the present
queen, both because of the general British convention that public
information is the private property of the government and because of

the particular circumstance that the Crown is more pathologically secretive than any other official institution. Occasionally we can get glimpses behind the veil. Richard Crossman recorded the fact that the Queen pressed a willing Harold Wilson to maintain censorship of the theatre in 1967. The Labour Whips made it clear to Willie Hamilton that his views on the monarchy would preclude him from the ministerial office which he was otherwise well qualified to hold. According to an unpublished memorandum from Eisenhower to Dulles, even the Duke of Edinburgh possesses 'a certain amount of political influence'.

In theory, of course, the monarch advises, encourages and warns the government. In practice, the constitution being unwritten, she exercises an authority which stems from the fact that she is the most experienced politician in the country. With her passion for horses and dogs, for ceremonies and uniforms, for parlour games and jig-saw puzzles, the Queen may appear to be the very model of an Edwardian country lady. But no one has better cause to realise that knowledge is power and even Margaret Thatcher, driven on by an over-active thyroid, is not more meticulous about 'doing her boxes'. Furthermore, the monarch remains the fount of a great deal of patronage, some direct (such as grace and favour residences, discretionary honours like the Order of Merit, and invitations to hob with the nobs), some indirect (but clandestine). How much of a say does she have, for example, in dishing out other baubles of rank, such as knighthoods to accommodating journalists, or in top military and ecclesiastical promotions?

The trouble is that we don't know and have no means of finding out. What is more, the Queen's popularity largely derives from the people's ignorance, or rather from their belief that she is above the grubby fray of politics. Like God, she is a figurehead who may be praised for any good that occurs to her subjects but cannot be blamed for their ills. She is the embodiment of the Establishment, of its wealth and social status and unknowable power, yet she does not appear to bear any responsibility for how it operates. She exercises power, or at any rate influence, without responsibility – and we all know whose prerogative that is. It is surely absurd that at the heart of our supposed democracy there is a hereditary institution, whose most crucial activities are secret and unaccountable, and which regards change as something to be embraced only in the last resort – in other words, as the old Duke of Cambridge used to say, 'when you can't help it'.

In fact, the most important role of the monarchy may be in enforcing a compelling ethos of conservatism, convention and 'discretion' at the top levels of public life. Desperation for the ludicrous anachronism of peerages and knighthoods as our only token of secular success dulls and vitiates once innovative and dissident minds in all professions and political persuasions. Yet even if the Queen were inclined to become a bicycling, people's monarch on the Scandinavian model, she would be unable to do so. For to preserve the mystique of majesty she must remain aloof. Of course, possessing perhaps the country's largest private fortune – and the only one exempt from tax – the sovereign is insulated from the world of her subjects anyway. Fish and chips in front of the telly, helping the state-educated kids with their homework, worries about the gas bill – how different from the home life of the monarch. But she is cut off even more effectively by protocol, pageantry and pomp. As the focus of countless more or less irrelevant bits of mumbo-jumbo, the royals are treated like animated icons. Divine right has disappeared but not the divinity that doth hedge a king.

Everything tends to promote a sacrosanct monarchy. Radio and television mention royalty in tones of hushed awe, and certain broadcasters have elevated sycophancy to the level of an art form. A recent commercial for some royalist publication had as its slogan, 'The family we love as well as our own.' Normally quite sensible biographers like Elizabeth Longford treasure up the sovereign's most banal remarks as oracles and pen adulatory drivel that would disgrace a Mills & Boon romance.

The press, which (a few tiffs and a Beaverbrookian vendetta or two notwithstanding) gives the royal family both the publicity and the privacy they want, is particularly culpable. It treats the natural functions of royalty, especially (to cite a current instance) the business of breeding, as well-nigh miraculous. No doubt pictures of the Princess of Wales sell popular newspapers, but how can our 'quality' papers justify printing her photograph so often and so prominently? No doubt she is a glamorous figure but the present emphasis on her reproductive capacities, both physical and pictorial, smacks of relentless propaganda on behalf of the Establishment. Royal ageing is only slightly less miraculous, the survival of the Queen Mother to 84 years old last month being treated by the most obsequious papers as little short of a divine blessing for her inner saintliness.

We can read the journalistic harpings on the peccadilloes of lesser royals; but though not without its snide aspects, these actually enhance the myth of monarchy. For the British attitude towards the royal family is strangely ambivalent. They require it to be at once godlike, above reproach, and to be human, fallible, united with the people (to paraphrase Lord Randolph Churchill) in the bonds of a common immorality. Yet is it common? The carryings-on of a dissolute divorcée like Princess Margaret, the frolics of Randy Andy, the arrival of a seedy

photographer like Tony Armstrong-Jones or a nouveau-riche upstart
like Princess Michael, even the tedious marital problems of Princess
Anne, are not of the same order as the fornications, tiffs and social
climbing of 'ordinary' people for they are burnished by a glamour and
wealth which lifts them into the realms of popular fiction or a mega-
Dynasty soap opera. Their promiscuous buzzing contrasts with, and
distracts attention from, the dull primness of the middle-aged Queen at
the centre of the hive.

Walter Bagehot correctly understood the monarchy's role, its way of
satisfying the irrational appetites of the community. As he put it, the
masses deferred to 'what we may call the "theatrical show" of society
... a certain charmed spectable which imposes on the many and guides
their fancies as it will'. Bagehot thus transformed into a national glory
what Tom Paine had earlier seen as a national disgrace – the common
people, who ought themselves to be sovereign, treated as 'a herd of
beings that must be governed by fraud, effigy and show'. As a
conservative race we are, of course, adept at such cosy metamorphoses,
at discovering contemporary justifications for obsolete institutions. So
all sorts of current rationales are urged on behalf of the monarchy –
that it is the surest social cement in a pluralist society, the
personification of the State at home and Britain's trademark abroad,
the emblem of Commonwealth unity.

These are romantic, not to say superstitious, notions and they
assume that communities will disintegrate unless held together by some
living myth or symbol. Perhaps this is true. If so, the monarchy as now
constituted is the wrong kind of symbol. It is a resounding anachronism.
It smacks of a past full of inherited privileges, social injustices,
Victorian values and other horrors. It is, as H.G. Wells said, 'a
profoundly corrupting influence upon our national life, imposing an
intricate snobbishness on our dominant class, upon our religious,
educational ... and combatant services generally'. The present
monarchy symbolises a determinedly retrogressive Britain, a museum of
quaint customs and antique attitudes, a caste-ridden, horse-riding,
philistine nation, throttled by the old school tie, full of excrement living
off increment.

On the other hand, it is quite possible that a mature, democratic
nation does not, in a scientific age, need to gravitate round a human
totem located variously in Buckingham Palace, Windsor Castle,
Sandringham and Balmoral. As a republic we might purge ourselves of
the archaic influences that still degrade our character, deform our
society and retard our progress. We might substitute rational judgment
for ritual, incantation and fantasy. We might recognise that the
Commonwealth is no more than the ghost of Empire, and that our

place in the world depends not on conjurations with a colourful past but on the present implementation of realistic and enlightened policies. We might conclude that the best place for princesses is in fairy tales and that princes should be turned, not into frogs perhaps, but at least into ordinary human beings.

At the moment, needless to say, all this is about as much of a pipe-dream as Voltaire's ambition to strangle the last king with the entrails of the last priest. It is more a plea that the voice of republicanism should once again be heard in the land than a blueprint for constitutional reform. But it should not be thought that, if as a nation we could ever be educated out of besotted monarchism, no simple, democratic alternative exists – as seems to be the case where the widely discredited House of Lords is concerned.

In a republic Big Brother would by no means supersede Big Mother. On the contrary, a cheap, efficient system could easily be devised whereby (say) some annually elected mayor of the palace carries out such official functions as are necessary. At the end of his term of office he could perhaps be ushered out in a ceremony of mock garrotting on Horse Guards Parade, which would symbolise the nation's commitment to hardy republican virtue. It would also attract hordes of tourists from America, where they have been getting on fine without a monarchy ever since the time of George III, who, as we know ... but that was where we came in.

Piers Brendon, 17 August 1984

EDWARD PALMER THOMPSON, perhaps the finest polemicist as well as one of the most distinguished historians on the libertarian and socialist Left today (and I write as someone who not uncommonly finds E.P.T.'s style infuriating), relaunched mass anti-nuclear protest with this extended appeal to come out of apathy, which appeared in the Christmas 1979 NS.

An Alternative to Doomsday

I am concerned with the management of opinion. This has a long history. But the history which concerns me now is that which led up to Britain's zealous advocacy, at Brussels on 12 December, of the deployment of Cruise missiles on our own soil and on that of NATO allies.

We may commence in October 1979. On 6 October Brezhnev attempted to pre-empt NATO plans by announcing some limited and unilateral local withdrawal of his forces from East Germany. This was like a nuclear 'red alert' to the propaganda organs of NATO and the British State, whose operators – television 'experts', defence correspondents, editorialists – were 'scrambled' and instantly sent aloft upon their long-prepared offensive against the public mind.

We were informed that NATO was just on the point of deciding to deploy about 600 nuclear-tipped Cruise or Pershing-2 missiles upon nominated hosts within NATO: 108 Pershings and 464 Cruises (or Tomahawks) to be exact:

> Britain would take the largest number of Cruise missiles (160) followed by Italy (112), West Germany (96 plus the 108 Pershings), Holland (48), and Belgium (48). (*Guardian*, 14 November)

These figures, 'released in the Hague', might not be wholly acceptable to Holland, and even created a little concern in Belgium (we were informed in mid-October by a defence 'expert' on BBC news) but they were (it seems) wholly acceptable to 'Britain'. The fact that these missiles, of the NATO 'alliance', would remain within the control of US forces, who would alone keep the ignition keys, aroused concern in Italy but not (it seems) in 'Britain'.

The processes by which 'Britain' made up its mind, and came to this remarkable consensus, remained obscure. Wherever one looked, the decisions had already been taken, or was just about to be taken, by someone else. 'Britain May Take Cruise Missiles' was the headline for Clare Hollingworth's account in the *Telegraph*, but her account commenced: 'The Government *will agree to* . . .' (31 October). 'Britain *has already agreed* to accept Cruise missiles,' she announced two weeks later (12 November). Then Henry Stanhope of *The Times* announced that 'Britain *has been* one of the strongest supporters of the American package,' and had even volunteered to take *more* of the missiles than originally intended 'because West Germany found that it did not have room for its whole quota' (14 November). The question 'is largely decided', Gregory Teverton, Assistant Director of the International Institute for Strategic Studies, informed the *Observer* (18 November): 'Britain and Germany are committed . . .'

The 'mind of Britain' – and Britain's 'quota' – were made up, it seems, not in this country but in The Hague, by a NATO committee known as the High Level Group, whose instructions were passed on in turn to a thing called NPG, or NATO's Nuclear Planning Group (*The Times*, 13 November). Three features of the strategy by which 'Britain' was instructed that its mind was already decided may be noted.

The first we will call subliminal indoctrination: that is, the decision was presented as if agreement was already *assumed*. Viewers and readers were informed that 'Britain' had decided, and it was a matter of consensus. The second was that of suppression. The facts were disguised (so far as possible) from public knowledge that Norway, Denmark, France and Turkey had refused to have these missiles on their soil, and that the decision of Holland and Belgium hung in the balance of an alert and disturbed public opinion. The third was that of devaluing the issue. The decision was presented, not as one of high and controversial political concern, but as a trivial question of *technology*. The key-word in this strategy has been 'modernisation'. Only Luddites or seditionists could oppose *that*!

Within this obliterating barrage of opinion-management there was one discordant theme. This concerned the question of a successor to Britain's own independent nuclear weaponry (Polaris), to which Robin Cook alerted readers of the *New Statesman* in a remarkable article early this year (12 January 1979). The mind of 'Britain' on this matter did turn out to be divided – not as to whether we should burn money up on an 'independent' nuclear arsenal ('Britain' has, it seems, a seamless consensus in favour of doing that), but as between two options: should we replace Polaris with trident missiles, at a cost of £5,000 million, or take the cheaper option of buying a few Cruise missiles of our own, to which the Americans might even allow us to have our own ignition keys?

This question (it turned out) had also been 'decided': 'A firm decision has been taken at the Ministry of Defence' in favour of buying Tridents, David Fairhall informed the *Guardian* (1 November). Even so, the mind of Britain remained divided, because the Chief of the Defence Staff is an admiral, who, for obvious reasons, is keen on the Trident submarine strategy, whereas army and air force chiefs would prefer Cruise missiles which would fall within their own constituencies, and which option would also leave hundreds of millions over for their other expensive toys.

This savage in-fighting over the war budget, as our service chiefs seek to mobilise minuscule sectors of elite 'public opinion' upon their side, builds up a terrific pressure in the bladder of Official Secrecy. Suddenly, on such occasions, ordinary viewers and readers find themselves sprayed from on high by conflicting official leaks. We are once again back in the universe made familiar to us by Chapman Pincher (*New Statesman*, 10 November 1978). Admirals and generals and senior officials of the MoD stand against the wall of Fleet Street and leak in the public interest.

A lot of 'official secrets', in the form of Official Information, have been sprayed around in the past two months. We have been told the exact range of Cruise missiles; what kind of warhead is going on the Tridents; where the Cruise missiles will be sited (Lakenheath, Upper Heyford and Sculthorpe). We are told that 'a US air force team has been touring the UK', examining possible sites ('at least a dozen'). We are given a précis of highly-secret reports from NATO secret committees. And so on and on.

Since these breathtaking secrets usually appear simultaneously in rival establishment sheets, I think that we may take it that all this leaking is very much in the public interest. There is no imminent danger of Ms Clare Hollingworth, Mr David Fairhall or the secretariat of the International Institute for Strategic Studies being clapped into jail for betraying the secrets of our country.

Let us now consider this material. We may commence with some observations on official secrets. First, an Official Secret is not defined by an objective criterion of secrecy, such as 'the national interest', but according to who tells it and how. If it is to *inform* public opinion, then it is an awesome secret, defended by State sanctions and threats of up to 14 years' imprisonment. If it is to *manage* public opinion, by established persons, then it is not. If Mr Duncan Campbell or I had come into possession of information as to decisions of the defence staff, the plans of NATO secret committees, or as to the warheads of missiles and their siting, and if Mr Bruce Page had been incautious enough to publish these, then we should all now be under arrest and awaiting trial before vetted juries.

Second – and following upon this – the foulest damage to our political life comes not from the 'secrets' which they hide from us, but from the little bits of half-truth and disinformation which they *do* tell us. These are already pre-digested, and then are sicked up as little gobbets of authorised spew. The columns of defence correspondents in the establishment sheets serve as the spittoons.

That is, the Official Information which we *do* get is only the other side to the medal the Official Secret Acts. A new breed of journalist has emerged in the last decade (and, very certainly, not only in 'defence'). These never have to get off their arses, poke around, move about the world, or investigate anything. They simply taxi to official briefings in Whitehall, Westminster, Brussels or The Hague. They serve as supine vectors to convey to their readers official pap. Their only skills are those of managing minds, or of chatting up public relations persons at this Ministry or that, so as to express from their official bladders the last few drops of exclusive leak.

Official Secrecy is not only a way of denying us honest information. It is a way of selling us pre-packaged decisions, accompanied by dishonest data and normative noise. Official Secrecy, in controlling *all* information in forbidden areas, controls even more what we *do* know than what we don't. In the moment of offering us any information whatsoever it attempts to control also what we are permitted to think.

Third, the function of Official Secrecy is not to deny knowledge to any 'enemy' but to delude and manage the opinion of the native population – that is, us. A nice example of this primary function came some weeks ago when the *Omaha World Herald* disclosed that we came within a hair's breadth of radioactive disaster in July 1956 when a B47 bomber crashed at Lakenheath. If the TNT component in three nuclear bombs had been ignited by fuel blazing all around their hideaway, then (a retired US airforce general said) 'it is possible that a part of eastern England would have become a desert'. Plutonium would have been released into the air, 'spreading radiation over a very wide area, giving cancer to those in contact and making the locality uninhabitable'.

Now this is, exactly, what an Official Secret *is*. It has been a well-kept secret, even though (it seems) it was known to members of Eden's government, senior service staff, and officials at the MoD. The secret was kept, of course, from us, and not from any 'enemy', just as the Soviet nuclear disaster in the Urals (which Zhores Medvedev has disclosed) is still kept as a secret, not from us, but from the Russian people.

In those distant days, I and other readers were tramping the Aldermaston road in support of the Campaign for Nuclear Disarmament. We carried some part of public opinion. We carried churches and trade unions. We carried the Labour Party conference, until the entire media swung around behind Gaitskell to fight our resolutions off. If the near-disaster at Lakenheath had then been known to the public, I have little doubt that we would have carried the country. Neither Cruise missiles nor £5,000 million for Tridents would be on the British agenda today.

It is enough to make one tired. It is even enough to make one angry. One does not have all that much life to spend on little meetings and tramping down roads. What other near-disasters are being kept under civil service hats until the *Nevada Cosmos Tribune* sees fit to let us know?

There is also that other little bit in the *Omaha World Herald.* Official secrecy was essential in 1956, it seems, because 'the Eden government had concealed from the British people the fact that American atomic bombs were being stockpiled in the UK'. As the former US air chief said: 'Orders came down to keep "nukes" out of the records. Officially they did not exist.'

One does not have to be a defence 'expert' to see that what is going on now is imbecile. There is the matter of where these missiles are going to be sited. At first we were told, on telly, that they were going to be scattered around in woods across East Anglia and the South Midlands. Then (David Fairhall) that the missiles will be kept together in a few sacred US sanctuaries:

> The individual missile launchers are mobile and if war threatened they would be scattered round the countryside. But to minimise costs, and perhaps more importantly the political and environmental impact of this unfamiliar weapons system, the peacetime deployment plans now being prepared in the Ministry of Defence envisage concentrating them in two, or possibly three locations. (*Guardian*, 31 October)

And, reassuringly, the Cruise 'makes no noise and the only inconvenience the local population will experience is the occasional sight of the missile launchers on the roads' (*Telegraph*, 31 October). That is likely to be no small inconvenience to the nerves of 'the local population', since we are also told that 'the missiles would begin to move around the countryside only in times of extreme tension' (*Observer*, 18 November).

And what is a time of 'extreme tension'? Is it a time, perhaps, when there are sudden oil embargoes, or when truculent students occupy US embassies in Asian cities? If Cruise missiles were already here, the local population might have noticed much movement around the countryside in recent weeks.

If nuclear war breaks out it is not going to be after a formal ultimatum and a gentlemanly count-down to zero, so that missile launchers can be sent down minor roads and across hayfields and into prepared emplacements in the woods – and only then can we all start fair together. The only possibility of genocidal 'victory' lies in the pre-emptive strike. The warning-time, which was once placed at 48 hours, is now calculated by 'experts' at 30 minutes, or even at 15 (*Telegraph*, 12 November; *Now!*, 16–22 November).

Whether war starts by accident or intent, it will start without more than a few days' warning, and (from the standpoint of the civilian population) it will finish in a day. (The high politicians and the service chiefs, in their deep strategic caves, submarines or stratospheric command posts, may slog it out for a few more weeks.) While NATO might be willing to write off the 'local population' (that is, us), it would not put its Tomahawks to an 'inconvenience' of that kind.

If the missiles come, they will be stationed to strike, or the whole operation is fantasy. I write this as a very knowledgeable military expert who, regrettably, has not yet found employment with the *Observer* or the BBC. In the last war I once arrived at a battle half an hour late, owing to the distance to be travelled and the difficult nature of Italian country tracks; fortunately the infantry whom my tanks were supposed to be supporting had not yet been over-run.

NATO is not going to have its expensive hardware bogged down to the axle in East Anglian byways. (More happens in thirty minutes now than used to happen then.) Nor is NATO going to start dispersing its missiles around the place only when 'extreme tension' has already arisen, since any such dispersal would be monitored by satellite observation and would be the instant signal to an enemy to press a pre-emptive ballistic button.

But, look where you will, there is no end to the insanity of the whole operation. One might suppose that 'modernising' NATO's nuclear armament might, at the least, allow us to spend less on conventional weapons and armies. Not at all. Mr Francis Pym, the Defence Secretary, in an exclusive interview given (as it happens) not to the House of Commons but to Sir James Goldsmith's *Now!* (9–15 November), has explained patiently that the more nuclear 'deterrence' there is, the more dangerous the situation becomes, and hence the greater the need to raise the level of conventional armaments as an alternative option to nuclear war. It is 'very important not to let our conventional forces run down, because if you do the result is to lower the nuclear threshold and weaken deterrence'.

This is not just a closed circle of 'deterrence', like a horse-gin, in which we must plod round and round for ever grinding out terror until something snaps or the horse falls dead on its side. It is a manic spiral of proliferating terror and proliferating expense, with misjudgment, hysteria, or accident becoming statistically more inevitable every day. And *why*, since there is already terror enough, ten times over, ballistically poised at both ends of Power's great divide, do we need this intermediate additive of terror at all? Ah, it is a safeguard to *prevent* the ultimate horror of a Soviet/US total nuclear war! It is to 'localise' nuclear war: that is, to keep nuclear war local to us, and to West and East Europe, and away from America.

Britain's 'primary role is to survive as a forward NATO base' (*Now!* 9–15 November). Or not to survive, as the case may be. Mr Gregory Teverton (who, we should recall, is an *international* expert) tells us that the threat of a Soviet nuclear attack on Western Europe might 'put American cities at risk'. 'Missiles in Western Europe would give the American President an intermediate option' (*Observer*, 18 November). No wonder the US service chiefs are determined to keep control of the ignition keys to 'our contribution' to NATO, since if such an 'option' had to be taken, the 'local population' might not be so keen to opt.

Three further comments. The first is self-evident. The whole operation of Official-Secrecy-cum-Prepackaged-Official-Information carries with it another kind of threat – that of internal terror. For if all the organs of the State and the media combine to impose a 'consensus' upon us, then it follows that the other side of the consensus (or those who fall outside it) must represent 'treason'.

There is a lot of this kind of talk around, as you may have noticed. *Now!* is very explicit as to the motives of anyone opposed to the consensus: 'Severe disruption of national life by Soviet special forces, operating together with undercover KGB "teams" and fifth columnists would take place days or hours before the first air strikes on Britain (9–15 November).

Good heavens, if such traitors and fifth columnists are lying in wait, then they must already be here! 'Speak for Britain, Mrs Thatcher!' squeals Peregrine Worsthorne (who has always had difficulty in distinguishing his own liver condition from the National Interest). 'Barbarians' are not only 'at the gate', they are 'within our own borders'. They burst forth, in their 'alien style', in the industrial troubles of last winter:

> Those brutal, angry faces seemed scarcely human, let alone British, arousing reactions of dismay among all classes rather as would the emergence of strange creatures from the nether regions. ... There seemed to be a stench of evil in the land. (*Sunday Telegraph*, 2 December)

Much the same thought, in more elegant terms, has occurred to the Regius Professor of Modern History at Oxford, Hugh Trevor-Roper: 'It is the function of MI5 to keep an eye on suspect contacts, and who can say exactly where, in the amorphous Labour Party, the eastern frontiers are now drawn?' (*Spectator*, 24 November). It is a chilling image, and chilling, when it comes from that high table of cultivation. Against the geographic eastern frontier we must mount the Pershing-2 and the Tomahawk; against the 'eastern frontier' of the human mind and moral sensibility, what modernised weapons will Trevor-Roper now grant to MI5?

The second comment is that all this has gone on, and for months, not through any open democratic process but behind democracy's back. There has not even been, prior to the decision of 'Britain' at Brussels, any debate in Parliament. I don't know that this greatly matters, seeing how rabbity parliaments are these days and how servile the opposition front bench. But there *are* some honest MPs, who would have asked awkward questions, to which answers must have been given. And for form's sake there could have been gestures – a White Paper, a debate.

Why does the Defence Secretary make his most luminous statements
to *Now!* or to Brian Walden on ITV's *Weekend World*? And why can
we be told, by the *Times* defence correspondent (15 November), that,
in relation to the siting of Cruise missiles,

> Mr Pym is understood to be considering ways in which this should be
> presented to the British public – particularly in East Anglia and Oxford-
> shire. . . .

when one might suppose that he would also be considering how to
solicit the assent of Parliament?

But that is the giveaway phrase: 'ways in which this should be
presented to the British public.' Politics has nothing left to it now but
this: lies, disinformation, the management of opinion, the theatrical
show of legitimation. Decisions are taken elsewhere: by NATO's High
Level Group, by defence and service chiefs. Politicians are the servile
and oily-tongued liars, the shady brokers who put these decisions
across.

Which leads one to ask – *what* has the Parliamentary Labour Party
been up to? Labour's official policy, as founded on conference
decisions, and as declared in its 1974 manifesto, was unambiguous: 'We
have renounced any intention of moving to a new generation of
strategic nuclear weapons.' 'Renounce' is a word without ambiguity: my
dictionary gives, *inter alia*, 'revoke', 'disown', 'reject', 'give up', 'consent
formally to abandon', 'repudiate', 'refuse to recognise longer',
'withdraw from', and (please note) 'not to follow suit at cards'. That
would seem to be clear. It does not say 'go along with in privy and
devious ways, following every suit that NATO leads'.

My dictionary, like the Authorised Version, no doubt needs
modernising. And Mr Callaghan can show us how this should be done.
For he modernised Labour's clearly-stated policy in the election
manifesto of this year (without consulting either the Parliamentary
Party or his own National Executive) by inserting some slippery
provisos:

> We reiterate our belief that this [i.e. renunciation] is the best course for
> Britain. But many great issues affecting our allies and the world are involved,
> and a new round of strategic arms limitation (*sic*!) negotiations will soon
> begin. We think it essential that there must be full and informed debate about
> these issues in the country before any decision is taken.

Yes. And how much has Mr Callaghan done to drive forward this 'full
and informed debate'? Inside the House? No. Inside the Party? No.

Outside the House? No. If we can trust some further official secrets leaked in *The Times* (4 December), his mind has been on other things. For it seems that, during the last 18 months of his administration, a 'small ad hoc committee' of the Cabinet was being convened by Mr Callaghan, so immeasurably secret that the Cabinet was not informed of its existence. This committee, or gang of four, was so very privy that it did not even have a name or number: it was an unconstitutional and secret faction of the Prime Minister, Dr David Owen, Mr Healey and Mr Mulley.

> In Mr Callaghan's judgment the matter was too delicate to put before the Cabinet's Defence and Overseas Policy Committee, upon which sat one or two sticklers who might have reminded him of the party's manifesto commitment.

It was not, however, too secret to have a slate of senior civil servants in attendance on it, headed by Sir Antony Duff of the Foreign Office, nor too privy to be leaked, in due course, to *The Times*. The function of this committee, or gang, was precisely to prepare for the next generation of nuclear weapons.

With this, Official Secrecy advances its frontiers to the very verge of the authoritarian state. The 'eastern frontiers' are now drawn through the elected government itself. One 'stickler' who was denied knowledge of the Cabinet's own operations was perhaps the Deputy Prime Minister, Mr Michael Foot, and, if so, his exclusion from this gang is to his credit. What is now officially secret is what leading Cabinet members, and the Deputy Prime Minister, may not know.

For the 'all-party consensus', and *especially* the submissions of the PLP to the 'consensus', is the linchpin of the whole operation. It is this fiction which legitimates all that is done to us – the suppression of information, the manipulation of the media, the exclusion of critical questions from the arena of national political life. And what an ineffably craven and captive set those PLP 'leaders' – those cringing uncles and tailor's models and thugs of the rostrum and inept conference wheeler-dealers – are!

The final comment is that, in the past three months, the British people have been publicly shamed, not only in their own self-esteem but also in the esteem of Europe generally. If we had had a debate, some kind of a row about it all, then – even if sanity had lost the day – people would at least have known that there was still a little breath in the lungs of British democracy. But there has not even been a little moan. There has been *worse* than a moan, for 'British public opinion', like one of those animated corpses in a Hammer horror film, has been sent around Europe to cajole *other* nations to act against their consciences.

Mr Francis Pym has proudly proclaimed that 'we' want to 'keep our allies up to the mark' (*Now!* 9–15 November). At the West German SPD conference this month, Chancellor Schmidt has been able to use our name to confuse his own critics. And our press has seen fit to deliver editorial homilies to the reluctant Dutch:

> The Alliance does not usually ask much of the Dutch, who lead a comfortable and prosperous life at the heart of Western Europe.

Thus the *Financial Times*, 19 November (whose readers are not noted for their austerity and self-sacrifice), which goes on to chide the Dutch for being 'smug and hypocritical'. I do not know what concerned Norwegians or Danes or Dutch think of 'Britain' today; but if they think of us with contempt I could not argue that this is unjust.

As to the facts of the matter, the supposed nuclear balance or imbalance, between Soviet SS-20s and backfire bombers and NATO F-111s and Polaris and Poseidon submarines, I can only recommend readers to turn back to Robin Cook's succinct summary in these pages (30 November). In half a column he conveyed more information than in sheet after sheet of the established organs. It is his conclusion that 'the overall nuclear line-up remains entirely unfavourable' to the Soviets.

Whether Cook is right or wrong (he is usually right), there are manifest and sufficient reasons for accepting the official Labour policy of *renouncing* a new generation of nuclear weapons (whether NATO or our own): reasons rational, ethical, and even tactical, which I cannot – and need not – now rehearse. But I must, at least, refuse the false choice which we are so often offered, between NATO and the unending inflation of mutual nuclear terror on one hand, and a moralistic 'gesture' of national self-exemption on the other.

I am not critical of moralistic gestures. They are often the signs of a deeper realism, and those Christians in Holland who advocate this have my respect. What I am opposing is the notion that renunciation of the means of nuclear terror entails *any* kind of opting-out from the discourse of the world.

The alternative which some of us have advocated on the Left for more than twenty years is the policy of 'active neutrality'. We argued this policy within the counsels of CND. We argued it again in the *May Day Manifesto* in 1967–8. And we argue it still. It has never been a position of sufficient propriety to permit its discussion (as a 'viable option') in the media, although I have noticed plenty of editorials and telly programmes aimed *against* its unexpressed and misreported theorems. For a good many years (I am sad to report) it was not even possible to state the position in this journal.

I will restate it now, as concisely as I can, as theorems.

1. The present nuclear status quo is inexpressibly dangerous and increasingly unstable. It is exceedingly probable that it will at some point detonate in global nuclear war, whether through accident, miscalculation or hysteria.

2. The status quo is a stationary state. It is (from the standpoint of democratic practices) a degenerative state: that is, it generates authoritarian tendencies, and is supportive of secretive and authoritarian bureaucracies within both halves of the divided world.

3. The bureaucratic elites engendered by this condition develop, in turn, a distinct *interest* in maintaining this condition. Moreover, in a curious manner, the two opposed elites (Soviet and US) develop a *common* interest in repressing any unseemly development or popular initiative within the system which might create instability within this delicate strategic equilibrium. Thus, the US held back from 'taking advantage' of the Czech unrest in 1968, and the Soviet Union did not 'take advantage' of this year's revolutionary situation in Iran. Both powers loathe democratic initiatives – and their possible contagion.

4. Hence to wait for ultimate *détente* fro initiatives at the top – to wait for some SALT treaty in 2079 – is futile. For the state of permanent terror affords to these elites their purchase upon internal and external power.

5. Hence the system must be made to crumble at the bottom before it will give way at the top.

Twenty years ago we argued that Britain should not only renounce nuclear weapons, but should also renounce NATO and initiate new policies of active neutrality. We should resume initiatives towards a Europe which included Stockholm, Belgrade and Warsaw, as well as towards India and the 'Third World' or non-aligned powers.

We were told, in those days, that this would leave Britain 'naked in the conference chamber' and without allies. That was rubbish then, but in the last twenty years developments in Europe and in the Third World have converged to enforce the realism of our policy. Greece and France have detached themselves from NATO, and the skies have not fallen. Yugoslavia has maintained its stubborn national integrity. Romania has edged into a curious position of truculent dependence. Within NATO itself, second and third tiers are discernible – Norway, Denmark, Holland, and Iceland, Portugal and (shortly) Spain – which are refusing nuclear hardware and keeping open other initiatives.

What a British Labour government might have done – might even still do – with a policy of democratic socialism at home and of active neutrality abroad would be to re-enter into an international discourse which would invigorate democratic practices both East and West. As a new neutralist heartland re-emerged in Europe, a hundred forms of political and cultural bonding would go on, not only between socialist and radical movements in West and South Europe, but also with the huge reserves of 'dissidence' in East Europe – and within the Soviet Union itself.

That such a policy would be complex, delicate and entail great risks, as the US and Soviet elites felt the ground begin to crumble beneath them, is evident. If we were to leave NATO, in fact as well as form, we could expect revenges from Washington and Bonn, just as in the Soviet Union would exact revenges upon any Eastern European nation which responded in the same neutralist kind. There would be 'red alerts', and missile launchers would scurry down West and East German lanes.

But that will happen anyway. It will very certainly happen if Mr Pym and Mr Callaghan get their way. We are already at risk – Britain, Europe, civilisation, the human project – whatever big name we wish to put upon it. The difference between us is this. In the 'new generation' of nuclear weapons we might subdue for a while immediate and manifest risks while centralised authoritarian power (and its concomitant management of the mind) encroached further year by year, and we drifted towards some unpredictable and unplanned contingency, an ultimate detonation. In the policy of active neutrality we would take an immediate and conscious risk, which if we survived, would engender a new generation of human possibilities.

But we will not take that risk. NATO will not permit it, and Mr Pym, Mr Callaghan and the controllers of the public mind will not permit it even to be discussed. There is only one freedom left to us now: the freedom to get out of our chairs and turn the television off.

E.P. Thompson, 21/28 December 1979

ROGER WODDIS, 'Sagittarius's' worthy successor as weekly satiric versifier, updated her 'Nerves' (see pp. 97-8) to illustrate the fears of which Thompson had spoken.

Nerves, 1980

After 'Nerves – 2 September 1939' by 'Sagittarius')

I think I'll get a paper.
I think I'll break a date;
I think I'll have an early night,
I think I'll stay out late.

It's like the Cuban missiles
In 1962.
I can't think why I'm shaking.
Perhaps it's just the 'flu.

I couldn't eat a morsel.
I think I'll cook some grub.
I feel like getting good and pissed,
I can't afford the pub.

They're moving the Olympics
To Mablethorpe-on-Sea.
The Russians are in Pakistan,
It doesn't bother me.

I think I'll take a shower.
I'd better pay some bills.
I can't decide between the box
And taking to the hills.

No point in being nervous,
The nation's standing fast.
Suppose there is another war,
It's sure to be the last.

Roger Woddis, 25 January 1980

Perhaps the most inspiring symbols of resistance to nuclear insanity to emerge from the second wave of CND were the peace camps established outside the death factories at Greenham Common and elsewhere. As I write, theirs has long become a desperate, defensive movement, fighting internal strife and intense physical hardship as well as state repression – but the Washington INF accord finally gave their efforts some reward, and the example of women like LYNNE JONES, who went singing to prison time and again for their beliefs, will last.

A Week in the Life of a Greenham Prisoner

Tuesday

I woke nauseated, cold, stuffy, and confused. Where was I? Newbury nick. Why? Oh, yes, I refused to pay my fine – God, how stupid, why on earth didn't I pay it immediately and get out of here. Gradually, the fog of waking lifted. I ate the egg sandwich thrust through the door and contemplated for the hundredth time the vast amount of Greenham graffiti on the cell walls: 'We're not just good, we're bloody perfection!' 'We're all going off to sunny Holloway, no more Greenham for a week or two. ...' And gradually I worked my way back to the position I had taken yesterday when I had told Stipendiary Barr that I thought my £50 fine for criminal damages could be better spent.

Speaking out clearly for one's beliefs is one thing. Spending the night in a dirty green cell because Holloway is full, and contemplating 14 more days of the same, is another. I am someone who finds tube trains and aeroplanes terrifyingly claustrophobic, so what was I doing voluntarily locking myself up? Liz visited me yesterday afternoon and asked if I was sure I wanted to go through with it, as she would happily pay the fine. It took all my willpower to say yes. I had no commitments, no children, £50 was a lot of money and I might learn something. This way, at least, I was exercising choice. Even here the fact that I could leave at any point by paying meant that I was in control.

They moved us at midday to this south coast prison, rather benign looking buildings of honey-coloured brick; except for the barred windows, double electric gate and high mesh fence topped with barbed wire, they looked like a modern housing complex. The fence reminded me of Greenham. 'Brought your bolt cutters?' one of the police officers asked.

There were four of us, Katrina, who has been here before, Alexis, Anna and me. They were having a party in the road on New Year's Eve: seven days for refusing to pay a £5 fine. Sitting in reception we could see through the glass doors to women waiting for medication. Sarah was there, pale and drawn from fasting. 'She hurts no one but herself,' the officer checking my belongings remarked. 'No one cares that she is doing it. It's pointless.' It obviously bothered this officer. I knew that I couldn't do it.

My clothing was returned to me along with a green booklet of prison regulations and a white sheet describing the prison routine: breakfast in cell, work or education, meals in the dining room, daily exercise and evening association. 'Don't take any notice of that,' a red-haired woman said. 'We've had all our meals in our cells for the last two weeks because there was a fight in the dining room: and more often than not there is no association because they are too short-staffed.'

An officer showed me my cell: 12 by 8, peagreen walls, a bed, table, a chair, a locker and a cupboard with a small loo and sink in an adjoining room. Women's symbols and peace signs stuck on the walls showed that Greenham women had been there too. 'All right, love?' the officer asked. 'Why, yes, thanks,' I replied, surprised to be asked. The heavy, handleless door, with a pillbox slit of glass, slammed shut behind me.

Wednesday

Sarah caught me in the line for breakfast this morning. She told me that she had been put in a solitary strip cell for 24 hours for insisting on her right to a newspaper. 'They don't say you can't have it, just that it takes too long to process.' She looked exhausted. 'I asked not to work because I was fasting, but they made me. It's supposed to be voluntary, but it's slave labour, isn't it?'

In fact we're not working today. They are too short-staffed to let us out of our cells. I'm beginning to understand the expression 'doing time'. That is exactly what it is: a tangible substance, hanging heavily over you, clogging your senses. Life becomes the stretches between the sound of keys and any break in the monotony is welcome. I try to discipline myself to read and think, but instead find myself dozing or staring absently through the small strips of glass set in concrete that make up a window.

We did get association this evening. I came out of my cell into a corridor of dark, laughing women. The association room, a bleak bare affair of grey lino and plastic covered chairs was filled with women switching the TV channel every five minutes and queueing to do their ironing.

K. has taken the Greenham women under her wing. She got us second helpings of supper (tea and cake) and sat with us. 'Shoplifting,' she replied to the inevitable question, 'to feed my habit. Mind you, if you women keep coming in, they'll have to stop sending us down.

"Deferred," the judge will say, "deferred, deferred, deferred, there's no room!"' She roared with laughter. The women here sum up their 'crimes' in one-word terms: 'cheques', 'smack', 'shoplifting'. There are three lifers and a few others with long-term sentences. The women's reactions to us ranged from friendly indifference to avid support. We've been in and out so often that they are very well informed. 'Soon as I get out, I'm coming to visit,' Q. says.

Thursday

Today we were allowed to work. This is probably the only time in my life that I am going to regard scrubbing floors as a privilege. Really it is just the relief of being able to stretch my arms and legs. Anne and I work together on the top corridor, at first being extremely conscientious, sweeping, scrubbing on our hands and knees, then wiping down. We quickly realised that everyone else was simply wiping down, as it made no difference to the streaky grey lino, besides which it gave us more time to hang out and chat. There is a work hierarchy here: wing cleaners at the bottom, librarians and hospital orderlies at the top. You work your way up by good behaviour and length of stay. Greenham women are mostly wing cleaners. We were sitting on the steps reading K. her letters from her sister (she can't read herself) when an officer came along. 'You girls finished?' 'Yes,' said K. 'I said girls, not convicts.'

We were locked up again after lunch. Theoretically each work shift gets gym four times a week. However, the gym's being cleaned and the instructor is away. But I've acquired yesterday's *Guardian* from N., one of the lifers. She stopped me in the corridor. 'Are you a Greenham woman?' 'Yes.' 'Well, I want you to know I am really with you in spirit.' she insisted that I come and look at the 'LIFE AGAINST DEATH' poster in her cell. 'You've made it beautiful in here,' I said, noting the curtains, books, potted plants and pictures with which she has transformed the cell. 'God, you have to, when it's your home.' 'How do you stand it?' I asked. 'It's like a bloody luxury liner after a submarine,' she replied. 'I was in Durham.'

It isn't the physical discomfort. I have a great deal more space and warmth than in my bender at Greenham. The whole thing, in fact, bears a distinct resemblance to my smart South Coast girls' boarding school, from the stodgy, unpalatable, overcooked food to the pop stars' posters stuck up with toothpaste in an attempt to make one's room a home. No, it is the small, endless, petty human humiliations: the plastic cutlery, bowl, plate and cup; the strip search by uniformed officers, and the fact that while being called 'girl', or 'love', or 'pet', whatever your age, is at least friendly, it also diminishes you and places you firmly at the bottom of a hierarchy. You could scarcely respond in the same vein.

Your life is completely exposed, watched through doors, every letter read and everything must be asked for, with no guarantee that your request will be granted. Refusal is a fine art. No one actually ever says no. You are faced instead with a smiling officer who says, 'Ask the wing officer,' who says, 'I'd really like to help, but you'll have to ask the governor.' And the little white request forms pile up and pile up, like my daily request for my notebook, or A.'s repeated request to move back to the wing where her friends are. We are like small children. The only power we have is to cause trouble and who wants to risk losing remission?

Friday

I've started taking pain killers for sciatica which is the only way I could think of getting a twice daily walk along the corridor to ease the cramp brought on by lack of exercise. In the queue for medication everyone was restless and bad-tempered at being 'banged up' for yet another day, as half the officers were sick – no work, no association. 'I'd rather be in Holloway,' one woman said, 'at least you get out twice a day.' 'They have to let us out to the kitchen,' another said. She was dressed in gum boots and a dirty apron, had straggly red hair pulled back in an elastic band and the pasty complexion that everyone acquires after a few weeks here. 'How long have you been here?' I asked. 'Four months, I got 18, for possession. I expected 6 but not 18, but the judge was biased. It makes you really bitter. I might as well have done armed robbery. You end up thinking ... cor, when I get out, I may as well be bent.' 'What did you do before?' 'I was at college and everything, doing secretarial. You'd have thought it would have counted, but he didn't care.' 'Can't you go on with it here?' 'I thought I could, but the education department here is hopeless, hopeless! I went to one class, Beauty Culture. I could have taught it better myself. ... My appeal is coming up Monday. I'm trying not to think about it. other girls get very down afterwards.'

She rolled a cigarette, split the match she was holding carefully, placing half back into the box. 'Why didn't you go to Holloway?' she asked me. 'Too crowded.' 'I guess it's 'cos everyone's short after Christmas.' 'Sorry?' 'Everyone's short,' she repeated patiently. 'So they nick things – shoplifting – that's the most common, I s'pose it's easier than drugs.' 'Where are you, then?' another woman asked me. 'Third floor,' I replied. 'Hard luck,' she said, a look of pity on her face. 'Why?' I asked. 'Well, it's darkest Africa up there, isn't it?' We lined up at the hatch to get our drugs. Q. came out grinning. 'She gave me an extra dose of valium – I'm just going to glide through my last few weeks.' We met K., face haggard, walking down the corridor, clutching her belongings. 'I'm really strung out. I'm going into the sick bay for a few days. I just can't keep my head together, can't get any rest.'

It's never quiet on the wing, even at night; there is always a subterranean murmur of music playing on radios, women's voices, a shout, water running, hard heels in the corridor. But the noise level has been rising steadily all day until I am convinced that I must be the only one still locked in my cell and that everyone else must be outside the door. But it's only women shouting to each other.

Saturday

They let us out for the whole morning, it felt like a holiday, with the library being open and Woo and Tim emerging from their cells to swoop me up in an enormous embrace. They had done a 6-hour journey the previous day cooped up in mesh cages in the back of a police van. It saves on staff. However, Tim is close on six feet tall, so it meant that her knees were up to her chest and her head bent down. 'Next time they'll have to carry me into it,' she said.

Sunday

N. told me, this morning, that she had heard on the radio they were definitely going to evict the whole camp on Monday. There's no way of confirming it, so I sat all morning trying to think what to do: to stay on a point of principle or pay off the remainder of my fine and get back to the camp. Woo and Tim feel that you should never pay them a penny, but they leave tomorrow anyway.

In the end I decided I couldn't bear sitting here wondering if the camp was being shredded, and that I could be more useful there. Could I make a phone call to raise the money? 'No, it's Sunday. You'll have to ask permission from Welfare tomorrow.' 'But I'd like to leave tomorrow, as early as possible, so I need to raise the money today. My little green book says "consult your wing officer". And that's you.' 'I'm sorry, I can't help.' 'Is there SOMEONE you could ask?' 'I'll ask the chief.' An hour later she returned. 'The chief says no!' 'Why? Did you explain?' 'I'm sorry, you can't' 'May I talk to the chief?' 'No!' She shut my cell door to cut off further conversastion.

I sat raging, furious, also with myself. What about Emma Goldman, two years for leafleting on birth control? What about Louise Michel? What about the women tortured and 'disappeared' in Chile, El

Salvador, South Africa? What about the women in here for months and years, for goodness' sake? What did two days matter? ... I was still raging.

We got association this evening for a second time in a week. I sat and talked with B., in for eight years, for supposedly allowing bombs to be made in her kitchen. A quiet, warm, middle-aged woman, knitting a children's jumper; it was impossible to believe, listening to her, that she was guilty. 'I didn't jump bail because I believed I could prove I was not guilty. And here I am.' She has been trying for eight years to get her trial reopened. 'Of course, I didn't do it. I don't even know what nitroglycerine is. I can't stand the way the IRA work. I'll have nothing to do with violence of any kind. They wanted Irish bodies, they got mine. I remember the officer saying – because first they charged me with murder – "If we don't get you for this, we'll get you for something, you Irish bastard!" They won't give us a re-trial because they are scared of the compensation they'll have to pay, but I don't want the money, all I want is an apology, and if it takes the rest of my life to get one, I'm going to do it.'

I sat looking at the pictures of her children grown up and married while she was in prison, and the Pope, to whom she had written. 'What you women are doing, that's the way to change things,' she went on. 'You don't sound bitter. I would be.' 'Not bitter,' she replied, 'Just hurt, very hurt.'

Monday

'I'm sorry, you can't phone yet, Welfare's busy.' It was 10.30 a.m. A phone sat unused on the table between the wing officer and myself. Now that I had made the decision to go every minute lost was exasperating, especially as women kept coming up and hugging me and asking me to write. 'Come back later,' she smiled. Eventually she phoned for me. Yes, my friends would be down.

Today, of course, we had work, gym, a bizarre visit from the chaplain who chatted about his wife's home birth and I finally got to see the chief officer. 'I don't suppose there is any point in discussing anything, as you are going,' she said after she had signed my travel warrant. It was a statement not a question, and I was out of the door before my now theoretical points about access to notebooks, newspapers and association could be answered.

The search on leaving was a curiously arbitrary process. I was stripped naked and asked to show the soles of my feet, yet my clothes and books were bundled unchecked into my bag. 'X. got her appeal. She's out,' one officer said. 'Oh good,' replied the other. 'I hope you've

no complaints,' she said to me, 'because that will take a lot more time.'
She thrust a form in front of me and I signed under 'no complaints'. I
walked past the women banging and grinning and waving from the sick
bay door into a cold, wet February afternoon. 'Come back soon!' Q.
mouthed to me. 'Probably,' I mouthed back.

Lynne Jones, 30 March 1984

*If to many the women of Greenham Common represented an inspiring
emblem of a new politics, the great mining industry strike of 1984–5 was
widely seen as the last desperate gasp of a dying class politics. CHRIS
BURKHAM talked to miners on the picket lines in the early stages of the
dispute, MICHAEL IGNATIEFF proposed some provocative ideas
about its wider significance towards the end.*

Last Stand at the Alamo

At Cortonwood colliery, where this miners' strike began, there is little
sign of the 'fifth column of political activists', all 'handpicked men, who
have Communist, Marxist or Trotskyist backgrounds' whom the *Daily
Express* last week alleged were running the strike. In the Strike Control
Centre an unknown hand has penned a notice: 'BEWARE! A vulture
is going round the estates of Brampton offering a few quid for watches,
bracelets, rings, etc.' And next to it, in a bolder hand: 'Beware. A
vulture is going round the coalfields offering a few quid for your jobs.'
Other 'fifth-columnist' material offers advice on how to get rent and
rates 'frozen' and on where meat parcels are available (1 lb mince, 1 lb
frying steak, 1 lb sausages and 1 lb liver for £2.50). It was Cortonwood
which sparked the present dispute – when, two days after they had been
told the pit had another five years' life and three weeks after 80 colliers
had been transferred there, the NCB announced that it must close.

'We're not militants, we don't strike for the sake of it,' explains Mick
Carter, Cortonwood's NUM representative, 'we're fighting for our
bloody existence.' It was formerly a 'moderate' pit which didn't vote for
the left-wing area leadership. Now these Yorkshire colliers, who still
dissociate themselves from 'political campaigning', are behind the
politics of Arthur Scargill and support them with flying pickets and the
intent to continue for 'seven years, if necessary'. Across the county
border, one Nottinghamshire miner describes the same Scargill as 'a
deceitful little bastard'.

For the men at Cortonwood who without the strike would already be out of their jobs, the deceit is in the action that suddenly ended five years' employment, mining the accessible and high-quality seam of silkstone coal. Nineteen other collieries are marked for closure this year. They trust Scargill to secure them a safer future, not Westminster.

With no solution in sight, one of Mick Carter's flying pickets is still firmly holding his ground: 'MacGregor wants our jobs and Maggie wants our union cards – they're having neither.' Further south this attitude is endorsed by two Derbyshire strikers, although without the same resolve. Already one is taking note of his wife's urging him to return to work and bring in the wage packet. In place of fiery resource, they have a stoicism towards the events overtaking them, splitting their time between long walks and picket duty.

For them, mining has no heroism. It is just a job and if there is work for them to do, it will be done. Theirs is the silent presence which follows where others lead and whose barely concealed envy for the hefty wage packets available in Nottinghamshire has constantly threatened further splits in the strikers' ranks.

A group of Notts miners militantly defended their passivity: 'In Nottinghamshire the pickets have met a hell of a lot of resistance, because we've turned round and said, "Sod you, we'll have an area ballot." So 78 per cent of our members said they'll work and they're not stopping us because we believe in democracy. *We* had a democratic ballot, and if *they* want to strike they can.'

At Cortonwood, the pickets have made their stand in a frontier-style lean-to shack, named 'The Alamo'. From there, they greet such answers with snorts of derision. 'Some of them can't see what's going on, they think they're safe because their directors have told them that there will be no closures in the Nottingham coalfield this year. They haven't been told about what will happen *next* year. All they're thinking about is next week's pay packet. Well, I'm afraid I can't think about next week's pay packet because I haven't got one.'

There is an air of semi-permanency to 'The Alamo': battered easy-chairs form a half circle around a brazier with a blackened kettle boiling up water; in the shelter there is an electric light bulb, copies of the *Daily Mirror* and *Reveille*, various eating utensils and a loaf of Mother's Pride for the chip butties at lunch-time. A group of miners, from one who can only have recently finished his apprenticeship to one who has already retired, pass the time, as they guard a deserted pit, with jokes about the supreme bogey-man, MacGregor. One has a photocopy of a poem from 'Anon – A miner's wife' which describes him as 'a decrepit Yankee pensioner' and concludes: 'The Sheriff of

Nottingham can't help him now because we'll be back for more/We will show this foreigner just how we won the war.'

'Our wives are 100 per cent behind us. If my wife saw me crossing a picket line she'd leave me.' Brampton already has an unemployment figure of 25 per cent in an area where the only industry is coal mining – 'it's not a beautiful place, it's a colliery village.' And the support of the village is still strong, drawn from the whole community. As well as the cut-price foodstuffs, all but five of 130 local businessmen have signed a petition backing them.

Survival on £11.75 a week for a 21-year-old man who already has a wife and two children is not easy, and even less so when compared to the 'dirty money' available to the strike-breakers. Miners still at work can earn £70–80 a day in bonus alone. On top of that they get their wages, so it can be £110–120 every day. More salt in the wounds of men who are held back from the strike-breakers by police, who may well be collecting bonus pay of £200 each week.

They may welcome the police presence, which helps them take away that hefty pay packet; but the strike-breakers also suffer the consequences. 'I have to carry my locker key around with me to prove I live in my home village,' said one Notts miner. 'I appreciate what they're doing, they're protecting our right to work. Then again, when you're stopped every 20–30 yards along a public footpath and asked where you're going, what you're doing, and who you're doing it with and why ...'

Police and pickets are engaged in a continual cat-and-mouse game, starved of information about each other's tactics. One morning the pickets at Bolsover all returned to their cars and left the colliery entrance only to drive round in a wide circle, arriving back at their starting point once their foes had moved elsewhere to head them off. The next day Mick Carter dispatched pickets south, who were all stopped before they left Yorkshire and threatened with arrest if they are even seen in Nottinghamshire again. On another day, police arrested pickets who were being driven to court, preventing them from appearing.

Such incidents make good stories – but they are not the rule. 'All you read in the media is biased, totally biased. Take this morning: I went to work at 5 o'clock and there were two men at the pit, two pickets from Yorkshire, who didn't threaten me at all. They just explained their situation to me and that they had the backing of their national union, which they did. So I said I believed in what they were doing and turned back. It's just the papers which are stirring it.' The week before, this same miner had ducked bricks and bottles to get to work, defiant because of the intimidation.

Underneath the plastic sheeting of 'The Alamo's roof the miners say the current situation is only serving to consolidate the gap between rich and poor, 'masters and slaves, upstairs and downstairs and in my lady's bloody chamber'. Strengthening their resolve to maintain the strike until they are victorious is the belief that the government is manoeuvring itself into a position where it can use the dispute to destroy the power of the NUM – and through that destroy the power of trade unions.

'I'm getting letters from all over the country, all trade unions, all walks of life who say, "If you don't win this one then what chance have we got?" Because the GCHQ has had far greater connotations than what people might think, the reverberations that went through the trade unions from that are still rumbling. As far as I'm concerned, if we lost this then every trade unionist – and I should imagine that you're trade unionists, and if not you can bugger off now – might as well tear their card up. It won't be worth anything.'

There is little common ground on what democracy means. Where the Nottingham miners harp on about the democracy of their decision to continue working, Mick Carter sees that: 'Every newspaper in the country, every television station is all telling us we should have a ballot. But did anybody ballot MacGregor into his job? Did anybody ballot Maggie Thatcher into hers? Did they tell the men [*sic*] at GCHQ that they could have a ballot? We have already balloted with our feet.'

Chris Burkham, 27 April 1984

Strangers and Comrades

I

After nine months of the miners' strike, any ordinary television viewer knows the terms of a potential settlement. Guarantees about the future of miners' jobs were given in the NACODS agreement and could be made iron-cast; the threatened pits could be given a reprieve; an arbitration board could be appointed to adjudicate the issue of closures on a case by case basis; the NCB's projected reduction in capacity could be shelved: the strike has made it irrelevant in any case. The miners could pay their fines, purge their contempt and return within the pale of the law. Even the vexed presence of Mr Ian MacGregor could be disposed of – after a decent interval.

A formula of words thus exists which would enable Mr Eaton and Mr Scargill to appear together under the hot lights on the steps of ACAS in St James's Square each claiming victory, or, at least, honourable vindication. Yet as any ordinary television viewer knows, this is unlikely to happen. Much more likely is a bloody fight to the finish. Whoever is still left standing on the field of battle, the result will be the decimation of a great industry and a great union. How has this been allowed to happen? Why is British political culture, one of the most venerable and successful instruments ever devised for the containment, suppression and adjudication of social conflict, proving so ineffective in this case? The simple answer is that neither side trusts the other to honour the terms of a compromise.

Compromise itself has been reduced to a synonym of capitulation, and the business of conciliating social interests – once thought to be the very art of government – has come to be seen as an exercise in appeasement by the government in power. There has been virulent and abusive language on both sides of the dispute, but the government bears a heavier responsibility for the degradation of political argument, precisely because it is not simply one side in the dispute: it is elected to represent the common interests of the country, chief among which is the maintenance of a language of mutual respect in political controversy. The Prime Minister's Carlton House speech about the 'fascists of the Left' simply guaranteed that when the Welsh taxi-driver was so shamefully murdered her attempts to speak for a common outrage were heard as a self-serving attempt to regain the higher moral ground she had abandoned earlier in the week.

When children say 'sticks and stones may break my bones, but words will never hurt me', they of course mean the opposite. The hurt of words endures long after the ache of truncheons has subsided. Miners have reason to feel bitter about the way they have been represented in the language of Parliament and the press as they are about the way they have been treated by the police and the social security system. When the Barnsley miners' wives formed their support group for this strike, they did so, in the first instance, to counter the image of the miners portrayed on the television screens and in the press. Fairness and balance – the *summum bonum* of Fleet Street's good conscience – does not begin to convey what miners and their wives want from the press: not merely the chance to present their case, but also the chance to be heard with simple respect. When the aged Earl of Stockton felt it necessary to remind his party and its press that the miners had fought and died for their country, one realized how far the language of the Right had abandoned the ground of common decency.

The erosion of a language of respect on the Right must be connected to the economism of the government's conception of the common good. The Chancellor of the Exchequer's assertion that the destruction of a great union and the immiseration of thousands of men, women and children is a sensible investment in the future of the British economy must be read against the same Chancellor's inability to define the country's collective purpose in any higher terms than containing inflation and reducing unemployment. This economism does not merely lack any idea of what 'one nation' is supposed to be 'one nation' *for*, it also lacks any accounting terms for measuring the social cost of laying waste to communities and to their painfully acquired heritage of skills.

Into the void in Conservative rhetoric where an idea of the common good ought to be, Mrs Thatcher has cast the language of law and order, as if the national interest were synonymous with the police interest.

Only a government bereft of any conception of the nation's good could define a reasonable settlement of the dispute in terms of the destruction of the NUM. What kind of victory would it be to leave behind a community of defeated and embittered miners? People have memories, and they have pride: 1926 is as much a cause of 1984 as Mr MacGregor. What is appalling about a political strategy explicitly seeking to smash the NUM and to 'isolate' the miners from respectable political discourse is that it mortgages the future of class relations in this country. Any victory won on these terms will bequeath a legacy of bitterness which will plague industrial relations for every government which comes after hers. The government's grotesque charade of non-involvement in the dispute – insisting that the NCB must negotiate for itself, while cutting strikers' benefits – is nothing less than an abidication of its responsibility towards the national interest.

II

In the normal course of events, a government which fails to uphold the national interest eventually forfeits its electoral support. Judging from the opinion polls, it is Labour rather than the Conservatives which is paying the higher electoral price for the strike. The miners' case – that their cause is the cause of all workers – has failed to persuade working people. A gulf is perceived to exist between the miners' interest and the national interest, and the Labour Party, being structurally dependent on the unions, is seen as being incapable of defending the latter against the former.

One reason why the miners' interest has not been seen as the national interest is that 1984 is not 1926. Their opponent now is not Capital, the sectional economic interest of mine owners, but the State itself. Any confrontation between a union and a nationalised industry and between the unions and the courts is thus seen by the general public as a conflict between a sectional interest and the national interest. The miners may say that the laws they are defying are capitalist laws, but that is not how the whole fabric of law, as opposed to the Employment Act of 1981, is seen by the country at large. By taking on every institution of the national interest at once – the courts, the police, and the government – the miners have inevitably been seen as acting against the collective good.

It is no use complaining that the State is arrayed against you: only the most painstaking observance of the law is likely to win over the watching national audience to the view that the State is actually acting against the national interest. Only non-violence in the face of provocation will convince a watching audience that the State has overstepped its bounds. In the event the State has acted with great brutality upon occasion, without losing any of its legitimacy except in the mining communities. Miners who have acted with self-discipline and restraint have had the bitter experience both of being assaulted by the police for their pains and then being branded collectively as criminal outcasts. Of course, when the State brands you as an outlaw, it becomes that much easier to behave like one. Violence is a spiral which only legitimises the State.

The fact that it is the State, not Capital, which is against the miners also transforms the *casus belli* – the definition of the uneconomic pit – into an issue about the social allocation of common resources. If the mines were in private hands, the argument that there are *no* economic grounds for closure might have sounded like a dignified socialist refusal to allow the law of profit to dictate the future of working people's communities. But the mines are a collective social asset. To say there are no economic grounds for closure in this context is to say there are no limits in principle to the amount taxpayers can be asked to pay.

This is not a dignified refusal to be dictated to by the capitalist law of profit: it is simply a refusal to submit the claims of the mining communities to the democratic process by which taxpayers' money is allocated between competing uses. Whatever the party in power, there will always be 'economic' grounds for closure, simply because there are choices to be made over public expenditure, between increasing the subsidy to miners, for example, and raising old age pensions. The appeal of the miners' case was fatally damaged by the failure to admit that their claim on collective resources was as limited as any other social group's.

The fact that the State is the employer in this dispute creates a conflict of loyalties for those workers asked to join sympathy strikes. Arthur Scargill has appealed for the power workers to turn out the lights on the rest of us, and those on the Left who believe in class politics believe the strike would have been over long ago had they done so. Yet most workers in the public sector are both producers and consumers of State services, and responsible public sector unions have to reconcile the claims of union solidarity against their obligations to the public. In this most obvious conflict of loyalties, power workers appear to have decided that the miners' interest and the general interest do not coincide.

No conflict of principle has cost the labour movement so dear in the past 20 years. Most of the major industrial struggles of the past generation have pitted Labour against the State, not Labour against Capital, and in the struggle workers have been divided against themselves. The public sector strikes of 1973–1979 destroyed the moral legitimacy of the union movement and prepared the electoral basis for Thatcherism within the working class itself. Many workers believe that if the price of victory in this or any dispute is plunging old age pensioners huddled before single bar fires into the freezing dark, then the price is too high.

The price is also too high if solidarity has to be built upon victimisation. There has always been a conflict which socialist politics has to reconcile between the sovereignty of private judgment – the individualism rooted in the Nonconformist working-class tradition – and the claims of solidarity enshrined in trade unionism. If there is a current of sympathy among working people for working miners it is because the claims of private judgment have always been valued as highly as the claims of solidarity. In a democratic union, the way to reconcile solidarity and private judgment is through a ballot. The call for a national ballot, heard from Ministers and the Tory press, is simply a way of demanding that the strike be called off. Yet the demand for a ballot is as legitimate as the demand that union members be asked whether the union should seek financial support from Arab dictators. In both cases, denying the men a ballot and making secret deals with Colonel Gadafy, the miners' leadership treated their own membership with a contempt which forfeited the support of other trade unionists.

It is also up to the leaders of the union to make sure that the claim of solidarity is not used as a moral permission for acts of hatred. Solidarity is a precious tradition of self-discipline and self-restraint: it is being traduced and betrayed by men who hurl bricks through their workmates' windows and beat them up in their own houses. The first task of leaders is to conserve the legitimacy and authority of the traditions entrusted to them. Can the miners' leadership honestly say that they have bequeathed that tradition of solidarity intact to future generations?

III

There are those on the Left who maintain that the miners' strike is a vindication of a class-based politics after decades in which the agenda of the Left was defined by cross-class campaigns like feminism and CND. Yet the strike demonstrates the reverse: a labour movement which is incapable of presenting a class claim as a national claim, which can only pose its demands in the language of total victory, which takes on the State and ends up on the wrong side of the law cannot hope to conserve its support and legitimacy among the working-class public. The miners' strike is not the vindication of class politics, but its death throes.

In the analysis of why this should be so – why steel workers and power workers do not come out in support of miners, or why workers do not vote Labour as they once did – argument often focuses on the claim that property ownership and post-war consumerism have transformed the working-class voter into a selfish individualist, for whom political allegiance is a floating and contingent accoutrement of life style. The intense passions raised by the miners' strike far away from the coalfields demonstrate the incorrectness of this view: political identity remains as much at the centre of people's sense of themselves as moral actors as it ever did.

What seems to be happening is not that workers are becoming more individualistic, but that their loyalties are more divided and conflictual than ever before. Political commitment is now a matter of choice in ways it never was when a man or woman was a member of a small, self-contained industrial or rural community. No one lives apart from the national community, not even the miners. If the pit communities are defended with passion, it is not because they are ancient, but because they are recent: fragile islands built against the tide of migration from pit to pit which has been the miners' lot since 1947.

All workers nowadays are both producers and consumers, both members of a local community and members of a national community, enemies of the State upon occasion, and also its dependants. The locus of political socialisation has shifted from the family, the workplace and the community to the great meeting place of the society of strangers: the media. Radio and television have made us a nation in ways we never were: every local conflict, every local tragedy is now a national event. Appeals by miners or by anyone else to a national audience to support their sectional interest increasingly fall on deaf ears for a television public whose primary concern is to understand how the conflicts unceasingly represented on the screens can be adjudicated and reconciled. In this conflict over the adjudication of national conflict, the battle for political opinion – for control of collective representations of the national interest – becomes the dominant form of struggle.

Toward these developments, Labour typically faces both ways, welcoming – for example – the freedom of women to make up their own minds politically, while lamenting the decline of old working-class loyalties. It would be more consistent to welcome the decline of all residual, fixed and automatic political loyalties and to embrace a political culture in which individual opinion is shaped and re-shaped by the nightly battle of representations on the television screen. In this struggle, the crucial requirement for political success is a believable image of national purpose and identity. Parties no longer win by making contradictory promises to a loose conglomerate of competing minority groups: they win by articulating a vision of common purpose which moulds minorities into majorities.

The Left crucially overestimates Mrs Thatcher's electoral appeal if it believes she has succeeded in monopolizing the language of 'one nation'. Her authoritarianism divides as much as it unites, and her idea of uniting strangers in a common purpose is to turn the nation into a limited company: first British Telecom, then Great Britain Limited.

The Left may scorn the idea of reducing citizenship to stock ownership, but Labour's own economics of national purpose – nationalisation – is equally bankrupt as a means of bringing the country together. Its image of the common good – the just community – is also crucially equivocal about how the goods of equality, community and justice can be reconciled. The left wing of the party who argue that Labour lost its electoral legitimacy because it lacked the courage of its egalitarian convictions are correct. Yet egalitarian justice is the most divisive of human virtues: one person's justice is another's injustice. A society which tries to live by justice can also die by it, unless it leavens justice with reconciliation. The trouble with Arthur Scargill's politics is not that it doesn't have justice on its side, but that it utterly lacks a conception of how competing classes, regions, races and religions can be reconciled with each other in a national community.

What the Left needs is a language of national unity expressed as commitment to fellowship among strangers. We need a language of trust built upon a practice of social comradeship. Labour's record in municipal government has severely tested the public's confidence that socialists know how to build and manage public housing parks, schools, swimming pools and hospitals in such a way that every citizen feels they are being treated with respect. We need, in short, a politics of public goods to set beside a politics of justice: this requires a practice of popular planning at local level which will restore ordinary people's faith that public goods can be made responsive to their needs, and beyond that, that living together in the multiracial city of strangers is actually desirable.

A language of the public good is not a middle-class liberal abstraction. In a society tied together by a division of labour and an electronic nervous system which turns every local conflict into a national conflict, a common language of social trust, and a shared system of public goods are the most urgent social needs we have. Common social attachments can be battered apart by intemperate and hate-filled speeches. They can also be bled to death by the social expenditure cuts undertaken by both Labour and Conservative government. Public goods are the membrane of social trust.

There are those on both sides in the miners' strike who openly welcome the end of the age of compromise and consensus in British political life, who welcome the dawn of an era of the politics of class versus the politics of the market. Future generations who will have to restitch the common fabric of social tolerance will not judge them kindly.

Michael Ignatieff, 14 December 1984

After several further bouts of inner-city uprising since that which prompted the following, with the weapons stakes being raised on both sides each time, ROGER WODDIS's prediction of April 1981 has become more horribly apt than he could have wished.

Frontline

And it will come again,
The phoenix fury rising from the ashes,
The raised arm after the raised profile
Even the blind foresaw.
And it will come again.

And it will come again
In other places and out of the same
Decay. There will be more than bricks
The next time, more than flame
And shattered glass and looted shop.
More than the gentle rain
Of missiles, more than the amatory

Clasp of hate and the indistinguishable
Blood.

And it will come again.
The unbelieving hand will be raised
In horror, the bewildered word
Will spew from microphone and press
And it will come again
From the picture-randy camera eye.
And nothing will be understood.

And it will come again.
The symptom will be solemnly recorded
As the disease. And most will forget
The red blood and the white law
And the bland unseeing blue.
And the black despair.

Roger Woddis, 17 April 1981

*British politicians have generated few isms. With the marginal exception
of Gladstone's obscure coinage 'Beaconsfieldism' – a Dizzy label which
never caught on – Thatcher is the first national leader to attain such a
dubious honour. Here ANGELA CARTER tries to explain what, for
her, induces the peculiar compulsion and revulsion which Mrs T. has
generated.*

Masochism for the Masses

Of all the elements combined in the complex of signs labelled Margaret
Thatcher, it is her voice that sums up the ambiguity of the entire
construct. She coos like a dove, hisses like a serpent, bays like a hound;
a protean performance that, on occasion, rises to a clarion call or
rallying cry. When she clarions, one imagines she can hear herself
crackling over the radio waves to outposts of the Empire: 'Britain
calling.'

It is, in a real sense, a voice from the past. Apart from anything else,
it has adopted a form of 'toff-speak' now reminiscent not of *real* toffs,
but of Wodehouse aunts. A voice as artificial, both in its well-
modulated, would-be mellifluous timbre and its over-precise diction, as

that of duchess in a farce or a pantomime dame. In itself, a voice with connotations so richly comic it's a wonder her perorations aren't drowned by peals of mirth each time she opens her mouth, and unpleasantly significant that they are not. Because just what makes her sound so ludicrous are the barbarous echoes of past glories that shape her vowels and sharpen her consonants; yet it is also these echoes that make some of us, as a reflex action, snap to attention and touch the forelock.

But how come the voice's perpetrator is not sometimes helplessly overcome by its funny side? Rallying the Scottish Tories at the election campaign kick-off: 'Let us go forth from Perth. ...' How did she manage to spit out that phrase from the elocution class with a straight face? God knows, there've been sufficient pompous windbags at the helm of this nation before, but never one who's combined a script straight out of *The Boys' Own Paper* circa 1909 with the articulation of Benny Hill *en travestie*. And got away with it. That's the grievous thing.

But, when Thatcher modulates from the dulcet if bellicose contralto with which she cajoles her own side to the shriek, as of ripped linen, with which she subjugates the Commons – and which, interestingly enough, she also uses to address open-air meetings, so it may be involuntary – then, it chills the blood. For, then, hers becomes the very voice of the implacable, arbitrary, irrational authority known and feared in childhood. Voice like a slap on the wrist. Voice that broke in on your game with the little boy next door: 'What *are* you doing? Put your knickers back on, this instant!'

Small wonder, then, she is widely known as 'the nanny' and, on television during the campaign, has given the impression that if you don't vote for her, she'll tan your bottie. (She'll tan your bottie even if you do, unless you're very rich, but as is well known this is *le vice anglais* and the rich have always got it in the private sector; certainly Thatcher has democratically extended the joys of masochism to the entire population.)

The Nanny. Although Anthony Barnett scrupulously refined the image – rather, the governess who feels a cut above the rest of the staff whilst despising her bosses, and has now kicked out the squire since she knows far better than her employers what's good for him.

But, of course, we're *not* the rest of the staff and though the squires in the Tory Party might have been foolish enough to first promote her within their enclosed little world, they are no longer her employers. *We* are. Her contract is up for negotiation again, now, and it is, perhaps, characteristic of the overweening upper servant that she appears to believe there is no chance it will not be renewed.

But most of us have little direct experience of hiring staff and have
seen nannies and governesses only on television, the medium, of course,
by which she has infiltrated every home. A rather less cosy association,
and one which gives the client less choice in her appointment, is with
the lady magistrate who sends the menopausal housewife – as it might
be one's mum; or oneself – down for two years for shoplifting.
('Society must be protected from women like you.' Thatcher is fond of
protecting society from people, as if people did not constitute societies.)

Certainly she rams home the point of the atavistic middle-class
authority figure with her lady magistrate's two-piece costumes and her
lady doctor 'sensible' shoes. Never one to miss out on the exploitation
of her gender by fair means or foul, she, unlike Shirley Williams, has
always known what garb intimidates. Yet, even when you cannot see
her, even on the radio when she's occupying the Jimmy Young Show
like an army with banners – and what other politician than this
Housewife Superstar would have spotted the potential of the Jimmy
Young Show – her scouring voice identifies her instantly as Class
Enemy Number One.

Well, it does to me. It does to the bloke next door, who doesn't
believe in hanging because it's too good for her. It does to all those who
are not dissipating their energies during this election campaign by
engaging in the voluptuous but non-productive luxury of Thatcher-
hatred – I'm told the Bingo callers in Sheffield say: 'Number ten,
Thatcher out' – as though she were somehow greater than the sum of
her party and, if she saw the light and joined the Poor Clares tomorrow,
the Tories would be perfectly all right. As they used to be, under
decent, magnanimous, welfare socialists like Heath. (Remember Heath,
who gave us the three-day week?) One of the wickedest things
Thatcher has done is to make other Tories seem tolerable.

Yet she and her media advisers, and how odd it is one should discuss
a British Prime Minister in terms of those who tell her how to powder
her nose, have worked damn' hard to blot out the Class Enemy bit, to
turn the Tory Party's greatest liability, both in terms of gender and
fanaticism, into a comicbook superheroine. ('Superwoman', as Jean
Rook of the *Daily Express* calls her.) They've done this, not by toning
down her patent absurdity but by playing it up. If her colonial war
helped, then it did so only with the aid of the most cynical manipulation
of blood lust and militaristic nostalgia of a kind we can ill afford. By
turning the absurd into something ineffable, something glorious.

All the qualities that make her like the 'bad guy' in wrestling, the 'Man
You Love to Hate,' like Mick MacManus, have gone into the resultant
Thatcher package. She is loathsome for precisely those reasons for

which she is most admired. For conviction, read monomania. For strength of purpose, read pig-headedness. For cleverness, read low animal cunning.

If the media were as besotted with Michael Foot as they are with Thatcher, he could be transformed overnight from the shambling loony as which they now present him into a lovable eccentric, vastly wise, figure of almost saintly heroism, whose sheer greatness of heart – there's Jean Rook's headline! 'Mr Great-Heart' – shines through the somewhat out-moded rhetoric originally designed to address a packed Welsh mountainside rather than to suit a tête-à-tête with a television camera. (In fact, that's all that's wrong with Foot on TV. He persists in addressing it as if it were a public meeting, while Thatcher knows very well she is partaking in a soap opera, with a role somewhat like, say, Alexis Carrington in *Dynasty*.)

Indeed, if Foot were Tory leader and not Labour leader, think what the notorious Jak, the *Standard*'s cartoonist, would do with him. Every time he tripped over his terrier's lead, it would be proof his mind was on higher things, such as saving the working class from the rapacity of the trade unions or voluntarily repatriating Siamese cats to Bangkok. All this is to do with the *artificiality* of the presentation of Thatcher, which is stressed by the constant emphasis on her personal appearance, in which she appears enthusiastically to condone the sexism of the media, gladly giving information about her tinted hair and the hours spent in the dentist's chair (what courage!) having her teeth capped.

We are told exactly how she does it and then invited to applaud her appearance of youth: 'Four years on and looking ten years younger', by Jackie Modlinger, Fashion Editor, *Daily Express*, Monday 23 May. Even if one might be forgiven for assuming that, like a latter-day Elizabeth Ba'thory, the Countess Dracula of Hungarian legend, she retained the appearance of youth by bathing each day in the blood of unemployed school leavers.

The ends to which this youthful radiance are put are balefully iconic. That face of Thatcher is more stylised than even her voice, and nothing about it is comic, especially its striking Aryan quality. The blonde, immaculate hair; the steel blue eyes glittering like bayonets, and always with a glazed expression as if fixed on the vision of some high Tory apotheosis such as the crucifixion of Arthur Scargill. The up-thrust chin, as if cresting the waves, like the figurehead as which Steve Bell has so often depicted her. Possibly, hideous thought, to her secret satisfaction, since, for Thatcher, the image is more important by far then the meaning behind it and a figurehead remains a figurehead, whatever its satirical intent.

It is the face, and the pose, too, of a Person of Destiny – and there seems no denying she has personally associated herself with that 'fulfilment of our nation's destiny' of which she spoke to the Scottish Tories, no doubt in serene confidence there was not one devolutionist amongst them who might have queried the appropriateness of the posessive pronoun.

However, the nature of that 'destiny' is as imprecise as the location of the 'Shining city on a hill' invoked as the destiny of the USA by Ronald Reagan during his pre-election debate with Jimmy Carter on American TV. Possibly her destiny and his destination are, in fact, the same city, luminous with radioactive dust and no longer identifiable.

Latterly, she's been sporting a silver and enamel Union Jack on her lapel, as emblematic a jewel as the accessories in the portraits of Elizabeth I as Gloriana. She's also developed a tendency to look vaguely red, white and blue, all over, unless the strain of all this is beginning to tell on me, as it is on Steve Bell's *Guardian* penguin. Union Jack jewel, patriotic colours – all convey the same story, that hers is a transcendent Britishness rising above mere sectarian strife such as the class struggle. Her cult of the personality, establishing her as an emotionally unassailable figure divorced from the sordid business of party politics, peaks on the cover of the *Economist* for 14–20 May. This shows her (up-thrust chin, commanding eyes, as ever, but with a new, positively Mussolini-esque meditatively brooding expression she must have practised in front of the mirror for ages) beneath a rampant Union Jack. The flag, for once, is out of focus, either an oddly tasteful touch or an indication that Thatcher is even more patriotic than it. The legend on the cover of this self-styled centrist publication: 'The issue is Thatcher.'

For the point of the *Economist* cover, constantly emphasised by Thatcher's appeal to the metaphysics of Britishness, is that a vote for Thatcher is a vote, not for the Tories, but for Britain. If you believe in Britain, clap your hands, and Britain, like Tinkerbell in *Peter Pan*, will rise from her deathbed. And. And then, do what? But what Britain will do after this, to change the metaphor, Lazarus-like resurrection is also left vague, except, like any revenant, she will be less corporeally substantial and, presumably, no longer need nourishment, health care, education or employment.

The scarcely credible words of the Thatcher campaign song – and it is a *Thatcher* campaign song, not a Tory campaign song – concentrate on those undoubted qualities of leadership she shares with charismatic lemmings. The song also leaves unstated the place to which she proposes to transport us. 'Who do we want, who do we need, It is a leader who is bound to succeed – Maggie Thatcher, Just Maggie for me.'

Yet the issue in this election is most emphatically *not* Thatcher, who is no more than the representative of certain vested interests, and it is only her vaunting personal ambition and readiness to use the dirtiest resources of right-wing populism that give the illusion she is 'Mrs Big', as Jean Rook calls her. Me, I'm only a writer of fiction and a coarse semiologist by profession and must use the words of a far greater person than I, Theodor Adorno, to sum up adequately what Thatcher represents and a vote for her means:

> Whatever was once good and decent in bourgeois values, independence, perseverance, forethought, circumspection, has been corrupted utterly. ... In losing their innocence, the bourgeois have become impenitently malign. ... The bourgeois live on like spectres threatening doom.

He saw it all, years ago, and said it in *Minima Moralia.*

And here she is, spectre not at the feast but at the famine, symbol – though only a symbol – of our bane and, possibly, an eventual enlightenment, like the plague in Camus's novel, except we may more easily be rid of her than Oran could purge itself of *pastorella pestis.* She can be exorcised with a mere cross on a voting slip. However, what then?

Years ago, during the February 1974 election campaign, the cover of the French news magazine, *L'Exprès,* carried the question: 'La Grande Bretagne: Chile ou Suède?' Curiously enough, this is the very choice Thatcher herself has offered us in this campaign, between 'a society coerced and a society free under the rule of law', although she might not agree the former phrase is an apt description of Chile under Pinochet while for me the latter sums up Sweden, with all its petty regulations and amazing virtues, well enough. In those days, the electorate pondered, wavered and finally plumped for the Swedish option. And the Labour government they put into power blew it. Blew it so badly that, as a result, this time round, a real choice might no longer exist.

Perhaps it was inevitable that in our post-imperial anomie, the hangover after the two-hundred year spree, Britain should throw up the apparatus to create a twopenny halfpenny demagogue of the kind known and feared throughout the Third World. Should release the madwoman who'd always been gibbering in the Tory attic, with its lugubrious lumber of Union Jack draped gallows, the personification of the Tory lady who'd grounded successive Tory Party conventions in a morass of meanness and cruelty. And should give this symbolic entity the keys to the whole asylum.

But nothing is inevitable; history seems inevitable only by virtue of hindsight. There is a conspiracy to create the impression that Thatcher is the kind of leader who goes down in the history books. I rather suspect that, should these islands survive so long, the ethnically complex, polyglot, joyously egalitarian inhabitants of these islands in 2083 will think of Thatcher only as a footnote to the history of graphics. 'Gave inspiration to Steve Bell, Ralph Steadman, Gerald Scarfe, q.v. See, also, under Mère Ubu.'

Angela Carter 3 June 1983

The Falklands/Malvinas adventure was the nadir of the imperial atavism, the deranged popular xenophobia that disfigures this island now. For this reader, BRUCE PAGE's finest moment was in denouncing Thatcher's war. Later, with cooler, slow-burning anger, ANTHONY BARNETT dissected the dishonest apologetics of the Franks Report into the war's origins.

Mad Margaret and the Voyage of Dishonour

The owl of Minerva, said Hegel, flies only at dusk. By this he meant that human societies take a dangerously long time in learning from history.

In the case of Britain and her post-imperial pretensions, the owl trundles down the runway again and again. But she never shows any sign of getting into the air.

It is not easy to believe that even a government as stupid and amateurish as Mrs Thatcher's can actually be sending some of the Navy's costliest and most elaborate warships to take part in a game of blind-man's buff at the other end of the world. The revenue cost of the enterprise can't be less than £50 million, which would be more than enough to give the Falkland Islanders the fresh beginning in life which this country certainly owes them. The capital cost, if ships and aircraft start going into action and taking casualties, could make the revenue cost look trivial.

And the cost in blood? One is not talking here of using a few highly-trained SAS men to knock over a captured embassy with its garrison of half-demented terrorists. The task is to take and hold a group of islands defended by some 5,000 professional soldiers, who have air and naval support from a tolerably-handy home base – while our people have to operate at the end of an 8,000 mile ocean supply line.

Some other late flutters of the post-imperial heart – notably, the Anguilla episode – had their comic side. But if any serious shooting starts in the Falklands, a lot of young men, British and Argentinian, are likely to get killed and maimed. And in what cause will this be done?

If you read the *Daily Mail*, or listen to Tory MPs, you might imagine that the cause was liberty and democracy. (These are the same people who suddenly became passionate trade-unionists when Jaruzelski's army crushed Solidarity.) If you believe *The Times*, you are committed to thinking that the cause is the rolling-back of an aggression more evil and portentous than Hitler's invasion of Poland in 1939. WE ARE ALL FALKLANDERS NOW says *The Times*, having apparently failed to notice that the government on which it now fawns went to some trouble, last year, in its Nationality Bill, to ensure that we are *not* Falklanders – and to ensure that no such colonial bounders could be mistaken for members of the homeland club.

Certainly the Argentine Government, in spite of changes of regime, hasn't for many years been off any sensible observer's shortlist of the world's most noxious regimes. But until the weekend's rhetorical orgy swept leader-writers and Parliamentarians into its embrace, no Labour or Tory ministers had found any serious inconvenience in that fact. Till now, British governments have gone out of their way to truckle to Argentina – and if that means abandoning the Falklanders, OK; if it means turning a blind eye to torture and fascist repression, fair enough.

There was a brief tiff in January 1976, when Buenos Aires broke off ambassadorial relations after Lord Shackleton paid a visit to the islands. But by March 1979 the Labour Government had agreed to exchange ambassadors again.

The truth is that relations between Britain and Latin America are dictated not by ministers, but by the Foreign Office and by an assortment of business-oriented lobbyists like Lord Chalfont and Viscount Montgomery. When Mr Nicholas Ridley was supposedly in charge of our Latin American affairs in 1980, he gave a touchingly honest account of the government's actual expertise: complaining of the whole continent, he said, 'It's very far away, it's very expensive to get there, and what's more they mainly speak Spanish or Portuguese.'

Labour ministers have not been better than Tories at taking a detached view of the 'advice' offered to them. A letter sent from Edmund Dell, Trade Secretary, to David Owen, Foreign Secretary, in 1978 deserves quotation in some detail:

> Evan Luard may have told you of the dinner given by the Lord Mayor recently ... for the purpose of bringing together those with significant

interests in Latin America. There was a free exchange of views, during which several speakers expressed concern about the effect which our stance on human rights was having and would continue to have for some time on our trade interests there.

Since then, George Nelson of GEC has written to Fred Catherwood, who as you know is chairman of the British Overseas Trade Board, following up their discussion at the dinner. Apart from reiterating his concern over our long-term trade interests generally, he has particularly drawn attention to GEC's and British Aerospace's interest in selling the Hawk aircraft to Argentina (worth about £100 million). ... I understand that you are at present considering whether or not General Agosti, Argentine Chief of Air Staff, should be invited here and received at the appropriate level. Nelson and Catherwood both urge that we should invite him. ...

No surprise, then, that during the 1970s Britain provided nearly one-third of all major weapons purchased by Argentina – including ship to air missiles and ship-to-ship missiles which could be used against our own fleet in the event of Mrs Thatcher's somewhat hysterical 'diplomacy' going adrift.

In October 1979 William Whitelaw received hearty Argentine congratulations on ending the visa programme for Latin American refugees. In August 1980 Cecil Parkinson, Minister for Trade, visited the Argentine and enthused about the trading possibilities and was followed by Peter Walker in 1981. Meanwhile, in all sorts of penny-pinching detail, the social infrastructure of the supposedly-treasured Falkland Islands was steadily handed over to the Argentine regime: as the British Government never followed up Shackleton's recommendations for a long-range airstrip on the island, the Falklanders' communications go via Buenos Aires, and via a small airstrip built by Argentine soldiers who no doubt made the most of their reconnaissance opportunities.

Supposedly, the emphasis is now on 'diplomacy', in which Mrs Thatcher's chum Ronald Reagan is expected to play some part. The likelihood of the double-act's success should be assessed in terms of its immediate past performance – which is the remarkable one of driving the Argentine dictatorship into the arms of Cuba and the Soviet Union.

Until last week, Buenos Aires backed Reagan's anti-Communist crusade all the way: sending 'advisers' to the Salvadorean and Guatemalan armies, and to the Somocieta camps in Honduras; withdrawing ambassadors from Havana and Managua in support of American aims.

Only last November the Americans gave General Galtieri a banquet in Washington and described him as a 'majestic personality'. Demented by flattery, Galtieri appears to have concluded that the Americans would support him in his Falkland Islands, and was thunderstruck to receive a long, distinctly hostile phone-call from Reagan just before the invasion went in. 'Whose side are you on?' he is reported to have asked Reagan, in understandable puzzlement.

But the Soviet Union – which will take 80 per cent of Argentina's grain exports this year – has been carefully cultivating the General for some time, and there is excellent historical precedence for hasty marriages of convenience between totalitarian regimes of 'left' and 'right'. Already the Argentine ambassadors are on their way back to Cuba and Nicaragua. And next month Galtieri's foreign minister will go to Havana to discuss ways in which Argentina might become more active within the 'non-aligned' movement of which Fidel Castro is president.

To support Britain's dubious, irrational enterprise, the whole armoury of patriotic rhetoric and flim-flam has been deployed. *The Times*, predictably, reached out for one of the two literary passages which even Fleet Street leader-writers know (the other being Yeats's remark about things falling apart when the centre fails to hold), and in which by endless repetition even John Donne's prose has acquired the overtones of cliché:

> No man is an island, entire of itself ... therefore never send to know for whom the bell tolls; it tolls for thee.

A slightly wider acquaintance with Donne's works might have yielded this, from the *Verse Letters* (and the title, *To H.W. in Hibernia Belligeranti*, ought to remind us that amid all this mimicry the Secretary of State for Northern Ireland is trying to transact some serious business):

> Went you to conquer? and have so much lost
> Yourself, that what in you was best and most,
> Respective friendship, should so quickly die?

The puzzle that the thing we call 'Britain' presents to the world is that of a community of people perhaps as civilised, and humane of temper, as any who may be found – yet which is led, again and again, into enterprises which are as self-defeating as they are dishonourable. The reason, of course, is that the thing we still have to call our government – the United Kingdom state – was never designed to rule a group of democratic, European industrial nations such as the English, the Scots, the Welsh and the Irish are capable of being. It was brought into existence to run, by bluff and cheapskate contrivance, a shabby world-wide empire that was assembled by blunder, force and fraud in varying proportions. Like an old, mangy lion, it knows no other trick, and so long as it has its dominion over us it will betray us – and make us pay the price of betrayal in our own best blood.

Bruce Page, 9 April 1982

To Be Absolutely Franks ...

LADY BROCKLEHURST: If I had been wrecked on an island, I think it is highly probable that *I* should have lied when I came back. Weren't there any servants with them?

LORD BROCKLEHURST: Crichton the butler. Why Mother you are not going to –

LADY BROCKLEHURST: Yes I am George, watch whether Crichton begins any of his answers to my questions with "The fact is," because that is always the beginning of a lie.

(J.M. Barrie, *The Admirable Crichton*)

It was widely thought that the Franks Report would be an investigation into the causes of the Falklands War, a war that is rightly held to have been unnecessary. Here, at last, we were to be given an account of what went wrong, with some stringent conclusions about how to prevent any recurrence. It would be one of those reports for which the British fancy themselves and in which they take inordinate pride. Americans may mount endless public investigations, the French indulge in scandals, but the British will produce – as it were out of the hat of disaster – a report by a committee that has met in secret that will be accepted as authoritative – because it is factual, unpartisan and true.

How very disappointing, then, that the blame which is made to stick by the Franks Report seems as harmless as bluetack. It peels off without resistance to leave the surface to which it was applied virtually unblemished. The war was unfortunate, but fundamentally nothing serious went wrong. It was just one of those things.

Indeed the Franks Report serves as a justification of the war. In so far as it calls for some surgery in the machinery of government, it merely demands plastic surgery in the way we are governed.

Its terms of reference, which refer to the way the government discharged its responsibilities towards the Falklands, seem to ask why there was a needless war in the South Atlantic. Implicitly, however, the Commission has asked why it *came to be necessary* to fight for the

Falklands. It presumes the rightfulness of British sovereignty – the key issue at question in the conflict itself.

In its concluduing chapter the Report asks 'Could the present Government have prevented the invasion?,' and then takes the question back over a period of 17 years to 1965. It says: 'There is no simple answer to it.' This is rubbish, especially over such a period of time. There is an obvious answer: Yes, successive Governments could easily have prevented the invasion by ceding some part of formal sovereignty over the Falklands to Argentina.

This is the crucial issue. We do not need a committee of 'The Great and the Good,' six wise men or even seven dwarfs to tell us that is so. But it seems that we *do* need such a committee – I mean of six wise men, they must be given all the respect they are due – to confuse us on this central question. In its conclusion the Report states that the British government 'had to act within the constraints imposed by the wishes of the Falkland Islanders'. It did not 'have' to do so in any passive way.

Over the page, the Report's first Annex states: 'Ministers and officials made clear to Argentina on numerous occasions that the wishes of the Falkland Islanders were paramount.' But this is not what is stated in paragraph 338. After all, if the Islanders' wishes were 'paramount,' these would hardly have been a 'constraint' for they would have been policy itself. Furthermore, as we shall see, there were a number of occasions over the years when Ministers were careful *not* to make the wishes of the Islanders the 'paramount' dictate of policy, some of which the Report itself cites. The Commission's account thus seems to be internally contradictory on the major and decisive issue of substance with which the war was concerned.

Before asking why this should be, what does the Report tell us about past party policies?

In August 1968 the Wilson government drew up a Memorandum for public agreement with Argentina. It stated that the UK would recognise Argentinian sovereignty over the Islands, provided that the 'interests' of the Islanders were safeguarded and guaranteed to the satisfaction of the UK. There was no mention of the 'wishes' of the Islanders themselves. (It thus seems that by the time they got to page 89 the Franks Committee had forgotten what they reported on page 6.) That government also planned to make clear when it released the Memorandum that the transfer of sovereignty would take place only when it was 'acceptable' to the Islanders. But again this is quite different from their 'wishes.' They might 'wish' the Islands to remain British, but given the fact of the UK's commitment to transfer sovereignty, they would have had to ensure 'acceptable' terms. But, 'critical' public and press reaction made the Government retreat from its plan. The Falklands were not worth a fuss, it seemed.

However, economic relations between the Islands and Argentina were strengthened, by the Heath government in particular. It formulated the idea of a *condominium* with Argentina, perhaps linked to joint development in the area but presumably not 'wished' by the Islanders either. But then Heath was ejected from office.

When Wilson returned, a further approach was made by the British to extend joint development. Whereupon Vignes, the then Argentine Minister for Foreign Affairs, suggested that this should be linked to 'a transfer of sovereignty followed by a simultaneous leaseback for a period of years'. Thus the leaseback proposal – in which nominal sovereignity would become Argentina's while the *actual* government of the Islands, and their population would remain British – was originally proposed by Argentina itself. The Wilson government turned this down. But the Report does not tell us why.

Naturally, the rebuff seems to have caused extreme resentment on Argentina's part, which was exacerbated by the dispatch of Lord Shackleton's team to investigate the development potential of the Islands. Actually, Shackleton concluded that an agreement with Argentina over sovereignty was an essential pre-condition to any satisfactory and lasting improvement on the Islands. However, the Franks Report does not tell us this.

But by July 1977, even the Callaghan administration had decided that 'substantive negotiations were necessary' and concluded that it 'would be forced back in the end on some variation of a leaseback solution linked with a programme of joint economic development'. Yet when Ted Rowlands went to New York to negotiate on that government's behalf in December 1977, he 'was able to avoid proposing leaseback'. One can almost hear the Franks Committee breathe a collective sigh of relief.

When Thatcher replaced Callaghan, Nicholas Ridley was sent out to the Islands. He found that there was 'little enthusiasm for the idea of a leaseback'. Such is the delphic truth, the teasing objectivity of the Franks Committee prose. Of course, we can be quite sure that there was no *enthusiasm*, no banners or T-shirts saying 'GIVE US LEASEBACK', however wise such sentiments might in fact have been. But what we want to know from this authoritative account is whether and on what terms the Falklanders would have found leaseback acceptable – over how many years and with what accompanying compensation? Perhaps if they had also been offered half a million pounds each they might *even* have been a little enthusiastic.

Meanwhile, the Foreign Office concluded that there had to be *substantive* negotiations, or there would be a high risk of military confrontation. And the report makes clear that from around 1980 the Thatcher government was aware at the very least that it was taking a risk. The Falklands were far more a matter of concern, if still a secondary one, than the public realised.

In November 1980 it was decided by the Defence Committee that Ridley should return again to the Falklands, 'to discover the level of support there' for a leaseback arrangement, which it had already been agreed would be the best basis for a settlement. But at this meeting, according to a later report in the *Economist* which seems to have been rather accurate (19 June 1982), Ridley was given a 'fearful mauling', by Thatcher. She was against making any concessions to Argentina and appears to have prevented Ridley from going to the Islands with a clear mandate of government support for a sovereignty settlement. Despite this, the visit found that, although a 'substantial minority' of the Islanders opposed leaseback on the Falklands, the 'majority' remained 'undecided', according to the Franks Report.

It does not tell us about how these proportions were arrived at. What sort of majority was it? How big was the 'substantial' opposition? Perhaps the latter just means loud, rich and influential. At any rate this evasion seems to bear out the argument made by some Islanders, that had Ridley gone with a firm mandate and generous terms he could have gained even majority endorsement in the Islands for a leaseback. Mrs Thatcher, concerned about back-bench resentment of the Zimbabwe settlement, blocked any such move, we can say almost certainly. We cannot be more certain than that, because the Franks Report just does not tell us about Thatcher's role at the crucial meeting. But we are certainly justified in thinking that the 'wishes' of the Islanders have been played with by politicians in Westminster, in particular by the Prime Minister, to further their own short-term ends.

But not only by Thatcher. For when Ridley returned he could not present the House of Commons with the Islanders' assent. Instead, Peter Shore leapt upon him to assert the 'paramountcy' of the Islanders' wishes, something that was never Labour's policy but which would henceforth bind them to Thatcher's chariot.

Even after his Parliamentary ambush, Ridley continued to press for a campaign to sell the policy of leaseback to the Islanders and to warn opinion in Britain, given the mounting risk of a military showdown. Carrington thought the effort hopeless, evidently because he could not get the Prime Minister's support – but again the Report does not tell us anything specific on this score. Instead, while concern about a confrontation mounted it was decided to withdraw the *Endurance*. Thus the Thatcher government decided simultaneously to continue to negotiate, to concede nothing and to reduce its guard.

Now why, after the humiliating excesses of the Falklands War, should we have to suffer the further embarrassment of this grovelling whitewash? There are a number of different, supporting answers. At least one of them concerns the general approach to world affairs of Britain since the war. There can be few better places to look for an expression of this approach than Lord Franks's own Reith Lectures in 1954, delivered when he returned from being our Ambassador in Washington. He titled his keynote address to the nation 'Britain and the Tide of World Affairs'. It was an extended advocacy of what he observed to be the governing impulse of British political life. Although Parliament seems to be full of noisy divisions and disagreements, Franks noted that on major issues decisions were quite uncontested: the creation of NATO, the positioning of troops in Germany, the rebuilding of the 'Sterling Area', the commitment to a nuclear programme. This consensus flowed from an accepted principle, Franks argued: 'It can be stated very simply. Britain is going to continue to be what she has been, a Great Power.' His lectures were dedicated to arguing that this is indeed the case.

He then went on to prescribe the future course for British politics. Take the Commonwealth for example. Younger readers of the *New Statesman* in 1983 will be forgiven if they think that the Commonwealth is an athletic association. For Lord Franks it has been something different. The Commonwealth, above all else, 'enables us to play in the big league with the continental powers'. Indeed, 'the basic condition for the continuing greatness of Britan is a vigorous Commonwealth'. It is a club, true, 'but never before has there been anything like it in the world'.

Franks's world view was, even in 1954, a ludicrous anachronism; and there is little evidence that it has changed since. In *The Times* the day before his Report was published, a magnificent puff was emitted. Lord Franks, its headline states, has 'an alpha treble plus mind', with an exceptional capacity to penetrate to the facts. His Reith lectures, however, are a charivari of wishful thinking.

And something in the attitude of the present report was foreshadowed succinctly by one Franks passage in 1954:

> Little argument is needed to show the necessity of the Commonwealth to Britain's continuing greatness. It is a truth which the British people have intuitively perceived: they do not require a demonstration. What is this small island with its 50,000,000 inhabitants if it has to go it alone?

The answer, of course, is that it *is* the British people! But for Lord Franks this is not enough, such a people would have to be part of Europe or a dependency of the United States. The British people, however, according to Franks, will always

> carry through what they believe necessary for the continuing greatness of their country.

In other words, they will work two shifts (that was in 1954) and keep down wages, or today suffer unemployment, and keep down wages, so as to ensure that the Frankses of this country, and the Thatchers, can believe themselves to represent a world power, in the 'big league'.

This is what the Falklands was about. And this is why the Report is hopelessly inadequate as an *explanation* of why something that should not have happened did take place. J.M. Barrie observed that when people answer a question with 'The fact is', then that is the beginning of a lie. When a diplomat leans forward and says to a reporter in confidence, and off-the-record 'to be absolutely frank', then you can be sure that while what follows may not be lie, it will always in some way be misleading. At least that is so in my experience.

So perhaps we should now coin a new phrase: 'To be absolutely Franks.' It has nothing to do with lying. It is not a form of mendacity of the sort that we 50 million tadpoles are concerned with in our mundane island. No, it is an altogether higher form of misleading. To be absolutely Franks combines utter self-assurance with complete self-deception. Each statement may be exact. Each step from one proposition to another will seem quite unimpeachable. Yet the whole thing is simply off the wall.

Anthony Barnett, 21 January 1983

No journalist in recent years has hit the headlines more often, brushed with the agents of the secret state more frequently, exposed more governmental scandals, blunders and routinised encroachments on our freedom, than DUNCAN CAMPBELL. His role in awakening attention to the creeping authoritarianism of modern British government has been unique. Here he reflects on the wider implications, and the personal costs, of watching the secret watchers.

The Chilling Effect

They have been watching me. For at least seven of the last nine years, they have tapped my telephone. Sometimes, they followed me around. And I am not paranoid. They really were out to get me, if they could. I am of interest to surveillance organisations as a journalist who investigates technology and its role in military or intelligence matters. But many other people also fear their phone might be tapped, their mail opened, their movements followed.

At first, my answers to these anxieties seem comforting. Almost nobody's phone is tapped. Ask yourself how much it would cost every week to record, transcribe, examine, read and take appropriate action over the average person's calls. And even then, what value does tapping have? In seven years' tapping of my own phone, nothing was accomplished except to make me angry, not afraid.

Almost nobody is watched. Think how much it costs to train, employ and equip the necessary dozen or more people needed for the full time physical surveillance of one person. Remember to allow for overtime payments, sick pay, national insurance ... and luncheon vouchers. Even the secret police have to eat.

Even when the secret police are not at lunch, their efforts can rival the Keystone Cops. I was once tailed round London by a convoy of identical brown Hillman Hunters – with identical members of the brown raincoat brigade inside. Of course we aren't being watched full time. And even if it sometimes happens, there may very well be no result.

But many people are certainly scared that the watchers and listeners are out there, unseen. What they experience is the 'chilling effect' of government behaviour. One woman who has felt that cold breath wrote to ask: 'Why should I be watched? I've never been involved in crime or politics.'

This is a 'democratic society'; yet she equates politics with crime. Lots of people do – and they are, as a result, very much afraid to exercise their rights as citizens.

In the United States, the Supreme Court has brought many judgments on the 'chilling effect'. They explain it this way: If the conduct of government and other public agencies is such that the ordinary person may have cause to fear the intrusion of officials in the course of the lawful exercise of individual rights and human liberties, then that government behaviour has an unlawful 'chilling effect' on freedom.

Surveillance technology intensifies the 'chilling effect'. With advanced, sophisticated technology, a totalitarian or authoritarian state may try to determine and control efficiently the ways that its subjects are permitted to think and act.

At present rapid progress is being made in the ability of computers to 'comprehend' speech and recognise visual images. When these developments become more sophisticated, computers will be able automatically to transcribe and, to a limited extent, interpret human speech. Telephone tapping could then become a widespread, completely automatic process.

Visual recognition techniques are also developing fast. The first glimmering of tomorrow's technologies of this kind include computerised scanners. They have already been tried out on three British motorways. The scanner computers automatically read vehicle number plates, and flash a warning signal if the vehicle is of interest of police.

Giant computer databanks necessarily play a central role in the demonology of Big Brother technology. This is not without good reason. The power that computers have to bring together information, then sort and collate it has been growing exponentially for three decades. It will continue to grow.

One remarkable system of recording information about the population at large is being developed fast but with no accompanying publicity. Since 1966, all police forces have been asked to appoint Local Intelligence Officers usually inside major police stations. These Local Intelligence Officers – sometimes called 'collators' – are required to assemble a 'memory databank' on anyone and everything in their area. Individual area constables – nowadays they've called 'community police' – are required, as their first duty, to feed information to the databanks.

In these national, official job specifications, community police are instructed that they should aim at recruiting 'at least one informant in every street'. The community constable is instructed to cultivate the confidence of other officials whom the public trusts, and anyone 'who is in a position to give information' gained through personal confidence. The instructions say that the 'amount of information' passed to the Local Intelligence Officer by an area constable 'will indicate his effectiveness'.

The basis for a nationwide network of informants and memory databanks is thus already in place. About twenty per cent of the entire adult population are already on local police files. The files include not just those accused, convicted or suspected of crime – but also all the victims of crime, the witnesses and anyone else who 'comes to notice' of the police.

Cross referenced against each personal dossier may be addresses, vehicles used, often the names of children, parents, or relatives, the type of home they have and any piece of gossip, rumour, or observation that has ever been recorded.

A second facet of this national information system is the Police National Computer. This is the most active official computer databank now in operation in Britain. In the ten years since it was set up, the number of files stored has grown from a few hundred thousand to over 50 million.

Another facet of this technology is the linking of computers. One effect of linking the Police National Computer to many other computers has already been to create a system of partial population registration – without asking parliament. Since 1974, through the vehicle and driving licence computer, more than half the adults in the country have had to keep the police computer notified of their current address.

The DHSS's new Departmental Central Index will be a comprehensive and efficient population register. It will contain almost everyone's age, address, financial status and family circumstances, taxes paid and benefits claimed. Its contents may be transferred, almost at whim, to police, tax, or security computers. Yet in making its plans for the Central Index, the government has not seen fit to debate the issues of principle involved. In the planning of this new scheme, I have yet to see a single reference to the issue of human rights or the dangers to liberty involved in creating a national population register. Nor has there been any reference to the need for greater public accountability of the officials involved, or a discussion of how to provide independent safeguards on how information may be used.

If we do ever get to a complete 'Big Brother' central databank, the first people I will blame will be the efficiency experts, who built the things just to make the system work better. They mean no ill, of course, but they owe no duty to making democracy work as well as their computers do.

If you find that news of computer databanks discomfiting, I ask you to remember that the computers did not create these threats. The problem throughout has been the cavalier attitudes and actions of bureaucrats – and the subsequent public acquiescence in what they have done.

By focusing on technology alone, the problem of resisting authoritarianism as a political system inevitably appears as remote and inhuman, as something which the ordinary person can never hope to control. Such an approach puts beyond reach the problem of protecting privacy and freedom from the encroachment of technology.

Big Brother was and is a *political* vision. The threats which technology poses for liberty are also political in their origin and effect. To look at the danger of totalitarianism through its technology alone misses the point. It means we blunt or sacrifice our vital protective instincts on behalf of liberty.

For an illustration, take telephone tapping. People frequently express fears about tapping, whereas they do not seem to fear the possible presence of informers and snoopers in the guise of friends. I have never received a letter which suggests that a friend is an informer to the political police or the state security service.

Yet the most important way in which all secret police forces acquire personal data – other than from open sources – is from informants inside a group under surveillance. They may be planted agents or simply recruited. Understandably, it is easier to believe that if one is being watched, it is by the impersonal agent of a telephone tap, rather than by a friend or colleague. Yet it is they who are the main source of information about us.

The most critical question about state surveillance is: what is done with the information gathered? Information on its own is of no consequence. It may as well not exist if it is not used.

The Police National Computer system provides a good example of the active use of information. It has a rapid communications network extending across the country, with video terminals in every major police station. From there, a radio system connects the computer to every police officer out on the streets. Information is normally made available within a few seconds of an inquiry being made.

This rapid access to information affects how the police deal with the public. Without the computer, police officers must make close and co-operative links with the whole community to obtain the information needed to clear up crime.

But with the computer networks, with the Local Intelligence databanks, society as a whole is put under surveillance, and the police objective alters. In order to be able to use the PNC most effectively, police officers must make as many checks as possible on each individual, in order to find the few that the computer singles out for special action. This process is called stop-checking. It requires no social support; indeed, it sacrifices any.

The random stopping of citizens to make a check on police computer records has *no* lawful basis. But it happens. This year, there will be over 10 million police computer checks on innocent people. According to the police and the government's own reports, between 90 and 99.5 per cent of all checks are on innocent people. This is not surprising – the idea is to check on what the computer has to say about as many people as possible.

On the basis of databank information – which may or may not be accurate, may or may not be legally acquired – those in authority can decide how to treat individuals. The police can, for instance, inflict extra-judicial punishments, such as harassing a citizen without the sanction of a court, or the process of publicly testing evidence. Inside security agencies, this practice is called 'countering'. It means actively disrupting the lives of those who do not accept the status quo, even though what they do and say is wholly within the law.

Last year it was shown that wholly inaccurate and extremely damaging information had for years secretly been passed on by the security services to managers of the BBC, blighting the careers of prospective television and radio employees.

Vetting processes which depend on a supply of secret personal information are also prevalent in the civil service and in British industry. This information has been used systematically to deny employment opportunities to people whom those in power considered to hold 'subversive' opinions.

Subversion is a dangerous word. The evident view of many in authority is that to disagree with the status quo is inherently anti-social. Official instructions to police Special Branches order them to keep watch on anyone who, in their view, might at some future time do something which might have an effect on public order. These official instructions allow this peculiarly political police force to extend the watch on so-called subversives as widely as they wish, or have resources for. This has in the recent past included mothers organising demonstrations for better crèche facilities. They were systematically watched and photographed as they and their infants celebrated outside local authority offices.

The existence of camera technology did not create such a situation. Arrogantly unaccountable and undemocratic police practices, and a complacent executive, did.

It is that sharp end of surveillance that matters most. It was the same in the novel *1984*. It was not Big Brother's omnipresent telescreens that actually caused oppression, but the public knowledge of what happened when you said something out of line in front of them. Above all, it was the fear of what would follow behind the windowless façade of the Ministry of Love.

Totalitarian systems of political control are about influencing the behaviour of many by the calibre of treatment that a few receive. The boundaries of freedom are determined by the behaviour of the state towards those who approach or cross the boundaries the state tries to set.

From this, it follows that the safety mechanisms needed to combat oppressive technology are, of necessity, political. They should address not the technologies *per se*, but instead create countervailing legal and bureaucratic structures which protect liberty, and ensure a plural, democratic society.

The first safety mechanism we need is a system of checks and balances, of controls on executive activity. To start with, that means a parliament, judiciary, press, who are independent of – not subservient to and worshipful of – the executive. Today, these institutions are increasingly dominated by supplicants and patrons of the current regime.

The second safety mechanism is the robust defence of fundamental human rights. Far too often, those who wish their privacy and liberty to be defended are asked: What have you got to hide? Such questions cannot be serious. There is nothing unreasonable in insisting that individuals should have rights to control how personal information about them is handled. To argue otherwise is to suggest that the agencies and organisations who act in our name are always benignly motivated, act without prejudice of view, are even-handed in their objectives, staffed at every level with individuals who operate with impeccable care, total honesty and consistent diligence. What nonsense!

The third and most important safety mechanism is to strengthen the democratic accountability of the institutions permitted to hold a monopoly of the use of force. The problem here is to make these administrators accountable to the community – not the other way round.

The propriety of the law, and the legitimacy of the police force derive only from the common desires and aspirations of the civic community. When, as is happening, that community feels the 'chilling effect', it is not a sign of their growing unreason. It is a signal that the institutions of government are losing balance and becoming authoritarian.

So do not be distracted by computers and video screens. Recognise the enemies of liberty for who they really are, and who they always have been. Recognise the instruments of the enemies of liberty for what they always have been.

Where there is trouble now, in El Salvador and Guatemala, in Johannesburg, Cape Town and Soweto, it is not computers or monitor cameras that are taking lives and freedom. It is the old, familiar, ugly apparatus – the acrid-smelling end of the policeman's gun, the heavy riot stick lancing the air, the boot in the kidneys. It is the quieter violence of being forced into poverty and silence. It is the same here in Britain.

What we need are checks and balances: effectively enforceable fundamental rights; democratic accountability of the police and other institutions; freedom of information. Have these needs not already widely been recognised? So the problems of controlling oppressive technology are then not hopeless?

Yes, but – in Britain now, the trends of government action are all away from accountability, and democracy, and against human rights. New laws and practices have greatly extended coercive powers, and diminished accountability.

Technology can be controlled. It is under control already. But by the wrong people.

Duncan Campbell, 24 January 1986

Depressed and depressing thoughts about the state of the nation – especially as expressed in the political travelogue – have become a major literary genre in the 1980s. ROBERT CHESSHYRE in the following gloomy reflections on return, now expanded in his book The Return of a Native Reporter *(1987), provided one of the most powerful indictments.*

The Poverty of Their Desires

It was 7.00 am, not a good hour when one has just flown the Atlantic economy class. I was stiff from spending eight hours in a seat like a straitjacket, shivery from lack of sleep, and vaguely queasy from inhaling the stale air that gathers in a Jumbo towards the end of a long flight. Half the lavatories, as ever, had been out of action, and somnambulant passengers had lined the aisles from the Irish coast till the seatbelt sign went on. Our sense of slumming it had been rubbed in by the occupation of the first-class cabin by mail bags and their escort of two security men slumbering in the wide luxury of their seats. That put *us* literally in our places. But if there is one thing worse than travelling through the night, it is the chaos of arriving before dawn.

'British rail welcomes you to Gatwick' read a big sign: 'London, Victoria, trains depart every 15 minutes'. It was still dark, and a cutting wind drove along the buried platforms as if propelled by icy bellows. Someone – vandals? British Rail itself? – had skilfully removed the seats: the holes where the bolts had been showed mockingly in the tarmac. A loudspeaker barked: 'Britain Rail regrets. ...' It was one of those deliberately articulated third-person announcements that make the inefficiencies of public transport appear like acts of God. Not one, but three Victoria express trains had been cancelled.

I had always enjoyed coming home. I recalled – as our train, filling with unknown yet familiar people, rattled its slow way towards London – the contentment I had felt as a small boy more than 30 years earlier when flying into Northolt Airport aboard a DC-3 of British European Airways. Then, as the plane made its approach, I had peered with high excitement to catch sight of the red-tiled roofs of Middlesex suburbia, which – drear though they might have been – to me were like a lighthouse to the returning sailor, the first glimpse of an anxiously sought land. My parents lived then in France, and it was a journey I had made three times a year for three years to return to school in England, and I had never been disappointed.

Nothing could have tested my nerve more than arriving on a commuter train at the height of the rush-hour on a bleak, cold February morning. Commuting everywhere depresses the spirit; passengers exist in limbo, their personalities temporarily on hold. Once the obviously resented disruption of the air travellers – several of them over-apologetic Americans whose tartan bags blocked the gangway – and their luggage had been absorbed, that morning's London-bound workers resumed their quotidian routine. The elderly dozed, the young listened to headphones, from which the 'boom-de-boom' rhythm of percussion leaked, and those of in-between years read newspapers suitable to their station in life.

Looking around, I realised with a shock that, although I had been living in the United States for over three years, I could none the less make a shrewd guess at the circumstances of most of my fellow travellers – their education, their income, their prejudices, their places in the pecking order, even perhaps where they took their holidays. It was not something I had been able to do in the States – neither, several friends told me later, could Americans – and I had grown accustomed to being among people less easy to read. George Orwell, in his study of *The English People* written after the Second World War, had reached a similar conclusion: 'The great majority of the people can still be "placed" in an instant by their manners, clothes and general appearance.'

The reminder that so little had changed was both comforting and alarming. I had been stimulated by living in an unpredictable and still largely unexplored society, but I had missed deeply the sense of belonging, of being among familiar, small-scale landscapes and buildings, of being with people whose outlook had been shaped by the same influences as mine had been, and of being wrapped in history and traditions that stretched in the mind's eye back almost to the beginning of recorded time.

If anything dampened my enthusiasm for home, it was, without doubt, British insularity. Watching the commuters that morning; eavesdropping on conversations about late trains – 'I went for the five-oh-seven last night, but they'd cancelled it'; the perils of winter holidays abroad – 'the change in temperature's too great. You come back and within a few days get a stinking cold'; I felt a degree of panic. A study of the news-stand at Gatwick Airport had brought to mind Ernest Bevin's observation of 40 years earlier that 'the working class had been crucified on the poverty of their own desires'. The papers carried front-page headlines about Princess Michael; stories on football thugs; pictures of royal children; hue and cry over 'sex fiends'; stories about 'Dirty Den', a television character rather than a sex fiend; one tabloid led its front page with a 'he deceived me' story about a professional footballer. A hurried perusal of the shelves turned up six magazines with front-page pictures of Princess Diana. Little had changed, certainly not the names.

Little had changed either, so I was to discover, at the 'serious' end of public affairs. I woke on my first morning to a sycophantic radio interview with a complacent junior minister, bound together in a cosy conspiracy of first-name terms. Apart from Mrs Thatcher herself, there appeared to be only three figures in British public life whose opinions were worth airing – Roy Hattersley, Norman Tebbit and (most over-exposed of all) David Owen – who were interviewed on every topic that arose, appeared, often together, on every discussion show, wrote leader-page articles, and between them set the national agenda. There was only one man of greater national consequence, Terry Wogan, the apotheosis of the prevailing national infatuation with glitz.

I knew the aspects of American life I was going to miss, the optimism, the classlessness – it is a canard, put about by apologists for the British class system, that the United States is a class-ridden society, with snobberies undreamed of even by the English; there are very small pockets of virulent class, money and 'who-do-you-know?' consciousness, but they mean nothing to most Americans – the wide variety of the country, the feeling renewed almost every morning that anything is possible means that for 70 per cent of Americans, equality of opportunity is a reality: they are launched into life with enormously positive impulses. Virtually every child stays in school until he is 18: to leave sooner is to be branded a 'drop-out'. An English schoolteacher, who had worked for many years in the States, wrote to me that in American schools one factor was common, 'that was a desire to learn, to get ahead (not always perhaps in a manner of which you and I might approve), but the drive was there. And of course class distinction – still nauseously rife throughout Britain – was non-existent.' In our Washington neighbourhood, packed with successful migrants from every corner of the States, educational and 'class' differences not only did not matter, but also were all but invisible.

I was, of course, aware of the harsh realities at the bottom of American society. Under Ronald Reagan, as under Mrs Thatcher, poverty and genuine destitution have grown sharply. As a child I had often wondered what it would have been like to be a Victorian, when the gap between rich and poor was so great. Inner city and rural black people are not among the 70 per cent of equal citizens. A 'southern' city like Washington is still effectively segregated in many ways. Fellow workers go home at six o'clock to different parts of the town. A study carried out shortly before I left found that a distinctive black argot was becoming more common in urban ghettos. Many black children have not spoken with a white person by the time they go to school. Homeless kids go hungry, and grimy vagrants roam the streets of major cities, cheek by jowl with some of the most affluent people in the world. Many black people are wealthy, but the majority – except those blessed with supreme sporting talents – are locked out of the American Dream.

Britain had obviously been changed by the often dramatic events of the previous years. One assumption that I had been raised on – that no government would long survive if unemployment rose above one million – was dead and buried. Weren't you surprised, several leftish acquaintances asked, not to find Britain in flames? No, I could answer in all honesty. We may have begun to hate with a frightening intensity those with whom we disagree, but we will endure real privations with bovine patience. Orwell had watched the poor coping with the great depression: 'Instead of raging against their destiny, they have made things tolerable by lowering their standards.'

But what I was not ready for was the deterioration in the daily quality of life, in people's tolerance for each other. The national cohesion that had been built so painstakingly in the post-war years was fragmenting fast. People were harder, more selfish, less caring, less 'wet'. The hard Right had captured not just the political high ground, but also the 'intellectual' and moral high ground. Whatever the economic gains of Thatcherism, they appeared to carry a high human price tag. To be poor was to have failed: pensioners and the unemployed, drawing their money from the Post Office, were a legitimate object of scorn, even hatred, to the stamp-buying classes who read Auberon Waugh.

I was converted to the virtues of what has become known as 'an enterprise culture', not by Mrs Thatcher's hectoring, but by the example of what I had seen in the United States. Nine million new jobs were created while I was there, almost entirely by small enterprises. In retrospect, it was shocking that my generation in Britain had been brought up with the sole presumption that we would work for someone else, no matter whether we left school virtually illiterate or emerged from university with a first-class degree. The only people who thought in business terms were those whose families had been in business, and the cultural pressures were on many of them to 'improve' themselves by joining the professional classes.

This declining tolerance has spilled over into everyday life. The British even drive more aggressively than they did. The once common British saw of 'giving credit where credit's due' no longer seems to have any validity. The chief executive of a northern new town said: 'A lot of people do want to get things back to where they ought to be. However, a lot don't unless they get the kudos, so they set themselves against it. Some actually don't want to see things improve: their role in life is to keep things festering. We are retreating into tribal divisions.' That seemed a fair, if horrifying, summary of the Britain I found on my return.

Robert Chesshyre, 18 September 1987

Finally, ZYGMUNT BAUMAN looks to the future of socialism.

Fighting the Wrong Shadow

At the end of this development the intellectuals of the opposition asked themselves in all seriousness: is there still a proletariat? Is there still a ruling class? Whereas they would have been more justified in asking: is there still an intellectual opposition?

Short-term hopes are futile. Long-term resignation is suicidal.

Hans Magnus Enzenberger

The Left is characterised by its lack of humour. This has set it apart from other forms of opposition to capitalism, e.g. avant-garde art. The latter's irony, self-mockery and playfulness was a *lèse-majesté* to the Left as much as it was to the priests of the establishment. *Epâter-le-bourgeois* has never been a left strategy, because the Left has treated *le bourgeois* seriously as the author of a project the Left thought worth fulfilling and as the hindrance to its fulfilment at the same time.

The Left was and remained until recently the counter-culture of capitalism. It could only come into being once capitalist culture launched a programme geared towards achieving a rational society. Logically, it made sense only by 'taking capitalism at its word' – a demand to deliver on the capitalist promise. Liberty, Equality and Brotherhood were capitalist passwords. The Left had nothing to add. It only took the capitalist programme seriously and asked everyone else to do the same.

The Left was indebted to capitalism for a number of ideas: that one can change the world by relying solely on human resources; that the world can be improved by rational human intervention; that to do this it is sufficient to increase the material wealth at mankind's disposal, and to make nature useful, first by learning its secrets and then relating it to human needs and ignoring the rest; that, as material wealth grows, so do the possibilities for happiness, understood as the lack of want but also as freedom from natural necessity; that this freedom will promote liberty, equality and brotherhood among people and, given the possibility of this rational choice, people will select a way of life best suited to their needs; that the value of 'really existing' societies can be measured by the degree to which liberty, equality and brotherhood have been attained and by the chances for their further growth.

Because it had borrowed all these capitalist ideas and treated them seriously, the Left had become a critic of capitalist practice. Eager successfully to complete the process, the Left questioned the qualifications of its current managers. Capitalist practice had to be rejected because it could not fulfil the capitalist promise and because it threatened to waste the opportunities opened up by the capitalist revolution.

The critique of capitalist practice had to be on two grounds – moral and rational ones. The newly attained material wealth had not been used wisely, i.e. it had not been used to promote liberty, equality and brotherhood; or capitalist administration of production generated far less wealth than could be achieved.

Disenchanted with the capitalist administration of social production, the Left looked for a more appropriate historical agent, better suited to the tasks on the historical agenda. For most of the Left, the industrial working class seemed the natural option.

A number of reasons spoke in favour of this – at least at the time.

1) As an historical agent, the propertyless working class had no track record and thus was not discredited. 2) The working class was rapidly growing to the point of eventually encompassing the nation as a whole. 3) Unlike other disaffected classes, industrial workers were subject to uniform rhythm and discipline, technically trained and organically tied to rational production. 4) They showed proclivities to militancy; their often violent rebellion against the rise of capitalism could be easily misread as resistance to capitalist administration. 5) For reasons of militancy, industrial workers had already been defined as the 'dangerous classes' and a threat to capitalist order. Here the Left only accepted the dominant view. 6) Industrial workers were a particularly tempting choice, as they clearly needed the guidance of the educated elite, of which most left critics were a part.

All these considerations have now turned into their opposites. Industrial workers are now the most rapidly shrinking part of the population. It is projected that within a generation they will be reduced to the size of agricultural labour at the beginning of this century. Employees who have displaced traditional industrial workers are transient, unorganised, scattered and unskilled – unlikely candidates to rule a rational society. Organised labour's militancy is now defensive in nature and particularistic in vision. Far from being a 'dangerous class', organised labour has become the staunchest defender of law and order. Rather than listening to the spokespeople of reason, it has been seeking illumination from the entertainment industry.

The changes in the nature of industrial labour have not made today's capitalist society more rational or just. If anything, poverty and suffering are still increasing. But poverty is no longer associated with organised labour. It has become much less romantic and politically interesting. It is now a suffering that does not entail redemption but calls for more bureaucracy and – if heeded – this call would only strengthen the oppressive grip of the capitalist state. In addition, this new kind of poverty, the poverty of flawed consumers, sees the rich and powerful not as enemies, but as role models and as the measure of their own inadequacy. Thus, it is difficult to see the new poor as agents of historical transformation.

To the extent that the Left seeks to retain its identity as the counter-culture of capitalism, it finds itself without any historical agent to complete the capitalist project. This absence of a plausible agent creates an unprecedented situation. It is at the root of the present 'disenchantment' and 'loss of direction' or, more simply, the contemporary crisis of the Left.

There are two common reactions to this sense of crisis. The first is to dismiss this loss of direction as another case of middle-class intellectuals getting cold feet when confronted with successive spells of misfortune. Thus it is claimed that organised labour's revolutionary potential is far from exhausted and that it must remain the benchmark of left politics. Such a reaction is reinforced by the Left's collective memory.

This reaction doesn't produce a unified politics. One possible politics is to translate loyalty to the working class as the historical agent to loyalty to organised labour. In practice, this means uncritically supporting organised labour, whatever its interests and demands may be, as 'by definition' anti-capitalist. This may occasionally re-establish credibility during brief periods of trade union militancy. In the long run, however, it is likely to reinforce the divisive 'policy of closure' pursued by a class in retreat. Whatever the value of this policy, its left credentials are, for these reasons, in doubt.

Another offshoot of this reaction is a politics privileging an orthodox philosophy of history. If 'really existing' workers do not behave according to the pattern suggested by this philosophy, all the worse for 'really existing' workers. Their deviation from the projected pattern may be easily explained in terms of ideological state apparatuses, police repression, consumerism, social democratic betrayals, bribes or the weakening of the left intellectuals. As a temporary abnormality, the behaviour of 'really existing' workers is dismissed as a possible refutation of a policy grounded in the philosophy of history. In practice, this is a sectarian policy of retreat into ever smaller groups of faithful who reinforce their collective legitimacy by imputing to workers (as they should be and not as they are) their own middle-class spiritual tribulations.

The second reaction is the very opposite of the first: it proclaims the 'end of modernity' and the coming of 'postmodernity'. Accordingly, the times of 'universal projects', of a world which made such projects plausible, are over. From this point on, however, the theorists of postmodernity split. Some dwell on the growing plurality of the contemporary world, on the autonomy of 'language games', 'communities of meaning' or 'cultural traditions' which are impervious to objective evaluation since they themselves individually provide the ground of all authority that any evaluation may claim. Others do not feel obliged to refer to the changing world to justify a plurality of ideas. The difference between postmodernity and modernity appears to them as another chapter in the history of thought. They abandon the futile search for universal standards of truth, justice and taste, and modestly claim that there is nothing but our own conviction to justify our decision to pursue values we claim worth pursuing. In varying degrees, both forms of postmodernist theory are philosophies of surrender. Both resign themselves to the impossibility, or unlikelihood, of improving the world, aware of the powerlessness of critique in influencing other communities.

Doomed romance

The left intellectuals' current flirtation with postmodernity can be accounted for by the desperation with which new inspirations are sought within a context which appears increasingly as a theoretical void. This romance of the Left with postmodernity, however, is bound to prove another case of unrequited love. Indeed, while condemning as futile the hopes that bourgeois values can ever be universalised, postmodern theory at the same time declares the futility of the Left. There is no conceivable way a realistic left programme could be patched together out of postmodernist theory. There can be no Left as a counter-culture – i.e. a positive and effective critique of neglects, drawbacks and mismanagements in implementing the cultural promise of a better society – without the conviction that this cultural promise is viable and in principle realisable. There can be no Left without the belief that society can be improved and history brought to our side. There can be no Left without the idea that, among different things, some are good and some are wrong, and that the first can be made more numerous than the latter.

If these two responses are either backward-looking or unpromising, it may be advisable to look for a third. And this third response is the reconstitution of the left critique as the *counter-culture of modernism* – a response which may avoid the drawbacks of the other two, while inserting the Left in the most crucial moral issues of Western society today.

A 'counter-culture of modernism' differs from a 'counter-culture of capitalism' in several respects. The counter-culture of capitalism was predicated on the possibility of the emancipation of labour from capital. It saw present and future society the way capitalism did: as a society whose members were primarily engaged in labour, a society organised around the task of replenishing the labour supply. This task, the counter-culture of capitalism maintained, was ill-served by capital. Realising the first task introduced an auxiliary task: removing capital from the administration of the productive process and replacing it with another version of the self-administration of labour.

The unanticipated effect of left pressure, and of the politics of industrial labour it generated, turned out to be the very opposite of what had been expected. Instead of the emancipation of labour from capital, what happened was the emancipation of capital from labour. Today, capital depends less and less on labour. Instead of engaging the rest of society as producers or servants of the productive process, capital today engages society as consumers or servants of consumption. The most obvious consequence of the changed mechanism of the reproduction of capital, and of the new form of systemic domination, is the obsolescence of the self-management of producers as a valid alternative to the present system. There are, however, other less self-evident consequences.

For the revelation of these other consequences, the Left is indebted, as so often in the past, to the system's political administrators. They were the first to draw practical conclusions from the newly acquired freedom of capital from labour and the newly acquired freedom of politics from the task of recommodification of labour. The present upsurge of neo-conservative politics, the reappearance of notions which the previous network of class-based checks and balances rendered for many a decade unmentionable, indicates that such conclusions have been drawn.

The outcast poor

To start with, the poor are less and less important to the reproduction of capital in their traditional role as the 'reserve army of labour'. They are no longer the object of concern for the twofold political task of recommodification of labour and limitation of working-class militancy. The previously taken-for-granted principle of social responsibility for the survival – and, indeed, the well-being – of that part of society not directly engaged by capital as producers has suddenly come under attack. In view of the progressive emancipation of capital from labour, the reaffirmation of the principle cannot be left to the rationality of the productive process. It has to be re-negotiated and re-imposed by appeal to those aspects of the counter-culture that capitalism tended to underemphasise: political democracy, as distinct from the self-management of producers.

Without this new anchorage, today's poor are under a threat worse than the misery of the early capitalist work-houses. Those were at least institutions of 'social rehabilitation' in terms of the requirements of rising capital in acute need of a rising labour force. Today, the rehabilitation rhetoric in which welfare payments are wrapped may only be used, in view of its phoniness, as a device to confirm the inadequacy of the poor and their ineligibility for social assistance. The same Social Darwinist rhetoric which once served to reforge small producers into disciplined industrial labourers today firmly and irreversibly stamps the poor as stigmatised, permanent outcasts of the consumer society, undeserving of citizen status. It is unlikely that welfare payments will be eliminated. The obsessive public ritual of counting 'the costs of welfare' immediately translated as the 'taxpayer's sacrifice' is a tool used to raise a wall between the 'fit' and the 'unfit' and deepen the stigma attached to poverty.

Quite real, however, is another threat: that of welfare payments becoming instruments of disenfranchisement and the withdrawal of citizenship rights for that rising minority of the consumer society who cannot prove their citizenship in the only way a consumer market admits. The reality of such a threat has been documented by the legally enforced interference of welfare agencies with the private and family life of their 'clients': an imposed 'infantilisation' of welfare recipients through denial of their rights to autonomous decision-making and the dense network of surveillance which consumes an ever growing slice of welfare funds. Thus the poor are not just growing poorer. They are being made into a deviant category: a section of the population defined as a separate entity by the withdrawal, or at least suspension, of political and personal rights which were thought to be the lasting and universal achievement of modernity.

The poor are the first to experience the threat to democracy and citizenship rights – and to experience it in the most tangible form. But they are not the only ones under threat. The political arena is in the process of acquiring a new role in the reproduction of the social system. Its function in systemic reproduction was, throughout most of the modern era, confined to guaranteeing the general conditions for the smooth reproduction of capital-labour relations. Capital, engaging the bulk of the population as producers and servants of production, could be relied upon as the major drilling and disciplining force. Emancipated from labour, capital cannot and need not carry on this function. The reproduction of the structure of domination becomes directly the matter of law and order, rather than indirectly the matter of the 'work ethic'. Systemic reproduction, in other words, has become more than ever before the responsibility of the political state.

Under these circumstances new pressures come to bear on political democracy and the modern form of public life in general. Indeed, with the new and enhanced function of the state, the political game cannot be left to 'democratic' politicians. Considerable freedom of political opinion and organisation, which virtually all interests enjoyed through a better part of modern history (the quality of modernity which the Left came to see – or rather not see – as unproblematic), was more than tangentially related to the relative innocuousness of political conflict in a system where domination was guaranteed primarily through non-political means. Too much hangs on political conflict today to expect this situation to last. Two kinds of assaults on political democracy as we know it are to be expected and, indeed, signs of both are already discernible.

First, there will be attempts to preserve the façade of political democracy while draining the substance of politics from public forms of democratic life. This can be seen in the shifting of real decision-making from ostensibly democratic institutions to government bureaucracies unaccountable to democratic control. The growing hysteria around 'state secrets' is an instrument to remove the daily work of the state from control by its subjects. This is facilitated by technological means presently at the government's disposal, which allow the most seminal decisions affecting the citizen's survival to be taken and implemented before democratic institutions have a chance to intervene. For example, modern warfare no longer requires the mobilisation of popular emotions, for waging wars. Indeed, it does not even require informing the population that they are in a state of war.

Second, the range of issues open to discussion within the democratic process is shrinking. This is brought about by proclaiming a growing number of radical attitudes out of the bounds of democracy; by lowering the threshold of opinions considered subversive; privatisation of a growing number of functions previously performed by the state; and, with the help of technological media, reducing the visible side of the democratic process to popularity contests, where issues evaporate in public relation exercises.

One of the consequences of the emancipation of capital from labour may be, therefore, the even more crucial emancipation of political power from democratic institutions. This is all the more important given the state's enhanced destructive power and the deeper penetration by state bureaucracies within spheres hitherto relegated to private life.

The severity of the first factor cannot be overestimated. We live under the shadow of mass destruction. This has rendered possible the end of history and of the human race. As such, it goes beyond the scope of a traditional politics meant to deal with everyday problems of human welfare. But the existence of weapons of mass destruction is also crucial for internal politics. As the ultimate weapons permitting the total annihilation of 'external enemies', they also allow the state to become emancipated from control by its own society. This is the decisive link in the chain of factors which threaten the survival of the democratic achievements of modernity. No definite progress can be made by the Left without the destruction of the weapons of mass destruction. This is not merely another concern of the Left, but the key to the viability of its identity as the counter-culture of modernity.

The second factor which renders emancipation of political bureaucracies from democratic control particularly sinister is the growing penetration of the 'private' sphere by the state. This penetration, of course, further strengthens the autonomy of the state: the deeper the penetration, the less realistic are the chances for democratic institutions to recapture those areas of control from which they have been evicted. Thus, in addition to having an instrumental political relevance, this penetration also has moral ramifications and has to be resisted on both accounts.

Going to market

Resistance to these developments is unlikely to generate a mass movement because the encroachment on individual autonomy and subjective freedom by state bureaucracies has its counterpart in solutions to the problem of autonomy provided by the market. In the same way that early capitalist conflicts about control over the producers' body and spirit were redirected and neutralised as conflicts over the distribution of surplus value, today the energy generated by the drive towards individual autonomy and political subjectivity is redirected and neutralised as a need to construct individual uniqueness and authenticity out of mass-produced commodities. In early capitalist societies organised around production, every call for autonomy tended to be translated immediately into increased pressure on the redistribution of surplus value, while, in the present consumer society, calls for autonomy tend to be translated into intensified preoccupation with the opportunities offered by the market. This circumstance renders the left critique of individual autonomy as self-defeating today as it was in the past. Contrary to its intention, it ends up contributing to the retrenchment of the system it wished to reform.

What ultimately feeds the intense preoccupation with market varieties of autonomy is the politically-induced limitation of individual freedom. Because of this, members of the consumer society seek redress in the market. Thus, enhancement of individual autonomy may be better attained by attacking the sources rather than their effects. Rolling back the bureaucratic invasion of the private sphere may relieve the pressure to seek the kind of autonomy that the market can provide.

All of today's critical issues point to the same central problem: the threat of the political state detaching itself from democratic control, and the resulting freedom of state bureaucracies to colonise the everyday world, thereby rendering their own domination permanent. This central problem defines the Left today.

If the Left as the counter-culture of capitalism located the causes of the failure to realise the promises of the capitalist revolution in capital's control over production, the Left as the counter-culture of modernity should seek such causes in the failings of political democracy and personal autonomy. The emphasis shifts following seminal transformations in the social system. When it engaged society in the role of producers, capital was the very force seeking the expansion of both political democracy and individual autonomy. Today capital is, at best, indifferent to both; it may well consider them costly nuisances. Thus, today, democracy and autonomy cannot be taken for granted. They must be consciously and stubbornly defended.

Unlike the counter-culture of capitalism, the programme of the counter-culture of modernity does not unequivocally privilege any particular social group as its primary or 'natural' target. In this sense, it is a programme without an easily identifiable 'historical carrier'. As the counter-culture of capitalism, the Left has long lived in the shadow of an historical agent. An artefact of the programme, this agent lulled the Left into forgetting its origins and legitimation. More often than not, the conclusion turned into the premise and the Left identified itself as a collective spokesperson for the class to which it imputed its own concerns. Memory of those long years make today's Left uneasy. It has yet to learn to live without an historical agent. It must see through what today may be only a delusion, straight into the only firm foundation of its purpose: the conviction that the values promoted by the bourgeois revolution need to be defended and can be defended only by exposing the mechanisms which prevent their fulfilment.

Living without an historical agent has its discomfiting aspects. It also has its virtues. Making shortcuts unattractive is one of them, maybe the main one. Revolution is a shortcut in its purest form: an attempt to force history where the agent is not ready to take it (if it was, revolution would not be needed). Revolution is hence an act of violence on history and on its assumed agent. This is what makes the shortcut morally odious and ineffective as the means to bring history where it was intended to be brought. In history, most shortcuts appear to be *culs-de-sac*.

Living without a hope for a shortcut is another thing today's Left has to learn. Indeed, to repeat Enzensberger's motto: short-term hopes are futile and long-term resignation is suicidal. But the virtue of living without an historical agent is that the futility of short-term hopes does not lead to long-term resignation. Resigning short-term hopes saves long-term ones from futility.

Zygmunt Bauman, 25 September 1987

INDEX OF CONTRIBUTORS